The Ailsa Mellon Bruce Studies
in American Art

VOLUME ONE

Copley in America

SELF-PORTRAIT 1769

John Singleton Copley

In America 1738-1774

Jules David Prown

Published for the
NATIONAL GALLERY OF ART · WASHINGTON

1966
HARVARD UNIVERSITY PRESS · CAMBRIDGE · MASSACHUSETTS

Distributed in Great Britain by Oxford University Press, London

Typographer ~ Burton L. Stratton

Library of Congress Catalog Card Number 66–13183

Printed in the United States of America by the Harvard University Printing Office
and the Meriden Gravure Company. Binding by the Stanhope Bindery.

This book is dedicated to my
father and mother
Max and Matilda Prown

Foreword

THIS IS THE FIRST BOOK TO BE PUBLISHED IN THE SERIES OF THE AILSA Mellon Bruce Studies in American Art sponsored by the National Gallery of Art. With the generous donation of Mrs. Bruce it is planned to publish at intervals scholarly monographs related to American art, with especial emphasis upon outstanding individual artists. We are fortunate to be able to begin the series with this distinguished biography and catalogue *raisonné* of the work of John Singleton Copley by Professor Jules David Prown of Yale University.

It is particularly fitting that the first book in the series should appear at this time, since it commemorates two anniversaries: the one hundred and fiftieth anniversary of the death of Copley, who died in 1815, and the twenty-fifth anniversary of the opening of the National Gallery of Art on March 17, 1941. To celebrate the first of these the National Gallery, the Metropolitan Museum of Art, and the Boston Museum of Fine Arts held a comprehensive exhibition of the works of Copley in 1965 and 1966. Mr. Prown was the author of the catalogue of that exhibition, and his manuscript for the present text was completed in that year.

One can easily imagine how much Copley would have appreciated the masterpieces from every country that now enrich our museums. The artistic handicaps of eighteenth-century America no longer exist. The trip to Europe in search of further instruction, which took Copley permanently from our shores, is no longer considered essential. Instead the American school today influences European painting.

John Walker, *Director*
National Gallery of Art

vii

Acknowledgments

WHEN I BEGAN MY DISSERTATION ON COPLEY'S CAREER IN ENGLAND at Harvard University over eight years ago, I received particularly warm encouragement and good advice from Louisa Dresser, Curator of Paintings at the Worcester Art Museum; from Barbara Neville Parker, co-author of the outstanding book on Copley's American work; and from Professor Benjamin Rowland, my dissertation adviser. The friendly tenor of the advice I received then has characterized the help I have had from scores of people over the long course of completing this work, which now covers Copley's English and American careers. I cannot hope to express adequate specific thanks here to all who deserve them, but I do want to broadcast my gratefulness to everyone who helped me along the way.

Mrs. Parker has unreservedly shared with me information gathered since the publication of her book and has given constant encouragement to this work from beginning to end. I am particularly grateful to her. Professor Rowland has given me the continued benefit of his knowledge and support, and I appreciate not only the quality of his criticisms but the practical advice he has given me along the way.

During the period that my dissertation on English Copley was being written, I had the privilege of being an assistant to Professor John P. Coolidge, Director of the Fogg Art Museum, Harvard University. His continual emphasis on the importance of the academic side of university museum life, his willingness to tailor my job to accommodate my needs for Copley research and writing time, and his subsequent reading of the dissertation and advice on converting it into a book have contributed significantly to the realization of this work. For his continuous help, and for his example, I am deeply grateful.

I should like to acknowledge a particular debt of obligation to Wendell D. Garrett for his careful scrutiny of my manuscript and his welcome suggestions, and also to extend my thanks to him and to his wife, Jane N. Garrett, for their warm and steady interest in this work.

Elliott and Mary Perkins have a proprietary interest in this book, most of which was written at Little River. Their encouragement and advice have materially aided my work.

It is doubtful that the book would have seen the light of day had it not been for the generous financial support I received during its preparation. The Edward R. Bacon Art Scholarship from Harvard University allowed me to spend the academic year 1958–59 in England on research. A grant from the American Philosophical Society in 1964 was exceedingly helpful in enabling me to acquire photographs with which to illustrate this book, and a subsequent grant from the National Gallery of Art (Ailsa Mellon Bruce Fund) made it possible for a number of objects to be especially rephotographed for this publication. A fellowship from the John Simon Guggenheim Memorial Foundation for 1964–65 was decisive in enabling me to complete the book.

I should like to express my gratitude to Mrs. Ailsa Mellon Bruce for establishing the Studies in American Art, of which this book is the first to appear.

My thanks are also extended to Yale University for granting me a leave of absence in order to work on these volumes. I am particularly indebted to Sumner McKnight Crosby, Chairman of the Department of the History of Art while this book was being prepared, and to Andrew C. Ritchie, Director of the Yale University Art Gallery, for their support of the Copley project and their effective and valued efforts to assist in its realization. The expenses of using the Yale Computer Center were largely absorbed by the center itself, and incidental charges were met by the Department of the History of Art at Yale. A timely grant from the Yale Graduate School covered some of the secretarial expenses involved in the preparation of the manuscript.

I am grateful to all of those who typed the manuscript for this book and the related correspondence, particularly to Marilyn Paige who prepared most of the final manuscript.

To G. B. Warden I extend more than a statement of thanks; he must share the credit (the author will take the responsibility) for the study of Copley's American patronage in the first volume. Engaged initially as a research assistant to gather data for the computer, Mr. Warden not only accomplished that task with diligence, energy, and apparent ease, but subsequently collaborated with me in preparing the material for computation, in shepherding it through the computers, and in analyzing the results. His impressive knowledge of eighteenth-century Bostonians has time and again been helpful, and he has used his familiarity with the subject to construct the genealogical charts found in Volume One.

Pictures by Copley seem as a rule to be owned by particularly kind and helpful people, and obviously this book owes a great deal to the cooperation of the owners. Their names appear in my catalogues and lists of illustrations, and I thank them all for allowing me to photograph and reproduce their paintings.

A few institutions have been subject to my recurrent calls for information or assistance. I want to acknowledge the essential help received from the staffs of these institutions, and particularly from: Edward Croft-Murray, Philip Pouncey, and Reginald Williams at the British Museum, London; Sir Anthony Blunt, Peter Murray, P. O. Troutman, and Cylla Mount at the Courtauld Institute of Art, London; Hannah J. Howell, Jr., Mildred Steinbach, and Helen Sanger at the Frick Art Reference Library, New York; Albert TenEyck Gardner and Stuart P. Feld at the Metropolitan Museum of Art, New York; Perry T. Rathbone, Peter A. Wick (now at the Fogg Art Museum),

ACKNOWLEDGMENTS

Kathryn Buhler, and especially Thomas N. Maytham and his staff in the Department of Paintings at the Museum of Fine Arts, Boston; K. Lindsay-MacDougall, Michael S. Robinson, and Edward H. H. Archibald at the National Maritime Museum, Greenwich; David Piper and John Kerslake at the National Portrait Gallery, London; Sidney C. Hutchison at the Royal Academy of Arts, London; Dennis Farr (now Curator of the Collection of Mr. and Mrs. Paul Mellon) and Martin Butlin at the Tate Gallery, London; and Graham Reynolds at the Victoria and Albert Museum, London.

For help in a variety of ways I should also like to thank: John Alden, Winslow Ames, Hugh Murray Baillie, Geoffrey Beard, Mrs. J. Lloyd Berrall, Violet Bourgeois, James D. Boyd, David S. Brooke, R. Brooke-Caws, Charles E. Buckley, William P. Campbell, James M. Carpenter, Charles Chetham, Charles D. Childs, Elizabeth Clare, Anthony M. Clark, Mary Bartlett Cowdrey, Bernard Crick, Abbott L. Cummings, William S. Curran, Jere R. Daniell, William F. Davidson, Morris Davis, George E. Dix, Edward H. Dwight, A. C. W. Edwards, O. W. Eggleston, Mrs. Raymond Emerson, Hon. David Erskine, Dean A. Fales, Jr., James T. Flexner, Brinsley Ford, Henry S. Francis, Anthony N. B. Garvan, William H. Gerdts, Hugh J. Gourley III, L. H. G. Greenwood, Denis Gwynn, Wendell S. Hadlock, George Heard Hamilton, Henry Hawley, Bartlett H. Hayes, Jr., Brigadier H. A. Hayes, Norman Hirschl, John Holmes, Graham S. Hood, Carol Hopkins, James L. Howgego, Robin Hutchison, Elizabeth Jones, Sheldon Keck, Patrick J. Kelleher, Katherine A. Kellock, John T. Kirby, John T. Kirk, Thomas W. Leavitt, Bertram K. Little, Mrs. M. S. Stewart Lockhart, Thomas J. McCormick, Thomas McGreevy, Donald C. Mackay, David McKibbon, Ruth S. Magurn, Oliver Millar, Charles W. Millard III, Charles Mitchell, Charles F. Montgomery, Denys P. Myers, Milo M. Naeve, Harry Shaw Newman, Earle W. Newton, Benedict Nicolson, Andrew Oliver, John H. Ottemiller, Robert O. Parks, Phyllis Polson, Edgar P. Richardson, Albert S. Roe, Caroline Rollins, E. J. Rousuck, Anna Wells Rutledge, Marvin S. Sadik, Marvin Schwartz, Josephine Setze, Frank Simpson, Theodore Sizer, J. Peter Spang III, Victor Spark, John Sweeney, Frederick A. Sweet, Davidson Taylor, Helmut Von Erffa, Robert C. Vose, Jr., Mrs. Alan Wace, Robert R. Wark, Ellis K. Waterhouse, H. Wade White, Walter Muir Whitehill, Ben F. Williams, Reginald Winder, Ingeborg Wittichen, Rudolf Wittkower, William E. Woolfenden, and Hiller Zobel.

My most resounding vote of thanks is lovingly extended to my wife, Shirley Martin Prown, who has lived with this book since its inception and has had to put up with Copley as well as with the author. Her contributions to the book have ranged from preparing card files to reading and criticizing the manuscript in all its stages. Her clear-headed judgment has been consistently helpful, and she has my deepest gratitude.

September 1965   J.D.P.

Contents

Illustrations

(Abbreviations for photo credits: B — Brenwasser, New York; Cushing — George M. Cushing, Jr., Boston; BMFA — Museum of Fine Arts, Boston; FARL — Frick Art Reference Library, New York; Met — Metropolitan Museum of Art, New York. Unless otherwise indicated, photo supplied by owner.)

Introduction

Introduction

THE UNEXPECTED BLOSSOMING OF A MAJOR EIGHTEENTH-CENTURY artist in colonial Boston, a small provincial city precariously perched on the Atlantic seaboard of the vast North American continent, is one of the most remarkable episodes in the history of art. John Singleton Copley's rise from humble beginnings to world renown has long fascinated writers on American art. Unfortunately much of the early literature on Copley, and some recent popular writing as well, has been marked by a chauvinistic approach which has sought and found in his achievement proof that America, unsullied by the decadent and corrupting influences of Europe, could produce its own great artists. For writers in this vein, Copley makes a particularly intriguing case study because his career is not a complete success story in the Abraham Lincoln–Horatio Alger vein: the story has a poignantly tragic twist. According to them, Copley is a flawed hero, with his decision to leave America at the zenith of his career spelling his doom as an artist. Copley, a self-taught artist, had first expressed through his honest American portraits the vigorous realism of an essentially American outlook on life. But when he went abroad to study and paint, he adopted the facile and vacuous techniques of European academic art. Like a character out of Henry James, the story goes, he withered and decayed when removed from the life-giving soil of his homeland.

Recent literature on American art, on the other hand, has been particularly concerned with debunking the excesses of the "nativist" school of scholarship. Scholars in this later camp have assiduously searched for and have often found antecedents in European art for virtually everything produced in this country, ranging from design-book sources for American architecture and furniture to compositional sources in European engravings, particularly English mezzotints, for American paintings. This process of finding European prototypes has now been carried to the point where the old and somewhat truculent arguments about "what is American in American art" have been largely replaced by equally truculent counter-demonstrations that everything in American art is of foreign origin.[1]

The present study of Copley attempts to avoid the Scylla of patriotic flag waving and the Charybdis of finding nothing American in the work of this American artist. My purpose is to bring together the widely scattered materials that exist on Copley and to

---

[1] The older tradition has been creatively renewed recently by John W. McCoubrey, *American Tradition in Painting* (New York, 1963). Although McCoubrey's approach is markedly different from that of such predecessors as Oskar Hagen in *Birth of the American Tradition in Art*, the goal of discovering distinctive qualities in American art is the same.

1

examine objectively his achievement both in the American colonies and in England. Although it might be pleasant to think that this American artist flowered with such brilliance solely through his own genius and the nourishment he received from his native soil, the evidence is clear that Copley's early development as an artist was shaped by a variety of outside forces. Boston, despite its small size and limited population of approximately sixteen thousand, was nonetheless a flourishing outpost of Western civilization (Harvard College was over a hundred years old when Copley was born). In Boston Copley absorbed a number of artistic influences, not as an uncreative copyist of things European, but as an alert and uncommonly resourceful individual who made all sorts of visual material grist for his mill, creating objects that far transcended the sum of their parts. But even though Copley was steeped in the European tradition, his character as a provincial American was not erased by that tradition. When he finally went to England, he achieved a significant mode of artistic expression that bore the indelible imprint of his American experience. Along with his fellow American, Benjamin West, Copley in his realistic history paintings made one of the first important American additions to the mainstream of Western art.

The essential character and strength of American art is not the result of independence from the Western artistic heritage: rather it results from the intense, almost greedy, drive on the part of American artists to absorb as much of that heritage as possible while at the same time, with enterprise and ingenuity, transmuting it into artistic statements that are distinctively, if not always consciously, American. A peculiarly American art has gained in vigor and definition over several centuries until in our own time it has become a primary cultural force. Because Copley was one of the first American artists to play a major role in the history of Western art, it is fitting and important that we attempt to get a clearer picture of his contribution.

The present state of Copley scholarship is somewhat imbalanced: far more attention has been paid to the American years, prior to 1774, than to the artist's subsequent career in England. Since Copley lived and painted for forty years in England, whereas only twenty-one of his thirty-six years in the colonies were artistically productive, this seems out of proportion. Historians of American art have tended to lose interest in the work Copley produced after he became, for all practical purposes, an English artist. At the same time, historians of English art have had only a limited concern for his English career. This is largely because Copley was primarily a history painter in England, and there has been little interest in English history painting since Allan Cunningham stopped writing and John Ruskin began a century ago. These factors have combined to cast the English career of Copley, a history painter of provincial origin, into nearly complete obscurity. In the great Exhibition of British Art, c. 1000–1860, held in 1934 at the Royal Academy of Arts in London, a comprehensive exhibition that included over fifteen hundred items with more than one work representing such contemporaneous figures as Jeremiah Myers, William Pars, and John Hamilton Mortimer, not a single painting by Copley was shown.

Copley's American career has not been neglected in this way. There has been a good deal written on the subject (although not always with perception or precision). The studies of Copley's American career culminated in 1938 with the excellent catalogue by Barbara N. Parker and Anne B. Wheeler, which recorded all of Copley's American work and cleared away much of the previous confusion by assigning a number of works incorrectly attributed to Copley to their proper authors. It also brought together a useful body of biographical information about the subjects of Copley's American portraits.

The absence of studies of Copley's English career and the existence of an ample catalogue of his American portraits have imposed two different scholarly requirements on the present book. Thus Volume Two, which deals with the unsung English years, contains a comprehensive catalogue of the English pictures, whereas Volume One simply contains a checklist of American paintings, revising Parker and Wheeler where necessary and incorporating materials or emendations that have become evident since the publication of their work. But the different art-historical needs and opportunities in regard to a study of Copley's two careers have shaped my study in more than catalogue requirements.

Copley, living in late eighteenth- and early nineteenth-century London, belonged to a well-organized, cosmopolitan society, and there is a wealth of primary source material available. County, town, and parish records in regard to baptisms, burials, marriages, wills, and property taxes are relatively complete. Numerous newspapers reported the activities of such artistic organizations as the Royal Academy and the Society of Artists, and individuals participating or interested in the arts kept diaries, many of which have been published. Nevertheless, there are serious lacunae in our knowledge of Copley's English work. Many paintings and drawings found their way into private collections at the large auction sale held by Christie in 1864 after the death of Copley's son, Lord Lyndhurst, and some are still unlocated. Biographical information about the subjects of English portraits is sometimes lacking, and on occasion, through the curtain of intervening years, it is difficult to perceive the full significance and implications of Copley's history paintings for his contemporaries.

In contrast with all of this, there are few records casting light on Copley's artistic activities in Boston. There were no public exhibitions attracting notices and reviews, no artistic organizations to leave historical footprints, and no townsmen interested enough in artistic activities to keep informative journals. The basic historical facts about Copley's life in Boston are indeed meager. But, as if to compensate, there apparently is a higher rate of survival of the pictures painted in America, and much more is known about the subjects of these pictures. This situation exists because of the relatively limited society, both numerically and geographically, for which Copley painted, and because of the familial sense of genealogically minded generations of descendants who have preserved the portraits of their ancestors and have recorded vast quantities of data about the sitters. We have the publications of the Massachusetts Historical Society, the Colonial Society of Massachusetts, and the New England Historic Genealogical Society; *Sibley's Harvard Graduates*; published histories of Boston in general, and specific studies of families and of groups like the loyalists; and the biographical compilations in Parker and Wheeler — through such sources a great deal of information is available about the people whose portraits by Copley survive in such quantity.

Obviously, then, the present state of knowledge for Copley in England and Copley in America is uneven, and the resources available for filling the gaps require the use of different scholarly techniques. The study of Copley in England is largely historical, pulling together scattered pieces of documentary information and recording as many of Copley's English pictures as possible. The study of Copley in America, with the scarcity of documentary information, uses the remarkable resource available in the objects themselves. My study of American Copley has thus involved not so much a search for pictures and documents as an attempt to find out what can be deduced from the great body of surviving visual evidence, the pictures themselves, and from the facts relating to these objects. As a result Volume One depends heavily on visual or stylistic analysis of objects, with particular emphasis on clarifying chronological sequence, informed by a supplementary statistical analysis of available information about the paintings and the sitters. This analysis of two hundred and forty individuals whose portraits were painted by Copley between 1753 and 1774 was made with the aid of a digital computer, and the results are included in the second part of this volume for the benefit of readers who do not mind wading through statistical lists and charts.

Because Copley's career so neatly divides itself into two periods that are discrete in locale, in the nature of the work produced, and in the life Copley led, there has been a widespread unconscious tendency to consider the man as two artists rather than one. Although my two volumes are necessarily disparate in character, they do unite to give a full and, it is hoped, cogent account of the life and work of the artist, putting this sadly bifurcated Copley back together again. The view presented here of Copley as a stylistically consistent but ever-changing artist, who produced major works on both sides of the ocean, serves to clarify his role as a major figure in the art of the eighteenth century.

Copley in America

Family, Childhood, and Early Artistic Influences

I

1738-1752

JOHN SINGLETON COPLEY WAS BORN ON JULY 3, 1738. HIS MOTHER, Mary Singleton Copley, was one of three children of John and Jane Bruffe Singleton, Quinville Abbey, County Clare, Ireland. Richard Copley, his father, was probably the son of Alderman Charles Copley, one of the sheriffs of Limerick. Family tradition has it that Mary and Richard Copley were married in Ireland around 1735 and emigrated to America in the following year. This would make it likely, though by no means certain, that John Singleton Copley was born in Boston.[1]

In Boston Richard Copley became the proprietor of a tobacco shop on Long Wharf. Although he is thought to have died in the West Indies shortly after his son was born, again according to family tradition, this must have occurred after he initiated a lawsuit

[1] Martha Babcock Amory, *The Domestic and Artistic Life of John Singleton Copley, R.A.* (Boston, 1882), p. 226, letter from Mrs. John Singleton Copley, London, to Mrs. Gardiner Greene, Boston, July 26, 1802; Henry Wilder Foote, "When Was John Singleton Copley Born?" *New England Quarterly,* X (March 1937), 111–20; Henry Watson, Limerick, to John Singleton, Esq., Aug. 24, [early nineteenth century], Lyndhurst Papers, Trinity College, Cambridge; Sir Theodore Martin, *A Life of Lord Lyndhurst* (London, 1883), p. 3. There is still some question about Copley's date and place of birth. Foote specifically examined the question of whether Copley was born in 1737 or 1738 and concluded in favor of 1738. An additional bit of evidence supports this. When Joseph Farington recorded in his diary on Jan. 1, 1794, the ages of all members of London's Royal Academy, he listed Copley's age as fifty-five, further indicating that Copley was born in 1738 ("Farington Diary," typescript copy in the British Museum of the manuscript original at Windsor Castle). But in a deposition of Jan. 22, 1812 (Society for the Preservation of New England Antiquities), Copley gave his age as seventy-four, which points to 1737 as the year of birth. Still, the weight of evidence favors 1738.

Since no birth or baptismal records for Copley have been located, he could have been born in Ireland or even en route to America, although the probability is strong that he was born in Boston. Gerard B. Warden has found a document in the Massachusetts state archives, dated March 17, 1741/42, which lists a Richard Copley as one of a group of petitioners to William Shirley, governor of the Massachusetts Bay Province, asking that their tract of land on St. George's River [St. George's Lower Town, founded in 1741, deserted in 1745–49], in what was then York County, be made a township (James P. Baxter, *Documentary History of Maine* [Portland, Maine, 1908], XI, 237–39; Cyrus Eaton, *History of Thomaston* [Hallowell, Maine, 1865], I, 51). The land in question was Samuel Waldo's tract in the Lincolnshire Company Grant in Maine. During much of the 1730's Waldo had served as the company's agent to recruit Irish and Dutch immigrants to settle the new tract. It is therefore possible, though highly conjectural, that Richard Copley, the artist's father, may have been one of the Irish settlers of Waldo's tract before settling in Boston. This might account for the absence of any record of Copley's birth.

to recover a bad debt in 1741.[2] But Richard Copley was undeniably dead by 1748. On May 2 of that year Mary Copley, widow, was granted administration of the estate of the late and intestate Richard Copley of Boston, tobacconist. An inventory of the household goods of Richard Copley, made on May 6, 1748, suggests clearly that the home on Long Wharf in which young Copley spent the first ten years of his life was indeed a modest one.[3]

In the Yellow Chamber

One Feather Bed, Boulster Curtains & 2 Blankets	£42.10.–
One Old Desk	7.–
One Looking Glass	17.–
Six Prints & Pictures	3.5.–
Twelve Bound Books &c	3.
Three Table Cloths, Two Towels	5.
Six Old Chairs	2.

In the Green Chamber

One Suit of Green Curtains	2.
Two Chests	2.
One Quilt	2.10.–

In the Kitchen

Six Dishes, Seven Plates Pewter	6.12.6
One Spit	.8
One Bell mettle Skillet	1.5.–
One Brass Sauspan	.5
Two Brass Candlesticks	1.10.–
Two Iron Do Old	.2
Two Flat Irons	.6
One Brass Skimmer	1.
Old Tenr	£97.13.6

There is very little here to suggest any roots for the artistic career Copley was to follow. On May 22, 1748, the widow Copley married Peter Pelham, an engraver, portrait painter, and schoolmaster, at Trinity Church.[4] The *Boston News-Letter* carried the following advertisement on July 11, 1748:

[2] Richard Copley, tobacconist, of Boston filed suit in 1741 to recover £200 from James Hamilton, mariner, also of Boston, to whom he had lent £180 on May 18, 1739. The summons was issued on June 15, 1741. Early Court Records, Suffolk County Courthouse, Boston, file no. 53765, vol. 345, fol. 133, July 1741, Copley v. Hamilton.

[3] The letter of administration, the inventory, and the administration bond (the widow Copley posted £100, with the bondsmen listed as Peter Pelham, gentleman, and Robert Skinner, peruke maker) comprise Probate no. 8979, Probate Court, Suffolk County Court House, Boston.

[4] This was the second marriage for the widow Copley and the third for Peter Pelham, who already had four sons and one daughter. See "The Copleys and Pelhams of New England," *Heraldic Journal,* IV (Boston, 1868), 175–82, and Guernsey Jones, ed., *Letters and Papers of John Singleton Copley and Henry Pelham,* Vol. LXXI, Massachusetts Historical Society Collections (Boston, 1914), pp. 3–11; hereafter cited, *Copley-Pelham Letters.*

Mrs. Mary Pelham (formerly the widow Copley, on the Long Wharf, Tobacconist) is removed from [to] Lindel's Row, against the Quaker's Meeting-House, near the upper End of King Street, Boston, where she continues to sell the best Virginia Tobacco, Cut, Pigtail and spun, of all Sorts, by Wholesale, or Retail, at the cheapest Rates.

Peter Pelham was an engraver of mezzotints who found it necessary to make his living through a host of other activities, such as teaching young gentlemen and ladies "Dancing, Writing, Reading, Painting on Glass and all sorts of Needle Work." [5] He advertised in the *Boston News-Letter* on September 12, 1748:

Mr. Pelham's Writing and Arithmetick School, near the Town House (during the Winter Season) will be open from Candle-Light 'till nine in the Evening, as usual, for the benefit of those employ'd in Business all the Day; and at his Dwelling House near the Quaker's Meeting in Lindell's Row; All Persons may be supply'd with the best Virginia Tobacco, cut, spun into the very best Pigtail, and all other sorts; also Snuff, at the cheapest Rate.

Thus the marriage of the widow Copley and Peter Pelham brought together two diverse businesses that, for a while at least, flourished jointly. It also took young Copley, aged ten, from a tobacco shop on Long Wharf to the home of Peter Pelham who, although a jack-of-all-trades, was first and foremost an artist and engraver. The boy was thrust into direct contact with a creative and experienced artist and his studio.

Peter Pelham (c. 1695–1751). Pelham began his artistic career in 1713 in London as an apprentice to John Simon, a mezzotint engraver. Between 1720 and 1726 he published twenty-five engravings in London and appears to have been quite successful. Nonetheless, for some reason, he left London in 1727 and emigrated to Boston. There was little opportunity for him to produce mezzotints in Boston; indeed, to secure a portrait as the basis for a mezzotint it was necessary to paint it himself. This is what he did in the case of his famous 1727 likeness of *Cotton Mather* (now at the American Antiquarian Society). The arrival of a superior painter, John Smibert, in 1729 was more of a blessing than a blow to Pelham, since in theory at least he could concentrate on his own craft of engraving while Smibert produced portraits from which he could take the engravings. But in practice there appears to have been a slim market for his prints in Boston, and his production of mezzotints before 1750 was limited. He scraped a single mezzotint in each of the years 1728, c. 1732, c. 1733, 1735, 1743, and two in 1747. In 1750–51, however, Pelham had a burst of activity and produced seven prints. This means that, during the very period that young Copley was in his house, Pelham was particularly active as an artist. This happy state of affairs was cut short by Pelham's death late in 1751.[6] Peter and Mary Pelham had been married only three and a half

---

[5] Advertisement in *Boston Gazette*, Jan. 16 and 23, 1738, printed in George F. Dow, *Arts and Crafts in New England* (Topsfield, Mass., 1927), p. 12.

[6] Anne Allison, "Peter Pelham, Engraver in Mezzo-

tinto," *Antiques*, LII (Dec. 1947), 441–43. In his American career Peter Pelham made a total of seven prints after his own paintings, five after paintings by Smibert, one after John Greenwood, and years and had one child, Henry Pelham, born February 14, 1749. Copley was almost ten when his widowed mother married Peter Pelham; he was thirteen when Pelham died and his home was again fatherless. Although he had older stepbrothers who undoubtedly helped to support the family, Copley apparently felt a particular responsibility for his once more widowed mother and his infant half brother. Despite his youth, Copley determined to contribute to the family income by the means that lay immediately at hand: Peter Pelham's studio with its equipment for making mezzotints and paintings. In 1753, at the age of fourteen or fifteen, he produced his first works, which were a mezzotint of *Rev. William Welsteed* (fig. 5) and a handful of portraits and mythological scenes.

Copley must have had innate artistic talent and a strong natural inclination to express it. But there is no certainty that he would have become a working artist if his interest in art had not been quickened by his fortuitous contact with Pelham, an artist who had lived among artists in London and who undoubtedly could supplement his demonstrations of skill with colorful anecdotes of artists he had known. There was also the exposure to the physical environment of an artist's studio, with its fascinating array of equipment. Pelham and his studio, moreover, were focal points for other artistic influences that touched the young Copley. Through Pelham, for example, Copley certainly knew John Smibert, whose studio and shop were just a few short blocks away.

John Smibert (1688–1751). Smibert's arrival and permanent settlement in the colonies had been the most important single event in the history of American art prior to Copley's time, and until mid-century Smibert was the foremost painter in America. He was born in Edinburgh and at the age of twenty-one went to London for a period of apprenticeship. Subsequently he spent three years in Italy and from 1720 to 1728 was a portrait painter in London, enjoying some success but never the highest levels of patronage. During this period it is likely that he knew his younger colleague, Peter Pelham, who was active in London until 1727. Smibert came to Rhode Island with Bishop Berkeley's party late in 1728, en route to a post as professor of painting and architecture in Berkeley's projected college at Bermuda. But he separated himself from the abortive Bermuda project and in 1729 began to paint actively in Boston.

In his strong early American works, such as the large 1729 group portrait of *Dean Berkeley and His Entourage* (*The Bermuda Group*; fig. 1), and the powerful likeness of old *Nathaniel Byfield*, Smibert established himself as infinitely more skillful than any artist who had yet appeared in the colonies. In addition to being a competent painter, Smibert was something of an impresario. He had brought with him, presumably for use in his projected teaching assignment in Bermuda, an important collection of copies of old-master paintings, plaster casts of ancient sculpture, and prints, all of which he had assembled during his travels in Italy, France, and Holland and during his years in

one after Joseph Highmore, the English painter. He was buried at Trinity Church, Boston, Dec. 14, 1751 ("The Copleys and Pelhams of New England," p. 179).

England. From the beginning, in the winter of 1729–30, Smibert regularly exhibited his collection in Boston along with his most recent paintings. Located in what became Scollay Square, his studio and the adjacent shop from which he began to sell prints and art supplies became the leading and virtually the only art center in colonial America. Smibert was unrivaled as a painter in Boston during the 1730's and maintained his pre-eminence well into the 1740's, when the first important generation of American-born painters (Robert Feke, John Greenwood, Joseph Badger) began to work. Despite the marked deterioration of his artistic abilities in the 1740's, accompanied by a physical decline, particularly failing eyesight, he was still the grand old man of American painting. This Scotsman had found in provincial Boston a congenial spot where he was not merely a run-of-the-mill portrait painter, as he had been in London, but the peerless artistic leader.

Although Smibert was the first and for a long time the only major painter in colonial America,[7] he exerted remarkably little influence on subsequent American art, except indirectly through the prints that he brought with him or imported for sale in his shop and through his collection of old-master copies and plaster casts, which were studied, and on occasion copied, by younger artists (including eventually Charles Willson Peale, John Trumbull, and Washington Allston). Smibert was the first major practitioner of the Lely-Kneller baroque tradition in American painting. However, his own works were decreasingly effective exercises in this mode, becoming over the years less cosmopolitan and less polished, possibly as a result of his failing health, the absence of competition, or his adoption of provincial aesthetic standards. By contrast, the succeeding generation of native-born artists, especially Feke, Greenwood, and Copley, traveled in the opposite direction, becoming less provincial and more cosmopolitan. They embraced the newest English styles eagerly, moving easily from the stolid baroque style into the brighter and more spritely rococo phase that followed it.

As for any direct influence from Smibert, even Copley's earliest portraits indicate that he had already left Smibert's old-fashioned style bobbing in his wake. With the passion of any youth for *le dernier cri*, he picked up the stylistic thread where artists younger than Smibert, specifically Feke and Greenwood, left off. Except for a general awareness of Smibert's precedent in full-length portraiture and in the conservative convention for bust-length portraits of ministers in painted oval spandrels, the stylistic influence of the older generation on Copley was minimal. Still, the illustrious Smibert and his colleague, Peter Pelham, must have made a deep personal impression on the boy, as the two old friends told stories and reminisced about art and artists during the last few years of their lives.

Robert Feke (*1705/10–after 1750*). The most active painter in Boston during the impressionable early years that Copley spent in Pelham's studio was Robert Feke. An

[7] There were, of course, other artists working in the colonies before Smibert arrived, such as Henrietta Johnston, Justus Englehardt Kühn, and John Watson, but their achievements were limited in comparison with Smibert's.

artist of irritatingly obscure beginnings, Feke appeared in Boston in 1741 as the painter of the impressive group portrait, *Isaac Royall and Family* (fig. 2). In 1741 Smibert was still the leading artist in Boston, although business had fallen off sharply from the halcyon days of 1729–1735 when clients were in good supply and he produced more than half of all of his Boston paintings. The attrition in Smibert's patronage can be attributed variously to the sated market, hard times, the decline in his skill, and the fading novelty of having a trained portrait painter in town. But Feke's commission from wealthy young Isaac Royall to paint the family portrait in 1741, surely the commission plum of the decade, apparently resulted not from any belief in Feke's superiority as a painter, but rather from some indisposition that made it impossible for the faltering Smibert to do the job.[8] Although Feke received the Royall commission, Smibert's influence on the finished picture is evident. Whether as a result of the client's insistence, Feke's choice, or the necessity of following a model, *The Royall Family* clearly echoes *The Bermuda Group* of a dozen years earlier in the general arrangement, pose, and sequence of figures grouped around a rug-covered table. As in Smibert's picture, the male figures are much better painted than the females, while the infants are almost grotesque.

After completing the *Royall* group, Feke seems to have been artistically inactive for a few years, living in Newport, but in 1745 he produced a splendid portrait, *Rev. Thomas Hiscox*. In the following year Feke was painting in Philadelphia. In 1748, the year that Copley and his mother moved from Long Wharf to Lindall's Row, Feke was in Boston, and he entered upon a remarkably productive period lasting some two years. In 1750 he disappears from view again, and that is the last we hear of him. Whereas Smibert's influence upon Copley tended to be mostly personal, Feke is a shadowy influence personally but seems to have wielded considerable force through his paintings. In part Feke's influence on Copley and others may be the result of his position as the first major American-born painter. His stylistic progression is almost diametrically opposed to Smibert's retreat from a relatively sophisticated London style. Feke moved steadily in the direction of sophistication, although his pictures always retained the mark of his provincial origin. The painted backgrounds of his portraits tend to be uniplanar theatrical drops against which the figures are merely set in place. Each area on the picture surface is clearly defined. Marked contrasts of light and dark are reinforced by pleasing, broad coloristic contrasts of warm against cool or vice versa. Figures are not integrated with their landscape settings spatially, but linearly: lines in the figure — the outline of a shoulder or the zigzag of a laced dress front — are repeated in the line of a hill or the meander of a stream. The intense light-dark contrasts seem to reflect an artistic vision nourished and shaped by mezzotints. American-born painters like Feke also tended to see and re-create in terms

[8] Smibert wrote to Arthur Pond in London, July 1, 1743, "my health [is] better than I could have expected, having near 3 years ago recovered from a dangerous ilnes [sic]." Henry Wilder Foote, *John Smibert* (Cambridge, Mass., 1950), p. 86.

of flat planes and in strong color contrasts that reinforce planarity; and a linear stress, perhaps also reflecting the influence of prints, works to define the edges of planes and resists the sculptural modeling of solid forms in space. Feke carried this essentially provincial mode of artistic expression — the two-dimensionality of folk art as opposed to academic mastery of plastic forms realized in a convincing spatial ambient — to new levels of achievement. His art was appealing to later American artists presumably because they tended to see and to react to visual experience similarly, and were equally innocent of academic techniques. Many of the stylistic characteristics found in Feke are essential to Copley's style as well, but in Copley this artistic language is carried to a still more effective level of expression.

John Greenwood (*1727–1792*). In 1741, the year of Feke's *Royall Family*, John Greenwood began a craft apprenticeship to Thomas Johnston, a Boston line engraver, sign painter, and japanner. Four years later, at the age of eighteen, Greenwood struck out on his own and for the next seven years painted actively in Boston. Like Feke, Greenwood was native-born and his style shares the same characteristics of linearity, planarity, clarity, and strong value and color contrasts that mark the work of colonial painters in general. Greenwood was clearly influenced by Feke, as can be seen by a comparison of his portrait of *Benjamin Pickman* (Essex Institute) with Feke's *William Peters* (Historical Society of Pennsylvania), or his *Robert Jenkins*, c. 1750 (fig. 25), with Feke's *James Bowdoin II*, 1748–1750 (fig. 23), in which he reverses the pose.

In addition to his paintings, Greenwood produced one engraving in Boston, *Jersey Nanny*, in 1748. The only person in Boston from whom it appears Greenwood could have learned the mezzotint technique was Peter Pelham. So it is quite possible that Greenwood was at least informally a pupil of Pelham's at the time young Copley arrived in Lindall's Row in 1748. Apparently Greenwood decided after producing a single mezzotint, as Copley was to do several years later, that engraving was not the form of artistic expression to which he was best suited. In the following year he had Pelham engrave his portrait of *Rev. Edward Holyoke*.

Stylistically Greenwood was, like Feke, wedded to a provincial tradition. Having been apprenticed to a painter of signs and hatchments, he was particularly alert to the design possibilities of the picture surface rather than to the spatial possibilities achievable through perspective and modeling. This is evident in *The Greenwood-Lee Family*, c. 1747 (fig. 3), a group portrait indebted to Smibert's *Bermuda Group* and Feke's *Royall Family*, with the artist himself appearing in the background as in Smibert's picture. Greenwood liked the unbroken, though occasionally agitated, movement of line on the surface plane, bounding areas of pigment that were frequently simplified to assume basic geometrical shapes — the head as an oval, an arm as a cylinder, the body as a triangle. Like Feke, Greenwood did not secure his figures in space: they exist in a vacuum; there is no atmosphere. As with all print-influenced native artists, Greenwood's value contrasts are pronounced, although the lights and darks are lumpy as in a Pelham mezzotint.

13

Unaccountably, in 1752, despite the fact that he enjoyed a virtual monopoly of Boston painting with Feke gone, Smibert dead, and Copley too young, Greenwood left the colonies and never returned.

Nathaniel Smibert (*1735–1756*). A still younger artist, Nathaniel Smibert, the son of John Smibert, was also on the Boston scene for a brief moment. After the departure of Greenwood in 1752, he was one of the potential bright lights of American painting. His premature death in 1756 at the age of twenty-two left eighteen-year-old Copley as the sole remaining artist of promise in Boston.

Joseph Badger (*1708–1765*). There was one other artist working in Boston who must be considered a possible influence on Copley. Joseph Badger was of Feke's generation and, like Feke, emerged as a recognizable artistic personality in the early 1740's. Badger, whose major period of activity was the decade 1750–1760, can almost be called a folk artist, more closely related to the anonymous limners of the seventeenth century and the so-called primitive painters of the nineteenth century than to his style-conscious, Europe-oriented contemporaries. With the exception of the use of a Badger portrait as the source for his mezzotint of *Rev. William Welsteed* (figs. 5 and 6), it seems evident that Copley accepted little or no influence from Badger. Indeed, if there was any flow of influence between the two, it went the other way, from the younger to the older artist.[9] Copley's taste ran to fresh, strong colors, fluid brushwork, smooth surfaces, and clearly defined areas. Some of his early pictures (*Joseph Mann*, fig. 21; *Jonathan Mountfort*, fig. 26; *Ann Tyng*, fig. 38) show a Badgeresque tendency toward rough brushwork, which allows the underpaint to show through darkly in flesh areas, and the portraits of the 1750's reveal a penchant for dark, smoky landscape backgrounds — but these are occasional stylistic similarities that do not seem to reflect any direct or purposive influence. Copley's paintings generally have a sort of professional sleekness about them, and this could never be said of Badger's work. The earth colors are somber and muted, the lines smudgy, the backgrounds hazy, and the paint surfaces thin but not smooth. In his later work Badger has an interesting way of setting his figures against an indistinct landscape background that is almost oriental in the laconic adumbration of a tree or a hill, but Copley appears to have found little visual inspiration in these paintings.

[9] Badger was extremely receptive to outside influences. For example, to cope with one large full-length-portrait commission, *Captain John Larrabee* (1760, Worcester Art Museum), he adopted the military full-length pose used by Feke in his excellent portrait of *Brigadier-General Samuel Waldo* (1748–50), which in turn had been derived from a recent mezzotint engraving of the Thomas Hudson portrait of *Admiral Ogle*. Badger does not seem to have let false pride stand in the way of taking an occasional idea from the younger Copley. His portrait of *Samuel Torrey*, probably dating from the late 1750's, seems very close to the pose of John Gore in the 1753 Copley group portrait of *The Brothers and Sisters of Christopher Gore* (fig. 29). The pose of *Rebecca Orne Cabot* (c. 1758), is reminiscent of the pose of one of Copley's *Gore Sisters* (fig. 30). Badger reveals his tendency to borrow from colleagues clearly in his 1757 portraits of *Mr. and Mrs. Timothy Orne*. Mrs. Orne is related to Blackburn's *Susan Apthorp* of the same year. Mr. Orne has a pose like Feke's *James Bowdoin II* (fig. 23) and similar paintings, but also has something of the quality of Copley's earlier *Joseph Mann* (fig. 21) and the roughly contemporaneous *Thomas Marshall* (fig. 52).

II   A Career Begins

1753-1757   WHEN COPLEY STARTED HIS CAREER IN 1753, A SCANT QUARTER century had passed since the arrival of Smibert. Yet a distinct and important period in American art was already ended. Feke disappeared in 1750; Smibert and Pelham died in 1751; and Greenwood departed for Surinam in 1752. Only Badger and the ill-fated Nathaniel Smibert were still on the scene when Copley began to paint.

The pattern of artistic patronage over the previous quarter century had begun with a sharp burst of portrait commissions from 1729 to 1735, occasioned by the arrival of the skillful Smibert in Boston. This was followed by a slack period, 1735–1745, in which painting seems to have been in the doldrums. Smibert's production was relatively low during that decade, and he turned out less than half as many paintings as during his first six years. Over the same period Pelham produced only one mezzotint; Feke painted *The Royall Family* and perhaps a self-portrait and a handful of other canvases; and Badger also produced very little. But in 1745 Feke, Badger, and Greenwood became active, and Smibert had ahead of him his important commissions for full-length portraits of the heroes of Louisburg. Pelham renewed his work as a mezzotint engraver in 1747, and , by the time young Copley arrived in his studio the following year, artistic activity was flourishing in Boston.

Copley, then, did not launch his career in a vacuum: there was a vigorous if unsophisticated tradition developed by Smibert, Pelham, Feke, and Greenwood in which he could and did follow, even though the artists themselves had gone. He seems to have begun in 1753 by stepping neatly into his late stepfather's shoes, the studio being conveniently at hand, with a mezzotint portrait of *Rev. William Welsteed* (fig. 5), the recently deceased minister of New Brick Church. As one would expect, Copley's mezzotint is stylistically close to the work of Pelham; in fact it is identical in some parts with Pelham's 1743 mezzotint of *Rev. William Cooper* (fig. 4). The young Copley, practical from the beginning, had simply selected an appropriate Pelham plate that was lying around the studio; planished out the head, the collar area, and a few selected parts of the inscription below, including the names of the previous artist and engraver, the last name of the sitter, and two digits from the age of the sitter and the date; and substituted Welsteed's head and collar, last name, age, and date, as well

15

as his own name as artist and engraver in the lower left-hand corner.[1] The altered areas in the Welsteed engraving are evident in the lighter penumbra of the rubbed area behind the head and in the palimpsest markings on the inscription. Although Copley put down his own name as the artist of the portrait on which the mezzotint was based, no such portrait is known and the likeness of the deceased Welsteed corresponds with the portrait now at the Massachusetts Historical Society (fig. 6), once attributed to Copley but almost certainly painted by Joseph Badger.[2]

The most profound influence of Pelham and his studio upon Copley, more lasting and significant than example or technical instruction or materials on hand, is the most difficult to document. This is the effect of Pelham's ideas about art and the ideas available in whatever books he owned or to which he introduced his stepson. Copley, while still in the colonies, was familiar with such books on art, architecture, and art theory as Count Francesco Algarotti, *Letters upon Painting*; Charles du Fresnoy, *De Arte Graphica* (possibly as edited by John Dryden, *The Art of Painting* [London, 1695; second edition, 1716]); Roger de Piles, perhaps *Abrégé de la Vie des Peintres* (Paris, 1699) or *The Principles of Painting* (London, 1743); Horace Walpole, *Anecdotes of Painting in England*; Daniel Webb, *An Inquiry into the Beauties of Painting*; Turnbull, *A Treatise on Ancient Painting*; and James Gibbs, *Book of Architecture*.[3] From the very start of his career, Copley seems to have been aware of and fascinated by the great unseen world of Western art that lay on the far side of the ocean. From his reading he developed an exaggerated idea of the sublimity of the works of the great masters, and of the importance of the artists themselves. Never having seen any masterworks, and with no experience of the actual role of the European artist in society, Copley developed his ideas in good measure from what he read; he was hardly able to know how much the art-theory books were given to overstatement. An example of the extent to which he was indoctrinated by his reading can be found in his comments on Benjamin West, in a letter sent some years later to John Greenwood in England: "I sincerely rejoice in Mr. West's successful progress towards the summit of that Mighty Mountain where the

[1] Copley's use of Pelham's *Cooper* plate was discovered by John David Summers as he was doing research on Pelham for my graduate seminar, "American Colonial Art and the Sources of Copley's Style," given at Yale University in the fall of 1963.

[2] The source could have also been an unlocated duplicate of this portrait formerly owned by the Unitarian Church, Waltham, Mass. Barbara N. Parker and Anne B. Wheeler, *John Singleton Copley: American Portraits* (Boston, 1938), p. 238, n. 3; hereafter cited, Parker-Wheeler.

[3] The reference to Algarotti is found in *Copley-Pelham Letters*, pp. 51–52, Copley to Benjamin West, Nov. 12, 1766. For the specific reference to Walpole and general references to De Piles and Du Fresnoy, see *ibid.*, pp. 170–71, Henry Pelham to Copley, Oct. 22, 1771; for the reference to Webb,

ibid., p. 303, Copley to Pelham, March 14, 1775. Copley, writing from Rome, mentions an account in Webb. He does not elaborate, since the book was available to Pelham in Boston, and the implication is that he too knew it in Boston. Copley's ownership of Gibbs and Turnbull is suggested by a letter in the Public Record Office, London, C.O./39, fol. 260, Henry Pelham to Mr. Knox, 1774. Pelham, serving as Copley's agent after Copley left Boston in 1774, requested the return of "Gibbs Designs in Archi[tecture]" and Turnbull on Ancient painting." There is another small piece of information concerning Copley's familiarity with European art. William Johnston, New Haven, sent Copley, Boston, Sept. 14, 1764, a life of Jan Steen and referred him for the lives of other artists to the 1763 supplement of *Gentleman's Magazine* (Public Record Office, C.O./38, foll. 52–53).

Everlasting Lauriels grow to adorn the brows of those Elustrious Artists that are so favoured of Heaven as to be able to unravel the intricate mazes of its rough and perilous Asent." [4] This is the kind of elaboration common in the theoretical literature of art — much of which was trying to establish painting as one of the liberal arts, in "reaction against the lingering medieval point of view which considered the arts as trades." [5] But it seems ridiculously naive when set forth so soberly in a letter to a friend. The strength of Copley's commitment to an idealized notion of art is clear from another letter that he wrote to a friend in England. Here, though enjoying enormous success as a portrait painter in Boston, Copley expresses his discontent at being restricted to a place where, "was it not for preserving the resembla[n]ce of perticular persons, painting would not be known in the plac[e]. The people generally regard it no more than any other usefull trade, as they somtimes term it, like that of a Carpenter[,] tailor or shew maker, not as one of the most noble Arts in the World. Which is not a little Mortifiing to me." [6]

Young Copley's somewhat unrealistic opinion of artists and their art also manifested itself in the kind of work he did. Copley learned from the writings of such theoreticians as Roger de Piles that all types of painting were not equal, that there was a hierarchy of the branches of painting, and that portraiture, the kind of socially useful art for which there was a demand in the American colonies, was of only middling importance. It ranked far below the highest branch of the profession, history painting, in which the great masters had achieved their glory. Aware that the imaginative depiction of historical, mythological, or religious scenes was considered the highest form of artistic expression, Copley produced at least three history paintings in his first few years of artistic activity. These were not audacious attempts to beat the masters at their own game — Copley had too much respect for his profession for that — but groping attempts at self-education. In the best academic tradition, he began to explore the problem of creating complex history paintings by copying the old masters. However, since Boston had little in the way of such paintings, Copley turned to prints.

Galatea (fig. 7) is based on an engraving by Augustinus of Lazarini's *Galatea Triomphe sur L'Onde* (fig. 8); the recently located *Return of Neptune* (fig. 9), which works as a pendant to *Galatea*, is based on an engraving of the subject by Ravenet after Casali (fig. 10); and although no print source has yet been identified for the *Mars, Venus and Vulcan* of 1754 (fig. 11), the source is almost certainly an eighteenth-century print. [7] Copley skillfully reproduced the compositions, but more important are the

[4] *Copley-Pelham Letters*, pp. 105–06, Jan. 25, 1771.
[5] Luigi Salerno, "Seventeenth-Century English Literature on Painting," *Journal of the Warburg and Courtauld Institutes*, XIV, no. 3–4 (1951), 234.
[6] *Copley-Pelham Letters*, pp. 65–66, Copley to Benjamin West or Captain R. G. Bruce, 1767 (?). I should note here that I have adhered closely to the texts in the *Copley-Pelham Letters* as edited by Guernsey Jones, who retained all of Copley's and his correspondents' idiosyncrasies of spelling, grammar, and punctuation (for two exceptions see Chapter V, note 8). All editorial emendations appear in brackets, whether introduced in the Jones edition or (infrequently) here; any parenthetical comment is part of the original text.
[7] Mrs. Samuel Cabot of Boston initially discovered the print source for *Galatea*, and I am grateful

variations he introduced. Not content simply to copy the sources, Copley let his mind and eye grapple with certain visual problems. Where he felt he could improve on the effect of the original, he attempted to do so. In the *Return of Neptune*, for example, he eliminated the shadows immediately behind the figures and introduced a real sea and skyscape. Although the print sources provided composition and a guide to the value range of lighting from bright to dark, they of course had no color. This gave Copley an opportunity to try his skills as a colorist, and his coloristic gifts are immediately evident. In later years the triumphs of Copley's art result more from his mastery of color than from any other stylistic factor.

Copley's essays into history painting at the very beginning of his career, when he was only fifteen or sixteen years old, reflect the intensity of his early artistic ambitions. He knew that an artist in colonial America had to earn his bread and butter by painting portraits; yet from the beginning he seems to have had a vision of achieving a place for himself in the pantheon of art alongside those heroes of whom he had read — Raphael, Rubens, Titian, Guido. In his early print-derived subject pictures, *Galatea*, *The Return of Neptune*, and *Mars, Venus and Vulcan*, Copley was unfurling his artistic wings for a flight that would ultimately carry him beyond the immediate task of winning worldly success as a portraitist. The playful figures cavorting in the water in *Galatea* and *The Return of Neptune* would someday become the tortured victims in *Watson and the Shark* and *The Siege of Gibraltar*.

During these first years Copley's curiosity and ambition impelled him to explore a variety of modes of artistic expression and to drill himself in the fundamentals of his craft. In the portrait of *John Rogers (the Protomartyr)*, fig. 12, he attempted to familiarize himself with old-master techniques by copying an oil painting, said to have been owned by Governor Thomas Hutchinson, which if not of very high quality had the essential attribute of availability. Copley practiced drawing, and the *Battle Scene* dated 1754 (fig. 13) is one of the exploratory ventures. Its source has not been identified, but another drawing (figs. 14 and 15), early though undated, is a study of a figure from Charles LeBrun's *The Battle of the River Granicus* from the Alexander series.[8] The figure has an interesting facial resemblance to the crouching figure on the left in *Mars, Venus and Vulcan*.

The most serious and painstaking of Copley's self-educative efforts was his careful preparation in 1756 of a book of anatomical drawings and texts. It digests and com-

---

to her for permission to publish this discovery. The source for *Neptune* was discovered and published by Albert TenEyck Gardner, "A Copley Primitive," *Metropolitan Museum of Art Bulletin*, XX (April 1962), 257–63. Parker-Wheeler, p. 131, first suggested an eighteenth-century engraving as the probable source for *Mars, Venus and Vulcan*. Margaret Hazlitt's diary refers to an unlocated painting by Copley entitled *Esau and Jacob*, which apparently is another of the youthful history paintings (W. Carew Hazlitt, *Four Generations of a Literary Family*, I [London and New York, 1897], 35–36).

[8] The identification of the LeBrun source for the Copley drawing and a further suggestion that it was probably taken specifically from the large Audran engraving after LeBrun were made by Jennifer Montague of London, and I am grateful to her for permission to publish the discovery.

presses material from two European anatomy books, Bernardino Genga and Giovanni Maria Lancisi, *Anatomy Improv'd and Illustrated* (London, 1723; first edition, Rome, 1691), and Jacob Van Der Gracht, *Anatomie der wtterlicke deelen van het Menschelick Lichaem* (The Hague, 1634; second edition, Rotterdam, 1660). The final sheet in Copley's anatomy book is a measured line drawing of the Medici *Venus* (fig. 17) from an unidentified third source, probably a contemporary drawing book, perhaps French, and probably the book he later mentioned in a letter to Henry Pelham as "the Book of the Antique Statues publish'd with their measures." [9] The alterations that Copley made in the texts, as well as the ways in which he combined and presented his material (see figs. 18–19), indicate that he was doing much more than transcribing source material from published works. He absorbed a substantial understanding of human anatomy, particularly the muscle functions, and put the material in a compact form that could subsequently serve him as a reference work. He kept the book with him throughout his life. Obviously Copley did not go to the considerable trouble of learning anatomy merely to improve himself as a painter of colonial portraits. Nonetheless, despite his long-range aspirations toward history painting, portraiture was the task at hand.

The influence of Feke and Greenwood on Copley is very evident in the early portraits of *Mr. and Mrs. Joseph Mann* (figs. 20–21), done in 1753 and 1754. These are closely related, in reverse composition, to Greenwood's half-length portraits of *Mrs. William Whipple*, c. 1752, and *Robert Jenkins* (fig. 25), which in turn are reflections in reduced scale of Feke's *Mr. and Mrs. James Bowdoin II*, 1748–50 (figs. 22–23). For *Mrs. Joseph Mann* Copley derived the specific composition from an Isaac Beckett mezzotint after William Wissing of *Princess Anne*, c. 1683. He was not the first American artist to use this particular source. Smibert used it directly for the portrait of *Mrs. Joseph Wanton* (Rhode Island Historical Society), and used parts of the pose and background in *Mrs. Nathaniel Cunningham* (fig. 24). When Feke used the same pose in his portrait of *Mrs. James Bowdoin II* (fig. 22), he reversed the landscape so that it opened to the right rather than the left. Greenwood, in *Mrs. William Whipple*, took the pose in reverse from Feke rather than the print source. Copley again turned directly to the print source for *Mrs. Joseph Mann*, but he continued the process begun by Greenwood of bringing the figure closer to the picture plane: the individual parts of the subject loom larger, and the figure more completely dominates the composition (in part this is also the direct result of using a smaller canvas size than Feke). [10] The

[9] *Copley-Pelham Letters*, p. 338. For a more extensive discussion of Copley's anatomy book and its sources, see Jules David Prown, "An 'Anatomy Book' by John Singleton Copley," *Art Quarterly*, XXVI (Spring 1963), 31–46.
[10] Charles Coleman Sellers, "Mezzotint Prototypes of Colonial Portraiture: A Survey Based on the Research of Waldron Phoenix Belknap, Jr.," *Art Quarterly*, XX (Winter 1957), pp. 429, 431; Waldron Phoenix Belknap, Jr., *American Colonial Painting: Materials for a History* (Cambridge, Mass., 1959), plate XX (hereafter cited, Belknap); Parker-Wheeler, plate 2; Alan Burroughs, *John Greenwood in America, 1745–1752* (Andover, Mass.,

Manns are depicted against a similar background of rock formations. Mrs. Mann is seated, and Joseph Mann stands. Copley's *Joseph Mann* is one of the few portraits, all early, in which the source of illumination is on the right. The use of broad, strong highlights suggests the influence of mezzotints, and a strong sense of color and clarity in the delineation of pictorial parts already distinguish Copley's manner. The portrait of the child *Jonathan Mountfort* (fig. 26), in which the light again flows from the right, is also quite pleasing in color. The rocky backdrop is that like that used in the *Mann* portraits, but the draftsmanship is less accomplished, suggesting that this may be one of Copley's very first paintings.

Copley's portrait of his stepbrother, *Charles Pelham* (fig. 27), is interesting in comparison with Greenwood's *Robert Jenkins* (fig. 25) for the gay vest and the linear treatment,[11] and it is closely related stylistically to *Joseph Mann*. The slightly stiff-necked dislocation of the head to the right, the treatment of the collar, and the pose and handling of the right arm, including the highlights and shadows caused by wrinkles in the jacket, are similar in both pictures.

A portrait erroneously identified as *Peter Pelham* (fig. 28) raises a few problems. The history of the picture, and its similarity in style to the portrait of *Charles Pelham*, fits the tradition that the picture is a portrait of a member of the Pelham family.[12] However, the subject cannot be Peter Pelham, Sr., who died in 1751 and was considerably older than this sitter at the time of his death. Peter Pelham, Jr. (born 1721), Copley's stepbrother, moved to Hampton, Virginia, before September 1750, when a son was born there, and the portrait cannot be of him.[13] It may represent a third stepbrother, William Pelham, who was born in 1729 and would have been about twenty-five at the time of this portrait: this does accord with the apparent age of the sitter. Unfortunately virtually nothing is known about William Pelham, and the engraving tools shown near the sitter may or may not support this identification.[14] Stylistically the treatment of the head, reminiscent of the manner of Feke, is quite like that of the standing figure in the center of *The Brothers and Sisters of Christopher Gore* (fig. 29).

At the beginning of his career Copley was very conservative and relied heavily on source materials at hand, as in the *Welsteed* mezzotint, the early mythological scenes, and the portrait of *Mrs. Joseph Mann*. At the same time, however, he steadily pressed against the limits of his ability, expanding his artistic vocabulary, which

---

1943), pp. 42–45, 67, 68. Belknap and Sellers, primarily concerned with sources rather than attributions, repeat the earlier ascription of *Mrs. William Whipple* to Copley. But Burroughs' attribution of the picture to Greenwood is convincing.

[11] Charles Pelham and Robert Jenkins knew each other. A letter from Charles to his father, Peter Pelham, written from Newport, Sept. 10, 1750, discusses Jenkins' apparent arrangement with Peter Pelham in regard to the sale of Pelham's mezzotint engravings in Rhode Island. *Copley-Pelham Letters*, p. 19.

[12] The suggestion that the sitter might be John Greenwood (Parker-Wheeler, p. 152) does not seem likely, since Greenwood left Boston in 1752, the year before Copley appears to have started painting.

[13] "The Copleys and Pelhams of New England," *Heraldic Journal*, IV (Boston, 1868), 179.

[14] It is only known that William Pelham was buried at Trinity Church, Boston, Jan. 28, 1760–61 (*ibid.*, p. 180).

explains the remarkable variety of such early ventures as history pictures, drawings, a mezzotint, and an anatomy book in addition to portraits. One of Copley's most ambitious advances occurred in several multi-figure portraits of children of the Gore family in Boston (figs. 29–30), done around 1755. The painting called, for the want of a more accurate title, *The Brothers and Sisters of Christopher Gore* (fig. 29) is almost a résumé of American colonial painting. The little girl on the left is reminiscent of Smibert's later portraits, such as *Jane Clark* (c. 1739, Massachusetts Historical Society). The little boy on the right is like Badger's children's portraits, particularly *Samuel Torrey* (c. 1757), possibly reflecting, as suggested earlier, Copley's influence on Badger. The central standing figure, perhaps John Gore (born 1745), derives from the work of Robert Feke in pose and treatment, the pose being the reverse of Feke's *James Bowdoin II* (fig. 23).[15] The varied positioning of heads is reminiscent of John Greenwood's earlier *Greenwood-Lee Family* (fig. 3). The movement is much more restrained and subtle here but, as in the Greenwood, the gaze of each figure is fastened upon the viewer. The clarity of the composition and the harmonious color arrangement are early manifestations of basic Copley characteristics. Although in this picture the palette owes something to Feke, Copley's vocabulary of brushwork in the application of pigment to the canvas comes primarily from Smibert, suggesting that young Copley learned technique from Smibert even though he turned to younger and more up-to-date artists like Feke and Greenwood for stylistic inspiration.

A recent discovery that adds to our knowledge of Copley and his stylistic debt to Feke and Greenwood is the three-quarter-length portrait of *Joshua Winslow* (fig. 31). Long thought to be by Greenwood, the picture was held by a militant minority to be an early Copley. This belief was substantiated when, upon cleaning, the painting was found to bear the signature "J Copley 1755." A related miniature head of *Winslow* done in oil on copper (fig. 32) appears to be of the same vintage and may be Copley's first miniature. In the large picture the figure, as in many of the early portraits, is posed against a background consisting of a rocky cliff on one side and an open landscape on the other. The pose is particularly reminiscent of Feke's *Isaac Winslow*, c. 1748 (fig. 33), in reverse, and somewhat less so of his *Tench Francis*, 1746 (fig. 34), the latter also having a similar placement of the tricorn hat under the arm.[16] Copley repeated the same pose the following year in the portrait of *William Brattle* (fig. 36) and, in a much more elegant fashion still another year or so later, in the portrait of young *Theodore Atkinson* (fig. 53). A noticeable difference between Copley's *Joshua Winslow* and the Feke prototypes is that young Copley did not try to emulate Feke's successful practice of laterally turning the figure so that the hidden

[15] The pose goes still further back to the pose of Isaac Royall, again in reverse, in the 1741 *Royall Family* (fig. 2) and Smibert's *Peter Faneuil* (Massachusetts Historical Society) of the same general period.

[16] Belknap, plate XIX, relates this general composition to a mezzotint by McArdell, c. 1757–67, after Thomas Hudson's *Lord Townsend*, but that seems to be too late to be the source.

rear shoulder recedes quite sharply toward the background, relating the figure to the landscape setting. The similarity of the linear style of this portrait to Greenwood's caused the confusion in regard to the attribution before the signature was uncovered. But Copley's color, as in the brilliant red and buff uniform here, is generally stronger, richer, and darker than Greenwood's, and his draftsmanship is more placid in comparison with Greenwood's nervous use of line. The portrait of *George Scott*, 1755–1757 (fig. 35), like the *Winslow* and *Brattle* portraits, is an early and fine three-quarter-length military portrait, striking in the eye-catching red-buff chord of the uniform.

Another link in our understanding of the development of Copley's style has been added with the recent discovery of the unidentified *Portrait of a Woman* (fig. 37), signed and dated 1755 as is *Joshua Winslow*. Like *Mrs. Joseph Mann* it is a traditional half-length portrait, related to any number of American colonial female portraits in the general pose of the figure and the disposition of the hands. In comparison with the *Mann* portraits, *Jonathan Mountfort*, and *Charles Pelham*, Copley seems to have gained in his ability to model the head and body as rounded forms in space, with a more sophisticated treatment of the highlights. Still the hands and arms remain crude and lifeless.

In 1755 Joseph Blackburn, a skillful English painter, arrived in Boston. A competitor working in the latest artistic fashion, he effected a major alteration in Copley's technique, adding the final formative elements that set him on the road toward his own personal and highly successful style. Blackburn was essentially a rococo artist. Intimations of the new style had already appeared in the work of native-born artists like Feke and Greenwood; they reflected in their lightening of the ponderous baroque manner of John Smibert the shift that was taking place in English art from the Lely-Kneller tradition to the style of Thomas Hudson and Joseph Highmore. The rococo influence on Feke and Greenwood was largely if not entirely print-borne, but now, a few years later, Blackburn introduced the style firsthand.

Blackburn had traveled from England to Bermuda in 1752–53 and then came to America in 1754, staying first in Newport and moving on to Boston the following year. With virtually no competition in Boston other than that provided by a precocious local teenaged painter (Copley), Blackburn enjoyed vigorous patronage during the next several years. Copley may have been unhappy at having to face this keen competition, but his paintings indicate that his positive reaction was to absorb quickly and eagerly everything from Blackburn's style that was compatible with his own. The first glimmer of this development is in the portrait of *Ann Tyng* (fig. 38). Ann Tyng was married to Thomas Smelt, a British army officer, in October 1756, and this portrait was probably painted before the wedding so that her family could have a keepsake. Unfortunately the portrait served as a grimmer memorial, since Ann Tyng died a month after her wedding. The portrait shows the general characteristics of Copley's first works — the rough-textured surface, the not completely successful modeling of the figure against a dark smoky background, long streaky brush strokes that sap the picture of vitality, particularly in the drapery highlights, and the tubular quality of the arms and fingers. In these elements the picture is not unlike the *Portrait of a Woman* (fig. 37), painted at about the time Blackburn first arrived in Boston. *Ann Tyng*, however, introduces a note of elegance that signals the initial impact of Blackburn's style. The relationship of Copley's *Ann Tyng* to Blackburn's similarly pastoral *Mary Sylvester Deering* (Metropolitan Museum of Art) has often been noted. Copley had grasped the general idea of the lightheartedness of Blackburn's rococo manner, although he had not yet mastered its vocabulary. But it did not take him long to learn what Blackburn had to teach. In his portrait of *Jane Browne* (fig. 40), also painted in 1756, we see that much of the heavy-handedness remaining in *Ann Tyng* from the earlier period has disappeared. Moreover, the new rococo emphasis on color seems to have released his remarkable capabilities as a colorist. Copley candidly acknowledged his debt to Blackburn in his adaptation of the painted spandrel, and he signed his picture on the spandrel in a style copied directly from Blackburn. The extent of Blackburn's stylistic effect is evident in a comparison of *Jane Browne* with Blackburn's *Mrs. Benjamin Pollard* (fig. 41) of the same year.

Blackburn's influence on Copley in 1756–57 was pervasive. *Anne Gardiner* (fig. 39) appears to have been directly influenced by one of the first paintings Blackburn did in America, the 1754 Newport portrait of *Mrs. Margaret Sylvester Cheeseborough* (Metropolitan Museum of Art), utilizing the same treatment of arm, hand, and drapery, although in an inverted position. The possible use of a common print source cannot be entirely ruled out. This is the case with the similar portrait of *Jonathan Belcher* (fig. 46), which is very much like the Blackburn portrait of *Joseph Dwight*, 1756 (fig. 42), both pictures deriving from a 1741 mezzotint by Faber, Jr., after Hudson, of *William Fortescue*. The companion portrait of *Mrs. Jonathan Belcher* (fig. 45), signed and dated 1756, introduces a shawl that is found in several Blackburn portraits, and it is based on a 1691 mezzotint by Faber, after Kneller, of *The Duchess of Grafton*.[17] *William Brattle* (fig. 36) is like Blackburn's male portraits in the high rosy flesh color used in the face, the yellowish cast of the highlights, and the generally light palette. The portraits of an unknown *Mother and Child* (fig. 43) and *Rhoda Cranston* (fig. 44) also seem ascribable to the period of early Blackburn influence.

Just as significant as Copley's assimilation of certain aspects of Blackburn's style is his resistance to others. Copley persisted in his own way of using light and shadow to model drapery and figures in space. Blackburn's light is often diffused, with very soft and subtle transitions from light to dark. Highlights on the surfaces of things occur in soft patches, like webs of light. Copley's value contrasts, however, are sharp and

---

[17] John Hill Morgan, *John Singleton Copley* (Walpole Society, Windham, Conn., 1939), p. 11; Belknap, plate XIV, 10 and 10A, and plate XLV, 56 and 56A.

crisp. Perhaps because his knowledge and experience of art came through prints, he appears to have seen things more literally in terms of black and white. In contrast with an academically oriented artist like Blackburn and like other American-born painters discussed earlier, notably Feke and Greenwood, Copley was more concerned with the pictorial possibilities of line and the picture surface than with the illusion of figures in space. Equally important to the individuality of his style was Copley's reaction to the liberating influence of the lighter, brighter palette introduced by Blackburn. Having already shown himself to be a strong colorist in such early ventures as *Mrs. Joseph Mann, The Brothers and Sisters of Christopher Gore*, and *The Return of Neptune*, Copley now gave color an even more telling role in the scheme of his paintings. Blackburn's colors were light and sweet, however, while Copley continued to use strong, bright, saturated colors. In painting drapery folds, Blackburn would introduce a variety of new colors, often gentle pastel shades, to get the desired effect. Copley, handling the same problem, controlled the play of shadow and highlights by using light and dark variants of the same color. Copley assimilated Blackburn's concern with the stuffs in a picture (drapery, jewelry, lace), but his treatment reveals a greater concern with the factual details of the thing being painted and an unwillingness to sacrifice the specifics of visual reality for general effect.

Jane Browne was painted in 1756, and Copley did matching portraits of her parents in the following year. The portrait of *Rev. Arthur Browne* (fig. 47), an Anglican minister in Portsmouth, painted in an oval spandrel, the head set high, is in the tradition of Smibert's ministerial portraits. The portrait of *Mrs. Arthur Browne* (fig. 48), more in the Blackburn style of her daughter's portrait, marks Copley's progress to still more advanced stylistic levels, transcending Blackburn's influence and pointing toward the effective, bold portraits of the next year, 1758. In *Rev. Arthur Browne* the striking use of sharp value contrasts is reinforced by the black and white of the clerical garb. In the portrait of *Mrs. Arthur Browne* the strong chiaroscuro is resoundingly echoed by the red-blue color contrast of dress and mantle, reminiscent of the portrait of *Mrs. Joseph Mann* painted four years earlier. Holding its own against the strength of these contrasts is the strength of character shown in the head itself. The face is painted in a flesh tint that almost constitutes a third primary color in its yellowness. Generously applied, the flesh pigment is worked into an effective realistic likeness. A number of Copley's other portraits of married women of this period have some of these qualities, but they are larger in size and tend toward stiffness and artificiality. For example, the portrait of *Mrs. William Stevens* (fig. 49) has a similar treatment of flesh tones, but the expanded format for the seated portrait leaves a large expanse of rather dull dress-filled canvas at the bottom. This is also true of the portraits of *Mrs. Daniel Rea and Her Daughter* (fig. 50) and *Mrs. Thomas Marshall* (fig. 51). The chairs and tables, adorned with heavy leaf and shell carving, are obtrusive, print-derived props. The portrait of *Mrs. Thomas Marshall* seems to be somewhat later in date than the companion portrait of her husband (fig. 52) — the latter appears to have been painted before Copley had seen the work of Blackburn — and might be dated around 1755. Since the Marshalls were married in 1757, one can only surmise that at the time of the marriage Mrs. Marshall had her portrait painted to go with her husband's picture done during his bachelor days. This practice was not uncommon, and a number of Copley's paired portraits consist of pictures painted in different years.

Copley had already been a professional artist for five years by the time he was twenty years old. During those years he experimented with various modes of artistic expression, but eventually settled down to concentrate on the kind of painting for which there was a consistent demand, portraiture. Although the arrival of Blackburn may have taken some of the wind out of his sails, the effect on his art was certainly salubrious. Becoming painfully aware of his shortcomings, Copley polished his style so that he could compete effectively with the new rival. The extent of his success is shown by a picture that reflects the influence of the older artist so clearly that for many years it was thought to be by Blackburn; even further, it was considered one of Blackburn's finest works and was used as the frontispiece of Lawrence Park's pioneer study of Blackburn (1923). This is the portrait of *Theodore Atkinson* (fig. 53).[18] In pose it echoes one of the first Copley male portraits to be influenced by Blackburn, *William Brattle* (fig. 36), as well as the 1755 *Joshua Winslow* (fig. 31). But Copley was no longer a novice wedding Blackburn's finesse to a home-grown style. In *Atkinson* he created a unified and elegant statement that absorbs and transcends Blackburn. The figure is posed with animation. One leg pushes forward and, as his torso twists slightly into space, Atkinson's head turns in the opposite direction, his eyes returning to the center to gaze steadfastly at the viewer. His left arm is thrust downward inside the pocket, its diagonal line reinforced by the edge of a background cloud formation, leading the eye to a gap between the trees where a river is shown winding its way up from the lower right. The pointing arm is an arrow playing against the curved bow of the other arm, which presses the silver-banded black tricorn hat against the subject's body. Atkinson is handsomely clad in an unusual lavender-brown suit over an ivory waistcoat.

This superb portrait indicates that by 1757, or 1758 at the latest, the twenty-year-old Copley had assimilated Blackburn's example into a successful style; for the moment at least, Blackburn had nothing further to teach him. Indeed, from 1758 on, the tide reversed itself and Copley seems to have exerted some stylistic influence on Blackburn. For example, Blackburn's 1758 portraits of *Mr. and Mrs. Jonathan Simpson* (Museum of Fine Arts, Boston) show greater realism, clarity, linearity, and stronger value contrasts than his earlier work.

Blackburn's presence in Boston seemed to have a healthy effect on the market for

[18] This portrait was properly reattributed to Copley, on the basis of its style, by William Sawitzky in 1943, in a seminar on American painting held at the Worcester Art Museum.

art, and, far from suffering economically from the competition, Copley enjoyed more business than before. Blackburn was proving that it was possible for an artist to support himself through painting alone. Smibert, to supplement his income, sold prints and ran an art-supply shop; Pelham painted a few portraits and was an engraver, but supported himself by teaching arithmetic, music, and dancing; Feke was a mariner; Badger was a glazier and house painter; and Greenwood, the closest of these men to being a full-time painter, had learned his trade from an engraver, japanner, and sign painter, and may have exercised these skills as well. In supporting himself fully as a portraitist, Blackburn obviously had more business than the earlier artists. During his years in America Blackburn averaged twice as many paintings per year as his predecessors, which clearly suggests that the number of portraits produced in Boston between the arrival of Smibert and the arrival of Blackburn was not limited by the availability of artistic talent, but by the restricted demand for portraits.[19] During that quarter century, Smibert, Feke, Greenwood, and Badger got most of their business (about half of the total) from merchants and their families. Ministers formed the next largest group of subjects, but this usually amounted to only one fifth to one quarter of the number of merchants, except in the case of Smibert, who painted approximately half as many ministers as merchants. Merchants and their wives tended to order larger portraits, whereas ministers' portraits were more modest, usually bust-length, as in the mezzotints made from them. Moreover, merchants were often painted in paired portraits with their wives, whereas the ministers were most often painted singly and invariably in ecclesiastical garb. Blackburn enjoyed more patronage from merchant families (about 60 percent) than any of the previous painters, but he painted few ministers. Reflecting the taste of the merchant families for large canvases, approximately three fourths of Blackburn's paintings were three-quarter-length portraits. This indicates that not only was he painting more pictures a year than his predecessors in the colonies, but he was painting larger pictures as well. Only a little more than half of his business came from Boston, as opposed to three fourths for Smibert or Badger; like Feke, Blackburn worked extensively elsewhere, notably in Newport after his arrival in the colonies and in Portsmouth, where he was very active in 1760–61.

Blackburn enjoyed a very high level of patronage in America, including numerous wealthy merchants and high-placed officials. His patrons were largely Anglicans and of what would soon be classifiable as a loyalist political bent. Copley's clients during his early years, though only occasionally equaling Blackburn's in position or wealth, were

---

[19] The statistical information given here for Smibert, Feke, Greenwood, Badger, and Blackburn is based on information gathered by my graduate students at Yale in the fall of 1963. It was estimated that the total production of these artists, including unlocated paintings, was: Smibert (110), Feke (70), Greenwood (50), Badger (90), and Blackburn (130). This meant that Smibert during his American career averaged about 5½ portraits a year, Feke 7, Greenwood slightly over 6, Badger 4½, and Blackburn 13. Although I now feel that these estimates should be revised upward, the ratios of productivity remain approximately the same. For Copley's rate of work, see the introduction to the appendices, pp. 97–99.

nonetheless fairly important people. One might expect that a tobacconist's son from Long Wharf and Lindall's Row, a young artist with a limited reputation, would have begun by painting local craftsmen and small shopowners, a predominantly lower-middle-class, Congregationalist clientele. Indeed this is generally true at the very beginning of Copley's career, with the portraits of his stepbrothers, the Manns, the Gore children, and young Jonathan Mountfort. But from 1755 on, though his sitters were not primarily the powerful officials and landowners he later painted, Copley did have some notable patrons. Lieutenant-Governor Theodore Atkinson of New Hampshire, Judge Jonathan Belcher, and General William Brattle were particularly prestigious individuals; Commissary General Joshua Winslow, Captain George Scott (later a general and governor of Granada), and Thomas Ainslie, collector of customs in the Port of Quebec, also held responsible positions. And Copley's patronage was surprisingly far-flung geographically, with a high percentage of sitters coming from outside Massachusetts, especially Portsmouth and Nova Scotia.[20]

[20] These sitters were all painted in Boston. Thomas Ainslie urged Copley to travel to Halifax and do some portraits there, but he never made the trip. *Copley-Pelham Letters*, p. 23, Oct. 8, 1757.

III   Artistic Maturity

1758-1761   By the time copley had come into his early twenties, he had formed a consistent style of his own. Surprisingly enough, the hallmark of the new style was not the polished elegance of the Blackburn mode, developing the possibilities suggested by the portrait of *Theodore Atkinson*, but instead a strong and vigorous ruggedness along the lines established in *Mrs. Arthur Browne* and *Mrs. William Stevens*. It is almost as if Copley had deliberately chosen a different path from Blackburn's, pursuing his own star artistically and possibly aiming for a different audience.

Three pairs of large portraits, *Mr. and Mrs. James Otis* (figs. 54–55), *Mr. and Mrs. Thomas Greene* (figs. 56–57), and *Mr. and Mrs. John Barrett* (figs. 58–59), painted in or close to 1758, mark the solid attainment of a mature style. The *Otis* portraits are early examples of Copley's successful formula for presenting married couples, one that he applied in a number of delightful variations over the next decade and a half. In this instance, though the two pictures are compatible, the sitters are not posed facing each other in order to make a closed compositional bracket. Since the heads face in different directions, however, the portraits can be hung as a pair, with the sitters' attention focused on a viewer in the center: they can also satisfactorily be seen separately, or in reversed positions, or on both sides of a corner. Mrs. Otis (fig. 55), in a composition reminiscent of *Mrs. William Stevens*, is elaborately clothed in an impressive array of satin and lace, with a necklace of large pearls around her sizable neck. She is seated in an upholstered armchair, a lush river landscape opening to the left beyond a drapery and column done in the grand manner. The note struck is one of domesticity and amplitude. James Otis (fig. 54) sits on a spare side chair at a cloth-covered table. There is nothing in the background except the architectural definition of the room itself. The dominant pictorial element is the strongly lighted head. Secondary highlights, the legs and hands, lead the eye to the outlines of the arms and jacket, which carry up to the head. The total effect is one of solidity and substance.

A similarly impressive pair of portraits represents *Mr. and Mrs. Thomas Greene* (figs. 56–57). Thomas Greene is seated on an upholstered backstool, holding a letter bearing the date September 25, 1758. The papers and standish at his elbow on the covered table underline his status as a man of business. A parted drapery in the upper

28

right reveals a ship, which more specifically suggests his mercantile interests.[1] Mrs. Greene is posed in an outdoor setting, one arm resting upon an embankment. The landscape crowding in close behind her on the left opens on the right to a river view. Copley achieves a rich and restrained color harmony in the brown dress, white lace and lining, black hair and yellowish flesh tones against the dark background. The paint is laid on in broad strokes, particularly in the face. Although his later works show increased sophistication and facility of execution, Copley never surpassed the painterly strength of this portrait.

A pair of portraits of Thomas Greene's younger brother, the silversmith *Rufus Greene* and his wife (figs. 61–62), appear to date from this same general period. They have unfortunately been drastically cut down, and may originally have been another in this series of paired three-quarter-length portraits.

Mr. and Mrs. John Barrett (figs. 58–59) may also be dated around 1758. John Barrett is seated on a Queen Anne side chair which, like Thomas Greene's upholstered backstool, appears to be of New England origin. His desk, like those of Thomas Greene and James Otis, is simply a fabric-covered table. This is common in Copley's American portraits, and actual desks appear rarely. The pose is quite like that in *James Otis*. The portrait of Mrs. John Barrett (fig. 58) almost exactly inverts the composition Smibert used for *Mrs. Daniel Oliver*, c. 1731 (fig. 60). Although this similarity may be explained by a common print source, there is a strong possibility that Copley actually encountered the Smibert portrait while doing a number of paintings of the Oliver family at this time. Andrew Oliver, a prosperous merchant, lived on the South Side of Boston, a section of town where Copley enjoyed considerable business in 1758–1761. Over three fourths of his Boston sitters during this period came from the South Side, including Mr. and Mrs. Thomas Greene, Mr. and Mrs. Rufus Greene, Anne Gardiner, Hugh Hall, and Thomas Aston Coffin, in addition to the Olivers. Although the Olivers were Congregationalists, the remainder of the South Side sitters were Anglicans, and Tories as well.

Copley painted two pairs of oil-on-copper miniatures of *Mr. and Mrs. Andrew Oliver* (figs. 63–66). They mark a technical advance over the comparatively crude head of *Joshua Winslow* (fig. 32), done about three years earlier, and this corresponds with the stylistic development we can note from the large *Joshua Winslow* (fig. 31) to *Mr. and Mrs. Thomas Greene* (figs. 56–57). Copley also did a larger oil-on-copper miniature of *Andrew Oliver* (fig. 67), in tandem with one of his brother, *Peter Oliver* (fig. 68), and these are related stylistically to a third oversize miniature, which represents *Samuel Danforth* (fig. 73).

[1] In this use of a ship in the background, Copley was following in the footsteps of Smibert, who wrote from Boston to his London agent, Arthur Pond, on March 24, 1743/4, ordering "A set of ships published by Lempriere and sold by H. Toms in Union court Holburn. These ships I want some-times for to be in a distant view in Portraits of Merchts etc who chuse such, so if there be any better done since send them. but they must be the modern construction." Henry Wilder Foote, *John Smibert* (Cambridge, Mass., 1950), p. 88.

Copley did a spate of oil-on-copper miniatures during this period. One of the earliest is a memorable likeness of *Nathaniel Hurd* (fig. 69), who later sat for a large picture. Stylistically this miniature goes back to *Joshua Winslow* and may be dated 1755–1758. Although Copley painted few craftsmen, he did portray several silversmiths, which suggests the possibility that he painted their portraits in exchange for merchandise. The excellent miniature of *Rev. Samuel Fayerweather* (fig. 74) in academic garb, done around 1758, is set in a superb but simple spiral gadrooned silver frame. According to Yale University Art Gallery records, the late John Marshall Phillips believed that the frame may have been made by Paul Revere, whom Copley later painted (fig. 272), and indeed Revere's Day Books contain a number of charges to Copley in the period 1763–1767 for gold and silver picture frames and gold locket cases and bracelets.[2]

Another silversmith or jeweler whom Copley painted at this time, although presumably as a member of the Oliver family rather than for business purposes, was *Andrew Oliver II* (fig. 71). This miniature and one of his sister, *Griselda Oliver* (fig. 72), are in simple black molded wood frames that seem original, like one on a similar but perhaps slightly earlier miniature of young *Anne Wentworth* (fig. 70). One of Boston's wealthiest citizens, *Thomas Hancock* (fig. 75), also sat to Copley for one of these early copper miniatures. This likeness became the basis for several later portraits of Hancock, including the large full-length oil done for Harvard (fig. 154). Copley also did a pastel of Hancock (fig. 76), perhaps copied from the miniature, the quality of which is obscured by its abraded condition. But there is no doubt that in 1758 Copley began to explore the pastel medium. That he used it well is attested to by the powerful study of the South Side merchant, *Hugh Hall* (fig. 77). In this rather crude but vigorous portrait, one can see the way in which Copley attempted to bend an obdurate medium to his will. There is a convincing sense of the physical presence of the subject, with the head very close to the picture plane and dominating the composition. This is not a pretty, effortless performance: the picture bears the scars of Copley's struggle to capture and model the subject successfully. What the picture lacks in elegance it more than makes up for in forcefulness, and it is a memorable document of an initial effort by an artist who became one of the leading pastelists in a century that produced a number of artists excelling in that medium.

[2] This fact has given rise to the widespread legend that many of Copley's paintings are still in an "original frame made by Paul Revere." There is no evidence that Revere, a metalsmith, ever did woodwork. Presumably he purchased frames, applied silver or gold leaf, and resold them. Although Revere in entering a charge to Copley in the Day Books (Massachusetts Historical Society, Boston) occasionally jotted down the name of the person for whom the frame, locket case, or bracelet was destined — more frequently he used an abbreviation of the name — this did not occur too often and the entry is usually indecipherable. On Jan. 1, 1763, Revere charged Copley £1.17.4 for a gold bracelet and £1.8.0 for the making of it, and the name given is Mrs. Bun or Brn [possibly Brown]. On Jan. 8 of that year there was a charge of £3.0.0 for a gold [locket] case for a picture of Mr. Nelson. On Feb. 1 Copley was charged £1.0.0 for a silver picture frame for Mrs. St — g [or "gs"], and £3.0.0 for a gold one for Gr — f [perhaps Greenleaf]. On Feb. 26 there were charges for gold picture frames and a gold case for Major and Mrs. R — gs [perhaps "Rogs" for Rogers]. Several entries in 1765 are not accompanied by names, but on Aug. 21, 1767, Copley was charged £3.11.4 for the gold, glass, and making of a gold bracelet for Mr. Wentworth. On Sept. 3 he was charged £3.10.0 for one that contained a little less gold for W. Brown. These entries suggest that a number of Copley miniatures have disappeared.

The small oil-on-copper miniature of a British colonel, *Sir John St. Clair* (fig. 79), signed and dated 1759, is somewhat more sophisticated than the miniatures previously examined, which further indicates c. 1758 as the date of Copley's *Oliver, Hurd, Wentworth, Hancock,* and *Danforth* miniatures. One final miniature of the period, quite different in character from the others, is a large oil-on-copper portrait of one of the sons of John Erving, probably *John Erving, Jr.* (fig. 80), seated at a round tiptop tea table. This miniature descended in the family of Anne Erving (*Mrs. Duncan Stewart,* fig. 188) and has long been considered a portrait of her father. The sitter is too young, though, and presumably is one of John Erving's sons, probably the son of the same name. Perkins in 1873 recorded a miniature of James Erving as "the first miniature in oil that Copley made," and this miniature may be related to that.

In addition to the oil-on-copper miniatures of the Olivers, Copley painted small oil-on-canvas portraits of *Elizabeth Oliver* (fig. 81) and her sister *Griselda* (fig. 82). The portrait of Elizabeth, an especially pleasing and effective example of Copley's style around 1758, displays clearly the qualities that are consistently found in Copley's best works throughout his career, including the late paintings done over a half century later: brilliance of color, clarity of forms, crisp definition of areas, and sharp value contrasts. To define each major area of the design, in this case the neck, chin, and forehead, Copley dragged a relatively dry brush along the outline so that there would be no confusion about where it begins and ends. With narrower strokes he did the same thing to outline the eyes, nose, and mouth. Lights are applied freely on top of darks, touching in the unshadowed parts of the ear and the light areas of the hair.

At about the same time he painted the Oliver sisters on small separate canvases, Copley painted a large double portrait of the two young sisters from another prominent family, *Mary MacIntosh and Elizabeth Royall* (fig. 83), daughters of Isaac Royall of Medford, whose young family had been painted in 1741 by Robert Feke (fig. 2). This was apparently Copley's last venture at painting more than one figure on a single canvas for fifteen years. The result is quite successful, although the two little girls are somewhat dominated by the competition of clothes, drapery, a dog, and a bird. This particular compositional weakness, a tendency to include too much peripheral detail, hurt Copley on two critical occasions in the future: in the portrait of *Mary Warner* [?] (fig. 164) and in the large conversation piece of *The Daughters of George III* (fig. 468), done in 1785.

The portrait of the Royall daughters has a strong color scheme of blue and white against red drapery, with an obtrusive bit of orange-yellow drapery in the center. The heads are strongly painted, a characteristic of the portraits of this period. The highlights on the drapery, perhaps reflecting the lingering influence of mezzotints, are vigorously brushed; in the next decade they become smoother and more realistic. Similarly the lace is roughly indicated with squiggles of pigment applied like fingerpaint, as opposed to the realistic delicacy of lace in Copley's later paintings. Nevertheless, the shorthand used for the lace and highlights is visually appealing. The same brusque handling can

31

be found in the portrait of *Mrs. Metcalf Bowler* (fig. 84), where it contrasts with the lighter and more graceful note struck by the pose and the bird cage.

Thomas Aston Coffin (fig. 85) is in the long tradition of portraits of children holding a bird, fruit, or something else in a hand passing in front of the body. The tradition had traveled from European, especially Flemish and Netherlandish, prototypes via East Anglia to America in the seventeenth century. Once here it survived from pictures like the anonymous 1670 portrait of *Henry Gibbes* through ones like Joseph Badger's portrait of his grandson, *James Badger* (Metropolitan Museum of Art); it continued deep into the nineteenth century in countless folk portraits of similarly posed children. Copley's picture, close in date to Badger's portraits of this type, is nonetheless much more polished, complex, and sophisticated. The overstated accessories, like the ornate furniture in *Jonathan Belcher, Mrs. Daniel Rea*, and *Mrs. Thomas Marshall*, suggest reliance on a print source.

A pair of portraits of children said to be twins of the Appleton-Greenleaf family (figs. 86–87) lacks the sophistication of *Thomas Aston Coffin* and probably predates it. The portrait of the boy, which has the smooth and overblown quality of *Coffin*, was based on a mezzotint by Smith, c. 1704, after Kneller, of *Lord Bury*.[3] The girl's portrait goes back to *Jonathan Mountfort* (fig. 26) and *The Gore Sisters* (fig. 30) and is perhaps closest to the child in the portrait of *Mother and Child* (fig. 43), done in 1755–1757.

A rather less polished portrait of a child (fig. 88), which like *Thomas Aston Coffin* includes a shuttlecock and battledore among the accessories, is traditionally presumed to represent a member of the Hancock family, once erroneously identified as John Hancock. The portrait is related compositionally to another picture sharing in the Hancock legend, the superb portrait of *Thaddeus Burr* (fig. 91). According to tradition, Burr, a close friend of John Hancock's, was painted as dressed for a dinner with Hancock. The story seems inaccurate but the fact of the Hancock association remains, and the compositional similarity of *Thaddeus Burr* and *Boy Called Master Hancock* suggests that there is some relation between the two paintings, even if it existed only in Copley's mind.

Copley struck a particularly bold and beautiful color chord in the portrait of *Thaddeus Burr*. The jacket is brown, the waistcoat blue with silver buttons and buttonholes embroidered with metallic silver thread. The brown drapery behind the head and the dark landscape on the right, with blue sky and brown clouds, repeat the primary color statement. The flesh tones of the hand and face are boldly painted. The portrait of *Mrs. Burr* (fig. 90) echoes this color scheme in the landscape, the brown drapery behind the figure, and the pedestal on which she leans in counterpoint to her husband's pose. Yet her rose and ivory dress, with its elaborately worked lace, is an effective visual counterweight to the strong portrait of her husband. The Burrs were married in 1759, and this is a reasonable date for the portraits in terms of style.

[3] Belknap, plate XXXIX, 47 and 47A.

After the burst of activity that produced the group of paintings ascribed to 1757–1759, there is an apparent lull in Copley's output. There are no dated pictures known from 1760 or 1761, the only years of Copley's American career for which this occurs. There seems to have been a decided general slack in business during this period. Perhaps it was an aftereffect of the great Boston fire of March 1760, which among other areas destroyed Lindall's Row, where Copley may still have been living. Whether or not the fire destroyed his studio, it probably took the minds of many potential sitters away from portraiture. This may also have affected Blackburn, who went off to Portsmouth to paint in 1760–61. Since there is no evidence that Copley was making serious inroads on his business, Blackburn presumably went to Portsmouth simply looking for greener pastures after the Boston commissions had fallen off.

Despite the absence of stylistic benchmarks in the form of dated paintings, there is a group of paintings that seems to belong to this general period, 1758–1761. A major canvas that fits the early part of the period is the splendid standing portrait of *Epes Sargent* (fig. 91). The pose of the figure leaning on a pedestal is obviously related to *Master Hancock* and *Thaddeus Burr*. The color is restrained, with the figure in a long gray coat seen against a dark and subdued landscape. Attention is pulled to the powerful head and to the centrally placed hand around which the entire composition pivots. Copley's portraits are often good in inverse proportion to the amount of paraphernalia with which they are cluttered, and this spare composition is particularly effective. In *Epes Sargent* Copley carries the strong brushwork of the 1758 portrait heads to a new level of accomplishment, applying heavy pigment in free slashes in modeling the head and in building up Sargent's memorable impasto-weighted hands.

The portrait of *Rev. Edward Holyoke* (fig. 92) has something of the rough-hewn quality of *Epes Sargent*, and like it belongs to the late 1750's or perhaps the earliest 1760's. These vigorous portraits of old men, in the vein of Smibert's *Nathaniel Byfield* and Feke's *Thomas Hiscox*, are among the strongest of Copley's artistic statements. His portraiture has many virtues, but generally speaking robustness is not one of them. Yet a basic strength of Copley's art is his ability to link suitable artistic means to desired artistic goals. These are sturdy portraits of tough-minded people, and very successful portraits they are. Edward Holyoke, president of Harvard College, in clerical robes and holding a book, is seated in the ponderous president's chair with college buildings in the background. The pose recalls *Mrs. William Stevens* (fig. 49) and *Mr. and Mrs. James Otis* (figs. 54–55), and, like the Otises, Holyoke is rather large-headed and short-torsoed in appearance. The chair, robes, and buildings make a clear statement about who and what Edward Holyoke is. The composition, which places the solid figure seated bolt upright in his chair, and the strong painterly technique employed serve to leave little doubt that this man is in complete control of his environment.

The portrait of the pensive *John Bours* (fig. 93) is one of the rare portraits in which Copley attempts to probe the sitter's personality rather than make a realistic statement about the physical appearance of the sitter and the objects that symbolize his station in life. As such it makes an interesting contrast with the similarly composed *Edward Holyoke*. Elegantly but simply garbed, Bours slouches in a gracefully curved Queen Anne roundabout or corner chair, in contrast to Holyoke's stern pose in a boldly turned seventeenth-century chair. The background does not consist of buildings, which reflect man's control of his world, but is a natural landscape enlivened by roiling clouds. Rather than confronting and dominating his environment like Holyoke, the poetic and introspective Bours seems almost eroded by it. In this portrait Copley does not stress the external aspect of Bours and his relationship to the world, but paints him engaged in thought — a thinker, not a doer. The book he holds is not a symbol of erudition, but an active agency in the picture: the sitter seems to have just set it aside while he reflects on what he has read.

John Bours is similar in pose and landscape background to the miniature portrait of *John Erving, Jr.* [?] (fig. 80), and like it may belong to the early part of this period. But in concept it is more closely related to an unusual study Copley made of his young half brother, *Henry Pelham* (fig. 95). With his customary artistic inquisitiveness, Copley apparently wanted to see if he could produce a picture artificially illuminated by candle or firelight, in the seventeenth-century vein of Honthorst or Georges de la Tour, a baroque tradition revived in the eighteenth century by a painter with whose efforts Copley's pictures were confused when first seen in England, Joseph Wright of Derby.[4] Copley sketched the young boy engrossed in reading, his hand raised to his head to shield his eyes from the warm and flickering light. This picture in turn makes an interesting comparison with a portrait of *Rev. Nathaniel Appleton* (fig. 94), who is placed in an unusual pose behind a table. Appleton, modeled like Edward Holyoke and Epes Sargent with heavy touches of opaque pigment, holds Watt's "Orthodoxy and Charity" and three other books rest on the table. The books, like the costume,[5] symbolize Appleton's profession and learning; in the *Pelham* portrait the book is not a prop, but an integral part of the picture.

The portrait of *Dorothy Murray* (fig. 96) can be considered both a summary of previous stylistic elements and a tentative start toward new things. With the ring of flowers her pose echoes that in *Jonathan Mountfort* (fig. 26); the treatment of the lace is close to Blackburn's manner; and the strong handling of paint on the head relates to the 1758 portrait series. But the scumbly dry handling of the embroidery on the badly abraded dress is novel and relates to two other portraits that appear to be of similar date, *Mrs. Samuel Quincy* (fig. 97) and *Jacob Fowle* (fig. 98). In later years Dorothy Murray's daughter recalled that the portrait showed her mother at the age of sixteen, which would date the portrait in 1761.[6]

---

[4] Copley's inspiration may have been the unidentifiable painting of the "Nun with a Candle," which he sold to Myles Cooper some years later.

[5] An X-ray in the records at the Fogg Art Museum indicates that the tab collar was added, apparently by another hand, over an earlier collar that lay flat. The lower section of the wig and face has also been retouched.

[6] Susan I. Leslie, *Recollections of My Mother* (Boston, 1886), p. 69.

The unusual portrait of *Mrs. Samuel Quincy* seems to indicate Copley's returning interest in elegance. The pose derives from Rubens' portrait of *Helena Fourment*, by way of some mid-eighteenth-century mezzotint after a painting by one of the group of English painters including Thomas Hudson and Allan Ramsay, who employed the drapery painter, Joseph Vanacken. Vanacken liked this particular Rubens source for costumes and used it several times with minor variations.[7] In each instance so far known, the figure holds a long feathered plume; Mrs. Quincy holds a flowering branch. Although Copley may not have been aware that he had chosen a source that traced its descent from Rubens, this is an early instance of his receptiveness to an artistic influence that was later to have special meaning for him as a history painter.

The three-quarter-length standing portrait of elderly *Jacob Fowle* shows a similar interest in texture, evident in the tree trunk and the embroidery on the clothes. The smoother, more sharply shadowed treatment of the head is another forward-looking stylistic element, although the pose is reminiscent of earlier colonial portraiture. Fowle leans against a stump holding a gun or fowling piece, which may be a pun on the family name.[8]

The handsome portrait of *Benjamin Pickman* (fig. 99) is inscribed with the sitter's age, twenty-one. This would date the painting in 1761, but in style it is more like such earlier portraits as *John Bours, Thaddeus Burr, Boy Called Master Hancock*, and the first painting of *Mrs. Metcalf Bowler*. The technique reflects more of the opaque bluntness of the early part of the period and less of the growing textural interest and softer modeling that appear at the end.

The period 1758–1761 stands out in Copley's career as somewhat atypical stylistically, perhaps as a result of a temporary reaction against Blackburn's facile style. The rough, vigorous brushwork contrasts with his subsequent smooth and polished manner. The darkened backgrounds and subdued color scheme also are particularly characteristic of this period, although they return in an altered form during Copley's last few years in America.

[7] Louisa Dresser, *Worcester Art Museum Annual,* IX (1961), 37; John Hill Morgan Notes, Yale University Art Gallery, New Haven, Conn.; John Steegman, "A Drapery Painter of the Eighteenth Century," *The Connoisseur,* XCVII (June 1936), 309–15. Louisa Dresser points out that the similarly posed Blackburn portrait of *Hannah Babcock* at the Worcester Art Museum was specifically based on the Faber mezzotint, after Hudson, of *Miss Hudson*, the artist's daughter.

[8] Parker-Wheeler, p. 73.

IV   Stylish Portraiture

1762-1764 THE PORTRAIT OF *Mrs. Daniel Rogers* (FIG. 100), SIGNED AND dated 1762, once more provides solid footing for establishing chronology.[1] It also signals the arrival of a new phase in Copley's stylistic development after such transitional portraits as *Dorothy Murray, Jacob Fowle,* and *Mrs. Samuel Quincy.* The basic characteristics noted earlier — linearity, strong value contrasts, intense color, and clarity of parts — are now orchestrated into works of greater sophistication and visual opulence.

Copley's new stylistic elegance was coupled with an increase in business.[2] The beginning of the boom coincided with Blackburn's departure from the colonies in 1762. There is no evidence that Copley drove Blackburn off by dint of his superior skill, since Blackburn consistently attracted a larger and higher level of patronage. But, whatever the reasons, Blackburn's departure left Copley as the leading painter in the American colonies, and portrait commissions flowed in.

Among the early successful pictures in the new elegant manner are a number of paired portraits. The Gloucester merchant *Nathaniel Allen,* 1763 (fig. 101), sits at a round table with ledger and letters at hand. No effort is made to disguise the two tufted growths on his face, which are prominently and realistically displayed. Handsome *Mrs. Nathaniel Allen* (fig. 102), the daughter of Epes Sargent, stands in a landscape setting. In contrast to her substantial husband, who is surrounded by business symbols, she is ensconced in a display of fashions, drawing on her glove and glazing at the viewer with piercing dark eyes from beneath her splendid broad-brimmed bonnet. *Mr. and Mrs. John Murray* (figs. 103–104) repeat a similar scheme, with the husband at his desk and the wife in a landscape setting. In a pair of smaller 1763 portraits, *Mr. and Mrs. John Scollay* (figs. 105–106), both sitters are in interior settings. In the following year Copley made pastel portraits of the same couple. *John Scollay* (fig. 107) is a replica of the oil, but *Mrs. Scollay* (fig. 108) looks off to the left rather than directly at the viewer. Copley had not done many pastels since 1758, but that he had maintained an interest in

[1] Before this time Copley had inscribed the date on less than a dozen pictures. From 1763 on, Copley dated his pictures quite regularly, especially during the period 1763–69. In all, one third of his painting can be ascribed with certainty to a given year by the date inscribed on the painting, the ex- istence of a bill, or specific recorded circumstances (such as the trip to New York in 1771).

[2] For an estimate of Copley's annual production of pictures, see the appendix, Analysis of Statistical Data, under "Period," pp. 128–129.

the medium is attested to by the remarkably uninhibited and slightly brassy letter he addressed to the Swiss pastelist, Jean-Etienne Liotard, in Geneva on September 30, 1762, asking him to send "one sett of Crayons of the very best kind such as You can recommend [for] liveliness of colour and Justness of tints." He continued:

> You may perhaps be surprised that so remote a corner of the Globe as New England should have any d[e]mand for the necessary eutensils for practiceing the fine Arts, but I assure You Sir however feeble our efforts may be, it is not for want of inclination that they are not better, but the want of oppertunity to improve ourselves. however America which has been the seat of war and desolation, I would fain hope will one Day become the school of fine Arts and Monsieur Liotard['s] Drawing with Justice be set as patterns for our immitation. not that I have ever had the advantage of beholding any one of those rare peices from Your hand. but [I have] formd a Judgment on the true tast[e] of several of My friend[s] who has seem em.[3]

In 1763, possibly using "crayons" sent by Liotard, Copley did a pastel portrait of *Mrs. Gawen Brown* (fig. 110), the daughter of Reverend Mather Byles and the mother in that year of the artist, Mather Brown.[4] Barbara Parker has identified the print source, perhaps the first one found for an American pastel, as a mezzotint by Thomas Frye, after an unknown artist, of *Maria, Countess of Coventry* (fig. 109), 1761.[5] In using this source he made important alterations, largely in the direction of simplification, omitting a collar band, earrings, and tiara, and replacing a band of lace falling over the shoulder from the tiara with a braid of hair. Copley also painted an oil portrait of *Mrs. Gawen Brown* (fig. 111), which is similar to the pastel. It eliminates the rest of the garb borrowed from the mezzotint, retaining only the pose and likeness.[6] Whereas his oils of *Mr. and Mrs. John Scollay* preceded the pastels, in this case the pastel, based on a print source and of superior quality, seems to have come first.

During this period Copley added one more string to his artistic bow. He painted a miniature portrait of *Deborah Scollay* (fig. 112) in watercolor on ivory, his first known essay in that medium, at about the same time that he painted her parents in oil, perhaps specifically to commemorate her wedding in 1762.

Copley painted *John Spooner* (fig. 113), in an oval spandrel, in 1763. *Mrs. Nathaniel Appleton* (fig. 114), done the same year, is a companion to the earlier portrait of *Nathaniel Appleton* (fig. 94). Mrs. Appleton is garbed simply in a white dress and bon-

---

[3] *Copley-Pelham Letters*, p. 26.

[4] Copley was apparently a good friend of the Byles and Brown families in Boston. In later years Mather Byles wrote to Copley in London, Dec. 5, 1780, recalling the birth of Mather Brown, the young man who now wanted to be an artist and to study in London with Copley and Benjamin West. Byles mentions that on the morning after Mather Brown was born, Copley came to the house "full of gaiety & animation." He congratulated the family, asked to see the infant, and then grabbed it and ran down the stairs, with an entreating nurse close behind. At the front door Copley carefully laid down the infant and left the house. George Atkinson Ward, *Journal and Letters of the Late Samuel Curwen* (New York and Boston, 1842), p. 495.

[5] Alfred Whitman, *Masters of Mezzotint* (London, 1898), p. 34.

[6] The painting appears to have been cut down from a 30" x 25" canvas.

net, a black shawl, and a green jacket that makes a pleasing coloristic sequence with the red of the chair and the table covering. Her head resting on her hand is similar to the pose in *Mrs. John Scollay*, painted in the same year and also on a "kit-cat" or 36″ x 28″ canvas. The portrait of *Mrs. Benjamin Pickman* (fig. 115) is dated 1763, the year after her marriage. Like *Mrs. Nathaniel Appleton*, it was painted to complete a pair with an earlier portrait of her husband (fig. 99).

In a three-quarter-length standing portrait, also dated 1763, *Mrs. Daniel Sargent* (fig. 116) wears a dress that seems virtually identical to Mrs. Pickman's. Mrs. Sargent was the mother of the artist Henry Sargent, who in later years reported that Copley had "painted a very beautiful head of my mother, who told me that she sat to him fifteen or sixteen times! six hours at a time!!" Once, after she had posed for many hours, Mrs. Sargent peeked at the canvas when Copley was out of the room and "found it all rubbed out." [7] The effort that Copley put into modeling the subtle and softly rounded head is apparent, especially in contrast to the brusque immediacy of portraits like *Mrs. Thomas Greene* (fig. 57), painted five years earlier. The remarkable portrait heads of Mrs. Sargent and Mrs. Pickman yield a more convincing impression of a plastic, three-dimensional form in space than anything produced up to that time by an American-born painter. The result was hard-won, not only by the artist but by his patient sitters. A penumbra of pentimenti visible around the head of Mrs. Pickman is surviving evidence of Copley's painstaking struggle to achieve his result. Without benefit of an academy in which to learn the more sophisticated techniques of his craft, Copley had to work out many of the problems himself, but a heavy price was paid in time and effort. In later years Benjamin West told Charles Robert Leslie that Copley "was the most tedious of all painters. When painting a portrait, he used to match with his palette-knife a tint for every part of the face, whether in light, shadow, or reflection." [8]

The pose of *Alice Hooper* (fig. 117) is the reverse of that in *Mrs. Daniel Sargent*, but the formal and stylistic similarities are clear and the portrait would date around 1763 also. Similar too is the second portrait of *Mrs. Metcalf Bowler* (fig. 119) and the unidentified *Lady in a Blue Dress* (fig. 118), inscribed 1763, who may be Sarah Oliver (Mrs. Thomas Hutchinson, Jr.). The portraits of *Mr. and Mrs. James Warren* (figs. 120–121) are of this same general period, or a little earlier, with a considerable amount of Blackburn influence evident in the palette and the composition of both paintings.

The portrait of *Hannah Loring* (fig. 122) is dated 1763, and the portrait of *Mrs. Roland Cotton* (fig. 123) seems stylistically related to it, as does *Mrs. Benjamin Blackstone* (fig. 125). The portraits of *Mr. and Mrs. Benjamin Blackstone* (figs. 124–125), Copley's first Maine sitters, have a compositional affinity with two other pairs of portraits, *Mr. and Mrs. John Gray* (figs. 126 and 171) and *Mr. and Mrs. Moses Gill* (figs. 128–129). The portrait of *Mrs. John Gray* (fig. 126), which apparently dates from 1763,

[7] William Dunlap, *History of the Rise and Progress of the Arts of Design in the United States* (New York, 1834), I, 126.
[8] *Ibid.*

the year of her untimely death, may serve as a summary of Copley's style in 1763. She stands, three-quarter length, putting on a pearl bracelet while looking at the viewer, a compositional device not unlike the use of the gloves in *Mrs. Nathaniel Allen* (fig. 102). Mrs. Gray's pose and the concern with drapery, pearls, and other stuffs of the material environment reflect the influence of Blackburn, who had just abandoned the field to Copley. Unlike earlier pictures, in which mezzotint-inspired slashes of light, boldly laid on with opaque pigment, zigzagged across the drapery, the highlights are now gentle and the darks, though deep, are soft. The picture is cleverly composed, with the diagonal of the shadow in the upper right carried through by the drapery in the lower left, and the vertical line of the architectural background stiffening the figure against the diagonal. An effort is made to round the figure convincingly in space. The head is moderately successful, though not equal to the plasticity of handling in *Mrs. Daniel Sargent*, whereas the fingers and forearm are poorly articulated. The portrait of *John Gray* (fig. 171) is dated 1766, three years after his wife died and two years before he remarried. His pose, which looks back compositionally to Robert Feke via the standing central figure in *The Brothers and Sisters of Christopher Gore* (fig. 29), is very much like that of *Benjamin Blackstone* (fig. 124), although more boldly off-center.

Mr. and Mrs. Moses Gill (figs. 128–129) were painted in 1764. Mrs. Gill's portrait is somewhat similar to *Mrs. John Gray* in costume and effect; *Moses Gill* anticipates *John Gray*, although he is posed more frontally against a paneled door, like *Benjamin Blackstone*. Copley also drew a pastel portrait of *Mrs. Gill* (fig. 130), presumably in 1764, which is similar to the oil except for the omission of pearls in the hair and over the shoulder and the relocation of the left upper arm. The pastel portrait of *Elizabeth Pitts* (fig. 131) also dates from the same general period, as does the extensively repainted but interesting portrait of *Timothy Folger* (fig. 132) leaning on a tall desk, inscribed 1764.

Mrs. Benjamin Davis (fig. 134) died in May 1764. Her portrait, like *Mrs. John Gray* and *Mrs. Gawen Brown*, appears to date from the year of her death. There is a family tradition that the portrait was posthumous.[9] This is possible, although Copley may have begun the picture and completed only the head when the sitter died. In either event he was faced with the problem of pose and dress. The solution appears to have been to take the arrangement of pearls over the shoulder and at the bodice and the diaphanous shawl over the sitter's left shoulder and bodice from the oil portrait of *Mrs. Moses Gill*. The sleeve with the serrated edge and pearl armband is found in the portrait of *Mrs. Samuel Waldo* (fig. 161). The portrait of *Elizabeth Deering Wentworth* (fig. 135), also in a painted oval spandrel, is very like *Mrs. Benjamin Davis* in costume and pose, but is reversed except for the head. *Elizabeth Deering Wentworth* may have been painted between the *Gill* and *Waldo* portraits and *Mrs. Davis*, although the sequence is uncertain. But it seems quite possible that the Gill and Waldo elements

[9] Parker-Wheeler, p. 69.

were woven together to complete the portrait of Mrs. Davis, and Copley was sufficiently pleased with the results to use them again in reverse in the portrait of Elizabeth Wentworth.

With Blackburn gone, Copley now pre-empted the market for social portraiture, especially stylish female portraits. As he bent to the task of satisfying the brisk demand, his portraits reveal a marked revival of the stylistic influence of Blackburn. The emphasis on drapery, a predilection for strands of pearls and diaphanous scarves, and the occasional use of painted oval spandrels are all adaptations of Blackburn's devices. The portraits of *Mrs. John Apthorp* (fig. 133), *Lydia Lynde* (fig. 136), and the pastoral *Mrs. Samuel Alleyne Otis* (fig. 137) echo Copley's first enthusiastic response to Blackburn, shown eight years earlier in *Jane Browne* (fig. 40) and *Ann Tyng* (fig. 38). In both the *Lynde* and *Otis* portraits Copley included the scalloped sleeve he used in *Mrs. Daniel Rogers* (fig. 100) painted in 1762 (the year Blackburn left), the picture that had put forward Copley's claim to Blackburn's mantle as the leading social portraitist in New England.

The portrait of *Mrs. Daniel Hubbard* (fig. 139), whose husband's portrait (fig. 138) is inscribed 1764, repeats the pose used the previous year in *Mrs. John Murray* (fig. 104). Copley used the identical composition once more at approximately the same time in the portrait of Mrs. Hubbard's cousin, *Mrs. John Amory* (fig. 140). All three pictures derive from a Faber mezzotint, after Thomas Hudson, of *Mary, Viscountess Andover*.[10] The attractive portrait of Mrs. Hubbard reflects many of Copley's artistic virtues, but it also shows one of his defects. Because his style, like that of virtually all American-born painters, tended to be linear, emphasizing the lines bounding clearly defined areas, Copley's paintings at first often attract attention for their use of line. Copley's drawing, however, is not nearly as sure as his use of color, and in his work one sometimes finds poor drawing, especially an impossible attenuation of limbs, as in the case of the arm resting on the pedestal here.[11] Linear awkwardness is a weakness that manifests itself on occasion throughout Copley's career, but except in the case of some English drawings it is not severe enough to mar the effectiveness of the objects he produced.

Copley painted two other paired portraits in 1764, *Mr. and Mrs. Samuel Phillips Savage* (figs. 141–142) and *Mr. and Mrs. Epes Sargent II* (figs. 144–145). As in virtually all of his pairs, only one picture in each set is signed and dated, in this case *Mrs. Sargent* and *Mr. Savage*. Both of the Savages are seated; the Sargents are standing. In

[10] Frederick A. Sweet, "Mezzotint Sources of American Colonial Portraits," *Art Quarterly*, XIV (Summer 1951), 153–54. Of the three Copley paintings based on this print source, *Mrs. Hubbard* is the most faithful to it.

[11] Oddly enough, the artist Charles Robert Leslie felt that, in addition to good composition and mastery of light and shadow, Copley was to be praised for his correct drawing and that he "was defective in colouring" (Dunlap, I, 127). Leslie is usually perceptive in his comments, but his opinion here had been largely formed during Copley's last years by Benjamin West, who was by then quite inimical to Copley. West had made similar observations on Copley's style as early as 1767, in discussing *Mary Warner*[?] (see Chapter V).

general Copley tended to pose younger people standing, middle-aged people and elderly women seated, and older men standing, although there are exceptions. In these two pairs all four figures face right, and, as in all of Copley's later paintings, the light comes from the left. Both men are placed in interior settings, both women out of doors.

Mrs. Epes Sargent II, wearing a handsome blue riding dress and holding a crop and a plumed blue hat, stands before an architectural backdrop, a landscape opening beyond a fountain to the left. *Epes Sargent II*, in an elegant gray suit against a dark red curtain, is, like the earlier portrait of his father, leaning on a pedestal; the composition opens on the right to trees and sky but then is filled in with a large column base and a low balustrade in the lower right. Although the handling is generally soft, the strongly contrasting lights and darks foreshadow the crisp chiaroscuro that will come later in such portraits as *John Erving* (fig. 319).

One of Copley's most effective portraits of 1764 represents the octogenarian *Mrs. John Powell* (fig. 143), the daughter of the first great American-born silversmith, Jeremiah Dummer. She is a little wizened bird of a woman, perched on and dwarfed by a large upholstered New England armchair. The painting is one of the first in a series of portraits of elderly women, all born in the seventeenth century, which rank among Copley's best American portraits. The similarly posed portrait of *Mrs. Joseph Calif* (fig. 147) belongs in the same category. So too does *Mrs. Samuel Hill* (fig. 148), an essentially conservative portrait in which the pose and the high placement of the head on the canvas — as in the earlier *Mrs. John Barrett* (fig. 58) — and the massive quality of the figure, dominating the chair and the pictorial space, are compositionally reminiscent of a number of late Smibert portraits. The simple restrained color scheme of brown, red, gold, and white is extremely effective.

In addition to *Mrs. John Powell*, which Copley painted for her son Jeremiah for eight guineas in a gold frame costing four pounds, Copley made a replica of the portrait (fig. 146), perhaps for another son. He also did pastel portraits of her merchant son *John Powell II* and his wife (figs. 149–150), which date from the same general period.

In the rather gruff, plain portrait of *Joseph Green* [B] (fig. 151), color is used sparingly, as in most of the early pastels, and is mostly restricted to the ruddy face. The gray suit against a black background and the white and gray in the wig complete the limited palette. The wig is created through the awkward convention of repeated semicircular white strokes on a gray ground. The figure is set close to the picture surface so that Green completely fills and dominates the space. The head is set high on the paper, as in most of the earlier pastels. In general it is true of both pastels and oils that, as the years went by, Copley placed the head lower and lower in the composition.

In 1764 Copley also painted his first large full-length portrait, the imposing *Nathaniel Sparhawk* (fig. 152).[12] Although the placement of the colonial merchant in

---

[12] Copley had earlier painted smaller full-length children's portraits, such as *Jonathan Mountfort* (fig. 26) and *Thomas Aston Coffin* (fig. 85).

such a grand architectural setting is at first disconcerting, Copley makes the picture work by not permitting the figure to be dwarfed by the enormity of the surroundings. This is accomplished by the use of a one-color costume so that the large rose-colored area of Sparhawk himself controls the canvas. A fairly substantial chain of colonial full-length portraits leads up to this picture, including such paintings as Smibert's Louisburg heroes *Sir William Pepperrell* (Sparhawk's father-in-law) and *Sir Peter Warren*, and his *Mr. and Mrs. William Browne*; Feke's *Samuel Waldo*; and Badger's *Captain John Larrabee*. But Copley struck free of precedents, and his relaxed and confident *Sparhawk* has no more than a general family relationship to the comparatively awkward full-lengths done by the others.

Sparhawk came from Kittery, Maine. Mr. and Mrs. Benjamin Blackstone were also from Maine, and Copley thus painted one half of his six known Maine sitters in 1762–1764. In the same period he painted the majority of his Gloucester sitters, mostly members of the Sargent family headed by Epes Sargent, whom he had painted earlier. These included Epes Sargent's daughter, Mrs. Nathaniel Allen, and her husband; his son, Epes Sargent II, and his wife; and their daughter-in-law, Mrs. Daniel Sargent. Later he painted young Judith after she became Mrs. John Stevens (fig. 310). Although Copley continued to enjoy patronage from South Boston, the area that provided a good part of his early business, he was also particularly active in Central Boston at this time.

Thomas Hancock, one of the wealthiest and most prominent Boston merchants, died in 1764. He left his flourishing business and large estate to his nephew John who, at twenty-seven, was only one year older than Copley. Perhaps as a token of his new position, young Hancock commissioned Copley to paint his portrait in the following year. *John Hancock* (fig. 153) is portrayed in the role of a man of affairs, a member of the substantial, reliable merchant class that Copley so often depicted. Rarely, however, was a man so young laden with such heavy symbols of mercantile activity as pictured here. Young men, such as Thaddeus Burr and Theodore Atkinson, were customarily presented in graceful standing poses. In this case there is a certain disparity between the youth of the sitter and the weight of responsibility implied by this pose in Copley's iconography. Copley was not quite able to resolve the problem, and the figure seems too slight and slender for the space he occupies — in contrast, for example, to the commanding *Epes Sargent, Nathaniel Sparhawk,* or *Edward Holyoke.* Even the bulk of the enormous ledger contributes to the sense that young Hancock still has to grow a little to fill his uncle's shoes. This is one of the few instances in which there seems to be a direct relationship between the commissioning of a portrait and the passing of wealth from one generation to the next. Although it was common to signal a marriage with portraits, it was apparently not the practice to have portraits painted upon inheriting the wherewithal to afford one: although the correlation between marriage and date of portrait is quite high,[13] that between inheritance and date of portrait is virtually nonexistent.

[13] See the appendix, Analysis of Statistical Data, under "Marital Status," p. 132.

John Hancock, however, was not devoid of familial piety or heedless of the source of his blessings. Thomas Hancock had founded a professorship of Hebrew and Oriental languages at Harvard. John Hancock, Harvard '54, apparently decided that it would be an appropriate gesture to present a portrait of its benefactor to the college. Copley was the natural choice as artist, and if Hancock asked Copley what was the most lavish and honorific type of portrait available, rather like inquiring about the most elaborate headstone or coffin, Copley would undoubtedly have indicated his recent venture into full-scale portraiture, the mammoth *Nathaniel Sparhawk*. Thomas Hancock and Nathaniel Sparhawk were both members of the Governor's Council, moderate Tories, and merchants, but Hancock was considerably wealthier. Obviously John could not let Uncle Thomas be outdone by a Sparhawk, and a large full-length was ordered.

The next problem was that of the likeness. The man was dead, but Copley had made a miniature portrait of Thomas Hancock (fig. 75) some years earlier, as well as a pastel (fig. 76), and the miniature seems to have been used as the source for the likeness. In the large *Thomas Hancock* (fig. 154), the subject is not as well integrated with his surroundings as was Nathaniel Sparhawk, perhaps because this was not a life portrait. As a result, there is a slightly amusing contrast between the simple and somewhat stiffly formal subject and the elaborate setting. The face seems detached from the wig, or superimposed on it pictorially, and the black garb sets the figure off sharply from the warm red drapery winding down the spiral column, disassociating it from the elegant surroundings.

While Copley was painting the full-length *Thomas Hancock* or shortly afterward, he also painted an oil-on-copper miniature of *Mrs. Thomas Hancock* (fig. 155), apparently in widow's weeds, as a pendant to the earlier miniature portrait of her husband (fig. 75). He also made pastel replicas of the pair (figs. 156–157), the one of Thomas Hancock dated 1766, the year that John Hancock presented the Copley full-length portrait of his uncle to Harvard College. That picture apparently set the precedent for a series of similar portraits of major benefactors of the college, particularly the donors of professorial chairs. In 1766 Copley painted for Harvard a seated portrait of *Thomas Hollis* (fig. 158), an early benefactor whose portrait by Joseph Highmore had been destroyed by fire in 1764. Copley's source for the likeness was a Cipriani portrait bust of Hollis that had been sent as a replacement for the destroyed portrait.[14] Although the figure is seated, the *Thomas Hollis* portrait is a mate to *Thomas Hancock*, with a similar painted marble floor. It is also reminiscent of the early miniature, *John Erving, Jr.* [?] (fig. 80). By 1767 another large Copley portrait, a now unlocated three-quarter-length portrait of *Governor Francis Bernard*, hung in Harvard Hall along with *Hollis* and *Hancock*, and in 1772, while John Hancock was treasurer of Harvard, Copley was called upon once more to make a full-length post-mortem portrait of *Nicholas Boylston* (fig. 330), whose bequest had endowed another professorship at Harvard. In

[14] Copley tried to keep the Cipriani bust from which he had made his copy, feeling that he had not been paid sufficiently for the full-length, but he was not allowed to do so. Parker-Wheeler, p. 105.

addition to their other virtues, the Harvard full-length Copley portraits of *Hancock*, *Hollis*, and *Boylston* are notable for the elaborate carved and gilded rococo frames in which they are encased, each of which has an escutcheon in the top center to accommodate the coat of arms of the sitter.[15]

During the years 1762–1764 Copley was most successful in his role as Blackburn's heir in the field of social portraiture. One consequence of this was that during the period two thirds of his sitters were females; before 1762 women had constituted only a third of his business, and the general average throughout his career was less than half. In 1762–1764 many of his sitters belonged to merchant families or to the landed gentry, and he produced an above-average number of the large 50″ x 40″ portraits favored by these groups. He did not paint a single sitter from the professions and was patronized by an unusually low number of holders of political, especially appointive, offices.

[15] President Edward Holyoke reported to Thomas Hollis, Jr., who had sent the Cipriani bust, that he had had the picture "drawn at large by a Painter, who takes a fine likeness." Holyoke requested Hollis to send him the family coat of arms so that it could be carved into the frame. W. L. Andrews, *Prospect of the Colleges, etc.* (New York, 1897), p. 35.

Fortune or Reputation?

V

1765-1766

IN 1765 COPLEY TOOK SOME STEPS THAT WERE TO INFLUENCE PROfoundly the subsequent course of his career. On the surface the year was not much different from the preceding one. Business was good and getting better. Commissions were rolling in. He continued to paint handsome female portraits in a later Blackburn vein, such as *Mrs. Edward Watts* (fig. 159) in its painted spandrel. For the splendid portraits of *Mrs. Samuel Waldo* (fig. 161) and *Mrs. Theodore Atkinson* (fig. 162), dated 1765, Copley posed the figures seated at a flat-top circular tea table, a device he used in a different way in *Thomas Hollis* (fig. 158). Mrs. Atkinson is seated in a Queen Anne side chair like that in *John Hancock*, her sleeve repeating the same scalloping found in *Mrs. Daniel Rogers, Lydia Lynde,* and *Mrs. Samuel Alleyne Otis.* Copley had painted Mrs. Atkinson's husband (fig. 53) several years before their marriage in 1761, and this picture completed the pair. Whereas Mrs. Samuel Waldo has fruit-laden cherry branches on the table before her, Mrs. Atkinson plays with a pet squirrel on a chain.

The motif of the flying squirrel on a chain was repeated twice more by Copley in 1765, in *John Bee Holmes* (fig. 160) and the remarkable *Henry Pelham* (*Boy with a Squirrel*; fig. 163). The portrait of Henry Pelham is one of the few pictures that Copley painted not on commission but for professional reasons. He wrote to a correspondent in February (probably Thomas Ainslie, who had urged him to come to Quebec for two or three months the following summer): "I have a large Room full of Pictures unfinishd, which would ingage me these twelve months, if I did not begin any others." [1] Copley's popularity can in part be ascribed to the absence of serious competition, and in part to general good times following the end of the French and Indian War. But most of all it was the direct result of his ability to give his patrons what they wanted. When Copley wrote to an English mezzotinter early in 1765 concerning a print after his projected portrait of *Rev. Joseph Sewall* (probably fig. 196), minister of Old South Church, he noted that, if and when he sent over the portrait for engraving, "I shall . . . depend on Your perticular care in the preservation of the likeness[,] that being a main part of the excellency of a portrait in the oppinion of our New England Conoseurs." [2]

[1] *Copley-Pelham Letters,* p. 33.

[2] *Ibid.,* p. 31, Jan. 25, 1765. The manuscript of the letter in the Public Record Office, London, C.O.5/38, foll. 51 and 51b, is dated 1764 on the front and 1765 on the back.

His clients wanted their portraits to be "like," to be realistic representations. How well he fulfilled these requirements is indicated in a letter Copley received from a satisfied customer — again Thomas Ainslie in Quebec, who some years before, perhaps as early as 1757, had sent a Copley portrait of himself back to his mother in Scotland. This useful function of the portrait as a surrogate for a departed or distant loved one was one of the reasons why people insisted upon realism, and it also helps to explain the popularity of portraiture in practical-minded America as opposed to other types of painting such as landscape, still life, or history. At any rate, Ainslie's fifteen-month-old son had recently gone to visit his grandparents in Scotland. Now Ainslie sent Copley a passage, "which does great honour to You," taken from a letter he had received from his father-in-law, giving an account of what had taken place when the child reached Scotland:

> We drank Tea with Grandmama Ainslie the afternoon of his Arrival, and being in the dineing Room, the Infant eyed your Picture, he sprung to it, roared, and schriched, and attempted gripping the hand, but when he could not catch hold of it, not gett You to speak to him, he stamp'd and scolded, and when any of us askt him for Papa, he always turned, and pointed to the Picture. What think [you] of this proof of the Painters Skill in taking Your likeness? [3]

This testimonial should have been enough to turn any artist's head, since it was a classic demonstration of superior skill in the Western artistic tradition of the genius who can fool the beholder, human or animal, into thinking that a painted object is real.

New England society in the mid-eighteenth century had an essential interest in securing the good things of this world. The achievement of worldly success was a sign not of crass materialism but of divine grace; there was no stigma attached to the possession of goods. Copley's portraiture celebrated his fellow colonials in their prosperity, and he did so in a language of pictorial realism that was most meaningful to them. The testimony of a child to Copley's powers as a realist was of considerable significance, and this was by no means lost on the artist. In his reply he confessed, "it gives me no small pleasure to receive the approbation of so uncorrupted a judgment as that of so Young a Child: it is free from all the fals[e] notions and impertinant conceits that is the result of a superficial knowledge of the principals of art." He modestly noted too that this "might tend to excite some degree of Vanity did not my diligence for Years past in the study of nature, most ef[ec]tually convince me of this sad truth, that all human productions fall infinitely short of the bea[u]tys of nature." [4]

Copley's clients wanted realism, and Copley gave it to them. Like any successful Boston dealer in a commodity for which there was a market, he reaped all the rewards this society had to offer. He found himself becoming wealthy, and there was the fringe benefit of rising social prestige that accompanied wealth in colonial America. But

[3] *Copley-Pelham Letters*, p. 30. [4] *Ibid.*, p. 33.

prosperity alone could not satisfy Copley: he had a hunger for glory as well. He wrote to Ainslie that, if he were to undertake any more work than he now had, it would

> retard the design I have always had in v[i]ew, that of improveing in that charming Art which is my delight, and gaining a reputation rather than a fortune without that: Tho if I could obtain the one while in the persuit of the other, I confess I should be so far from being indiferent about either that I would willingly use great diligence for the acquireing of both, and indeed the mutual assistance they would render each other in their progress must naturally excite in me a desire for both, tho in diferent degrees.[5]

Copley's impulse to achieve material success — and his financial squabbles throughout his life make it clear that he did have such a drive — was a natural reflection of the values of his time and place, perhaps intensified by his humble beginnings in the tobacco shop on Long Wharf. His dreams of achieving fame as an artist were rooted in his early exposure to art and theory in Peter Pelham's studio. They induced his early attempts at history painting and his dogged self-instruction in anatomy exercises, which were not at all necessary if he intended only to paint portraits in Boston. His dream of rivaling the great European masters had been formed early, but the more mundane pressures of earning a living had pushed the dream aside. The only kind of art for which there was a demand in this utilitarian society was the portrait. Copley had successfully pursued the task at hand; now the old ambitions began to stir in the back of his mind. It was fine to be a commercial success in Boston and to win the plaudits of its citizens — but how good was he in absolute terms? how good when measured against the leading painters in Europe? To find out, Copley decided on an experiment. He would paint a portrait and send it to London for exhibition at the Society of Artists.

So in 1765 Copley painted the memorable portrait of his gifted sixteen-year-old half brother, *Henry Pelham* (fig. 163), better known as *Boy with a Squirrel*. He sent the picture to a friend in London, ship's captain R. G. Bruce, informing him in a letter of September 10, 1765, that the picture had been sent and confessing, "I am under some apprehension of its not being so much esteem'd as I could wish: I dont say this to induce You to be backward in letting me know how far it is judged to deserve censure for I can truly say if I know my own heart I am less anxious to enjoy than deserve applause." [6] The die was cast, and Copley anxiously awaited the outcome.

Word began to filter back to Boston by letter and by the arrival of a few people who had seen the exhibition at the Society of Artists, and the news was good. The extent of Copley's triumph became apparent with the receipt of a report from Captain Bruce:

---

[5] *Ibid*. On the back of the manuscript of this draft letter, Copley jotted down a different ending to the paragraph, replacing "tho in diferent degrees" with, "tho I think if I know my own mind I should prefer a well founded reputation to a fortune singly" (Public Record Office, London, C.O.5/38, fol. 33).

[6] *Copley-Pelham Letters*, pp. 35-36.

It was universally allowed to be the best Picture of its kind that appeared on that occasion, but the sentiments of Mr. [Joshua] Reynolds, will, I suppose, weigh more with You than those of other Criticks. He says of it, "that in any Collection of Painting it will pass for an excellent Picture, but considering the Dissadvantages" I told him "you had laboured under, *that it was a very wonderfull Performance.*" "That it exceeded any Portrait that Mr. West ever drew." "That he did not know one Painter at home, who had all the Advantages that Europe could give them, that could equal it, and that if you are capable of producing such a Piece by the mere Efforts of your own Genius, with the advantages of the Example and Instruction which you could have in Europe, You would be a valuable Acquisition to the Art, and one of the first Painters in the World, provided you could receive these Aids before it was too late in Life, and before your Manner and Taste were corrupted or fixed by working in your little way at Boston . . ." At the same time he found Faults. He observed a little Hardness in the Drawing, Coldness in the Shades, An over minuteness, all which Example would correct. "But still," he added, *"it is a wonderful Picture* to be sent by a Young Man who was never out of New England, and had only some bad Copies to study." [7]

A young American artist in London, Benjamin West, also saw the picture at the exhibit and was moved to write to Copley. This letter was the first contact between Copley and West, two artists whose lives had run curiously parallel courses up to this point and whose careers were to be intertwined thereafter. West had been born near Philadelphia, in 1738 and in relatively humble circumstances like Copley, the son of a Quaker innkeeper. He was strongly influenced by the personality of an artist, as Copley was, in this case William Williams of Philadelphia, who showed and gave him engravings and books on art theory by Jonathan Richardson and Charles du Fresnoy. Like Copley, too, West swallowed the theoretical literature whole, overstatements and all, and was filled with the same burning desire to become not just a great painter but a great history painter. Whereas Copley felt obliged to stay in Boston to help support his widowed mother and his infant half brother, West was a freer agent. After developing his talent and absorbing local influences, West was exposed to the rococo vernacular in portraiture through the arrival of John Wollaston, just as Copley had been similarly affected by Blackburn; and West soon transcended Wollaston just as Copley artistically outstripped Blackburn. West's goal was Italy, and when the Philadelphia merchant John Allen offered him free passage on one of his ships bound for Leghorn, and when a group of New York and Philadelphia merchants offered to advance him funds against copies of old-master paintings to be made in Italy, West leaped at the opportunity. He studied in Italy from 1760 to 1763, and in 1764 settled in London. From the beginning, when young Matthew Pratt came over with Betsy Shewall, West's fiancée, to give away the bride and to study painting with West, West was interested in the training of young artists. He had a particularly tender spot

[7] *Ibid.,* pp. 41–42.

in his heart for artists who came from the American colonies. Within a few years West was running a flourishing studio, and Pratt's fascinating painting entitled *The American School*, 1766 (Metropolitan Museum of Art), depicts West instructing his pupils and apprentices.

With his colonial background and his interest in encouraging young American artists, it is not surprising that West was struck by the remarkable performance of the precocious young man in Boston. With typical generosity, West in his letter offered to give Copley a professional evaluation of the portrait of *Henry Pelham*, which he correctly assumed would be welcome. After some preliminary comments, he plunged directly into the core of his criticism:

> at first Sight the Picture struck the Eye as being too liney, which was judgd to have arose from there being so much neetness in the lines, which indeed as far as I was Capable of judgeing was somewhat the Case. For I very well know from endevouring at great Correctness in ones outline, it is apt to Produce a Poverty in the look of ones work. Whenever great Decision is attended to, the lines are apt to be too fine and edgey. This is a thing in works of great Painter[s] I have remark[ed] has been strictly avoyded . . . for in nature every thing is Round, or at least Partakes the most of that forme which makes it impossible that Nature, when seen in a light and shade, can ever appear liney.
>
> As we have every April an Exhibition where our works is exhibited to the Publick, I advise you to Paint a Picture of a half figure or two in one Piece, of a Boy and Girle, or any other subject you may fancy. And be shure [to] take your Subjects from Nature as you did in your last Piece.[8]

Copley had found out what he wanted to know, and the results must have gratified him. Not only was he good by the standards of colonial Boston, but his work had won acclaim in London. Of course he was not perfect. Both Reynolds and West had pointed out minor deficiencies in his work, but these did not diminish the dimensions of his triumph. The picture had been exhibited as the work of "William Copeley," surely only a minor blemish on the success of his experiment. And when he was immediately elected a fellow of the Society of Artists of Great Britain, this honor could not have been too much marred by the fact that it came to him as William rather than John.[9]

West had urged him to send another picture to the exhibition for the following year, and now Copley had a chance to rectify the specified errors, primarily the restriction to flat areas of local color (a feature prevalent in the work of all American-born painters). Both Reynolds and West, in pointing to this flaw (Reynolds had also criticized the coldness of color), had suggested his coming to Europe, where he could see deft modeling and subtle chiaroscuro in the works of master painters and more readily grasp the meaning of the criticisms. This was obviously true, but Copley had come so close to complete success, and the painterly sins pointed out by Reynolds

---

[8] *Ibid.*, p. 44. I have silently corrected the more difficult of West's innumerable spelling errors in the two longer extracts from his letters to Copley.
[9] *Ibid.*, pp. 45–46.

and West seemed so venial, that he could not resist the temptation to take up West's invitation and send another picture. This time he would try to warm up the palette and round out the forms in space, as directed.

Full of zeal, Copley decided to try something more challenging than a half-length portrait. During the final days of 1766 and the beginning of 1767, Copley worked on the portrait of *Young Lady with a Bird and Dog* (fig. 164), later known as *Mary Warner* [?], in order to complete it by mid-February, the deadline for shipping a picture to London in time for the exhibition. After it was sent off, there followed another trying wait of some five months while the picture crossed the ocean, went on exhibit, and letters came back to report its fare. In June Captain Bruce and West both wrote to Copley. Although they made heroic efforts to cushion the blow, the news this time was disappointing. Bruce wrote:

> The general opinion was that the Drawing and execution exceeded the last, and some went so far as to say it was the best Portrait in the Room in point of Execution; but you have been universally condemned in the choice of your Subject, which is [of] so disagreable a Character, as to have made the Picture disliked by every one but the best Judges who could discern the Excellence of the Painting; so that it has not so universally pleased as last years Picture . . . I waited on Mr. Rennolds on purpose to get his opinion, as of more Consequence than all the rest. He exclaimed against the Subject, but approved of the Painting, and perserveres in his Opinion that you only want Example to be one of the first Painters in the World. He dislikes your Shades; he says they want Life and Transparency. He says "your Drawing is wonderfully correct, but that a something is wanting in your Colouring." I begd him to explain it, that I might communicate it to You, but he told me "that it was impossible to convey what he meant by Words, but that he was sure (by what you have already produced) he could make you instantly feel it by Example, if you was here." [10]

West again sent some professional criticism:

> Mr. Reynolds when he saw it, he was not so much Pleased with it as he was with the first Picture you Exhibited, that he thought you had not mannaged the general Affect of it so Pleasing as the other. This is what the Artists in General has Criticised, and the Colouring of the Shadows of the flesh wants transperency . . . Your Picture is in Possession of Drawing to a Correctness that is very Surpriseing, and of Colouring very Briliant, tho this Brilantcy is Somewhat missapplyed, as for instance, the Gown too bright for the flesh, which overcame it in Brilency. This made them Criticise the Shadows of the Flesh without knowing from whence this defect arose; and so in like manner the dog and Carpet too Conspicuous for Excesry things, and a little want of Propriety in the Back Ground, which Should have been Some Modern orniment, as the Girle was in a Modern dress . . . I hope I shall have the Pleasure of Seeing you in Europe, whare you will have an Oppertunity of Contemplateing the great Productions of art, and feel from them what words

[10] *Ibid.*, pp. 53–54.

Cannot Express. For this is a Source the want of which (I am sensible of) Cannot be had in America; and if you should Ever Come to London my house is at Your Service, or if you should incline to go for Italy, if you think letters from me Can be of any Service, these are much at your Service.[11]

Copley's experiment had led to a dead end. When *Boy with a Squirrel* had been exhibited, he had been told that he was already superior to most of the painters working in London at the time; all he had to do was make a few minor stylistic adjustments and he would rival the greatest painters in Europe. On the basis of the verbal instructions received from West and Reynolds, he had tried to paint a picture that would rectify the shortcomings of the first. The result was a labored, unnatural, and considerably less successful picture. His critics found the subject unattractive, the dark shadows lifeless and opaque, the coloring overbright, and the peripheral details excessive and distracting from the portrait head. And Copley now knew that, although he was astonishingly good for a Boston artist, he was not equal to the best of Europe. Even if he only fell short by a little, he realized that he could not remedy his defects by verbal instruction alone. It was not possible to succeed by taking a correspondence course in Benjamin West's "American School." If Copley wanted to rival the great European painters, he would have to go to Europe to see what Reynolds and West were talking about.

This was simple enough, perhaps, but it put Copley squarely on the horns of a dilemma. If he followed his star to Europe, if he accepted the challenge of trying to scale "the summit of that Mighty Mountain where the Everlasting Lauriels grow," [12] he had a fairly good chance of succeeding. Certainly he seemed to have the skill and the promise. But success would mean exile. His Boston patrons only wanted realistic portraits, and these he was already giving them. The odds were that masterpieces of history painting would be far less salable in Boston than the pictures he was now producing. As a provincial portrait painter, Copley may not have been rivaling the great masters in quality, but economically he was doing very well indeed. As he wrote to Captain Bruce in 1767, this year of indecision, "I make as much as if I were a Raphael or a Correggio; and three hundred guineas a year, my present income, is equal to nine hundred a year in London." [13] A practical man with a deep respect for money, Copley was not the sort lightly to abandon a lucrative career in pursuit of chimeras. On the other hand, if he chose to remain in Boston, his artistic ambitions would be stunted and his dreams frustrated. Which would it be?

[11] *Ibid.*, pp. 56–58.
[12] *Ibid.*, p. 106.
[13] Allan Cunningham, *The Lives of the Most Emi-* nent *British Painters and Sculptors*, IV (New York, 1834), 140, Copley to Captain Bruce, 1767.

VI

Rising Fortune

1765-1767 WHILE COPLEY SOUGHT TO MEASURE HIMSELF AGAINST EUROPEAN standards by sending portraits to England, he was riding the crest of his career as a social portraitist in Boston. He now virtually monopolized the stylish portrait market. Stylistically he continued to develop the rounded modeling that had marked the portrait of *Mrs. Daniel Rogers* in 1762. The *Boy with a Squirrel*, which Reynolds and West found hard-lined and somewhat cold, is in fact one of the softest and warmest of Copley's American portraits, painted at the peak of this style and coming between the more planiform early works and the more linear and harshly chiaroscuroed style of the late 1760's and early 1770's.

Two portraits of 1765 demonstrate continuity in Copley's softer style. *Mrs. George Watson* (fig. 165) holds a Delft vase of flowers in her left hand. The composition is strikingly effective, with the figure superimposed on a diagonal recession of four distinct planes, starting with a dark greenish drapery in the upper left, then a light brown wall behind the figure, a light gray column against which the still life is seen, and finally a thin band of sky along the right edge of the canvas. The portrait of *Sarah Jackson* (fig. 166) echoes several earlier portraits in the fluted urn (*Mrs. Epes Sargent II*, fig. 144), the balustrade in the lower right (*Epes Sargent II*, fig. 145), and the pose of the hand at the figure's side and the placement of the white choker (*Mrs. Daniel Sargent*, fig. 116).

A pair of oil-on-copper miniatures of *Mr. and Mrs. Henry Marchant* (figs. 167–168) seems to date from the same period, probably shortly after the couple's marriage on January 8, 1765. *Mrs. Marchant* is similar to *Mrs. George Watson* and *Sarah Jackson*, while the unusual portrait of *Henry Marchant* is like *Boy with a Squirrel* in its concern with character rather than with the externals of status and occupation. Marchant places one hand over his heart, as if making a pledge. There is an awkward disparity between this hand, looming large in the foreground, and the gently modeled head, which is much further back in space. This adds, however, to the intensity of the emotional content in a way that a static and balanced composition would not. Although the pictures are close in size and are set in similar and quite possibly original oval wood frames, the drapery with tassel is of a different (yet related) hue in each picture;

and whereas the light in the portrait of Mrs. Marchant comes from the left, as usual, in her husband's portrait it comes from the right.

Sarah Jackson (fig. 166) embodies one of the most remarkable characteristics of Copley's American portraits of this period: a sense of presence, of the physical entity and personality of the sitter, which is conveyed across the span of two hundred years. The subject of the portrait appears as a distinct, knowable human being. This phenomenon is almost disconcertingly evident in the stunning immediacy of the portrait of *Mrs. Woodbury Langdon* (fig. 170), which seems to obliterate the void between past and present. This is not the case with the stiffer and more distant matching portrait of *Woodbury Langdon* (fig. 169), a Portsmouth merchant. Similar to it is the portrait of *John Gray* (fig. 171), dated 1766, probably a pendant to the earlier portrait of his wife, who had died in 1763 (fig. 126). The figure is dramatically off center to the left, but is anchored into the composition by the mass of the column and the edge of the drapery that passes in front of the column and behind the figure, its compositional line of force picked up by the open jacket. This continuation of diagonals is a compositional echo of the device used in the earlier portrait of *Mrs. John Gray.* Langdon leans on a pedestal, as did *Epes Sargent II*, and the pose echoes *Moses Gill* and *Benjamin Blackstone*, tracing its lineage back through Copley's earlier efforts (such as John Gore in *The Brothers and Sisters of Christopher Gore*) to prototypes by Robert Feke.

The portraits of *Mr. and Mrs. Joseph Scott* (figs. 172–173) present each figure seated and facing right, an elbow resting on a marble-topped table in the lower left and a green drape behind. Mrs. Scott wears a choker like Sarah Jackson's, but one of pearls, and like her pinches her shawl at the bosom. Like Mrs. George Watson she holds flowers in her extended left hand, though not in a vase.

The similarly posed portrait of the physician *Joseph Warren* (fig. 174), who later fell at Bunker Hill, is also reminiscent of *John Hancock* (fig. 153) in the angularity of the pose and the setting. Warren's arm rests on sheets of anatomical drawings in a direct reference to his profession. Copley introduces another pictorial reference to a subject's occupation in the portrait of *Nathaniel Hurd* (fig. 177). Hurd was a successful local engraver and silversmith, the son of silversmith Jacob Hurd. Rather than appearing in his best suit and wig, Hurd is posed informally in a dressing gown with a turban on his shaved head. The pose is not as informal as may have been initially intended, if the oil sketch showing Hurd in his shirtsleeves is any indication (fig. 176). The finished Hurd picture is Copley's first known use of the informal portrait, a device often employed in England by Hogarth, Hudson, and Highmore. It was obviously successful and was picked up in a trice by some of Copley's most well-to-do sitters. Hurd sits with two books on the table before him, as in the earlier *Mrs. Samuel Hill* (fig. 148). But the books are of particular relevance to Hurd's work, not mere decoration. The spine of one of them reads, "Display of Heraldry / I. Guillim." Guillim's

Heraldry was a basic source of information about family coats of arms, useful to Hurd in engraving silver, book plates, and such. The second book in the painting, unmarked, has been tentatively identified by Kathryn Buhler as Sympson's *Book of Cyphers.*[1]

The portrait of *Elizabeth Ross* (fig. 175) is based directly on Joshua Reynolds' *The Ladies Amabel and Mary Jemima Yorke* (Cleveland Museum of Art).[2] Copley continued to keep abreast of recent developments in English art through the medium of prints, and now it was Reynolds who piped the compositional tunes to which the colonial artists danced. The picture is dated 1767 by family tradition, the sitter then being sixteen years old. It shares with *Mrs. Woodbury Langdon* the disposition of drapery and hands. *Mrs. Benjamin Hallowell* (fig. 190) holds a similar but slightly more bellicose dove. Mrs. Hallowell was the daughter of *Mrs. Thomas Boylston* (fig. 178), whose splendid portrait by Copley is dated 1766. Its color scheme of an olive-brown satin dress and black lace shawl, set against the dull-yellow damask of the armchair and a dark green-black drapery backdrop, is particularly tasteful. Mrs. Boylston's small, intelligent face peers out of a white bonnet and dominates the composition.[3] The pattern in the damask is left incomplete, and the same muted effect in the hands suggests that Copley did not want peripheral detail to compete with the exceedingly successful head. This was a natural instinct, one he unfortunately abandoned in painting *Mary Warner* [?] in the same year.[4]

Copley painted two sons of Mrs. Thomas Boylston, *Nicholas Boylston* (fig. 182), in 1767, and *Thomas Boylston II* (fig. 183), probably in the same year. For these portraits Copley expanded the type of informal portrait in robe and turban, first used in *Nathaniel Hurd*, to three-quarter-length scale. On his death in 1771 Nicholas Boylston left £1500 to Harvard to establish a professorship of rhetoric and oratory. Following the precedent set with the full-length portraits of Thomas Hollis and Thomas Hancock, the President and Fellows of Harvard College decided in 1772 to

[1] Kathryn C. Buhler, "Three Teapots with Some Accessories," *Bulletin of the Boston Museum of Fine Arts*, LVI, no. 324 (1963), 53.

[2] James Thomas Flexner, *John Singleton Copley* (Boston, 1948), p. 32 and plate 3.

[3] The pose in *Mrs. Thomas Boylston*, the shawled figure seated in an upholstered, brass-studded armchair with one hand cupped over the other wrist, is repeated without any background elements in a number of other portraits. One of these, *Mrs. Sylvanus Bourne* (fig. 179), is signed and dated 1766, the same year as *Mrs. Boylston*, while a very similar portrait of *Mrs. James Russell* (fig. 275) appears to have been painted several years later. A third kindred portrait, perhaps cut down and apparently damaged and repainted, is *Mrs. Ebenezer Austin* (fig. 181). The portrait of *Mrs. Nathaniel Ellery* (fig. 180) also seems generally related to *Mrs. Bourne*, as does a later portrait of *Mrs. Michael Gill* [?] (fig. 276), which also uses the hand-on-

wrist pose. Copley adhered to a rather restricted formula for portraits of older female subjects, showing them seated three-quarter length and facing three-quarters right, but with head and eyes front, wearing a white lace bonnet and a shawl, the light coming from the upper left. This formula is also found in such earlier examples as *Mrs. John Barrett* (fig. 58), *Mrs. Samuel Phillips Savage* (fig. 142), and *Mrs. Samuel Hill* (fig. 148).

[4] In the portrait of *Mary Warner* [?] the child kneels awkwardly in front of the same damask upholstered chair in which *Mrs. Thomas Boylston* is seated. Chippendale chairs are not found in Copley's portraits until 1766, when they suddenly begin to replace Queen Anne chairs. It is of particular note that the type of Chippendale chair that first appears has a molded straight leg supported with a fret bracket and stretchers, a substructure that is customarily thought of as a late element in the Chippendale style in America.

obtain a copy of the original portrait. Copley thereupon made a full-length for the college (fig. 330), like the other two taken from another picture rather than from life and similarly placed in a handsome carved wood frame with an escutcheon in the top center.[5] In the large picture Copley fills the figure out to full length, endowing him with enormous slippered feet, and places the Chippendale side chair on a carpeted platform.

The portrait of *Thomas Boylston II* (fig. 183) is enlivened by the diagonal spatial recession from the left foreground leg through the figure, to the arched opening in the right background. The relaxed figure makes an interesting contrast to the similarly posed but more tense *John Hancock* (fig. 153). Copley also painted an informal portrait of *Thomas Hubbard* (fig. 185), John Hancock's predecessor as treasurer of Harvard, shown with keys as well as papers on the table next to him.

Copley did several portraits of daughters of Mrs. Thomas Boylston as well. For the 1767 portrait of *Rebecca Boylston* (fig. 186), he abandoned the seated three-quarter-length format and painted her as a standing figure, much like *Mrs. Daniel Rogers* (fig. 100), who also holds a basket; *Alice Hooper* (fig. 117), with the dripping fountain on the side; and *Mrs. Daniel Sargent* (fig. 116). Despite the opulence of the stuffs that surround Rebecca Boylston, there is once more a strong sense of the woman's identity. In Copley's portraiture elegance usually does not erode character, but serves to set it off like a precious gem.

The portrait of *Mrs. Duncan Stewart* (fig. 188) is similar in conception, the figure standing before a tree-covered embankment, a fashionable hat slung over one gloved hand, the ungloved hand holding a bunch of grapes. A natural waterfall is in the left distance. The pendant portrait of *Duncan Stewart* (fig. 189), dated 1767, compositionally looks back to *Woodbury Langdon* (fig. 169) and *John Gray* (fig. 171) and ahead to *Lemuel Cox* (fig. 282) and *Thomas Amory II* (fig. 303).

The portrait known as *Mrs. Timothy Rogers* [?] (fig. 187) poses something of a problem because that particular Boylston daughter, Lucy, died in 1759 at the age of thirty-three. This portrait seems clearly to date from 1766–67. The straight-legged upholstered Chippendale armchair in which the sitter is posed is the one used in *Mrs. Thomas Boylston, Mary Warner* [?], and others, and is stylistically too late for 1759 in Boston. The costume and the artist's style also point to a later date. This may be a post-mortem portrait,[6] but the painting may well represent another Boylston daughter: it is stylistically similar to other Boylston portraits, and there is a strong facial similarity to the other Boylston sisters, *Rebecca Boylston* (fig. 186) and *Mrs. Benjamin Hallowell* (Mary Boylston; fig. 190). Mrs. Hallowell is seated in a similar

---

[5] Thomas Hancock, who had given a portrait of his uncle to the college a few years earlier, this time paid Copley for the portrait as treasurer of Harvard.

[6] Timothy Rogers died in 1766. His brother Dan-iel was apparently painted by Copley in 1767 (fig. 217). *Mrs. Daniel Rogers* (fig. 100) was painted by Copley in 1762, in a portrait that has similarities to the 1767 *Rebecca Boylston*.

armchair, which is upholstered in red damask instead of yellow. Her husband *Benjamin Hallowell* (fig. 191) was painted in a format repeated in two other portraits, *John Gardiner* (fig. 193) and *Thomas Lewis* (fig. 194). *Benjamin Hallowell* and *John Gardiner*, the latter not datable before 1768 when the sitter returned from England, are especially close and slightly atypical technically; they recall *James Murray* (fig. 127) in composition. Benjamin Hallowell, in fact, is seated on a very similar if not identical upholstered backstool, a type of chair first seen in the portrait of *Thomas Greene* (fig. 56).

A masterly painting of this period is the 1767 seated portrait of *Martin Howard* (fig. 192). The scarlet judicial robes provide the kind of bold color Copley later used so effectively in his English pictures. The figure is set very close to the picture plane, which makes the color areas of the foreground even more emphatic. A warm primary chord of red-brown-black resounds against a cool blue-green background. A half-length portrait of *Harrison Gray* (fig. 195) is remarkably akin to *Martin Howard* in facial expression, the disposition of shadows, the position of the head, and the type and treatment of the wig. Gray is seated in a Chippendale side chair, with one arm casually hooked over the crest rail, coming back in front of the body where the hand holds a quill and letter. A portrait of the lawyer *Samuel Quincy* (fig. 197) is informal in pose like *Harrison Gray* without going to the extreme casualness of dress found in the *Boylston* or *Thomas Hubbard* portraits. In this case the informality of pose results in an eccentric composition, with the head substantially left of center, crowding most of the pictorial interest and the dominant area of light value into the upper left quadrant. A secondary light area is formed by the hand, cuff, pen, and paper on the table in the lower left, with the lonely balancing highlight of the other hand resting on the sitter's hip in the lower right. The composition of the figure is sinuously diagonal, but the lights are arranged in a rigid, form-maintaining right triangle that focuses attention on the head as effectively as would the more customary triangular composition built on a central axis. The portrait of Samuel Quincy is not as close compositionally to the earlier portrait of his wife, *Mrs. Samuel Quincy* (fig. 97), as it is to the contemporaneous portrait of his father, *Josiah Quincy* (fig. 198). Josiah Quincy is also posed with the head sharply off center, but the pattern of lights and the directional lines of the buttons, drapery, and outline of the figure tend to lead the eye to the head in a more regular and conservative composition.

In addition to his portraits of lawyers, Martin Howard and Samuel Quincy, Copley seems to have painted several clergymen in this same general period. One of these was *Rev. Mather Byles* (fig. 199), whom he painted again later (fig. 200). On January 25, 1764, Copley had written to an English engraver inquiring about the costs of obtaining a 14″ x 10″ mezzotint of "a good Old Decenting Cleargyman of this Town," Dr. Joseph Sewall, minister of Old South Church.[7] But Copley does not seem to have undertaken the project of painting a portrait for the projected mezzotint immediately.

[7] *Copley-Pelham Letters*, p. 31. The letter is erroneously dated 1765.

On November 12, 1766, he wrote to Benjamin West, "I have been painting the head of a Decenting Cleargyman," and again went into the question of what it would cost to have a 14″ x 10″ mezzotint scraped, asking West's advice about a good engraver.[8] There is some question about whether Copley completed this portrait, but the chances are that he did and that fig. 196, quite extensively restored, is the picture in question.

In 1767 Copley painted portraits of the fabled Marblehead merchant, "King" *Robert Hooper* and his wife (figs. 201–202). Robust Mrs. Hooper sits facing the viewer, her physical bulk dominating the canvas as in late Smibert portraits or Copley's *Mrs. Samuel Hill* (fig. 148). Her head seems to pop out of the cornucopia of stuffs poured around her, including pearls, lace, satins, grand-manner drapery complete with cord and tassel, a marble-top table, and a highly polished Queen Anne side chair. Blue-eyed "King" Hooper is posed sideways at a slant-top desk, which is covered with green baize and studded with brass tacks. This is one of the few portraits showing a desk rather than a cloth-covered table. Hooper is also seated in a Queen Anne chair, with a similar tasseled red drapery behind to establish the connection with the portrait of his wife. Like Harrison Gray and Samuel Quincy he holds a pen, and papers are in his hand and on the desk. The angled pose causes Hooper, though he too is rather corpulent, to dominate the picture plane less completely than his wife does. Yet he overtops the desk and its accessories, so that some sense of his control over his business affairs is implied. (Whether he controlled Mrs. Hooper is another question.) With the portraits of the Robert Hoopers, whose daughter Alice he had painted several years before, Copley began to enjoy an active patronage in Marblehead, largely from Hoopers and their relatives, rather like the earlier patronage he had from the Sargent family in Gloucester.

The middle years of the decade found Copley continually strengthening, refining, and varying his style. One of the major areas of enlargement was his increasing mastery of the medium of pastel. His early efforts, such as *Hugh Hall* (fig. 77), were attempts to force the powdered pigment into an illusion of a sculptured form in space. Often achieved with a minimal utilization of his gifts as a colorist, this effort culminated in the effective monochromatic portraits of *Mr. and Mrs. John Scollay* (figs. 107–108). At the same time, Copley began to explore a more decorative approach in pictures like *Mrs. Moses Gill* [A] (fig. 130). By 1765 Copley had hit his stride in the medium: during the next five years he created a series of pastel portraits that are without equal in American art, and indeed rivaled only by such contemporaneous European pastelists as Maurice Quentin de la Tour, Rosalba Carriera, and John Russell. In 1765 Copley did a pastel portrait, for four guineas, of *Mrs. Gregory Townsend* (fig. 203) who in August 1764 had married the subject of an earlier pastel, *Gregory Townsend* (fig. 78).[9] There is a clear stylistic affinity between this pastel and oil portraits of the same date, such as *Mrs. George Watson*. At this time Copley also did pastels of *Mrs. Edward Green* (fig.

---

[8] *Ibid.*, p. 52.
[9] *An Exhibition of Paintings by John Singleton* *Copley*, Metropolitan Museum of Art, New York (Dec. 22, 1936–Feb. 14, 1937), no. 15.

204), *Mrs. Samuel Henley* (fig. 205), *Mrs. Andrew Tyler* (fig. 206), and *John Temple* (fig. 207). In almost all of these middle-period pastels, the heads are placed high in the composition. For *Mrs. Green* Copley indulged in a coloristic splash of blue in both the dress and the sky, but the drawing remains rather tight and constrained. In the portrait of *John Temple*, however, Copley dramatically consolidated his powers as a pastelist, uniting the hard-won ability to model a plastic form in space with a new freedom in using color.

The sensitive pastel of *Peter Chardon* (fig. 209) in his lawyer's robes and white wig presumably dates from 1765 or 1766, the latter being the year of the young man's death. Copley's skill as a pastelist must have been bruited about in London in 1766, perhaps by Captain Bruce or others. When Benjamin West wrote to Copley about *Boy with a Squirrel* on August 4, 1766, urging him to send a picture for the following year's exhibition, he explicitly noted, "lett it be Painted in oil, and make it a rule to Paint in that way as much as Posible, for Oil Painting has the superiority over all other Painting." In his reply on November 12 of that year, Copley requested that "when you write next you will be more explicit on the article of Crayons, and why You dis[ap]prove the use of them, for I think my best portraits done in that way." To make his point, in 1767 Copley sent a currently unlocated or unidentified pastel for West's examination along with the portrait of *Mary Warner* [?]. But West did not even mention the pastel in his next letter, *Mary Warner* [?] being the principal subject.[10]

Copley produced a large number of pastels in 1767, including splendid pairs of *Mr. and Mrs. William Turner* (figs. 211–212), *Mr. and Mrs. Joseph Greene* (figs. 213–214), and *Mr. and Mrs. Joseph Green* [A] (figs. 215–216). *Mr. and Mrs. Joseph Green* have simple tonal backgrounds against which the figures stand out in sharp relief, projecting a strong sense of the physical presence of the subjects. Mrs. William Turner and Mrs. Joseph Greene — as well as *Mrs. George Turner* (fig. 210) and *Mrs. Andrew Tyler* (fig. 206), which appear to date from the same period — are seen against a background of light blue sky enlivened with white clouds; their husbands are posed in interior settings against a drapery background. The general color schemes are light, whether strong, as in the cool harmony of William Turner's ivory jacket against the blue drapery, or delicate, as in Mrs. Joseph Greene's lavender, yellow, and white costume against the pale skyscape.

The years 1765–1767 launched Copley upon the second half of his American career. This was more or less an intermediate period during which he weighed the possible future directions for his career, and unknowingly passed the midpoint in the production of his American pictures. His clientele was more balanced than usual among different types of sitters. Although he continued to paint a large number of rich merchants and landowners, and their wives and daughters, as in the previous three-year period, he did so less exclusively and began to paint more sitters from the professions.

[10] *Copley-Pelham Letters*, pp. 45, 51, 53.

58

VII To the Top of the Hill

1768-1770   COPLEY'S EXHIBITION OF *Young Lady with a Bird and Dog* [*Mary Warner?*] at the Society of Artists in 1767 had been something of a fiasco. If as a result he took the advice of West and Reynolds and went to Europe, it seemed likely that the experience might enhance his art. But if he settled in London, it was not certain that he could make as good a living as he had in Boston, "and," he wrote, "I cannot think of purchasing fame at so dear a rate." [1] He virtually asked West and another correspondent, probably Captain Bruce, to make his mind up for him by offering assurances that in England he could match or exceed the three hundred guineas a year he earned in Boston. In January 1768, while waiting for some reply, Copley sent for exhibit at the Society of Artists the portrait of "Mr. Rogers," presumably the 1767 *Daniel Rogers*[?], and (apparently undaunted by West's lack of enthusiasm for such pictures) an unidentified pastel of a "Young Lady." Having had his fingers burned the last time, Copley now cradled his offering in protective excuses. He complained to West that Mr. Rogers did not sit often enough and noted his own involvement with "a great [deal] of Business. Having no assistance I am obliged to do all parts of my Pictures with my own hand." Despite Copley's apprehensiveness, the picture met with general approval, and West felt that Copley had "nothing to Hazard in Comeing to this place." He urged Copley to go to Italy for a year before settling in England, adding, "My Friendship I freely give, and if ever you should Come hear, I begg you'll make my house your home." [2]

The portrait of *Daniel Rogers* [?] (fig. 217) is not as effective as the promise of its parts, which perhaps explains why Copley seemed to anticipate West's objections. The figure is seated sideways on a straight-legged mahogany Chippendale side chair, facing the viewer directly. As in Copley's best pictures of this period, there is a strong sense of the sitter's presence. Copley brings this about in several ways: rendering details accurately, setting the figure close to the picture plane so that it occupies most of the pictorial space and appears close to the viewer, modeling the figure with strong contrasts of light and dark to create the sense of a solid mass in space, and restraining the rich colors so as not to divert attention from the illusion of physical reality.

---

[1] *Copley-Pelham Letters*, p. 64, Copley to Captain R. G. Bruce[?], 1767[?].

[2] *Ibid.*, pp. 66–68, 72–73.

Joseph Sherburne (fig. 218), a prosperous Boston merchant, is similarly posed, seated on an identical side chair but dressed in the informal gown and turban Copley introduced so effectively in the *Boylston* and *Hubbard* portraits. This handsome picture contains one of Copley's most effective color harmonies, brown and blue. Copley, like Feke, often carefully created a play between warm foreground colors and a cool background, or vice versa, at times enriching the coloristic tension in a pair of portraits by having the pendant reverse the planar sequence of warm and cool colors. However, Copley departed from this coloristic convention as freely as his sensibility dictated. An intriguing aspect of this picture is its relationship to the portrait of *Mrs. Jerathmael Bowers* (fig. 219), the composition of which Copley took wholesale from the James McArdell engraving after Joshua Reynolds' portrait of *Lady Caroline Russell* (c. 1759).[3] Mrs. Bowers was the daughter of Joseph Sherburne by his first wife, Mary Watson. She married Jerathmael Bowers of Somerset, Massachusetts, in 1763, and her portrait has customarily been dated at about that time. But stylistically the picture fits better into the later rather than the early 1760's. The print-derived placement of the figure on a sofa, probably a painted wooden garden bench in this case, occurs in Copley's later paintings (notably figs. 284 and 286). The costume, though worn in England in the early 1760's, is apparently not found in America until the late 1760's. A sitter might select or approve a print source for a portrait if the dress were still fashionable, but it seems unlikely that one would choose to be painted in a costume that was as revolutionary as this dress would have been in Boston in the early 1760's. The sitter, moreover, looks considerably older than twenty-eight, Mrs. Bowers' age in 1763. Although age is difficult to estimate in a portrait, even when the subject is portrayed by a realist like Copley, the subject of this picture also looks older than thirty-three, which Mrs. Bowers would be if the date of the portrait is advanced to 1768. Albert S. Roe has suggested that the identity of the sitter may have been confused during the nineteenth century, and that she might be the third Mrs. Joseph Sherburne, Mary Plaisted of Salem, whom Sherburne married in 1750.[4] This suggestion is appealing because the painting makes an excellent and viable pendant to *Joseph Sherburne*. The two portraits then fit neatly into the stylistic development of pairs of wealthy merchants and their wives — from the *Robert Hooper* portraits of 1767 to the related *Isaac Smith, Jeremiah Lee, Joseph Hooper,* and *Ezekiel Goldthwait* pairs of 1769–70. Although it is not possible definitely to convert the identity of the sitter known as Mrs. Jerathmael Bowers from Sherburne's daughter to his third wife, the possibility must be acknowledged.

Copley's portrait of *John Amory* (fig. 220) is dated 1768 by an extant bill for fourteen pounds (Massachusetts Historical Society). The pose of the figure is borrowed

[3] Bryson Burroughs' publication of Copley's use of this print source, in *Metropolitan Museum Bulletin,* XI (March 1916), 76, was the starting point for the subsequent preoccupation with European print sources for American art. See also Belknap, plate

XLII.

[4] Albert S. Roe, Cornell University, to Stuart P. Feld, Metropolitan Museum of Art, April 15, 1964; Albert S. Roe, Cornell University, to the author, Aug. 18, 1964.

from the portrait by Thomas Hudson of the artist *Samuel Scott* (fig. 221), presumably through the medium of a print. Copley later modified the pose for his own figure in *The Copley Family* (fig. 344), painted in London. John Amory leans on the back of a chair that is quite outmoded for 1768. Virtually all other pictures by Copley datable after 1765 incorporate Chippendale furniture, except for Windsor chairs in several late portraits. The use here of an early New England Queen Anne side chair, a type that usually had a rush seat and Spanish feet, reflects the use of a similar spoon-backed chair with a vasiform splat in the Hudson prototype; perhaps it also served to make the portrait look a trifle dated and thus more compatible with the earlier portrait of *Mrs. John Amory* (fig. 140). The portrait of *George Watson* (fig. 222), dated 1768, roughly reversing the pose of *John Amory*, is similarly a pendant to an earlier portrait of his wife (fig. 165). But Watson was painted when he was a widower, a year after the death of his wife.

During the same year Copley also took the likeness of a prominent visiting New Yorker, *Rev. Myles Cooper* (fig. 223), president of King's College (Columbia). Upon his return to New York, Cooper on August 5, 1768, sent Copley his Oxford academic gown, hood, and clerical band to copy in finishing the picture. He also sent seven guineas as payment. Copley, however, did not feel he had completed the likeness satisfactorily and desired Cooper to sit again when he next came to Boston. Cooper had to ask for his picture once more, in January 1769, and was indignant that his gown had not yet been returned. The sharp letter achieved the desired result, and in August 1769 Cooper advised Copley that his picture was much admired; he also urged Copley to come to New York for a few months, where he was sure to find considerable business. Copley replied that he might make the trip later, as indeed he did in 1771. Cooper also paid Copley two guineas for a small picture, now unlocated, of a "Nun with the Candle before her" to start a public collection in the college library. This probably was a European picture that Copley had acquired, perhaps at auction, but the possibility does exist that it was a copy he had made himself.[5]

The year 1769 marked a milestone in Copley's personal life as well as a turning point in his artistic development. The ebullient style of the previous years, particularly evident in all the portraits of young and handsome social scions, was replaced by a more sober and restrained manner. It accompanied a changing level of patronage, as Copley painted fewer sitters of primarily social prominence and more sitters of political, professional, or fiscal importance. The personal event that triggered the change in Copley's career, or at least symbolizes it, was his marriage on November 16, 1769, to Susanna Farnham Clarke. Susanna (called Sukey) was the daughter of Richard Clarke, a rich and influential Boston merchant, and Elizabeth Winslow, daughter of Isaac Winslow and granddaughter of Sheriff Edward Winslow, the master silversmith. Copley was

[5] *Copley-Pelham Letters*, pp. 70–76.

joining one of the most prominent merchant families in Boston. The firm of Richard Clarke & Sons, operated by Clarke and his sons Isaac Winslow and Jonathan, was prospering. Through the marriages of several daughters, who had made more practical matches than Sukey had, the firm forged links with a number of other mercantile establishments. Sukey's eldest sister, Hannah, had become the second wife of Colonel Henry Bromfield (1727–1820) of Harvard, Massachusetts, whose son Henry, Jr., worked with his uncle, the merchant Thomas Bromfield, in London. Sarah Clarke married Charles Startin (d. 1799), who before the start of the revolution operated his mercantile enterprises out of Philadelphia. He subsequently settled and made his career in New York. A third sister, Mary, married Judge Samuel Barrett.

The Clarke family was distinctly loyalist in its politics. Richard Clarke was the Boston agent for the British East India Company, which necessarily affected his political attitudes. The family belonged to Jonathan Mayhew's Congregational West Church in Boston. But Reverend Mayhew gave a sermon on civil liberty after the arrival in Boston of stamped paper in consequence of the Stamp Act, and Clarke withdrew his family from the church. The family apparently then transferred to Samuel Cooper's Brattle Square Church. Although Cooper's political position could not have been much more palatable to Clarke, the church on Brattle Street seems to have been fashionable and merchant-oriented. Like Trinity Church and to a lesser extent King's Chapel, both Anglican churches, Brattle was very popular with Copley's merchant sitters but not with the professional class. Perhaps Clarke was attracted to this church, the most stylish of all the Congregational meetinghouses, because it was attended by fellow merchants, in preference to one like Hollis Street whose minister, Mather Byles, was a loyalist in politics but whose congregation, if we can judge by the small sample of Copley sitters, tended to include a higher percentage of professional people and fewer merchants. At any rate it was Samuel Cooper, the popular pastor of Brattle Square Church, who married Copley and Sukey Clarke on Thanksgiving Day, 1769. Copley was an Anglican, however, and apparently Sukey transferred to Trinity Church after the wedding.[6] Copley's union with the attractive Sukey Clarke was a long and happy one, and the tranquillity of his domestic life later provided a welcome shelter from the unpleasant battles and disappointments of his final years. The Copleys had six children, three of whom not only reached adulthood but like their mother achieved the age of ninety or more.

Copley's social ascent was accompanied by an actual physical ascent as well: a new residence for himself and his bride that was literally located at the top of the town, almost adjacent to John Hancock's property near the peak of Beacon Hill. Throughout

[6] The births of Copley's children were recorded in Trinity Church. Peter Pelham had been buried from there, as Mary Pelham was to be after her death in 1789. See *New England Historical and Genealogical Register*, XVIII (1864), 226; Alexander P. Rogers, "Some Notes on Richard Clarke, of Boston, and the Copley Portraits of His Family," *Old-Time New England*, XI (April 1921), 161; *New England Historical and Genealogical Register*, XLVI (Jan. 1892), 15–16, letter from Rev. Jonathan Mayhew to Richard Clarke, 1765, sent in by Daniel Denison Slade; Frederick Tuckerman, "Notes from the Rev. Samuel Cooper's Interleaved Almanacs of 1764 and 1769," *ibid.*, IV (April 1901), 149; Parker-Wheeler, p. 7.

his life Copley's professional, social, and economic progress was consistently reflected in his changes of address. The first decade of his childhood had been spent at the foot of town on Long Wharf. At ten he moved with his mother to Lindall's Row, probably on the corner of Exchange Place and Congress Street (formerly Leverett's Lane).[7] He continued to migrate westward and at least set up a studio, if he did not live there, at a new address which in 1764 he gave as Cambridge Street. In the previous year he had received a letter from Samuel Fayerweather, addressed, "To Mr. John Copley, Limner, Near the Orange Tree in Boston." The Orange Tree Tavern stood at the head of Hanover Street, on the northeast corner of Hanover and Court streets.[8]

Copley began to accumulate property on Beacon Hill in 1769, the year of his marriage. He first acquired a piece fronting on Beacon Street, west of what is now Spruce Street, which included present-day Louisburg Square (see fig. 224). This land had been the homesite of the first Boston settler, William Blaxton. In 1708–09 it passed into the hands of Thomas Bannister, and after his death in 1711 continued in the Bannister family. In about 1733 it was mortgaged to Nathaniel Cunningham, who eventually foreclosed and took over the property, and Copley bought it from the Cunningham estate. In 1770 Copley purchased the adjoining property to the east, land once owned by Francis East and acquired by Thomas Bannister after East's death in 1694. Finally, in 1770 and 1773 Copley completed his "farm" by purchasing the western half of a property of just under five acres that had been acquired by Samuel Sewall in 1692. This consisted of two lots next to Walnut Street, the Vinal and Cushing lots, owned at the time of purchase by Sylvester Gardiner, the apothecary-physician on Marlborough Street whom Copley painted in the early 1770's (fig. 318), perhaps in part payment for the property. The eastern portion of that property was eventually bought by John Joy in 1791.

Copley's total estate, then, was roughly located between Beacon and Mount Vernon Streets, running west from Walnut Street. He had acquired about eleven acres of upland property and nine acres of adjacent flats, plus three houses (two of which he bought from Sylvester Gardiner), a barn, and an orchard. The three houses on Copley's land are on the left in Christian Remick's 1768 watercolor view of part of Boston Common (fig. 225); John Hancock lived in the large house on the right. The easternmost Copley house (on the right), at what is now 39–40 Beacon Street, stood closest to Walnut Street. In the middle was a house at the site of 41–42 Beacon Street, now occupied by the Somerset Club. The house to the west, probably built before 1694, was in the southeast corner of Francis East's old pasture.

[7] Denison Rogers Slade, "Henry Pelham, the Half-Brother of John Singleton Copley," *Publications of the Colonial Society of Massachusetts*, V, Transactions, Feb. 1898 (Boston, 1902), 196, n. 4.

[8] Samuel Adams Drake, *Old Boston Taverns and Tavern Clubs* (Boston, 1917), p. 116. In 1766 Copley received a letter from Barbados, perhaps from a step-nephew, Peter Pelham, addressed to him "at his Seat near St. James Square, London Place, in Boston, New England," but this address seems to have been a jest, consistent with the humorous tone of the letter itself. *Copley-Pelham Letters*, pp. 28, 32, 40.

Most of Copley's property had been purchased at quite reasonable prices because of the forced sale of the Cunningham estate and because the title was not clear. Copley's risk in acquiring the property paid off when he won a clear title to the land in subsequent litigation. The case began in 1769 in the Inferior Court with the claim of John Bannister of Newport and Providence, grandson of former owner Thomas Bannister, to ownership of the eight and a half acres, the old house, and the barn on the property bounded on the south by the Common (or Training Field), on the east by the lands of the late Samuel Sewall (the Gardiner lots), and on the northeast by the Charles River and the lands of the late John Leverett and James Allen. The original defendant in the case was Ephraim Fenno, leather dresser, who sold cakes and ale and had a reputation as a "worthless fellow." Fenno lived in the old seventeenth-century house, the westernmost one on Copley's land, until 1785 when Mary Pelham, acting as Copley's agent, finally managed to get him evicted and had the old house torn down. Although Fenno was the original defendant, perhaps because he occupied the property, Copley was allowed to defend in Fenno's place, and ultimately he won in two courts, getting a favorable verdict and court costs. Final litigation in the Superior Court ended in February 1772.[9]

The estate that Copley put together was known in his time as Mount Pleasant. Well outside down-town Boston, this area of Beacon Hill in 1770 was completely rural, overrun with trees, bushes, and flowers.[10] Copley and Sukey decided to live in the middle house, one previously known as the King's Hospital, which had been occupied in 1760–1764 by John Vinal. The next task was the remodeling. Because of the disruption this would entail, Copley scheduled it to coincide with a trip he and Sukey made to New York during the second half of 1771. He left his capable half brother, Henry Pelham, in charge of supervising the work, which was executed by the housewright John Joy.

The middle or great house was two stories high in the front, one story high in the rear. It was decided to remove a rear addition and attach it to the house that stood on the eastern boundary of Copley's land, after first moving that house onto a new cellar. Then that east house was extensively remodeled, which involved raising the roof of the addition, adding two new chimneys, installing a new staircase with turned balusters in the front entry, putting in new chimney breasts in the two front rooms, and replacing or adding much new woodwork for windows, doors, dressers, kitchen shelves, and so on. A "piazza" was also added. This house was subsequently occupied by Mary Pelham, and probably by Henry Pelham as well.[11]

[9] Suffolk County Courthouse, Boston, Records, 1772, fol. 3, Bannister v. Fenno, and foll. 3–4, Bannister v. Jenkins and Bass; Early Court Files, foll. 91 and 105; Minute Book 95, Superior Court of Judicature, Feb. 1772, Continued Action 19. See also, Allen Chamberlain, *Beacon Hill: Its Ancient Pastures and Early Mansions* (Boston and New York, 1925), pp. 22–26, 50–54, 176–77. A number of documents pertaining to Copley's suit with John Bannister as well as other relevant material is owned by The Society for the Preservation of New England Antiquities, Boston.

[10] Chamberlain, *Beacon Hill*, p. 118.

[11] *Copley-Pelham Letters*, p. 152. John Vinal again rented the middle house in 1781 and continued to live there even after Copley sold the property.

At the great house, after the rear section was removed, a new addition of twenty by forty feet was attached to the back and a hipped shingle roof was placed over the entire enlarged structure, capped with a "neat Chinese Tarret" and a plain small look-out. A staircase with a twist rail was installed in the front entry. In the other rooms, identified in the agreement between Copley and Joy as parlor or best room, sitting room, kitchen, back room, kitchen entry, chamber over the parlor, chamber over the sitting room, kitchen chamber, and chamber over the back room, there were new windows, doors, casings, chimney breasts, closets, mopboards, panel doors, locks, and hinges. Joy built a new barn, thirty by eighteen feet, with stalls for horses and stanchions for cows. He even supplied "Seats to Houses of Offices." Joy was in fact the contractor for the entire job, and in the agreement obligated himself to obtain all materials and to do or have done the necessary work of the carpenters, masons, stonecutters, turners, diggers, and carters; the price was "£519–10 Lawfull Money," with alterations to be charged in proportion to the rest of the work.

It is clear from the correspondence between Copley in New York and Henry Pelham in Boston that the alterations were many, plus incidental jobs such as making boxes for pictures, books, and papers to be sent to Copley in New York, fencing in the pasture and garden, boxing trees on the Common, and making a hot-bed frame. As a result the bill came to just over £1000. Copley balked, and once more litigation ensued. Suit was brought by Joy at the end of 1772, and during the spring of 1773 three referees, George Erving, Gilbert DeBlois, and James Richardson, met numerous times over madeira, punch, and crackers to hear witnesses and to reach a just agreement. Joy and Copley agreed to abide by the majority verdict of the referees, which at the end was that Copley should pay £645.5 for the work that was done, with costs divided between plaintiff and defendant. It apparently was another victory for Copley in court.[12] Even so he had spent a great deal of money to acquire and refurbish his farm. The Copleys were at last able to move into their handsome new house early in 1772. Their enjoyment of it was short-lived, however, marred by the anguish and disturbances of the times. In subsequent years, after they had left America, the property was a source of income but also of considerable trouble. In 1779, with Copley in England, Mary Pelham petitioned that the estate be restored to her. In subsequent years, as her son's agent, she rented out the property and brought suit when tenants did not pay. The whole property problem reached a tumultuous climax in the 1790's, when Copley finally sold the property at about a fivefold profit and came to the conclusion, perhaps not entirely without justification, that he had been bilked.[13]

[12] Suffolk County Courthouse, Boston, Superior Court of Judicature, Office of the Clerk, Early Court Files, fol. 71, Jay v. Copley, Jan. 1773; various documents at The Society for the Preservation of New England Antiquities, including a deposition of William Homer, Oct. 8, 1810, a deposition of Thomas Chapman, Oct. 9, 1810, a survey of the property sent by Copley from England, the Mount Vernon partition of 1799, and the Mason partition of July 1809, wherein the land was divided by Mason, Otis, and Joy.

[13] *Journals of the House of Representatives of Massachusetts, 1778–1779,* 3rd sess., Feb. 22, 1779, p. 151; Suffolk County Courthouse, Boston, Early

With his marriage and the acquisition of property atop Beacon Hill, Copley had come a long way from the tobacco shop on Long Wharf. He had won wealth and position through the practice of his art, and had in fact achieved the general social and financial level of his sitters. In a manner of speaking he was now entitled to sit for himself, which he did, painting a pair of handsome pastel portraits of himself and his wife (figs. 226–227). For his own portrait Copley employed the informal dress that he had introduced in *Nathaniel Hurd* and had developed further in the 1767 portraits of merchants, *Nicholas Boylston*, *Thomas Boylston*, and *Thomas Hubbard*.

The first use of informal dress in a pastel had been in 1767, in *Joseph Green* [A] (fig. 215). The strong color injected by the silk damask banyan with satin lapels made a happy convention for male pastels, and Copley turned to it again and again, particularly for young subjects. One of the best of these is the fine portrait of *Jonathan Jackson* (fig. 228), who wears a blue damask robe lined with white over a white vest, strongly contrasted against a brown background. Copley used almost exactly the same pose for another well-to-do young merchant, *Joseph Barrell* (fig. 230). In his self-portrait Copley, the successful young artist, conceived of himself in pictorial terms that paralleled his treatment of successful young merchants like Barrell and Jackson. And Barrell's first wife (fig. 231), whom Copley later painted again in pastel (fig. 232), and Sukey Copley (fig. 227) are attractive counterparts to their elegant husbands.

A set of four pastels, *Mr. and Mrs. Ebenezer Storer* (figs. 234–235) and *Mr. and Mrs. Ebenezer Storer II* (figs. 236–237), poses several problems. These arise in part from the natural confusion of names, in part from numerous replicas and copies, and most of all from the fact that Ebenezer Storer appears much younger than his wife and almost younger than his son. The immediate temptation is to assume that the identification of the portraits of father and son had been inadvertently switched at some point, but reversing them does not make more compatible pairs. Moreover, early copies indicate that the pictures have long been paired as they now stand.

The two male portraits fit into the sequence of informal pastels between *Joseph Green* [A] and the *Barrell* and *Jackson* portraits. The coloristically restrained portrait of Mrs. Ebenezer Storer is reminiscent of the 1766 *Mrs. Thomas Boylston* (fig. 178). These pastels thus seem to date from the period 1767–1769, after the *Boylston* pictures, even though the elder Ebenezer Storer died in 1761. This apparent contradiction becomes understandable through an examination of his portrait. There is a disparity be-

Court Records, file no. 95292, vol. 540, fol. 14, John Singleton Copley, London, v. Samuel Gardner Jarvis, Boston, merchant, April 1784; lease of Copley estate to General Henry Knox, Dec. 6, 1784, Massachusetts Historical Society. For a comprehensive account of the final sale of the land, see the chapter entitled "Copley Title Complexities," in Chamberlain, *Beacon Hill*, pp. 61–69. The subject is also considered in the present work, Chapter XVII (vol. 2).

In 1800 Copley's daughter Elizabeth married Gardiner Greene of Boston and subsequently lived on Pemberton Hill, in a residence celebrated for its gardens. After Greene's death in 1832, that land was sold and graded into Pemberton Square. Mrs. Greene then purchased 32 Beacon Street and lived there for over thirty years, only a couple of houses removed from the site of her childhood home. Chamberlain, *Beacon Hill*, p. 16.

tween the lower part of the picture, which resembles Copley's other informal portraits of 1767–1769, and the head and turban, which look disturbingly like the work done around 1740. This strongly suggests that Copley in 1767–1769 copied the likeness from an early portrait of the deceased Ebenezer Storer, which had represented him as a relatively young man, and put him in a contemporary dressing robe to match the portrait of his son. The head of Ebenezer Storer is clearly in the tradition of English informal portraiture of the second quarter of the eighteenth century, which found expression in America in the work of artists like John Greenwood. The head, for example, is closely related to Greenwood's self-portrait in *The Greenwood-Lee Family* (fig. 3) or, somewhat less so, to his *Edward Bromfield, Jr.* at Harvard.[14] Perhaps a Greenwood portrait of Ebenezer Storer served as Copley's source. Greenwood was active in Boston 1745–1752, and a date of c. 1747 for the source picture, the presumed date of *The Greenwood-Lee Family*, would mean that Storer was depicted at the age of forty-eight, which accords with his appearance. On at least one other occasion Copley had copied the likeness of a deceased subject from a picture: the pastel portrait of *Thomas Amory* (d. 1728; fig. 240) painted for a son, John Amory.

The highest-ranking government official Copley painted in the colonies sat for a pastel. He was Governor John Wentworth of New Hampshire, who wrote to Paul Wentworth in London on October 27, 1769, "I expect Copley here next week to take my picture which I kindly thank you for accepting." If Copley arrived in Portsmouth at the time he was expected, he probably found things in a turmoil. Theodore Atkinson, secretary of the province, whom Copley had painted over ten years earlier (fig. 53), died on October 28, the day after Wentworth had written of Copley's anticipated arrival. He was buried on November 1, and ten short days later his widow (fig. 162), who was also his cousin, married her other cousin, none other than John Wentworth. Thus it is quite possible that Copley was painting a pastel portrait (fig. 229) of this important sitter at about the time the governor married the newly widowed Mrs. Atkinson. The pastel was sent to Paul Wentworth in London as promised, on January 6, 1770, and Copley sent a copy of the pastel to Portsmouth in the following spring.[15]

After 1770 Copley produced few pastels. In these, as in the oil portraits of the early 1770's, strongly lighted figures stand out in clear relief against extremely dark backgrounds. *Mrs. Joseph Henshaw* (fig. 238), done in the late 1760's or early 1770's, echoes the earlier portrait of *Mrs. Joseph Green* [A] (fig. 216). *Mrs. Henry Hill* (fig. 243),[16] painted in tandem with her husband (fig. 242), is one of the few sitters to wear an embroidered dress; she grasps her shawl in a pinching gesture reminiscent of earlier female portraits, such as *Sarah Jackson*, and of the *Jackson* and *Barrell* pastel pose. The strong, sober pastel of *Ralph Inman* (fig. 241) is particularly close in style to Copley's bust portraits in oil of the very early 1770's.

[14] Burroughs, *Greenwood*, p. 32, fig. 21.
[15] Lawrence Shaw Mayo, *John Wentworth* (Cambridge, Mass., 1921), pp. 68–69.

[16] Mrs. Henry Hill was the sister of Samuel Barrett (fig. 246), who married Susanna Copley's sister Mary (fig. 247).

Copley also produced a spate of miniatures during the late 1760's, and then pretty much abandoned that mode of expression along with pastels. The oil-on-copper miniatures, such as *George Green* (fig. 244) and *Peter Boylston Adams* [?] (fig. 245), more smoothly painted than the earlier ventures of 1758, are often ensconced in similar wood frames, although the width and depth of the moldings differ. Copley also did two miniatures in watercolor on ivory at this time. A splendid miniature self-portrait (fig. 250) is a replica of the pastel (it is unlikely that the reverse would be true), and its date of 176? (the last number is illegible) would seem to put it and the pastels of Copley and his wife in 1769, the year of their marriage. Copley also painted a miniature of *Jonathan Jackson* (fig. 251), which is not a replica of the pastel. This clear, strong miniature, in which the bluish cast of the miniature self-portrait is absent, appears to be a little later in date, and the subsequent inscription of "1770" on the back accords with the stylistic evidence.

Copley painted only one known pair of watercolor-on-ivory miniatures. These, *Mr. and Mrs. Samuel Cary* (figs. 252–253), have the restrained stipple-background technique and the overall blue or green-blue cast of the self-portrait, and presumably also date around 1769. The miniatures seem to have been painted before the couple were married in 1771, perhaps as tokens for separated lovers since Sarah Gray, the future Mrs. Cary, lived in Boston and Samuel Cary was a landowner in the West Indies. This pair fits into the quite sizable group of pastels and miniatures of 1768–1770 representing wealthy young people like the *Barrells*, the *Copleys*, and *Jonathan Jackson*. The remarkable series of paired portraits that Copley had painted over the years came to a climax in 1769: in miniatures with the *Cary* pair, in pastels with the portraits of himself and his wife, and in oils with such striking examples as the wealthy Boston merchant, *Isaac Smith*, and his wife (figs. 255–256), which rank among the highest achievements of Copley's American career.

Isaac Smith at the time of his portrait was fifty years old, his wife seven years younger. Like most of the successful merchants who sat to Copley, he did not have a college education. He was a self-made man. He and his wife were, like many others among Copley sitters, members of Samuel Cooper's Brattle Street Church. His political inclinations were Whig, but he was not a radical. Like many leading Whigs who were not part of the ruling Tory hierarchy, he had been made a justice of the peace and enjoyed the benefits of that office. At the time of the portrait, the Smiths had been married for twenty-three years.

Isaac Smith is shown at three-quarter length facing right, seated in a Chippendale side chair. On the table, covered with a blue fabric that matches the damask drapery behind, are writing implements and paper. He wears a plum-colored suit; the background is brown. The deep colors are fully saturated, providing a rich, resonant color scheme. The contrasts of light and dark are marked, with the highlighted portion of the head and wig, the cuffs and hands, the paper, the quill, and the stockings standing out sharply from the subdued remainder of the picture surface. The dominant area of light value is the head, which demands attention and dominates the picture. The light-stockinged legs form an arrow directing attention past the large white shirtcuff upward toward the head, and the light tracery of the pen also arches toward the head like a pointer. The outline of the back and shoulders, the inner edge of the jacket against the vest, and the dramatic and insistent rhythmic line of the gold buttons, again forming an arrow, force the eye to notice the head above all else. The edges of the drapery on the right and the back posts and crest rail of the chair on the left bracket the head, anchoring it in place in a tense equilibrium of opposing forces. Just as these elements enliven the picture with divergent lines of force, others, such as the horizontals of the chair seat, upper leg, and desk edge marked by the paper, stabilize the composition.

The various elements of the picture's construction — color, line, composition — work together to reinforce in stylistic terms an explicit assertion of the kind of man Isaac Smith is. This statement is made in the realistic likeness of Smith and in the careful depiction of the stuffs with which he is clothed and surrounded, the material things of his world. The subject matter itself makes it clear that Isaac Smith could afford to have fine damask draperies, clothes well cut from excellent cloth, a graceful mahogany chair; but the stylistic elements make an important indirect statement as well. The rich sonority of the color scheme echoes the richness of Smith's very environment. The colors are not frivolous or gay, but deep and sober, consistent with the serious mien of the man depicted amidst such occupational tokens as a desk, writing implements, and papers. Similarly the value contrasts in the picture are strong, crisp, decisive; and this element in the style spills over to become by implication a characteristic of the subject portrayed. The pictorial forms themselves are clearly and precisely delineated; there is no uncertainty about where one object begins and another leaves off. So the sense of well being, sobriety, strength, decisiveness, precision — all rubs off from the style onto the subject. There is little doubt left in our minds that here is a man of business affairs who is a success at whatever he undertakes. He has achieved wealth through his own ability. He sits calmly amidst the symbols of his trade, his hand resting on top of some papers, and there is no doubt that he is the master of his environment. As in many, but not all, of the male portraits, there is no rapport between the sitter and the viewer. Isaac Smith, staring off into space, may be looked at, admired, and respected, but he is occupied with other matters and does not return our gaze.

The pendant portrait of *Mrs. Isaac Smith* (fig. 256) represents the figure seated at three-quarter length facing left. She is not seated like her husband in a severe side chair, but rests rather more comfortably in an upholstered armchair. The yellow of the damask upholstery, the blue of the dress, the purple of the sacque, and the green of the collar are, like the colors in the matching portrait of her husband, richly saturated, but they are considerably lighter in hue. The palette is in a brighter, more light-hearted key. The figure, although seated, is not in a completely interior setting; a landscape opens

69

into the distance on the left. In her lap Mrs. Smith holds a ripe bunch of grapes. Whereas Isaac Smith was seen as a man of affairs in a businesslike attitude, Mrs. Smith, who steadfastly returns the viewer's gaze, is given an air of comfortable domesticity. There is a sense of lushness, abundance, fruitfulness.

In both portraits Copley dwells on the representation of things, whether they are chairs, draperies, or human bodies. He is not primarily concerned with character studies aimed at revealing what kind of sentient beings Mr. and Mrs. Smith were. Rather he is exploring the significant external reality of these people, showing them amidst the symbols of the world in which they live. As noted earlier, Copley's popularity as an artist in Boston resulted from just this concern with the material world, expressed in exquisitely crafted depictions that were the quintessence of contemporary values, just as the Dutch artists Vermeer and De Hooch had successfully celebrated the material facts of their world for a similarly Protestant, mercantile society a century earlier.

Since, by the values still dominant in Copley's New England, the achievement of worldly success reflected heavenly favor, there was nothing to be ashamed of in the successful stockpiling of goods. Whether or not Isaac Smith was in fact the superbly calm and confident, as well as wealthy, man of business, and whether or not Mrs. Isaac Smith was the comfortable, warm *mater familias*, this was the way in which they wished to see themselves. Although they did not want to be flattered — if they were homely that is how they wanted to be portrayed — they wanted to be represented, handsome or ugly, in the roles they had cast for themselves. Copley satisfied this demand through portraits that were not only realistic representations of external appearances, but also representations of these people in a particular social role. By giving his sitters what they wanted, and doing it supremely well, Copley found himself at the zenith of his American career with wealth and position that reflected the very values he was celebrating in his paintings.

The portrait of *Isaac Royall* (fig. 254), whom Feke had painted with his young family over a quarter of a century earlier, clearly follows the *Isaac Smith* pattern. Royall regards the viewer, but at the same time points toward his desk and the documents on it and holds letters in his other hand, making it clear that his mind is still on business. Copley also began a pendant portrait of *Mrs. Isaac Royall*, but after the likeness had been taken she died. The picture was completed a decade later (fig. 365), in vastly different circumstances.

The portraits of *Mr. and Mrs. Jeremiah Lee* of Marblehead (figs. 257–258) were Copley's first venture into full-length portraiture since the paintings of *Nathaniel Sparhawk* and *Thomas Hancock* five years before. Like the subjects of the two earlier full-lengths, Lee was a wealthy merchant. The *Lee* portraits repeat the pictorial means and effects of the *Isaac Smith* portraits, although in an even more exaggerated fashion. Jeremiah Lee stands in an elaborate setting, including a lavish carpet, a marble-topped table, and ornate drapery, posed against a landscape background. He too is presented as a man of business, standing at a table holding a letter, hand on hip, in full control of the situation. Again numerous lines, from the quill to the great embroidered banding on his waistcoat, converge on the head, and the gaze is directed off into space. The portrait of Mrs. Lee is, like *Mrs. Isaac Smith*, lighter in key but still rich in color. Against a setting of architecture and landscape, Mrs. Lee ascends a short rise of stairs; in her skirt she holds a still-life arrangement of fruit, a recurring symbol of fecundity in Copley's iconography.

An interesting and credible theory about these portraits and the position in which they were hung in the Jeremiah Lee mansion has been developed by Stuart P. Feld. Lee built an elegant late Georgian house in Marblehead, completed in 1769. The entrance, centered in a projecting central bay, opens into a hall with a double-rise stairway at the rear. The first flight ascends on the right to a landing below a large Palladian window, which opens to the gardens at the rear of the house, admitting light into the staircase and hall. Feld suggests that the portraits, painted in the year the house was finished, were intended to occupy particular places on the staircase. The portrait of Lee was, according to this theory, placed on the right side of the landing, from which vantage point the effigy looked out over the large entrance hall and could be admired from below. With a wall to the right and a landscape to the left in the painting, there is a convincing echo of the actual wall to the right of the portrait and the Palladian window opening on the left. The portrait of Mrs. Lee hung facing her husband's, on the other side of the landing, visible only when one had mounted part of the staircase or had reached the landing. Then *Mrs. Lee*, the landscape opening on the right in the painting as actually was the case with the Palladian window, led the way up a short run of steps to the second floor, hospitably bidding the guest to follow.

The *Lee* portraits are interestingly archaistic in pose. Jeremiah Lee's stance recalls poses that were commonplace a quarter of a century earlier in the work of Smibert and Feke.[17] Copley's portrait of *Mrs. James Smith* (fig. 259), also done in 1769 and very close in pose and treatment to *Mrs. Jeremiah Lee*, also looks backward in time. The relationship of the figure to the background and the treatment of the drapery are akin to prototypes in the Hudson-Theus-Hesselius vein. As in a number of Copley's portraits of large females, the figure is close to the picture plane, dominating the space and insistingly present.

The portraits of *Mr. and Mrs. John Greene* (figs. 261–262) date from the same year, and the relation in pose of John Greene to earlier portraits (*Hallowell, Gardiner*) sug-

---

[17] The portraits are reminiscent of Smibert's *Mr. and Mrs. William Browne*, in which the husband is placed on the left and the wife, holding her dress, on the right. Smibert ordered the full-length cloths for this pair of portraits in 1743 and probably painted them in 1744 as a well-planned decoration for Browne Hall in Salem, perhaps like Copley's portraits for the Lee mansion. Browne Hall was being built in 1740–45, and apparently appears in the background of Mrs. Browne's portrait.

gests that this pair might predate the *Smith* and *Lee* pictures. As in so many of the pairs, the husband is seated at a table in a working environment, while the wife is posed in an outdoor setting.[18]

The recently found portrait of *Mrs. William Eppes* (fig. 260), a widow painted several years before her marriage to *Sylvester Gardiner* (fig. 318), is related to the other three-quarter-length female portraits of this year in dress, hair style, an open panel of landscape to one side, color, and general treatment. The large oil portraits of 1769 mark a high point but not an end in the development of Copley's American style. In his smaller half-length canvases and pastels of this period, Copley was departing from his previous manner and beginning to create a related but decidedly different type of portraiture, evolving the style that marked his last years in the colonies.

[18] *Mrs. John Greene* seems to derive from the same source used by Charles Willson Peale in a 1776 portrait of *Mrs. George Washington*. See Belknap, plate XXXVI, 40A and 40B.

VIII   Stylistic Change and a Trip to New York

1769-1772   THE ESSENTIAL CHANGES THAT COPLEY INJECTED FIRST INTO HIS smaller pictures of the late 1760's and subsequently into his large portraits involved darker backgrounds, sharper contrasts of light and shadow, and a more somber palette. These stylistic mutations manifested themselves initially in pastels where the background became an abstract dark plane against which the figures stand out in strong relief. As contrast became increasingly important in setting off the figure, the range of light and dark was extended further away from the center of the white-gray-black scale toward the two extremities. This trend was carried forward notably in portraits of lawyers and ministers, whose black robes and white collars automatically provided the kind of sharp contrast that worked well against a dark background. The pastel of lawyer *Peter Chardon* (fig. 209) is an early case in point. If the identification of the sitter is correct, this portrait would have been made no later than 1766, the year of Chardon's death. On stylistic grounds alone, the pastel would appear to date several years later. In 1769 the stylistic change, quite possibly taken over from the successful pastels of 1768–69, becomes evident in the half-length oil portraits of *Rev. and Mrs. Alexander MacWhorter* (figs. 263–264). Both figures are rather archaistically placed in painted spandrels. The value contrast between intense highlighting that almost washes out detail and deep shadow that obscures detail is newly dramatic. The contrast is heightened by the natural black-white play of MacWhorter's robe, and by the very reserved color notes struck by the gray dress, black shawl, and white lace of Mrs. MacWhorter.

There is little coloristic or compositional difference between the two pictures, except that highlights on the fabric of the dress and cuffs in the lower part of Mrs. MacWhorter's portrait tend to make the effect slightly more decorative, drawing attention away from the head, which does not float in splendid isolation like that of her husband. In portraying merchants and other prosperous New Englanders, Copley often surrounded them with objects suggestive of their occupations. The intellectual tools of

73

the minister's trade were more difficult to portray. The long tradition in ecclesiastical portraits in Boston was to concentrate on the head, whether in the bust portraits favored for ministers' portraits or in the prints taken after them. In these likenesses there is little to detract from the clergyman's head, the source of intellect, where the eyes and the mouth that transfixed and transported an audience are prominent. Although the predilection of ministers for small portraits may have been an economic matter, since they were by and large not a wealthy class, the motivation for choosing simple, unostentatious portraits, which focused attention on the world of the spirit rather than on the worldly aspects of body and material possessions, seems to have been more than a matter of economy.

Alexander MacWhorter, a Presbyterian minister, and his wife were painted by Copley while they were visiting with Mrs. MacWhorter's widowed sister-in-law, Mrs. Alexander Cumming in North Boston, an area from which Copley suddenly received a considerable amount of business in 1768–1770. At about the same time, Copley must have painted the stylistically similar portrait of the minister of Brattle Square Church, *Rev. Samuel Cooper* (fig. 266), who had married Copley and Susanna Clarke in November. This was probably Copley's second portrait of Cooper; the first is slightly earlier in date, without a spandrel and having a lighter background. It is of interest to note in passing that more than half of Copley's Boston Congregationalist sitters belonged to Cooper's church, four times as many as the next most popular church, Old South.

Copley's portrait of Mrs. MacWhorter's sister-in-law, *Mrs. Alexander Cumming* (fig. 269), is dated 1770, but almost certainly was painted in sequence with the MacWhorter portraits and simply lapped over into the next year. The portraits of *Mrs. Samuel Watts* (fig. 270), in a painted spandrel, and *Mrs. William Coffin* (fig. 271) are similar. All place a strongly lighted subject against a dark background. The portraits work in terms of value contrasts rather than color. *Mrs. Coffin*, for example, is painted in an almost monochromatic range of white, gray, and black, except for a touch of pale brown-red in the lips. In this portrait and *Mrs. Cumming* attention is diverted from the heads, set low on the canvas, by the light value areas of fabric descending from the head to the bottom of the canvas; indeed Mrs. Coffin's bodice bows are brighter than her face, detracting from the forcefulness of the head. *Mrs. Watts*, with the head set higher on the canvas, has less distractions and is more effective.

Another half-length portrait in the new sober style is the sensitive depiction of *James Allen* (fig. 268), a rather romantic portrait that recalls the introspection of *John Bours* (fig. 93) or the soulful quality of *Boy with a Squirrel* (fig. 163). There is a greater effect of space between the subject and the viewer than usual, achieved by means of the intervening spandrel.

One of the most successful of Copley's half-length portraits, *Paul Revere* (fig. 272), was almost certainly painted before March 29, 1770. In a letter of that date Henry Pelham accused Revere of having pirated his engraving of the *Boston Massacre*, robbing him "as truly as if you had plundered me on the highway. If you are insensible of the Dishonour you have brought on yourself by this Act, the World will not be so. However, I leave you to reflect upon and consider of one of the most dishonorable Actions you could well be guilty of."[1] After this it seems unlikely that Revere would sit to Pelham's half-brother, or that Copley could paint such a sympathetic portrait of him.

Revere is presented almost full face to the viewer, seated behind a work table on which are scattered engraving tools. His left hand holds a silver teapot on a hammering pillow. He appears in his shirtsleeves and vest and, like James Allen, wears his own hair, not a wig. The informality of dress and pose is reminiscent of the earlier portrait of another silversmith, *Nathaniel Hurd* (fig. 177), who in an unfinished preliminary sketch (fig. 176) was also in shirtsleeves. In Hurd's portrait materials relative to his occupation, in that case books, were similarly placed on a table before him. Copley portrays Revere at a moment when the teapot has been completed, and the smooth surface awaits decorative tooling, and perhaps a coat of arms. Revere ponders the problem of design, one hand cradling the globular teapot, the thing created, and the other supporting his head, the source of mind and imagination. Copley ingeniously creates a compositional interplay between the two spherical forms, one in each hand, which echoes the significance of the moment portrayed. Copley's perceptive insight into his subject results from an understanding of a creative process that paralleled his own. Copley and Revere were both gifted craftsmen, the sons of immigrants who had risen from humble beginnings by creating objects of high artistic quality for wealthy and worldly New Englanders. Copley's genius for the realistic depiction of stuffs, an aspect of his art that had special appeal to his audience, is particularly evident in this portrait. The light flows in from the left, modeling and giving texture to the chill and gleaming silver, the warmly reflective mahogany, the glowing flesh and soft hair, the crisp shirt, and the vest. No other picture shows more clearly Copley's artistic kinship with Vermeer and De Hooch.

The strong value contrasts and the more restrained palette seen in these half-length portraits had become the standard mode of expression for pictures of all sizes by the time of Copley's New York trip in 1771. Although dated pictures are few for the period immediately prior to that trip, there is a group of large paintings that can be generally ascribed to 1770–71. The portraits of *Mr. and Mrs. Ezekiel Goldthwait*, for example (figs. 273–274), the only sitters from North Boston known to have ordered large portraits, can be quite securely placed before the New York journey both by style and by the bill that Henry Pelham receipted on July 1, 1771, on behalf of Copley in New York.[2]

[1] *Copley-Pelham Letters*, p. 83. [2] Document at the Museum of Fine Arts, Boston.

Ezekiel Goldthwait Esq. to Jnº Singⁿ Copley Dr.

To his Lady's portrait half length 14 Guiˢ	£19.12.0
To his own Dº	19.12.0
To two carved gold Frames at £9.0	18.0.0
To a Black Frame for Mʳ Cummings	1.8.0
	58.12.0

Boston July 1ˢᵗ:1771. Recᵈ the contents above for my Brother Mʳ. John Singⁿ Copley.

Henry Pelham, Attorney.

Ezekiel Goldthwait, registrar of deeds of Suffolk County and former town clerk of Boston, whose bold signature appears on so many Boston documents of the period, holds a quill that symbolizes the role he played in local affairs. Unlike the remote *Isaac Smith* and *Jeremiah Lee*, he looks directly at the viewer. The coloristic placement of the warm dark-red suit against the dark background, with the cool blue drapery off to the right, softens the effect, as does the lightening of the background behind the head, suggesting that the portrait belongs to an early moment in Copley's new severe style. In a particularly successful portrait Mrs. Goldthwait sits diagonally behind a round tip-top table, corpulent and friendly, her left hand extended over a bowl of succulent apples, peaches, and pears. The loving delineation of the objects in this picture celebrates the tangible reality of Mrs. Goldthwait and her world. The still life is again a barely disguised fertility sign, and Mrs. Goldthwait's extended hand emphasizes her identification with the symbol: she was the producer of fourteen children, and her elaborate gardens were noted throughout the community. The picture bulges with rounded forms, the figure of Mrs. Goldthwait herself, the fruit, the bowl, the oversized column in the background, the table, the pearls around the sitter's neck, and the cap framing her head, all of which emphasize the sense of amplitude and plenty.

Mrs. James Russell (fig. 275), seated in an upholstered armchair, echoes the earlier portraits of *Mrs. Sylvanus Bourne, Mrs. Ebenezer Austin,* and *Mrs. Thomas Boylston.* But the color contrasts, as well as the value contrasts, are much sharper, especially the striking chord of electric blue in the upholstery and the brown and white in the clothing against the neutral brown and gray-brown background. Her cap is virtually identical with that in *Mrs. Goldthwait.* The brushwork is less vigorous than in the earlier works, and the surface of the flesh and fabric areas is surprisingly smooth. Only the lace is animated with pronounced impasto.

A portrait traditionally identified as *Mrs. Michael Gill* (fig. 276) reverses the pose of *Mrs. James Russell.* It is another of Copley's superb portraits of elderly women. Mrs. Gill is placed in an upholstered easy chair with vertical scrolled arms, but she is not dwarfed by it (see *Mrs. John Powell,* fig. 145). Since Mrs. Michael Gill died in 1759 at the age of eighty-three, there seems to be little likelihood that this is her portrait. Perhaps the sitter is her daughter-in-law, Mrs. Michael Brigdon (Elizabeth Abbott; 1706–1788), the widow of John Gill (1701–1734) and the mother of Moses Gill, who

76

had been painted with his first wife by Copley about seven years earlier (figs. 128–129) and whose second wife was to be painted a short time later (fig. 326).

Copley repeats the hand-on-wrist pose in his portrait of *Mrs. Joseph Hooper* (fig. 278), although the general composition is novel. The portrait of *Joseph Hooper* (fig. 277), however, is a direct repetition of the portrait of *Mr. Daniel Rogers* [?] (fig. 217) of four years earlier, even to the color scheme. As in the contemporaneous *Ezekiel Goldthwait*, the head is rounded by a lightened background, in this instance a panel of lighter brown directly behind the shadow side of the head.

The portrait of Joseph Hooper's brother, *Robert Hooper II* (fig. 281), appears to date from the same general period, rather than contemporaneously with the portraits of his parents (figs. 201–202), which were painted about five years previously. Similar in pose to this picture, but in an interior setting and somewhat less sharply cut with contrasts, is the portrait of *Joshua Henshaw* (fig. 279). It in turn is closely related stylistically to the superb portrait of the lawyer *Richard Dana* (fig. 280). These portraits recall such early works as *Epes Sargent* (particularly Dana's prominently centered hand), *Thaddeus Burr*, and *Boy Called Master Hancock*. So too does *Lemuel Cox* (fig. 282), dated 1770, although the crisp lighting of the figure against a dark-brown background, lightened slightly behind the right side, also looks ahead toward *Samuel Adams* and Copley's later American portraits.

In the spring of 1770 Copley received a letter from his old friend John Greenwood, who, having left Boston almost twenty years earlier, was now settled in London where he worked primarily as an art dealer and auctioneer rather than as a painter and engraver. Greenwood wrote:

> It has given me infinite pleasure from time to time, to see your masterly performances exhibited here in London, and hope at the approaching Season to find no disappointment, as it will certainly be a very great one to me, if a Picture of yours is wanting. as it may hapen that subjects may frequently hinder your favoring us with them so often as one coud wish, I've tho't of one very proper for your next years Applause, and our amusement; I mean the Portrait of my Hond. Mother, who resides at present nigh Marblehead, but is often in Boston. as I have of late enter'd into conections, that may probably keep me longer in London than I coud wish, I am very desirous of seeing the good Lady's Face as she now appears, with old age creeping upon her. I shoud chuse her painted on a small half length or a size a little broader than Kitt Katt, sitting in as natural a posture as possible. I leave the pictoresque disposition intirely to your self and I shall only observe that gravity is my choice of Dress. I have desired her to write to you to be inform'd when 'twill suit you for her to come to Boston.[3]

Copley painted Greenwood's mother, *Mrs. Humphrey Devereux* (fig. 283), during the autumn of 1770, sending the portrait to Greenwood with a covering letter on Jan-

[3] *Copley-Pelham Letters*, pp. 81–82, March 23, 1770.

uary 25, 1771. A strong and effective portrait, it was exhibited at the Society of Artists in 1771. Mrs. Devereux, like Paul Revere, is seated at a table with one hand cupped beneath her chin. The Pembroke table does not run parallel to the picture plane, but recedes diagonally into space as in *Boy with a Squirrel*. Restrained in color, as Greenwood had requested, to bronzy browns, white, and black, except for the blue armchair, there is a maximum concentration upon the quick vitality of the sitter, her alert dark eyes flashing in her tanned face, as in *Mrs. Thomas Boylston* and *Mrs. Michael Gill* [?]. Clearly the strong, severe style that characterized Copley's later work in New York had already become well defined during 1770 and, in *Mrs. Humphrey Devereux*, was utilized for a splendid pictorial achievement.

The commission from Greenwood for a portrait to be exhibited in London revived Copley's old artistic ambitions and dreams of Europe, which had been forced into the background by his preoccupation with courtship, marriage, and the need to establish a home for his family. Copley had let his correspondence with Benjamin West lapse after sending him the portrait of "Mr. Rogers" for exhibition at the Society of Artists in 1768. However, on November 24, 1770, almost simultaneously with the arrival of his first child, Elizabeth Clarke, Copley resumed his correspondence with West. After expressing his regret that he had let two years go by without writing or exhibiting anything, he said: "When I wrote you last I menshoned some obstruction in my way to making such a tour, and you have doubtless heard before this time I have increased the dificulty; yet be assured, notwithstanding I have entered into engagements that have retarded my travilling, they shall not prevent it finally. I will make all give way to the predominant passion of cultivating our Art." Copley went on to note that he was painting a portrait of Greenwood's mother which might do for exhibit the following year, although the subject was not as attractive as a younger one would be. He also suggested the possibility of the portrait of young Wilkes Barber (now unlocated), which had been recently sent by the boy's father to the controversial John Wilkes. But Copley hedged this offer with a comment that illuminates his political attitude:

> the party spirit is so high, that what ever compliments the Leaders of either party is lookd on as a tassit disapprobation of those of the other; and tho I ought to be considered in this work as an Artist imploy'd in the way of my profession, yet I am not sure I should be, and as I am desireous of avoideing every imputation of party spir[it], Political contests being neighther pleasing to an artist or advantageous to the Art itself, I would not have it at the Exhibition on any account what ever if there is the Least room to supose it would give offence to any persons of eighther party.

West's reply of June 16, 1771, was rather shorter and cooler than usual, though not unfriendly. *Mrs. Devereux* had been exhibited and, according to West, did Copley "great honour"; the other portrait he had not seen. He expressed the hope that Copley would be coming to London before the year was out. West was obviously unaware that Copley had headed in the opposite direction and at that moment was just settling down for a half-year stay in New York.[4]

In April 1771 Copley had exchanged letters with Captain Stephen Kemble in New York in regard to a projected visit to that city. Kemble had enrolled a number of subscribers who agreed to be painted by Copley when he arrived. Copley's prices were forty guineas for a full-length canvas, twenty guineas for a 50" x 40", and ten guineas for a 30" x 25", except in the case of children where the necessity of adding hands could raise the price from ten to a ceiling of fifteen guineas per portrait. Although these prices were above Copley's regular scale in Boston, New York was delighted to have a portrait painter of Copley's skill as an alternative to less able local practitioners such as John Mare and John Durand. Kemble had obtained subscriptions for the equivalent of a dozen 50" x 40" portraits (two 30" x 25" paintings being considered equal to one 50" x 40").[5] Copley and his wife were in New York by mid-June, having left their daughter Elizabeth with relatives in Roxbury. By July 14 Copley had begun eleven portraits — four 50" x 40", six 30" x 25", and one 36" x 28"; by August 3 he had begun work on commissions worth £300, or the equivalent of thirty bust- or quarter-length pictures; on November 6 he estimated that he would finish these in a period of twenty weeks, two of which were spent on a trip to Philadelphia and thus lost to work; and by December 15 Copley's estimate for completed work was up to thirty-seven busts, implying a total income for the trip of a handsome £370.[6]

In New York Copley did not achieve the balance between Anglican and Congregationalist sitters, between Tories and Whigs, and among socialites, officials, and merchants that was his New England pattern. Instead he seems to have been patronized by a more homogeneous Anglican-Tory group. Since many of these people returned to England during the ferment of the revolutionary period, a number of the portraits were also removed to England, where some may still await reidentification (less than two thirds of the New York portraits are known today). One portrait (fig. 284) was formerly attributed to Nathaniel Dance but has now been correctly reattributed to Copley;[7] once known as Charlotte Ogle, it is convincingly held by Barbara Parker to be of *Mrs. Thomas Gage*, Charlotte Ogle's mother, and is still owned by the Gage family in England. Mrs. Gage was born Margaret Kemble, and her name heads the list of subscribers that Stephen Kemble sent to Copley in April. After the notable Boston preludes in his new style, *Paul Revere* and *Mrs. Humphrey Devereux*, Copley hit his full stride in New York with such fine portraits as *Mrs. Gage*. He knew he was painting well and on November 6 wrote to Henry Pelham, "I have done some of my best portraits here, perticulary Mrs. Gage's, which is gone to the Exibition. it is I think beyond Compare the best Lady's portrait I ever Drew; but Mr. Pratt says of it, It will be flesh and Blood these 200 years to come, that every Part and line in it is Butifull, that I must get my

[4] *Ibid.*, pp. 98, 116.
[5] *Ibid.*, p. 114.
[6] *Ibid.*, pp. 127, 136, 174, 179.

[7] Charles Merrill Mount, "A Hidden Treasure in Britain, Part II: John Singleton Copley," *Art Quarterly*, XXIV (Spring 1961), pp. 41, 43, and fig. 5.

Ideas from Heaven." [8] The portrait was exhibited in London at the Society of Artists in 1772.[9]

The matching three-quarter-length portrait of *Thomas Gage* (fig. 285) is also a striking picture. It had been painted several years earlier and was instrumental in securing Copley's reputation in New York prior to the trip. Captain John Small wrote to Copley from British headquarters in New York on October 29, 1769, "Your picture of the General is universally acknowledg'd to be a very masterly performance, elegantly finish'd, and a most striking Likeness; in short it has every property that Genius, Judgement and attention can bestow on it." [10] In the portrait a flood of light from the left creates strong light-dark contrasts, and the brilliant scarlet jacket with buff vest and black lapels is set off against a dark-brown rock formation. Outlines are sharp and crisp, with the head set low on the canvas. Reversing the frequent relationship of male and female portraits, Copley here sets the military subject, a man of action, in an outdoor landscape setting while his wife, resting her head on her hand — more like the earlier *Mrs. Nathaniel Appleton* (fig. 114) or *Mrs. John Scollay* (fig. 106) than the *Revere* or *Devereux* portraits — is indoors, seated at the end of a sofa.

A similar superb portrait of a woman on a sofa has been traditionally known as *Mrs. Thrale* (fig. 286), a logical identification in view of the resemblance of the sitter to Hester Thrale (1741–1821), Dr. Johnson's good friend, as she appears in other portraits and because of the long history of the portrait in the Keith–Lansdowne family into which Mrs. Thrale's daughter, "Queenie," had married. The portrait seems clearly a Copley on stylistic grounds, as comparison with *Mrs. Gage* indicates especially well. The sitter holds a letter dated 1771, which tends to confirm the stylistic similarity of this portrait with Copley's New York work. If the portrait is by Copley and if the date is authentic, and both conditions seem strongly credible, then the portrait cannot be of Mrs. Thrale, who never came to America. Nor could the portrait have been painted later when Copley was in England, since it is not consistent stylistically with Copley's English work. This raises the question of the actual identity of the sitter. Because of the similarity of the portrait with *Mrs. Gage*, one wonders if she might not be the other female subscriber for a 50″ x 40″ portrait that Stephen Kemble had entered on the list in his own hand (only the first few names were written down by Kemble), a "Miss Johnston." The subject has her hands placed in the hand-on-wrist position found in so many portraits after the 1766 *Mrs. Sylvanus Bourne* (fig. 179). A remarkable portrait, this is one of those few pictures in which Copley concentrates on the character of the

[8] *Copley-Pelham Letters*, p. 174.

[9] Also exhibited were two "half-length" (50″ x 40″) portraits of gentlemen, one of which could have been *Thomas Gage* (fig. 285), which was already in London. A review-guide to the exhibition, entitled "Candid Observations on the Principal Performances Now Exhibiting at the New Room of the Society of Artists . . . Intended as a Vade Mecum to that Exhibition," observed of Copley's pictures:

"This Artist's Portraits are all finely painted, and very highly finished; he has a good Chiaro Oscuro, and his attention to Truth is remarkable." James Hughes Anderdon, "Collectanea Biographica," XXII (London, 1853), Society of Artists files for 1772, Department of Prints and Drawings, British Museum, London.

[10] *Copley Pelham Letters*, pp. 77, 94.

subject rather than on external appearances. The woman, in a silver-gray dress, slumps back into the deep-red damask cushions of the sofa. She gazes at the viewer gently but fixedly with her brown eyes. There is a strong sense of the sitter's personality here, whoever she be, and a warm rapport is created between the viewer and the subject of the painting.

Copley's portrait of seventy-one-year-old *Mrs. Paul Richard* (fig. 287) is another in his series of strong portraits of older women. She is seated in a dark-green upholstered armchair reminiscent of the type used in a number of *Boylston* portraits, *Mrs. Sylvanus Bourne*, and *Mrs. James Russell*. Copley painted only one clergyman while in New York, the Anglican *Rev. John Ogilvie* (fig. 288), of Trinity Church, although earlier in Boston he had painted New Yorker Myles Cooper. Ogilvie is seated on what appears to be a short upholstered bench or window seat. The picture anticipates a number of Copley's later English portraits, particularly *Lord Mansfield* (fig. 429), in the prominent use of the diagonally placed book as a space-defining element.

The Verplanck family of New York gave Copley several commissions. *Gulian Verplanck* (fig. 290), turned with his arm resting on the crest rail of a Chippendale side chair, is the subject of a 36″ x 28″ portrait. His brother *Samuel* (fig. 289) ordered a modest 30″ x 25″, but commissioned a large 50″ x 40″ portrait of his son *Daniel* (fig. 293). In these portraits the drawing is crisp, the light-dark contrasts very strong, and the heads placed low on the canvas. In *Daniel Verplanck*, portrait of another boy with a squirrel, the head rests on an invisible line bisecting the center of the canvas horizontally. The portrait of *Mary Elizabeth Martin* (fig. 291) is rather stilted and awkward, something like *Mary Warner* [?] and the unidentified *Little Girl with Grapes* (fig. 292) of some years earlier, perhaps as the result of the compositional requirements of a square canvas painted for a specific overmantel setting.

A half-length portrait called *John Richards* (fig. 294), with the sharply lighted figure against a dark background as in *Samuel Verplanck*, may also date from this period, or it may have been painted a short time before. On July 14, 1771, just after his arrival in the city, Copley wrote to Henry Pelham: "When we came here Capt. Richards's portrait (At Mr. [Miles] Sherbrooks) [was] so much admired that vast numbers went to see it. Mr. [James] McEvers (from whom by the way we have received great civility) spoke to Mr. Sherbrook to send it to my Chamber where it is [as] much esteemed [as] I Could wish."[11] The color is warm and restrained, the brown jacket echoed in the brown eyes and brown hair and enhanced by the dark wine-red waistcoat. The color harmony anticipates the portrait of *Samuel Adams* (fig. 302).

A particularly striking New York half length depicts *Mrs. Roger Morris* (fig. 296) in an ivory dress and a rose shawl, her high-waisted dress cinched with a gilt-embroidered black band. The value contrasts are severe, as usual, and as in most of these later portraits the pigment is applied more thinly than in the earlier work, with constrained

[11] *Ibid.*, pp. 127–28.

brushwork and little or no impasto. The thin, harder style of the late period gives a rather metallic appearance to the drapery folds. The same effect can be observed in the portrait of *Mrs. Charles McEvers* (fig. 297), the sister of Samuel and Gulian Verplanck. The strongly illuminated figure is set against a very dark background on the left, with a lighter brown background behind the shadow side on the right and a panel of greenish drapery with a tan pattern on the far right. On August 17, 1771, Copley wrote to Henry Pelham: "Mrs. Copley and myself have this Even'g returned from Mrs. McEvers's at Blooming Dale where we have been two Days. I have been taking her portrait there." [12]

The Copleys finally left New York on Christmas Day, 1771, and after a seven-month absence were reunited with their family on January 3, 1772. Unfortunately, although Mount Pleasant had been the scene of much activity during their absence, the remodeling of the great house was not completed, and they could not move in until early in February.[13] Presumably the family was well established in the new home when Sukey delivered a second child, their first son, John Singleton Copley, Jr., on May 2, 1772. A third child, Mary, was born the following year.

It is not clear to what extent Copley himself planned the remodeling of the houses at Mount Pleasant. Certainly he had been much concerned with its progress during his stay in New York, and he bombarded Henry Pelham with written directions for alterations. Copley did have some ability as an architect. After his return from New York, when plans were afoot for rebuilding the Brattle Square Church, he submitted a plan and elevation for a meetinghouse complete with steeple. The plan was considered at a meeting of the church's building committee on June 11, 1772. Although "much admired for its Elegance and Grandure," Copley's plan was considered too ambitious and costly to execute and was discarded.[14]

Since the New York trip did not mark any break in Copley's stylistic development, there is some difficulty in determining whether a number of pictures should properly be dated before or after this interlude. For example, the portraits of *Thomas Flucker* (fig. 311) and *John Hancock* (figs. 300–301), because of stylistic affinities with the dated 1772 portrait of *John Newton* (fig. 312), might naturally be assigned to that year. *John Hancock*, furthermore, is akin to *Samuel Adams* stylistically, and it has been suggested that both portraits were painted in 1772. While Copley was in New York, however, Henry Pelham wrote: "I have rece[i]ved Money from Messers. Sargent, Fenno, Barrell, Goldthwait, Pepperell, Hancock and Mrs. Watts. I have about 90£ O.T. by me. Mr Jno. Green owes, as also Mr. Flucker, Mr. Loring and Mrs. Martin." [15] Fenno, who lived in the old house on Copley's property, presumably was simply paying his rent. The money paid to Pelham as Copley's agent by Sargent, Barrell, Goldthwait, Mrs.

---

[12] *Ibid.*, p. 141.
[13] *Ibid.*, p. 184.

[14] *Ibid.*, pp. 185–86.
[15] *Ibid.*, p. 162.

Watts, and John Green seems clearly for recently completed portraits. Flucker also may have owed for a recently completed half-length portrait, and the same is true of John Hancock, who had been painted five years earlier as well. So, although there is some stylistic evidence for moving the *Hancock* and *Flucker* pictures toward 1772, there is documentary evidence pointing toward 1770; and the portraits are not inconsistent stylistically with other Copley productions of that year, such as *Mrs. Humphrey Devereux*. Since Copley's sober style was fully developed by 1770, it seems appropriate to speak of a 1770–1772 style and not to define the pre- and post-New York portraits too precisely.

The *Flucker* and *Hancock* portraits typify Copley's late period in several ways. Hancock was a radical Whig, Flucker a high Tory. In both portraits Copley employed dramatic chiaroscuro and a somber palette that seem to reflect the darkening political skies. Although a clear causal relationship cannot be proven, there is no doubt that, as the storm clouds of revolution gathered over Boston, Copley's colors did become more muted and his backgrounds darker and more abstract, with a flood of light focusing more strongly on the figures, the *dramatis personae*, and less on their surroundings and the objects that typified or symbolized their place in society.

John Hancock and Thomas Flucker, both very wealthy men, chose surprisingly modest portraits. In fact Copley found that, after 1768, sitters increasingly favored the 30″ x 25″ bust portrait, and two thirds of his portraits of this size were painted during his last six years in the colonies. Smaller canvases cost less, of course, and this meant less income per sitter. Further, business appears to have been shrinking in the number of sitters as well as in the size of portraits, and Copley's level of income was maintained only by a raise in prices to offset the decline in volume. The decision to tap the rich supply of patrons in New York was most likely a direct result of this. Copley's answer to previous requests for his services in distant parts had always been that he was too busy with portraits in Boston. But demand had apparently tapered off at the very time that his marriage had involved him in sharply increased expenses, and the New York trip seemed wise, perhaps even necessary. Thus one might say that a decrease in income, a possible stylistic sensitivity to the disturbed political scene, and the fact that Copley's clientele was dividing into two strongly opposed political groups are all mirrored in the portraits of *Flucker* and *Hancock*.

One of the most effective and dramatic of Copley's portraits of 1770–1772 is laden with political symbolism and significance. This is the famous portrait of *Samuel Adams* (fig. 302), represented as he had appeared when confronting Governor Thomas Hutchinson after the Boston Massacre of March 5, 1770. The portrait could have been painted in 1770, but there is equally good reason to place it in 1772. The picture belonged to the Hancock family and is thought to have been painted along with one of the half-length portraits of Hancock a few days after the election of May 27, 1772, in which Hancock and Adams were re-elected to the House of Representatives. The purpose of the commission was to emphasize that the two men were still united politically, despite Hutchinson's hopes that Hancock had become disenchanted with radicalism.[16]

There is no other Copley portrait as taut with dramatic intensity as the somber *Samuel Adams*. The dominant pictorial element, the brightly illuminated head, stands out with clarity and force against the dark, warm background. The hands and the documents are secondary accents. Behind the figure, paired columns suggest the interior space, the front column lightened slightly behind the shadow side of Adams' head. The body, clad in a dark red-brown suit and slightly turned, looks small in relation to the head. A frontal presentation of the body would have conveyed a sense of physical bulk, but here the emphasis is on the full face, which gives a sense of the power and force of Adams' personality. The sharply drawn face is a mobile mask, the eyes fixed in the compelling stare of an actor or a fanatic. The slightly dishevelled hair and two open waistcoat buttons subtly contribute to a strong sense of the palpable presence of this shrewd, intense, unstable man. The picture is a masterpiece of Copley's late style.

A three-quarter-length portrait of *Thomas Amory II* (fig. 303), who leans on a column base and rests his hands on a long cane, is stylistically akin to *Samuel Adams*, but in pose it recalls the group of *Lemuel Cox* (fig. 282), *Robert Hooper II* (fig. 281), and *Joshua Henshaw* (fig. 279), and such earlier antecedents as *Thaddeus Burr* (fig. 91) and *Epes Sargent* (fig. 89). Copley painted *Mrs. Thomas Amory II* (fig. 305) at approximately the same time, but not in a matching portrait. Instead *Mrs. Thomas Amory II* was painted as a pendant to an earlier Blackburn portrait of Amory. Although this choice may have been partially economic, another factor could be that it put the portrait of Mrs. Amory, who was twenty years younger than her husband, in tandem with a portrait of Amory painted when he had been closer to her current age.

All of these portraits fall into the general period 1770–1772. In the portrait of *Joshua Henshaw II* (fig. 306), which is closely related to *Samuel Verplanck* and *John Hancock*, and in the matching portrait of *Mrs. Joshua Henshaw II* (fig. 307), the heads are set low on the canvas, and one suspects that these are closer to 1772, possibly even later. The same is true of the portrait of *Joseph Henshaw* (fig. 308). In these small pictures the hands are usually omitted, a measure that cut the cost of a portrait and perhaps reflected the kind of economies that were making life difficult for Copley.

---

[16] Herbert S. Allan, *John Hancock: Patriot in Purple* (New York, 1948), p. 126. This source does not document its statements in regard to dating Copley's *Samuel Adams* and *John Hancock* in 1772. If the information is correct, the portrait of Hancock must be one of the half lengths (figs. 300–301), and Hancock's name must have appeared on the list of individuals owing money to Copley which Henry Pelham had recorded the previous year (see above) for another reason. Henry Pelham was still trying diligently to collect money from John Hancock in July 1777, after Copley had gone to Europe, perhaps for the Adams portrait or one of the half-length portraits of Hancock. Pelham told Copley: "Coll. Hancock I have not yet been able to gett an audience of, tho he is so well as to talk of Heading his Company in a few Days. I have always the misfortune to go there [erased: "(which has not been seldom)."] when he has a Violent Headack, or when he is laying down" (*Copley-Pelham Letters*, p. 232).

Mrs. John Stevens (fig. 310) was married in 1769, and her portrait appears to have been done at some time after that. The name "Sargent" appeared on Henry Pelham's 1771 list of debts owed to Copley, and, although that could have been for money owed for the 1764 portraits of *Mr. and Mrs. Epes Sargent II*, it also could have been for this portrait of the former Judith Sargent. As in many of the later portraits, the subject wears an ivory-colored dress, with a dark-blue mantle and a plum or rose-lavender turban bound with pearls. The pose with flowers reminds one of the social portraits of the mid-1760's, but the strong contrasts, the restrained brushwork, the subdued palette, and the classicism of the dress all point to a later date for this handsome portrait.

Since only a few portraits can be placed with certainty in the year 1772, they become important evidence in the attempt to distinguish between pictures painted just before and just after the New York trip. The dated half-length portrait of *John Newton* (fig. 312) relates to a number of portraits, including *John Hancock* and *Thomas Flucker*, with the head set low on the canvas. The superb portrait of *Mrs. Richard Skinner* (fig. 315) also dates from 1772. It recalls earlier portraits of figures seated at polished wooden tables, such as *Boy with a Squirrel* (fig. 163), *Mrs. Samuel Waldo* (fig. 161), and *Mrs. Theodore Atkinson* (fig. 162), but its closest antecedents are the similarly posed *Paul Revere* and *Mrs. Humphrey Devereux*. The portrait of Mrs. Skinner's cousin, *Dorothy Quincy* (fig. 316), who is also placed behind a gate-legged table, is similar in pose and costume, but she sits in an armchair and is seen at three-quarter length.

Among Copley's late American masterpieces are several fine portraits of old men. *Eleazer Tyng* (fig. 317) was in his early eighties when Copley painted him in 1772, seated in Windsor armchair. The memorable portrait of *John Erving* (fig. 319), posed in the manner of innumerable merchant portraits of earlier years, also shows that sitter at the age of about eighty; *Sylvester Gardiner* (fig. 318), from whom Copley had recently acquired some property on Beacon Hill, is merely in his mid-sixties.

Copley's interest in a trip to Europe had blown hot and cold over the years. His first enthusiasm, prompted by Reynolds and West, had been chilled by the realization that artistic improvement would not necessarily be accompanied by economic improvement. His marriage and increased obligations had seemingly quashed his aspirations to study the old masters in Italy. Although the commission to paint *Mrs. Humphrey Devereux* for exhibition in London, perhaps coinciding with a slack in business at home, did revive thoughts of Europe, Copley apparently was still reluctant to give up his lucrative practice in the colonies for a study trip. Otherwise it seems unlikely that he would have made such a costly commitment in the extensive remodeling that he ordered done at Mount Pleasant while he was in New York. By the end of November 1772, however, Copley was unquestionably and earnestly contemplating a European jaunt. He wrote on the subject to West and also to his brother-in-law, Jonathan Clarke, who was on a business trip to London. Clarke replied on December 20, relaying West's approval of Copley's plan and of the suggestion that he go directly to Leghorn rather than to Italy by way of England. West, he said, believed that Sukey should not accompany her husband, since she would only distract him from his studies during the important period in Italy, and urged that she join him later. West, himself writing to the same effect on January 6, 1773, added specific recommendations about what Copley should study in Italy — antique sculpture, Raphael, Michelangelo, Correggio, and Titian — and promised to forward letters of introduction.[17]

Why at this point did Copley suddenly begin to think seriously of Europe, after so many years of toying with the idea? Comfortably ensconced on his estate, with an expanding family and considerable expenses, it would seem impractical for him to contemplate a trip that would involve a long period of outlays and no income. Presumably he needed all the work he could get, and, since Henry Pelham had attained a sufficient degree of artistic proficiency to assist with the backgrounds of pictures when necessary,[18] Copley could handle an increased volume of business. If more money was needed, he could also travel elsewhere, as he had done on his financially successful trip to New York. Before he went to New York, Governor John Wentworth had given him employment in New Hampshire, and John Hurd, in conveying the invitation from the governor, also noted that there would be other commissions in Portsmouth.[19] But commissions were getting harder and harder to come by, and clients were ordering smaller paintings. The problem apparently was not so much a matter of Copley's having exhausted the New England market as an actual drying up of patronage in the face of increased political turmoil. Copley's potential sitters had other, more urgent matters on their minds — this was not the time for having one's portrait painted.

Equally serious may have been the pressures on Copley himself to take sides in the struggle. His wife's family was solidly loyalist, but his own inclinations were considerably more on the rebels' side. Jonathan Clarke jokingly acknowledged as much when he wrote to Copley about the expense of living in London, "where money will go and you Sons of Liberty will find some times without your consent." [20] Copley's clientele was splitting into two factions that opposed each other with increasing vitriol. As he had told West two years earlier, he wanted to avoid "every imputation" of party spirit, for politics were neither pleasing to the artist nor good for art.[21] Copley saw in partisanship a clear threat to his work. Despite Tory friends and relatives, Copley had friends of long standing among the Boston radicals. If he had recently painted Thomas Gage, John Wentworth, and Thomas Flucker, he had also painted Paul Revere, John Hancock, and Sam Adams. Fence straddling was difficult, and if he took sides he would alienate half of his potential clientele, not only now but in the

[17] *Copley-Pelham Letters*, pp. 190–97.
[18] *Ibid.*, p. 197.
[19] *Ibid.*, pp. 84–85.
[20] *Ibid.*, p. 193.
[21] *Ibid.*, p. 98 (Nov. 24, 1770).

future. So the study trip to Europe no longer seemed so impractical; it became a logical and sensible way to avoid a difficult situation. Copley could enjoy a long-denied visit abroad and return after the tempest had blown itself out, presumably in short order, to resume his career without having given offense to either party. And, if worse came to worse and the political split in the colonies led to war, the experience of extended study in Italy would enable him to start a new career for himself in London, perhaps one in which he might fulfill his old dream of fame and glory as a history painter.

IX   An End and a Beginning

1773-1774   Once the practical advantages of the trip to Italy began to take shape in his mind, Copley made a quick decision. He intended to leave in the spring of 1773, although his family probably hoped, as Sukey's sister Sarah wrote to their brother, Isaac Winslow Clarke, that he would give up the idea.[1] Business had apparently not fallen off drastically, and Copley, perhaps yielding to family pressure, stayed on. A fellow Bostonian wrote to a correspondent in England on June 3, 1773, "One Mr Copley of this Town, has, by Genius & Application, made himself a great Master in that business & acquired a large Fortune in a few years. He now talks of going to Europe to make himself more perfect, but is so full of business, that he finds it difficult to get away."[2]

The portraits of *Daniel Henchman* [?] (fig. 320), *Nathaniel Perkins* (fig. 321), and *Mr. and Mrs. Jabez Bowen* (figs. 322–323) seem generally datable to 1772–73 by style and composition. In these portraits the heads of the sitters descend closer and closer to the center of the canvas, a standard characteristic of Copley's late period. Daniel Henchman [?] is placed in a painted spandrel as are *Benjamin* and *Joseph* [?] *Gerrish* (figs. 313–314), while Nathaniel Perkins and Jabez Bowen each have an arm looped back over the crest rail of their side chairs as in *John Erving* (fig. 319) and *Sylvester Gardiner* (fig. 318), roughly contemporaneous three-quarter-length portraits. Jabez Bowen's head is set much lower on the canvas than that of his wife, whose figure is more sharply turned laterally into pictorial space. As in the earlier works, the female portrait is relatively lighter and brighter in color, even though the palette in these late portraits is generally more subdued.

One of several impressive portraits Copley produced in 1773 is the three-quarter-length seated figure of the Newburyport Congregational minister, *Rev. Thomas Cary* (fig. 324), who is seated like *Eleazer Tyng* (fig. 317) in a Windsor armchair. Cary is seen in a professional setting, surrounded by books as is Nathaniel Perkins, but his raised eyebrows give him an unministerial puckish expression. The informality of pose and costume is unique among Copley's portraits of ministers. The portrait of the admiral *James Gambier* (fig. 325), dated 1773, echoes *Thomas Amory II* (fig. 303) in

[1] Feb. 6, 1773, Massachusetts Historical Society.
[2] Joseph Palmer, Boston, to Joseph Cranch, Kings- bridge, Devon, Autograph File, Houghton Library, Harvard University.

pose, with the similarity reinforced by the high pedestaled columns at the right. However, as with *Thomas Gage* (fig. 285) of several years earlier, the military subject is posed before an open landscape. The skyscape in the lower left is freely brushed, and the hands and cuffs are boldly outlined against the light background in a fashion that anticipates some of the later English portraits. Copley had apparently begun to move in the direction of his "English style" by 1773.

Rebecca Boylston, whom Copley had painted in 1767 (fig. 186), along with other members of her family, became the second wife of Moses Gill in 1773. Copley had painted a pair of three-quarter-length portraits of Gill and his first wife, Sarah Prince (figs. 128–129), in 1764. Now at the time of her marriage to Moses Gill he painted Rebecca Boylston again (fig. 326), this time in a companion piece to the earlier *Gill* portraits. All three portraits are similar in size and are placed in a set of handsome carved and gilded Chippendale wood frames. *Mrs. Moses Gill* [B] provides a revealing contrast with the earlier pair. The figure is set lower on the canvas and the value contrasts are naturally much sharper. The brushwork is vigorous and more assured than in the earlier pictures, looking ahead, like *James Gambier,* to subsequent achievements in England. Wearing a high-waisted blue dress with gold-embroidered maroon bands at her waist and along the top edge of her dress, the second Mrs. Gill is turned boldly into space, her large dark eyes directed at the viewer, with a gold-banded lavender turban entwined with pearls in her upswept hair. A column set on a high pedestal similar to others often encountered in the late portraits appears on the right, and on the left a glorious burst of lilies, framed by a large vine-entwined tree and a steep hill in front of an open landscape, springs from a large urn. The portrait, like *Mrs. John Stevens* (fig. 310), *Mrs. Thomas Gage* (fig. 284), and *Mrs. Thrale* [?] (fig. 286), proves that Copley's late American style, despite the sobriety and strength that made it so effective for male portraits, was also tellingly used in female portraits that equaled the more lighthearted earlier efforts.

In the same year Copley painted three-quarter-length portraits of *Samuel Winthrop* (fig. 329) and his brother *John Winthrop* (fig. 328), and a kit-cat (36″ x 28″) portrait of *Mrs. John Winthrop* (fig. 327). Samuel Winthrop echoes the unusual pose in *Samuel Quincy* (fig. 197), while the portrait of Mrs. John Winthrop, who is seated at a round tilt-top table and holds a cut bough of fruit, is a later and much reduced echo of *Mrs. Samuel Waldo* (fig. 161). John Winthrop, a professor at Harvard, sits at his telescope (still at Harvard and currently exhibited beneath the portrait in which it appears). The landscape opening to the right, infrequent in seated male portraits, is a functional necessity because of the telescope. Whereas in many of the late portraits the head is low on the canvas, with an uncomfortable amount of space above, here the reverse is true. The effect is rather unsatisfactory, as is the drawing of Winthrop's left hand, which appears disproportionately large.

Although Copley had painted several multi-figure portraits early in his career, notably the *Gore* children, and the *Royall* sisters (figs. 29 and 83), he subsequently avoided the inclusion of more than one figure in a picture during the 1760's and early 1770's. It is uncertain whether this reflected a preference of his patrons or a reluctance on his part to come to grips with the compositional complexities of multi-figure portraiture. But the latter explanation seems quite plausible, since Copley was somewhat intimidated by the theory books that made composition sound so difficult. Upon his arrival in Europe a few years later, one of Copley's first messages to his protégé, Henry Pelham, was an expression of relief that composition was a much easier matter than he had thought.[3] In 1773, however, Copley decided or was persuaded to paint a double portrait of a pair of prominent visiting Philadelphians, *Mr. and Mrs. Thomas Mifflin* (fig. 331). Certainly the finished picture is not bad, though it lacks the assurance of Copley's contemporaneous single portraits. Compositionally he simply juxtaposed two three-quarter-length poses, sliding Mrs. Mifflin into a foreground plane in front of her husband, who is set in a second plane. Mrs. Mifflin, pausing in her work at a fringe loom to regard the viewer, is seated at a spider-leg table like that in *Mrs. Richard Skinner* (fig. 315) and *Dorothy Quincy* (fig. 316). Her husband sits sideways on a chair placed behind the table, leaning on the crest rail. The figures are set in an architectural niche or pocket, with high pedestaled columns opening to a landscape on the right. Copley used this same architectural setting for the full-length post-mortem portrait of *Nicholas Boylston* (fig. 330), painted for Harvard in the same year. These two pictures were among several that appear to have exercised a strong influence on the young John Trumbull, then a student at Harvard. Trumbull had met Copley at Mount Pleasant the previous year, not long after the Copleys had moved into the remodeled house, and he later recalled in his autobiography: "We found Mr. Copley dressed to receive a party of friends at dinner. I remember his dress and appearance — an elegant looking man, dressed in a fine maroon cloth, with gilt buttons — this was dazzling to my unpracticed eye! — but his paintings, the first I had ever seen deserving the name, riveted, absorbed my attention, and renewed all my desire to enter upon such a pursuit." [4]

Copley painted the Mifflins during the summer of 1773, detaining them in Boston until August 25 so that he could finish the portrait. But the wait was worthwhile and, on the eve of the Mifflins' departure, S. Eliot of Boston wrote to William Barrell in Philadelphia that, with Copley's portrait, "this Town will have the Honour of furnishing Phil[a] with one of the best Pictures it has to boast." [5] The *Mifflin* portrait was painted not on regular canvas but on ticking. An invoice of merchandise shipped to Copley on August 17, 1771, by the Bromfields in London shows that Copley received both regular

[3] *Copley-Pelham Letters*, p. 226.
[4] Theodore Sizer, ed., *The Autobiography of Colonel John Trumbull* (New Haven, 1953), p. 11.
[5] S. [probably Samuel] Eliot, Boston, to William Barrell, Philadelphia, and Ruth Andrews, Boston, to William Barrell, Philadelphia, both Aug. 24, 1773, Miscellaneous Collections, Historical Society of Pennsylvania, Philadelphia.

"cloths" and "fine ticking," and apparently he used one and a half "half length Cloths" of ticking to make the canvas for the portrait.[6]

Thomas Mifflin was a Whig who, two years later, was quartermaster general of the revolutionary army and subsequently a member of the First Continental Congress and governor of Pennsylvania. The paradox of having a radical like Thomas Mifflin as an important client on the eve of a violent Whig outbreak directed against his in-laws dramatizes Copley's predicament. He confided to Mifflin his hopes to get to Italy, and Mifflin secured letters of introduction from Dr. John Morgan of Philadelphia, who had traveled in Italy over ten years earlier, addressed to several influential and knowledge-able people in Italy. Morgan sent these letters to Copley via Mifflin on November 24, 1773, and Copley had already obtained similar letters from Thomas Palmer of Boston, who in delivering them to Copley wished "him success, and cannot but say he wishes him gone." [7] The expression of such concern found its source in the fact that the political situation in Boston had become dangerously worse, and Copley was caught right in the middle of it. The precipitating factor was the arrival of the taxed tea from England in Boston Harbor. The firm of Richard Clarke and Sons was a major consignee of the tea as principal agent for the East India Company in Boston. Richard Clarke was the nephew of Governor Thomas Hutchinson, moreover, which made his position even more obnoxious to the increasingly fractious radicals. On November 17, 1773, a mob smashed the windows in Clarke's house.[8] Copley found himself cast in the role of mediator, shuttling between his merchant in-laws and the radical leaders. Threatened violence caused Clarke and his two sons to take refuge on Castle William in Boston Harbor, and Copley wrote his brothers-in-law there on December 1, 1773, about his experience at a meeting of the Sons of Liberty. He had been sent from the meeting to bring back the Clarke brothers so that they might state their position. The Clarkes, knowing full well the temper of the crowd, would not come. Copley reported that on his return to the meeting he had presented their position in the most conciliatory way possible. He had explained the obligation of the Clarkes as businessmen to fulfill the trust placed in them by their fellow merchants in London. The way was now open for the tea to be returned, but the Clarkes could not actively do this themselves. Copley had assured the meeting that the Clarkes were not in contact with or acting under the orders of the governor, a point on which the rebels were particularly touchy.[9]

Copley's efforts were not successful obviously, since the Sons of Liberty threw much of the tea into the harbor on December 16, and the Clarkes continued on Castle William for many months. In the interim Copley furthered the plans for his trip. On

[6] *Copley-Pelham Letters*, pp. 140–41.

[7] *Ibid.*, p. 202. Thomas Palmer gave Copley letters to James Byers, the antiquarian, in Rome and to Sir William Hamilton, the British minister in Naples. John Morgan sent letters to Rutherfoord, an influential merchant in Leghorn; Byers; Abbé Grant, like Byers an antiquary; and Isaac Jamineau, the British consul in Naples (*ibid.*, pp. 202–11).

[8] Herbert S. Allan, *John Hancock* (New York, 1948), pp. 135–36.

[9] *Copley-Pelham Letters*, pp. 211–13.

February 18, 1774, Charles Startin in Philadelphia wrote to Isaac Clarke that he was surprised by "Brother Jackys sudden determination to depart for England," wondering whether in view of attempts to defame the Clarkes this might not be seen in an unfavorable light, although Startin implied too that Copley might be able to exert some helpful influence in England.[10]

The temper of the times and their effect on Copley and his family is made clear enough in an account Copley sent to his brother-in-law, Isaac Clarke, at Castle William on April 26, 1774. On the previous evening at about midnight, a crowd had appeared at Copley's house, demanding to see Colonel George Watson of Plymouth, mandamus councilor and a prominent loyalist. Copley said he was not there. They wanted to know how Copley "came to entertain such a Rogue and Villin" (he had also painted Watson six years before — see fig. 222). He shrewdly replied that Watson had visited neighbor John Hancock, had then stopped at the Copleys', and had now left town. They went away, "but soon returned and kept up the Indian Yell for sometime." Copley again rose to reassure them that Watson was not there and asked them not to disturb his family. Further threats were voiced, but eventually the mob withdrew. Copley mused, "what if Mr. Watson had stayed (as I pressed him to) to spend the night. I must either have given up a friend to the insult of a mob or had my house pulled down and perhaps my family murthered." [11]

In this troubled year of 1774 Copley painted only a handful of pictures before leaving Boston. The most ambitious one, *Mr. and Mrs. Isaac Winslow* (fig. 332), is a double portrait of Sukey's uncle and his second wife, Jemima Dubuke, whom he had married in 1770. Winslow paid Copley twenty-eight guineas for the picture. Unlike the *Thomas Mifflin* double portrait, the composition is horizontal, and the two figures are better integrated spatially. Isaac Winslow, in a painted Windsor chair like those in the recent *Eleazer Tyng* and *Thomas Cary*, sits beside the *Mifflin-Skinner-Quincy* spider-leg table, which has both gates open and the leaves up, while his wife sits behind it.

The double portrait may have been Copley's last American picture, though that honor may also go to *Mrs. and Mrs. Adam Babcock* (figs. 333–334), who were briefly in Boston at this time. According to a letter Henry Pelham received from Joshua Wentworth in Portsmouth a year later, Copley had interrupted work on Mrs. Wentworth's portrait after she had sat for many days, and after Wentworth himself had sat once for his portrait, to undertake and complete "a Portrait for a Mrs Babcock." [12]

[10] Clarke-Bromfield Papers, Historical Manuscripts and University Archives Collection, Yale University Library, New Haven.

[11] *Copley-Pelham Letters*, pp. 218–19.

[12] *Ibid.*, p. 313. The Wentworths had been obliged to leave Boston before their portraits were completed. Pelham sent Wentworth a bill for Mrs. Wentworth's picture, perhaps having completed it himself, and Wentworth replied that he would be delighted to pay for it if the portrait were indeed finished, and would moreover gladly pay a like amount for his own portrait, which Copley had started. The case of the Wentworths is the only one currently known in which the rather punctilious Copley left unfinished work behind (in interesting contrast to the practice of Gilbert Stuart), presumably of necessity since the subjects left town.

Copley sailed from New England on June 10, 1774. Unquestionably the final decision to leave was difficult, but it had been a long time in the making. Certainly it must have become even harder when Copley discovered that he was not only leaving Sukey with three infants but with a fourth on the way: the fragile Clarke Copley was born in the following January (and lived for only slightly over a year). Yet Copley was acting in the ultimate best interests of his family by taking advantage of a nonpolitical reason for absenting himself from Boston — his old desire to study in Europe. It was this rationale for his departure that later enabled him to refute any charge of Toryism and to maintain his Boston property in the face of widespread expropriation of Tory holdings, even though he and his family had by then settled in London. Copley, furthermore, did not think that armed conflict would actually break out. It is reasonable to assume that at this point he intended eventually to return to Boston.

With Henry Pelham and her own family on the scene, Sukey Copley was not left without people to care for her. Richard Clarke, his son Isaac Winslow, and his youngest daughter Lucy boarded with her at Mount Pleasant. The actual funds for Sukey's needs were in the hands of the Clarke firm, on which Sukey could draw as necessary. Copley's account with them ran from the time he left Boston until Sukey's departure in May of the following year. She received three pounds a week board from the Clarkes, which helped to cut down expenses. But she did find it necessary to draw funds to buy wood for herself and Copley's mother and to get it sawed, to purchase such items as sugar, souchong tea, beef, fish from Salem, a small hog, and four fowls, and to pay for her general needs. On May 16, 1775, the firm records a sum of seventy pounds paid from the account to Captain Callahan for the passage to England of Mrs. Copley, her three oldest children, and a maid; an additional twenty-one pounds in cash was drawn for Sukey to carry with her to London.[13] War had broken out and Sukey left Boston, as did the rest of her loyalist family, planning to join her husband in London when he returned there from Italy. The infant Clarke Copley, too feeble to undertake the rigorous journey, was left in the care of Mary Pelham. Six months later Copley, at the age of thirty-seven, was reunited with his family in London, and a new life began. He never returned to America.

[13] Clarke-Bromfield Papers.

Appendices

Appendices

Copley produced approximately 300 extant paintings during his period of activity in the American colonies, from 1753 to 1774. In addition, there are another 50 unlocated or destroyed pictures that can be firmly attributed to him on the basis of reliable sources. Most of these 350 pictures are portraits, and the substantial amount of available factual information on the sitters provides a rare opportunity to study the relationship between an artist and his clients. For example, Copley was painting in Boston during the tumultuous quarter century immediately preceding the American Revolution. What was the effect of that imminent event on his business and on the character of his work? Did he paint an increasing number of Tories, or did the political distribution remain constant? Many similar questions come to mind. What general correlation for Copley's sitters is there between wealth and politics, between occupation and religion, between education and income? What effect could this have on Copley as an artist and as a member of this society? Did he paint more Anglicans as he himself prospered? Did his Anglican sitters tend to be Tories? Did the Whig sitters come from specific geographical areas? Did he paint members of families in clusters, indicating a way of obtaining commissions by word-of-mouth recommendation? Did certain occupation groups tend to order larger pictures, or pictures in certain media, in contrast to other groups? The list of questions can be extended almost indefinitely. Answers can be found through statistical analysis of available data concerning these painting and their subjects, but the answers are meaningful only if the surviving Copley paintings offer an adequate sample of his work. It is difficult to know with certainty how large a proportion of Copley's total these 350 pictures represent. Still a rough estimate of output can be made by applying what we know of the prices Copley charged for his work to his known pictures and comparing the result with Copley's own estimate of his income. He wrote to Captain Bruce and Benjamin West in London in 1767–68 that his income in Boston amounted to about 300 guineas a year.[1]

There is no information about the structure of Copley's prices prior to 1764, other than a bill for one guinea for a miniature of *Thankful Hubbard* in 1758.[2] In 1764–66 Copley was charging 8 guineas sterling for a 50″ x 40″ or three-quarter-length portrait (*Mrs. John Powell*, 1764; *Sarah Jackson*, 1765; *John Hancock*, 1765–66).[3] This portrait

---

[1] Cunningham, *Eminent Painters*, IV, 140; *Copley-Pelham Letters*, pp. 66, 68.

[2] Parker-Wheeler, p. 266.

[3] *Ibid.*, pp. 97–98. The portraits of *Mrs. John Powell* (bill owned by Ellery Sedgwick, Jr., Gates Mills, Ohio) and *Sarah Jackson* (bill at Boston Public Library) were priced at 8 guineas sterling and were paid for at the legal tender equivalent, which was £11.4.0. The gilt frame for *Mrs. Powell* cost £4.0.0, legal tender.

size, which in eighteenth-century parlance was a "half-length," was considered in size and cost to be literally the equivalent of one half of a full-length portrait, and twice that of a 30" x 25" or quarter-length portrait. Thus Copley's sterling price scale in 1764–66, and possibly earlier, was 16 guineas for a full-length (*Thomas Hollis*, 1766), 8 guineas for a 50" x 40" and 4 guineas for a 30" x 25" portrait (*Rev. Joseph Sewell*, price quoted c. 1765).[4] By 1767 Copley had raised his prices: a letter from George Livius, Portsmouth, to Copley on Sept. 14, 1767, notes that a price Copley had quoted "exceeds considerably what was customary with you when I was in Boston two years since." Copley's new price scale was 28 guineas for a full-length, 14 guineas (*Mr. and Mrs. Isaac Smith*, 1769) or pounds (*John Amory*, bill dated 1768) for a 50" x 40" portrait, and 7 guineas (*Myles Cooper*, 1768) or pounds (*Mr. and Mrs. Mackintosh*, bill dated 1769) for a 30" x 25" portrait. In February 1767, probably after the new price scale was in effect, Copley was getting five guineas for a pastel portrait (*Rev. Jonathan Mayhew*). Prices may have gone up again at about the time of Copley's marriage, since the 30" x 25" portraits of *Mr. and Mrs. Alexander MacWhorter*, 1769, cost £9.16.0, as did the portraits of *John Hancock* and *Daniel Henchman* billed to John Hancock.[5]

Prices were raised once more for the New York trip to 40 guineas for a full-length, 20 guineas for a 50" x 40", and 10 guineas for a 30" x 25" portrait. Subsequently Copley must have maintained a similar price structure in Boston, although there are some inconsistencies that are difficult to assess.[6] The ratio of 4–2–1 in pricing portraits from full-length to half-length to quarter-length made it easy to calculate proceeds in terms of quarter-length units. Thus when Copley in New York wrote to Henry Pelham that he had undertaken 37 pictures,[7] he meant that he had painted the equivalent of 37 quarter-length portraits, signifying, since the New York price for a quarter-length was 10 guineas, an income for the six months in New York of 370 guineas. The trip was highly successful financially for Copley. In half a year he earned more than the annual income of 300 guineas a year he had told Captain Bruce and West he was earning in 1767–68.

By applying Copley's price structure to known portraits, it is difficult to account for the claimed income of 300 guineas a year in 1767–68. On the basis of portraits now known, he would have averaged about 120 guineas per year in 1765–67, and 225 guineas per year in 1768–70; after his return at the end of 1771 from the lucrative New York trip, his income would have dropped back to the 1768–70 level.[8] This is consistent-

---

[4] Harvard College paid 16 guineas, or £22.8.0, legal tender, for the portrait of *Thomas Hollis*, twice the rate of the 50" x 40" portraits listed in the previous note (Parker-Wheeler, p. 105; *Copley-Pelham Letters*, p. 75). Copley noted his price for the projected portrait of Rev. Joseph Sewall as £5.12.0, legal tender (*Copley-Pelham Letters*, p. 32).

[5] *Ibid.*, pp. 22, 97–98, 101, 167, 184; *Copley-Pelham Letters*, pp. 61, 71, 284; Gratz Collection, Historical Society of Pennsylvania, case 7, box 39;

Perkins, p. 130.

[6] *Copley-Pelham Letters*, pp. 112–13. Whereas the 30" x 25" *John Hancock* of 1770–72 cost £9.16.0, *Thomas Flucker* of approximately the same date cost £14. The kit-cat or 36" x 28" portrait of *Mrs. John Winthrop*, 1773, cost only 10 guineas (Parker-Wheeler, pp. 72, 97–98, 211).

[7] *Copley-Pelham Letters*, p. 179, Dec. 15, 1771.

[8] These estimates of income were arrived at by determining first the number of pictures of each

ly below his claimed income. Perhaps he had other sources of revenue. Occasionally, we know, he restored damaged pictures. It is also probable that he made a profit on the frames he sold with portraits. Gilt frames such as those for the *Isaac Smith* portraits (1769) sold for £9 apiece, while the simple black frames on the small *MacWhorter* portraits (also 1769) cost only £1.4.0 each. Copley's profit on frames, which he had to buy, could have afforded him only a modest increment. He presumably also made a profit in the same way by reselling the bracelets for miniatures and the gold and silver miniature locket cases that he bought from Paul Revere.[9] But it seems unlikely that these sources of income could account for the entire difference between Copley's claimed annual increment in 1767 and the income earned from paintings now known. The remainder must be attributed to the likelihood that he painted more pictures than are currently known, although his claimed income may have been somewhat exaggerated since he was trying to sound out the chances of matching this sum in London. Perhaps he arrived at the income figure in 1767–68 by applying his newly elevated price scale to the previous year's volume of business.

From all of this it would seem reasonable to conclude that the number of Copley paintings now known approximates three-fourths of his actual production, acknowledging considerable margin for error on either side of this estimate. It is evident, then, that the known paintings form a more than adequate base for drawing some conclusions about Copley's career and the pattern of his patronage.

The following statistical study was based on a refined sample of 240 paintings. Drawings, mythological subject pictures, and portraits of unknown or uncertain subjects were necessarily eliminated from consideration. In selecting the sample and compiling data, it was considered more important to protect the purity of the sample than to make it as comprehensive as possible. So objects of only probable authenticity or of only probably correct identification of sitter were not included. Some portraits were located or verified too late for inclusion in the statistics, but the sample is sufficiently large that these additions would have little, if any, effect. The following categories of information were tabulated in the study (only the data for items marked with an asterisk are fully listed in this volume — other results are summarized when and if germane):

name of sitter *
date of birth *
date of death *
sex
place of residence *
occupation (or situation) *

education (college) *
church *
politics *
marital status *
office *
date of marriage

---

size Copley produced in each period in the statistical sample of 240 paintings. The price scale of each period was applied, and the result was then projected to cover the known production of 350 objects.

[9] *Ibid.*, pp. 84–85; Parker-Wheeler, p. 184; Gratz Collection, Historical Society of Pennsylvania, case 7, box 39; Revere "Day Books," Massachusetts Historical Society.

date of father's death (inheritance)	paired or single portrait
college class	date of portrait (if known) *
rank in college class	period of artistic production *
politics of husband or father	medium *
occupation of husband or father	size *
age	second portrait by Copley
estimated income *	family portraits by other colonial artists

The first appendix is a tabulation of the basic data (only the asterisked items are shown), arranged alphabetically by sitter's name. The next appendix breaks down this tabulation into the most important specific categories pertaining to the sitters themselves. The third appendix contains a summary of the most important data, with remarks on the relevance of particular facts to Copley's career. Finally, genealogical charts and tables are provided that give the statistical categories as they apply to the most important family groupings among the 240 sitters.

Insofar as possible, information recorded applies at the time the portrait was taken. Some of the conclusions have already been presented in the text; others are given below (see especially the section entitled "Analysis of Data"); and still others, only implied by the statistics, must await further interpretation.

Statistical Data for 240 Portraits

The pairing of columns does not indicate any special or more important connection between the respective categories; the pairing was effected solely for fit and for ease of reading. "Occupation" includes family situation (such as Daughter). "Period" refers to Copley's period of artistic production. For further discussion of the categories themselves, see the appendices that follow.

* Abbreviations used for medium: O.C. — oil on canvas; P. — pastel; W.I. — watercolor on ivory; O.Cp. — oil on copper; Eng. — engraving.

† More than one portrait painted of this subject. See checklist for other portrait(s).

‡ In the statistics the Carys were considered as a married couple since the miniatures were obviously made as an exact pair, even though the stylistic evidence suggests that they were painted before the date of marriage.

§ Included because identification seems reasonable.

** Counted as a single subject, although a multi-figure portrait.

†† Probably cut down from a larger canvas.

‡‡ Correct residence may be New London.

§§ Deceased at time of portrait.

Statistical Data for 240 Portraits

| | SITTER | | | | | | PORTRAIT | | |
NAME	BIRTH DEATH	RESIDENCE OCCUPATION	COLLEGE	CHURCH POLITICS	MARRIED	OFFICE INCOME	DATE	PERIOD	MEDIUM* AND SIZE (IN.)
Adams, Sam.	1722 1803	Boston Official	Harvard	Cong. Rad. Whig	Yes	Clerk, House of Representatives Medium		1771–74	O.C. 50 x 40
Ainslie, Thos.	? ?	Nova Scotia Official		High Tory	Yes	Collector of customs	1757	1753–57	O.C.
Allen, James	1734 1808	Boston Gentleman	Harvard	Cong. Mod. Whig	No	High		1768–70	O.C. 30 x 25
Allen, Nath.	1717 1778	Gloucester Shipper		Cong. Mod. Whig	Yes	Justice of peace High	1763	1762–64	O.C. 50 x 40
Allen, Mrs. N.	1729 1792	Gloucester Housewife		Cong.	Yes			1762–64	O.C. 50 x 40
Amory, John	1728 1805	Boston Merchant		Angl. High Tory	Yes	Very high	1768	1768–70	O.C. 50 x 40
Amory, Mrs. J.	1731 1777	Boston Housewife		Angl.	Yes			1762–64	O.C. 50 x 40
Amory II, Thos.	1722 1784	Boston Distiller	Harvard	Angl. Mod. Tory	Yes	Very high		1771–74	O.C. 50 x 40
Amory II, Mrs. T.	1742 1822	Boston Housewife		Angl.	Yes			1771–74	O.C. 30 x 25
Appleton, Nath.	1693 1784	Cambridge Minister	Harvard	Cong. Mod. Whig	Yes	Low		1758–61	O.C. 36 x 28
Appleton, Mrs. N.	1699 1771	Cambridge Housewife		Cong.	Yes		1763	1762–64	O.C. 36 x 28
Apthorp, Mrs. John	1744 1773	Boston Housewife			Yes			1762–64	O.C. 30 x 25
Atkinson, Theo.	? 1769	Portsmouth Official	Harvard	Angl. High Tory	Yes	Provincial sec. Very high		1758–61	O.C. 50 x 40
Atkinson, Mrs. T.	1745 1813	Portsmouth Housewife		Angl.	Yes		1765	1765–67	O.C. 50 x 40
Austin, Mrs. Eben.	1710 1800	Charlestown Widow		Cong.	Widow			1765–67	O.C. 36 x 28

Name	Dates	Place / Occupation	Education	Religion / Politics		Status	Year	Years	Size
Babcock, Adam	1740 1817	New Haven Merchant		Bapt. Mod. Whig	Yes	Medium		1771–74	O.C. 50 x 40
Babcock, Mrs. A.	1742 1774	New Haven Housewife		Cong.	Yes			1771–74	O.C. 50 x 40
Barnard, Edward	1720 1774	Haverhill Minister	Harvard	Cong. Mod. Whig	Yes	Low		1771–74	O.C. 30 x 25
Barrell, Jos.†	1740 1804	Boston Merchant		Angl. Mod. Whig	Yes	High		1768–70	P. under 30 x 25
Barrell (A), Mrs. J.	1744 1771	Boston Housewife		Cong.	Yes			1768–70	P. under 30 x 25
Barrell (B), Mrs. J.	1754 1777	Boston Housewife		Cong.	Yes			1771–74	P. under 30 x 25
Barrett, John	1708 1786	Boston Merchant		Cong. Mod. Whig	Yes	Town office Medium		1758–61	O.C. 50 x 40
Barrett, Mrs. J.	1711 1798	Boston Housewife		Cong.	Yes			1758–61	O.C. 50 x 40
Belcher, Jon.	1710 1776	Nova Scotia Official	Harvard	Angl. High Tory	Yes	Chief justice High	1756	1753–57	O.C. 50 x 40
Belcher, Mrs. J.	1727 1771	Nova Scotia Housewife		Angl.	Yes		1756	1753–57	O.C. 50 x 40
Blackstone, Benj.	1725 ?	Maine		Cong. Mod. Whig	Yes	High		1762–64	O.C. 50 x 40
Blackstone, Mrs. B.	1733 1807	Maine Housewife		Cong.	Yes			1762–64	O.C. 50 x 40
Blake, Jos.	1740 1817	Boston Mason		Mod. Whig	Yes	Medium		1765–67	O.C. under 30 x 25
Bourne, Mrs. Sylv.	1695 1782	Cape Cod Widow		Cong.	Widow		1766	1765–67	O.C. 50 x 40
Bours, John	1734 1815	Newport		Angl. Mod. Tory	Yes	Medium		1758–61	O.C. 50 x 40
Bowen, Jabez	1739 1815	Providence Lawyer	Yale	Cong. Mod. Whig	Yes	Medium		1771–74	O.C. 30 x 25
Bowen, Mrs. J.	1742 1800	Providence Housewife		Cong. Mod. Whig	Yes	Medium		1771–74	O.C. 30 x 25
Bowler, Mrs. Met.†	1732 1803	Newport Housewife		Angl.	Yes			1762–64	O.C. 50 x 40

Continued

STATISTICAL DATA *Continued*

| | SITTER | | | | | | PORTRAIT | | |
NAME	BIRTH DEATH	RESIDENCE OCCUPATION	COLLEGE	CHURCH POLITICS	MARRIED	OFFICE INCOME	DATE	PERIOD	MEDIUM* AND SIZE (IN.)
Boylston, Nicholas †	1716 1771	Boston Merchant		Cong. Mod. Whig	No	Very high	1767	1765–67	O.C. 50 x 40
Boylston, Rebecca †	1727 1798	Boston Daughter		Cong.	No		1767	1765–67	O.C. 50 x 40
Boylston, Mrs. Thos.	1696 1774	Boston Widow		Cong.	Widow		1766	1765–67	O.C. 50 x 40
Boylston II, Thos.	1721 1798	Boston Merchant		Cong. Mod. Tory	No	Very high		1765–67	O.C. 50 x 40
Brattle, Will.	1706 1776	Cambridge Military	Harvard	Cong. Mod. Whig	Yes	Council Medium		1753–57	O.C. 50 x 40
Brown, Mrs. Gawen †	1737 1763	Boston Housewife		Cong.	Yes			1762–64	O.C. under 30 x 25
Browne, Arthur	1699 1773	Portsmouth Minister	Trinity, Dublin	Angl. High Tory	Yes	Low	1757	1753–57	O.C. 30 x 25
Browne, Mrs. A.	? 1773	Portsmouth Housewife		Angl.	Yes			1753–57	O.C. 30 x 25
Browne, Jane	1734 1803	Portsmouth Daughter		Angl.	No		1756	1753–57	O.C. 30 x 25
Burr, Thaddeus	1735 1801	Fairfield Landowner	Princeton	Cong. Mod. Whig	Yes	Medium		1758–61	O.C. 50 x 40
Burr, Mrs. T.	1739 1805	Fairfield Housewife		Cong.	Yes			1758–61	O.C. 50 x 40
Byles, Mather †	1707 1788	Boston Minister	Harvard	Cong. High Tory	Yes	Low		1765–67	O.C. 30 x 25
Calif, Mrs. Jos.	1693 1772	Boston Housewife		Cong.	Yes			1762–64	O.C. 36 x 28
Cary, Sam.	1742 1812	West Indies Landowner		Cong. Mod. Tory	Yes‡	High		1768–70	W.I. under 30 x 25
Cary, Mrs. S.	1742 ?	West Indies Housewife		Cong.	Yes‡			1768–70	W.I. under 30 x 25
Cary, Thos.	1745 1808	Newburyport Minister	Harvard	Cong. Mod. Whig	No	Medium	1773	1771–74	O.C. 50 x 40

Name	Born	Died	Residence	Occupation	Education	Religion / Politics	Married	Status		Date	Category
Chardon, Peter	1737	1766	Boston	Lawyer	Harvard	Cong. Mod. Whig	No	Medium		1765–67	P. under 30 x 25
Coffin, Thos. A.	1754	1810	Boston	Minor		Angl.	No			1758–61	O.C. other
Coffin, Mrs. Will.	1707	1775	Boston	Housewife		Angl.	Yes			1768–70	O.C. 30 x 25
Cooper, Myles	1737	1785	New York	Minister	Oxford	Angl. High Tory	No	Low	1768	1768–70	O.C. 30 x 25
Cooper, Sam.†	1725	1783	Boston	Minister	Harvard	Cong. Rad. Whig	Yes			1768–70	O.C. 30 x 25
Copley, John S.†	1738	1815	Boston	Painter		Angl. Mod. Tory	Yes	Medium		1768–70	P. under 30 x 25
Copley, Mrs. J. S.	1745	1836	Boston	Housewife		Cong.	Yes	High		1768–70	P. under 30 x 25
Cotton, Mrs. Rol.	1730	1766	Woburn	Housewife			Yes			1762–64	O.C. 50 x 40
Cranston, Rhoda	1741	1763	Newport	Daughter		Angl.	No			1758–61	O.C. 50 x 40
Cumming, Mrs. Alex.	1733	1821	Boston	Widow		Cong.	No		1770	1768–70	O.C. 30 x 25
Dana, Richard	1700	1772	Boston	Lawyer	Harvard	Cong. Rad. Whig	Yes	Justice of peace Medium		1768–70	O.C. 50 x 40
Danforth, Sam.	1696	1777	Cambridge	Official	Harvard	Cong. Mod. Tory	Widower	Council Medium		1758–61	O.Cp. under 30 x 25
Davis, Mrs. Benj.	1741	1764	Boston	Housewife		Cong.	Yes			1762–64	O.C. 30 x 25
Devereux, Mrs. H.	1710	?	Marblehead	Housewife			Yes		1771	1771–74	O.C. other
Ellery, Mrs. Nath.	1692	1782	Gloucester	Housewife		Cong.	Yes			1765–67	O.C. 50 x 40
Eppes, Mrs. Will.	?	1780	Salem	Widow			Widow			1768–70	O.C. 50 x 40
Erving, John	1693	1786	Boston	Shipper		Angl. Mod. Tory	Widower	Council		1771–74	O.C. 50 x 40
Fayerweather, Sam.	1725	1781	Kingston	Minister	Harvard	Angl. Mod. Whig	No	Low		1758–61	O.Cp. under 30 x 25

Continued

| | SITTER | | | | | | PORTRAIT | | |
NAME	BIRTH DEATH	RESIDENCE OCCUPATION	COLLEGE	CHURCH POLITICS	MARRIED	OFFICE INCOME	DATE	PERIOD	MEDIUM* AND SIZE (IN.)
Flucker, Thos.	1719 1783	Boston Merchant		Cong. High Tory	Yes	Provincial sec. Very high		1771–74	O.C. 30 x 25
Folger, Tim.	1732 1814	Nantucket Shipper		Cong. Mod. Whig	Yes	Sheriff Medium	1764	1762–64	O.C. 50 x 40
Fowle, Jacob	1704 1778	Marblehead Merchant		Mod. Whig	Yes	High		1758–61	O.C. 50 x 40
Gage, Thos.	1721 1787	New York Military		Angl. High Tory	Yes	Medium		1768–70	O.C. 50 x 40
Gage, Mrs. T.	? ?	New York Housewife		Angl.	Yes		1771	1771–74	O.C. 50 x 40
Gambier, James	1723 1789	England Military		Angl. High Tory	No	Medium	1773	1771–74	O.C. 50 x 40
Gardiner, Ann	1741 1807	Boston Daughter		Angl.	No			1753–57	O.C. 50 x 40
Gardiner, Sylv.	1708 1786	Boston Physician		Angl. High Tory	Yes	Very high		1771–74	O.C. 50 x 40
Gerrish, Benj.	1717 1772	Nova Scotia Merchant		Mod. Tory	Yes	Council High		1771–74	O.C. 30 x 25
Gerrish [?], Jos.§	1709 1774	Nova Scotia Merchant		Angl. Mod. Tory	Yes	Council High		1771–74	O.C. 30 x 25
Gill, Moses	1733 1800	Boston Brazier		Cong. Rad. Whig	Yes	Town office Medium	1764	1762–64	O.C. 50 x 40
Gill, Mrs. M.†	1728 1771	Boston Housewife		Cong.	Yes			1762–64	O.C. 50 x 40
Goldthwait, Ezek.	1710 1782	Boston Merchant		Cong. Mod. Whig	Yes	Recorder of deeds High		1768–70	O.C. 50 x 40
Goldthwait, Mrs. E.	1713 1794	Boston Housewife		Cong.	Yes			1768–70	O.C. 50 x 40
Gore Children†**	? ?	Boston Minors		Cong.	No			1753–57	O.C. over 50 x 40
Gray, Harrison	1711 1794	Boston Merchant		Cong. High Tory	Yes	Council Very high		1765–67	O.C. under 30 x 25

Name	Years	Place / Occupation	Politics	Education	Status	Office / Social status	Year	Dates	Property
Gray, John	1713 1782	Boston Merchant	High Tory		Widower	Town office High	1766	1765–67	O.C. 50 x 40
Gray, Mrs. J.	1730 1763	Boston Housewife			Yes			1762–64	O.C. 50 x 40
Green, Mrs. Edw.	1736 ?	Boston Housewife	Cong.		Yes		1765	1765–67	P. under 30 x 25
Green, George	1742 1800	Boston Merchant	Mod. Tory		Yes	High		1768–70	O.Cp. under 30 x 25
Green (A), Jos.	1706 1780	Boston Distiller	Cong. Mod. Whig	Harvard	Yes	High	1767	1765–67	P. under 30 x 25
Green (A), Mrs. J.	? 1800	Boston Housewife	Cong.		Yes	High		1765–67	P. under 30 x 25
Green (B), Jos.	1703 1765	Boston Merchant	Mod. Whig		Yes	Medium		1762–64	P. under 30 x 25
Greene, John	1731 1781	Boston Merchant	Angl. Mod. Tory		Yes	Medium		1768–70	O.C. 50 x 40
Greene, Mrs. J.	1735 1785	Boston Housewife	Angl.		Yes		1769	1768–70	O.C. 50 x 40
Greene, Jos.	1745 1802	Boston	Angl. Mod. Tory		Yes	Medium	1767	1765–67	P. under 30 x 25
Greene, Mrs. J.	1745 1794	Boston Housewife	Angl.		Yes		1767	1765–67	P. under 30 x 25
Greene, Rufus	1707 1777	Boston Silversmith	Angl. Mod. Tory		Yes	High		1758–61	O.C. under 30 x 25††
Greene, Mrs. R.	1709 1768	Boston Housewife	Angl.		Yes			1758–61	O.C. under 30 x 25††
Greene, Thos.	1705 1763	Boston Merchant	Angl.		Yes	High	1758	1758–61	O.C. 50 x 40
Greene, Mrs. T.	1706 1784	Boston Housewife			Yes			1758–61	O.C. 50 x 40
Hall, Hugh	1693 1773	Boston Merchant	Angl. Mod. Tory	Harvard	Widow	Justice, inferior court Medium	1758	1758–61	P. under 30 x 25
Hallowell, Benj.	1725 1799	Boston Official	Cong. High Tory		Yes	Surveyor of customs Very high		1765–67	O.C. 50 x 40

Continued

[107]

STATISTICAL DATA *Continued*

		SITTER					PORTRAIT		
NAME	BIRTH DEATH	RESIDENCE OCCUPATION	COLLEGE	CHURCH POLITICS	MARRIED	OFFICE INCOME	DATE	PERIOD	MEDIUM* AND SIZE (IN.)
Hallowell, Mrs. B.	1722 ?	Boston Housewife			Yes		1765	1765–67	O.C. 50 x 40
Hancock, John †	1737 1793	Boston Merchant	Harvard	Cong. Rad. Whig	No	Representative Very high		1765–67	O.C. 50 x 40
Hancock, Thos.†	1703 1764	Boston Merchant		Cong. Mod. Tory	Yes	Council Very high		1758–61	O.Cp. under 30 x 25
Hancock, Mrs. T.†	1714 1777	Boston Widow		Cong.	Widow			1765–67	O.Cp. under 30 x 25
Henley, Mrs. Sam.	1741 1812	Charlestown Housewife		Cong.	Yes			1765–67	P. under 30 x 25
Henshaw, Jos.	1727 1794	Boston Merchant	Harvard	Cong. Mod. Whig	Yes	Medium		1771–74	O.C. 30 x 25
Henshaw, Mrs. J.	1736 1822	Boston Housewife		Cong.	Yes			1771–74	P. under 30 x 25
Henshaw, Joshua	1703 1777	Boston Merchant		Cong. Mod. Whig	Yes	Justice of peace High		1768–70	O.C. 50 x 40
Henshaw II, Joshua	1745 1823	Boston Merchant	Harvard	Cong. Rad. Whig	Yes	Medium		1771–74	O.C. 30 x 25
Henshaw, Mrs. J.	1746 1822	Boston Housewife		Cong.	Yes			1771–74	O.C. 30 x 25
Hill, Henry	1737 1828	Boston Distiller	Harvard	Rad. Whig	Yes	Medium		1768–70	P. under 30 x 25
Hill, Mrs. H.	1739 1822	Boston Housewife		Cong.	Yes			1768–70	P. under 30 x 25
Hill, Mrs. Sam.	1696 1765	Boston Housewife			Yes			1762–64	O.C. 50 x 40
Holmes, J. B.	1760 1827	Charleston, S.C. Minor		Cong.	No		1765	1765–67	O.C. 30 x 25
Holyoke, Edw.†	1689 1769	Cambridge Teacher	Harvard	Cong. Mod. Tory	Yes	Low		1758–61	O.C. 50 x 40
Hooper, Alice	1746 1826	Marblehead Daughter		Cong.	No			1762–64	O.C. 50 x 40

Name	Dates	Place / Occupation	Education	Religion / Politics	Married	Office / Status	Year	Period	Size
Hooper, Jos.	1743 1812	Marblehead Merchant		Cong. High Tory	Yes	Medium		1768–70	O.C. 50 x 40
Hooper, Mrs. J.	1746 1796	Marblehead Housewife		Cong.	Yes			1768–70	O.C. 50 x 40
Hooper, Robert	1709 1790	Marblehead Shipper		Cong. Mod. Tory	Yes	Justice of peace Very high	1767	1765–67	O.C. 50 x 40
Hooper, Mrs. R.	1727 1776	Marblehead Housewife		Cong.	Yes		1767	1765–67	O.C. 50 x 40
Hooper II, Robert	1747 1781	Marblehead Merchant	Harvard	Cong.	Yes			1768–70	O.C. 50 x 40
Howard, Martin	? 1782	Charleston, S.C. Lawyer		Angl. High Tory	Yes	Chief Justice High	1767	1765–67	O.C. 50 x 40
Hubbard, Daniel	1736 1796	Boston Merchant		Angl. High Tory	Yes	Medium	1764	1762–64	O.C. 50 x 40
Hubbard, Mrs. D.	1734 1808	Boston Housewife		Angl.	Yes			1762–64	O.C. 50 x 40
Hubbard, Thankful	1744 1772	Boston Daughter		Cong.	No			1753–57	under 30 x 25
Hubbard, Thos.	1702 1773	Boston Brazier	Harvard	Cong. High Tory	Yes	Council Very high		1765–67	O.C. 50 x 40
Hurd, Nath.†	1730 1777	Boston Silversmith		Cong. Mod. Whig	No	Town office Medium		1765–67	O.C. 30 x 25
Inman, Ralph	1718 1788	Cambridge Merchant		Angl. High Tory	Widower	Justice of peace Very high		1768–70	P. under 30 x 25
Jackson, Jon.†	1743 1810	Newburyport Merchant	Harvard	Cong. Rad. Whig	No	Very high		1768–70	P. under 30 x 25
Jackson, Sarah	1738 1771	Boston Daughter		Cong.	No		1765	1765–67	O.C. 50 x 40
Langdon, Woodbury	1738 1805	Portsmouth Merchant		Cong.	Yes	High		1765–67	O.C. 50 x 40
Langdon, Mrs. W.	1748 1827	Portsmouth Housewife		Cong.	Yes			1765–67	O.C. 50 x 40
Lee, Jeremiah †	1721 1775	Marblehead Merchant		Cong. Rad. Whig	Yes	Justice of peace Very high	1769	1768–70	O.C. over 50 x 40
Lee, Mrs. J.	1726 1791	Marblehead Housewife		Cong.	Yes	Very high	1769	1768–70	O.C. over 50 x 40

Continued

STATISTICAL DATA *Continued*

	SITTER						PORTRAIT		
NAME	BIRTH DEATH	RESIDENCE OCCUPATION	COLLEGE	CHURCH POLITICS	MARRIED	OFFICE INCOME	DATE	PERIOD	MEDIUM * AND SIZE (IN.)
Lewis, Thos.	1735 1801	Marblehead Merchant		Mod. Whig	Yes	Medium		1765–67	O.C. 50 x 40
Loring, Hannah	1742 1785	Boston Housewife		Angl.	Yes		1763	1762–64	O.C. 50 x 40
Lynde, Lydia	1741 1798	Boston Daughter		Angl.	No			1762–64	O.C. 30 x 25
McEvers, Mrs. Chas.	1745 ?	New York Housewife			Yes		1771	1771–74	O.C. 30 x 25
MacWhorter, Alex.	1734 1807	Boston Minister	Princeton	Presby. Rad. Whig	Yes	Medium	1769	1768–70	O.C. 30 x 25
MacWhorter, Mrs. A.	1740 1807	Boston Housewife		Presby.	Yes		1769	1768–70	O.C. 30 x 25
Mann, Jos.	1717 1807	Wrentham Distiller (tavern-keeper)			Yes	Medium	1754	1753–57	O.C. 36 x 28
Mann, Mrs. J.	1731 1798	Wrentham Housewife			Yes		1753	1753–57	O.C. 36 x 28
Marshall, Thos.	1719 1800	Boston Tailor		Rad. Whig	Yes	Medium		1753–57	O.C. 50 x 40
Marshall, Mrs. T.	1727 1794	Boston Housewife			Yes			1753–57	O.C. 50 x 40
Martin, Mary E.	1762 ?	New York Daughter		Angl.	No			1771–74	O.C. other
Mifflin, Thos. **	1744 1800	Philadelphia Merchant	Coll. Phila.	Quaker Rad. Whig	Yes	Representative Very high	1773	1771–74	O.C. over 50 x 40
Morris, Mrs. Roger	1730 1825	New York Housewife			Yes		1771	1771–74	O.C. 30 x 25
Mountfort, Jon.	1746 1785	Boston Minor		Cong.	No			1753–57	O.C. 30 x 25
Murray, Dorothy	1745 1811	Boston Daughter		Angl.	No			1758–61	O.C. 36 x 28

Name	Dates	Origin / Occupation	Education	Religion / Party	Married	Position	Year	Period	Portrait
Murray, James	1713 1781	Milton Landowner		Angl. High Tory	Yes	Council High		1762–64	O.C. 50 x 40
Murray, John	1720 1794	Rutland, Mass.		High Tory	Yes	Representative		1762–64	O.C. 50 x 40
Murray, Mrs. J.	1730 1768	Rutland, Mass. Housewife			Yes	High	1763	1762–64	O.C. 50 x 40
Newton, John	1725 1811	Nova Scotia Landowner		Angl. High Tory	Widower	Surveyor of customs Medium	1772	1771–74	O.C. 30 x 25
Ogilvie, John	1724 1774	New York Minister	Yale	Angl. Mod. Tory	Yes	Medium	1771	1771–74	O.C. 50 x 40
Oliver, Andrew †	1706 1774	Boston Merchant	Harvard	Cong. High Tory	Yes	Council Very high		1758–61	O.Cp. under 30 x 25
Oliver, Mrs. A.†	1713 1773	Boston Housewife		Cong.	Yes			1758–61	O.Cp. under 30 x 25
Oliver II, Andrew	1731 1799	Boston Jeweler	Harvard	Cong. Mod. Tory	No	Justice, inferior court High		1758–61	O.Cp. under 30 x 25
Oliver, Elizabeth	1738 1820	Boston Daughter		Cong.	No			1758–61	O.Cp. under 30 x 25
Oliver, Griselda †	1737 1761	Boston Daughter		Cong.	No			1758–61	O.C. under 30 x 25
Oliver, Peter	1713 1791	Middleboro, Mass. Merchant	Harvard	Cong. High Tory	Yes	Justice, superior court High		1758–61	O.Cp. under 30 x 25
Otis, James	1702 1778	Cape Cod Lawyer		Cong. Rad. Whig	Yes	Representative Medium		1758–61	O.C. 50 x 40
Otis, Mrs. J.	1702 1767	Cape Cod Housewife		Cong.	Yes			1758–61	O.C. 50 x 40
Otis, Mrs. Sam. A.	1746 1779	Boston Housewife			Yes			1762–64	O.C. 30 x 25
Pelham, Chas.	1722 1793	Boston Merchant		Mod. Tory	No	Medium		1753–57	O.C. 36 x 28
Pelham, Henry †	1749 1806	Boston Minor		Angl.	No		1765	1765–67	O.C. 30 x 25

Continued

		SITTER							PORTRAIT	
NAME	BIRTH DEATH	RESIDENCE OCCUPATION	COLLEGE	CHURCH POLITICS	MARRIED	OFFICE INCOME	DATE	PERIOD	MEDIUM * AND SIZE (IN.)	
Perkins, Nath.	1715 1799	Boston Physician	Harvard	Cong. High Tory	No	Town office High		1771–74	O.C. 30 x 25
Pickman, Benj.	1740 1819	Salem Merchant	Harvard	High Tory	No	High		1758–61	O.C. 50 x 40
Pickman, Mrs. B.	1744 1817	Salem Housewife			Yes		1763	1762–64	O.C. 50 x 40
Pitts, Elizabeth	1734 1810	Boston Daughter		Cong.	No			1762–64	P. under 30 x 25
Powell, Mrs. John †	1684 1764	Boston Widow		Angl.	Widow		1764	1762–64	O.C. 50 x 40
Powell II, John	1716 1794	Boston Merchant		Angl. High Tory	Yes	Town office Medium		1762–64	P. under 30 x 25
Powell II, Mrs. J.	1735 1774	Boston Housewife		Angl.	Yes			1762–64	P. under 30 x 25
Quincy, Dorothy	1747 1830	Braintree Daughter		Cong.	No			1771–74	O.C. 50 x 40
Quincy, Josiah	1710 1784	Braintree Merchant	Harvard	Cong. Rad. Whig		Justice, inferior court High		1765–67	O.C. 36 x 28
Quincy, Sam.	1735 1789	Braintree Lawyer	Harvard	Cong. High Tory	Yes	Medium		1765–67	O.C. 36 x 28
Quincy, Mrs. S.	1734 1782	Braintree Housewife		Cong.	Yes			1758–61	O.C. 36 x 28
Revere, Paul	1735 1818	Boston Silversmith		Cong. Rad. Whig	Yes	Medium		1768–70	O.C. 36 x 28
Richard, Mrs. Paul	1700 1774	New York Housewife			Yes		1771	1771–74	O.C. 50 x 40
Rogers, Mrs. Dan.	1739 1769	Gloucester Housewife		Cong.	Yes		1762	1762–64	O.C. 50 x 40
Ross, Elizabeth	1751 1831	Maine Daughter			No			1765–67	O.C. 50 x 40
Royall, Isaac	1719 1781	Medford Merchant		Angl. High Tory	Yes	Council Very high	1769	1768–70	O.C. 50 x 40

Name	Dates	Residence / Occupation	Education	Religion / Politics		Office / Status			Classification
Royall, Mrs. I.	1722 1770	Medford Housewife		Angl.	Yes		1769	1768–70	O.C. 50 x 40
Royall, E. and M.**	? ?	Medford Daughters		Angl.	No			1758–61	O.C. over 50 x 40
Russell, Mrs. James	1717 1778	Charlestown Housewife		Cong.	Yes			1768–70	O.C. 50 x 40
St. Clair, Sir John	1767	England Military		Angl. Mod. Tory	Yes	High	1759	1758–61	O.Cp. under 30 x 25
Sargent, Mrs. Dan.	1743 1818	Gloucester Housewife		Cong.	Yes		1763	1762–64	O.C. 50 x 40
Sargent, Epes	1690 1762	Gloucester Merchant	Harvard	Cong. Mod. Tory	Yes	Justice, inferior court High		1758–61	O.C. 50 x 40
Sargent II, Epes	1721 1779	Gloucester Merchant		Cong. Mod. Tory	Yes	Justice of peace High		1762–64	O.C. 50 x 40
Sargent II, Mrs. E.	1722 1788	Gloucester Housewife		Cong.	Yes		1764	1762–64	O.C. 50 x 40
Savage, Sam. P.	1718 1787	Boston Merchant		Cong. Rad. Whig	Yes	High	1764	1762–64	O.C. 50 x 40
Savage, Mrs. S. P.	1718 1764	Boston Housewife		Cong.	Yes		1764	1762–64	O.C. 50 x 40
Scollay, Deborah	1737 ?	Boston Daughter		Cong.	No			1762–64	W.I. under 30 x 25
Scollay, John †	1712 1790	Boston Shopkeeper		Cong. Mod. Whig	Yes	Justice of peace Medium		1762–64	O.C. 36 x 28
Scollay, Mrs. J.†	1719 1793	Boston Housewife		Cong.	Yes		1763	1762–64	O.C. 36 x 28
Scott, George	1720	Boston Military		Angl. Mod. Tory	Yes			1753–57	O.C. 50 x 40
Scott, James	1720 1798	Boston Brazier		Cong. High Tory	Yes	Medium		1765–67	O.C. 50 x 40
Scott, Mrs. J.	1733 1817	Boston Housewife		Cong.	Yes			1765–67	O.C. 50 x 40
Sherburne, Jos.	1710 1779	Boston Merchant		Cong. High Tory	Yes	Town office Very high		1768–70	O.C. 50 x 40
Skinner, Mrs. Rich.	1733 1822	Marblehead Housewife		Cong.	Yes		1772	1771–74	O.C. other

Continued

[113]

statistical data *Continued*

NAME	BIRTH DEATH	SITTER						PORTRAIT	
		RESIDENCE OCCUPATION	COLLEGE	CHURCH POLITICS	MARRIED	OFFICE INCOME	DATE	PERIOD	MEDIUM * AND SIZE (IN.)
Smith, Isaac	1719 1787	Boston Merchant		Cong. Mod. Whig	Yes	Justice of peace High	1769	1768–70	O.C. 50 x 40
Smith, Mrs. I.	1726 1786	Boston Housewife		Cong.	Yes		1769	1768–70	O.C. 50 x 40
Smith, Mrs. James	1726 1785	Boston Housewife			Yes		1769	1768–70	O.C. 36 x 28
Sparhawk, Nath.	1715 1776	Maine Merchant		Mod. Tory	Widower	Council High	1764	1762–64	O.C. over 50 x 40
Spooner, John	1728 1768	Boston Merchant		Cong. High Tory	Yes	Medium	1763	1762–64	O.C. 30 x 25
Stevens, Mrs. John	1751 1820	Gloucester Housewife		Cong.	Yes			1771–74	O.C. 50 x 40
Stevens, Mrs. Will.	1713 1778	Gloucester Housewife		Cong.	Yes			1758–61	O.C. 50 x 40
Stewart, Duncan		Boston†† Official		Angl. High Tory	Yes	Collector of customs Medium	1767	1765–67	O.C. 50 x 40
Stewart, Mrs. D.		Boston†† Housewife		Angl.	Yes			1765–67	O.C. 50 x 40
Storer, Eben.§§	1699 1761	Boston Merchant		Cong. Mod. Whig	Yes	Justice of peace High		1768–70	P. under 30 x 25
Storer, Mrs. E.†	1700 1771	Boston Widow		Cong.	Widow			1768–70	P. under 30 x 25
Storer II, Eben.	1730 1807	Boston Merchant	Harvard	Cong. Rad. Whig	Yes	Selectman High		1768–70	P. under 30 x 25
Storer II, Mrs. E.	1734 1774	Boston Housewife		Cong.	Yes			1768–70	P. under 30 x 25
Temple, John	1732 1798	Boston Official		Mod. Whig	No	Surveyor of customs Very high	1765	1765–67	P. under 30 x 25
Temple, Mrs. J.	? 1809	Boston Housewife			Yes			1765–67	P. under 30 x 25

Name	Dates	Place / Occupation	College	Religion / Politics	Married	Status	Year	Period	Portrait size
Townsend, Greg.	1739 1798	Needham		Cong. High Tory	No			1758–61	P. under 30 x 25
Townsend, Mrs. G.	? ?	Needham Housewife		Cong.	Yes	Medium	1765	1765–67	P. under 30 x 25
Turner, Will.	1745 1789	Boston		Angl. Mod. Whig	Yes			1765–67	P. under 30 x 25
Turner, Mrs. W.	1746 1824	Boston Housewife		Angl.	Yes	Medium	1767	1765–67	P. under 30 x 25
Tyler, Mrs. And.	1731 1783	Westwood Housewife		Cong.	Yes			1765–67	P. under 30 x 25
Tyng, Ann	1733 1756	Boston Daughter			No		1756	1753–57	O.C. 50 x 40
Tyng, Eleazer	1690 1782	Tyngsboro Landowner	Harvard	Cong. Mod. Tory	Widower	Justice of peace High	1772	1771–74	O.C. 50 x 40
Verplanck, Dan.	1762 1834	New York Minor		Angl.	No		1771	1771–74	O.C. 50 x 40
Verplanck, Gul.	1750 1799	New York Merchant	King's		No	Very high	1771	1771–74	O.C. 36 x 28
Verplanck, Sam.	1739 1820	New York Merchant	King's	Angl. Mod. Whig	Yes	High	1771	1771–74	O.C. 30 x 25
Waldo, Mrs. Sam.	1737 1817	Maine Housewife		Cong.	Yes			1765–67	O.C. 50 x 40
Warren, James	1726 1804	Plymouth Landowner	Harvard	Cong. Rad. Whig	Yes	Representative Medium		1762–64	O.C. 50 x 40
Warren, Mrs. J.	1728 1814	Plymouth Housewife		Cong.	Yes			1762–64	O.C. 50 x 40
Warren, Jos.	1741 1775	Boston Physician	Harvard	Cong. Rad. Whig	Yes	High		1765–67	O.C. 50 x 40
Watson, George	1718 1800	Plymouth Merchant		Cong. High Tory	Widower	Very high	1768	1768–70	O.C. 50 x 40
Watson, Mrs. G.	1737 1767	Plymouth Housewife		Cong.	Yes		1765	1765–67	O.C. 50 x 40
Watts, Mrs. Edw.	1741 1812	Maine Housewife		Cong.	Yes		1765	1765–67	O.C. 36 x 28
Watts, Mrs. Sam.	1715 1773	Boston Widow		Cong.	Widow			1768–70	O.C. 30 x 25

Continued

| | SITTER | | | | | | | PORTRAIT | |
NAME	BIRTH DEATH	RESIDENCE OCCUPATION	COLLEGE	CHURCH POLITICS	MARRIED	OFFICE INCOME	DATE	PERIOD	MEDIUM* AND SIZE (IN.)
Welsteed, Will.§§	1696 1753	Boston Minister	Harvard	Cong. Mod. Tory	Yes	Low		1753–57	Eng. under 30 x 25
Wentworth, Eliz.	1737 ?	Boston Daughter		Angl.	No			1762–64	O.C. 30 x 25
Wentworth, John †	1737 1820	Portsmouth Official	Harvard	Angl. High Tory	Yes	Governor Very high	1769	1768–70	P. under 30 x 25
Winslow, Isaac **	1709 1777	Boston Merchant	Harvard	Cong. High Tory	Yes	Council Very high	1774	1771–74	O.C. over 50 x 40
Winslow, Joshua †	1727 1801	Marshfield Military		High Tory	No	High	1755	1753–57	O.C. 50 x 40
Winthrop, John	1714 1779	Cambridge Teacher	Harvard	Cong. Mod. Whig	Yes	Low		1771–74	O.C. 50 x 40
Winthrop, Mrs. J.	1727 1790	Cambridge Housewife		Cong.	Yes		1773	1771–74	O.C. 36 x 28
Winthrop, Sam.	1716 1779	Boston Official		Cong. Mod. Whig	No	Clerk, superior court Medium		1771–74	O.C. 50 x 40

Categorical Listings

In the following section, data given in the preceding tabulation are recombined into these categories: residence, occupation, education (college), church, politics, office, and income. After each subject heading, the size of the sample is given in parenthesis, indicating for what number of the 240 sitters analyzed information in the category is applicable and available. After the subheadings, a numerical and occasionally a percentage indication of the size of that group is given parenthetically. Under *Residence* the pictures are grouped chronologically according to six periods in Copley's career, with the firmly dated objects and those associated with them listed first. Under *Education (college)* rank refers to the socioeconomic ranking system then in effect in the colleges, not to academic performance.

RESIDENCE (240)

MASSACHUSETTS (192; 80%)

Boston (126; 52%)

North End[1] (15)

1753–57
William Welsteed (1753)
Jonathan Mountfort

1762–64
Elizabeth Wentworth

1765–67
Joseph Blake
Mather Byles

1768–70
Alexander MacWhorter (1769)
Mrs. Alexander MacWhorter (1769)
Mrs. Alexander Cumming (1770)
Ezekiel Goldthwait
Mrs. Ezekiel Goldthwait
George Green
Henry Hill
Mrs. Henry Hill
Paul Revere

1771–74
Thomas Flucker

[1] North of Mill Creek.

West Side[2] (15)

1753–57
Gore Children

1758–61
Thomas Hancock

1762–64
Daniel Hubbard (1764)
Mrs. Daniel Hubbard
Mrs. Samuel A. Otis

1765–67
Mrs. Edward Green (1765)
John Hancock (1765)
Henry Pelham (1765)
Peter Chardon
Mrs. Thomas Hancock

1768–70
Samuel Cooper
John S. Copley
Mrs. John S. Copley
Joseph Sherburne

1771–74
Samuel Winthrop

[2] West of Tremont Street.

117

South End[3] (35)

1753–57
Ann Gardiner

1758–61
Thomas Greene (1758)
Mrs. Thomas Greene
Hugh Hall (1758)
Thomas Aston Coffin
Rufus Greene
Mrs. Rufus Greene
Andrew Oliver
Mrs. Andrew Oliver
Andrew Oliver II
Elizabeth Oliver
Griselda Oliver

1762–64
Hannah Loring (1763)
John Spooner (1763)
Mrs. Joseph Calif
Mrs. Samuel Hill
Elizabeth Pitts

1765–67
Joseph Greene (1767)
Mrs. Joseph Greene (1767)
Benjamin Hallowell
Mrs. Benjamin Hallowell

1768–70
Joseph Barrell
Mrs. Joseph Barrell (A)
Mrs. William Coffin
Joshua Henshaw I

1771–74
Samuel Adams
Thomas Amory II
Mrs. Thomas Amory II
Mrs. Joseph Barrell (B)
John Erving
Sylvester Gardiner
Joseph Henshaw
Mrs. Joseph Henshaw
Joshua Henshaw II
Mrs. Joshua Henshaw II

Central Boston[4] (52)

1753–57
Ann Tyng (1756)
Thankful Hubbard
Thomas Marshall
Mrs. Thomas Marshall

Charles Pelham
George Scott

1758–61
John Barrett
Mrs. John Barrett
Dorothy Murray

1762–64
Mrs. John Scollay (1763)
John Scollay
Deborah Scollay
Moses Gill (1764)
Mrs. Moses Gill
Mrs. John Powell (1764)
John Powell II
Mrs. John Powell II
Samuel P. Savage (1764)
Mrs. Samuel P. Savage (1764)
Mrs. John Amory
Mrs. John Apthorp
Mrs. Gawen Brown
Mrs. Benjamin Davis
Mrs. John Gray
Joseph Green (B)

1765–67
Mrs. Thomas Boylston (1766)
John Gray (1766)
Nicholas Boylston (1767)
Rebecca Boylston (1767)
Thomas Boylston II
Joseph Green (A) (1767)
Mrs. Joseph Green (A)
Mrs. William Turner (1767)
William Turner
Harrison Gray
Thomas Hubbard
Joseph Scott
Mrs. Joseph Scott

1768–70
John Amory (1768)
Mrs. John Greene (1769)
John Greene
Isaac Smith (1769)
Mrs. Isaac Smith (1769)
Mrs. James Smith (1769)
James Allen
Nathaniel Hurd
Ebenezer Storer[5]
Mrs. Ebenezer Storer
Ebenezer Storer II
Mrs. Ebenezer Storer II
Mrs. Samuel Watts

1771–74
Nathaniel Perkins

[3] South of Milk Street and Rawson's Lane.
[4] South of Mill Creek, East of Tremont Street, North of Milk Street and Rawson's Lane.

[5] Deceased at time of portrait.

Other and Unlocated Boston (9)

1762–64
Lydia Lynde

1765–67
Sarah Jackson (1765)
John Temple (1765)
Mrs. John Temple
Duncan Stewart (1767)
Mrs. Duncan Stewart
Joseph Warren (Cambridge)

1768–70
Richard Dana

1771–74
Mr. and Mrs. Isaac Winslow (Roxbury) (1774)

Marblehead (12)

1758–61
Jacob Fowle

1762–64
Alice Hooper

1765–67
Robert Hooper (1767)
Mrs. Robert Hooper (1767)
Thomas Lewis

1768–70
Jeremiah Lee (1769)
Mrs. Jeremiah Lee (1769)
Joseph Hooper
Mrs. Joseph Hooper
Robert Hooper II

1771–74
Mrs. Humphrey Devereux (1771)
Mrs. Richard Skinner (1772)

Gloucester (10)

1753–57
Mrs. William Stevens

1758–61
Epes Sargent

1762–64
Mrs. Daniel Rogers (1762)
Nathaniel Allen (1763)
Mrs. Nathaniel Allen
Mrs. Daniel Sargent (1763)
Mrs. Epes Sargent II (1764)
Epes Sargent II

1765–67
Mrs. Nathaniel Ellery

1771–74
Mrs. John Stevens

Cambridge (8)

1753–57
William Brattle

1758–61
Nathaniel Appleton
Samuel Danforth
Edward Holyoke

1762–64
Mrs. Nathaniel Appleton (1763)

1768–70
Ralph Inman

1771–74
Mrs. John Winthrop (1773)
John Winthrop

Braintree (4)

1758–61
Mrs. Samuel Quincy

1765–67
Josiah Quincy
Samuel Quincy

1771–74
Dorothy Quincy

Cape Cod; Nantucket (4)

1758–61
James Otis
Mrs. James Otis

1762–64
Timothy Folger (1764)

1765–67
Mrs. Sylvanus Bourne (1766)

Plymouth (4)

1762–64
James Warren
Mrs. James Warren

1765–67
Mrs. George Watson (1765)

1768–70
George Watson (1768)

Charlestown (3)

1765–67
Mrs. Ebenezer Austin
Mrs. Samuel Henley

1768–70
Mrs. James Russell

Medford (3)

1758–61
Elizabeth and Mary Royall

119

1768–70
Isaac Royall (1769)
Mrs. Isaac Royall (1769)

Salem (3)

1758–61
Benjamin Pickman

1762–64
Mrs. Benjamin Pickman (1763)

1768–70
Mrs. William Eppes

Needham (2)

1758–60
Gregory Townsend

1765–67
Mrs. Gregory Townsend (1765)

Newburyport (2)

1768–70
Jonathan Jackson

1771–74
Thomas Cary (1773)

Rutland (2)

1762–64
Mrs. John Murray (1763)
John Murray

Wrentham (2)

1753–57
Mrs. Joseph Mann (1753)
Joseph Mann (1754)

Haverhill (1)

1771–74
Edward Bernard

Marshfield (1)

1753–57
Joshua Winslow (1755)

Middleboro (1)

1758–61
Peter Oliver

Milton (1)

1762–64
James Murray

Tyngsboro (1)

1771–74
Eleazer Tyng (1772)

Westwood (1)

1765–67
Mrs. Andrew Tyler

Woburn (1)

1762–64
Mrs. Cotton

NEW YORK (11; 5%)

1768–70
Myles Cooper (1768)
Thomas Gage

1771–74
Mrs. Thomas Gage (1771)
Mrs. Charles McEvers (1771)
Mary Martin (1771)

Mrs. Roger Morris (1771)
John Ogilvie (1771)
Mrs. Paul Richard (1771)
Daniel Verplanck (1771)
Gulian Verplanck (1771)
Samuel Verplanck (1771)

NEW HAMPSHIRE (8; 3%)

Portsmouth (8)

1753–57
Jane Browne (1756)
Arthur Browne (1757)
Mrs. Arthur Browne

1758–61
Theodore Atkinson

1765–67
Mrs. Theodore Atkinson (1765)
Woodbury Langdon
Mrs. Woodbury Langdon

1768–70
John Wentworth (1769)

MAINE (6; 2½%)

1762–64
Nathaniel Sparhawk (1764)
Benjamin Blackstone
Mrs. Benjamin Blackstone

1765–67
Mrs. Edward Watts (1765)
Elizabeth Ross
Mrs. Samuel Waldo

NOVA SCOTIA (6; 2½%)

1753–57
Jonathan Belcher (1756)
Mrs. Jonathan Belcher (1756)
Thomas Ainslie (1757)

1771–74
John Newton (1772)
Benjamin Gerrish
Joseph Gerrish [?]

RHODE ISLAND (6; 2½%)

Newport (3)

1758–61
John Bours
Rhoda Cranston

1762–64
Mrs. Metcalf Bowler

Providence (2)

1771–74
Jabez Bowen
Mrs. Jabez Bowen

Kingston (1)

1758–61
Samuel Fayerweather

CONNECTICUT (4; 2%)

Fairfield (2)

1758–61
Thaddeus Burr
Mrs. Thaddeus Burr

New Haven (2)

1771–74
Adam Babcock
Mrs. Adam Babcock

OTHER (7; 2½%)

West Indies (2)

1768–70
Samuel Cary
Mrs. Samuel Cary

Charleston, S. C. (2)

1765–67
John Bee Holmes (1765)
Martin Howard (1767)

Great Britain (2)

1758–61
Sir John St. Clair (1759)

1771–74
James Gambier (1773)

Philadelphia (1)

1771–74
Mr. and Mrs. Thomas Mifflin (1773)

OCCUPATION (116)

BIG BUSINESS AND LANDED GENTRY (63; 55%)

Merchants (52)
John Amory
Adam Babcock
Joseph Barrell
John Barrett
Nicholas Boylston

Thomas Boylston
Thomas Flucker
Jacob Fowle
Benjamin Gerrish
Joseph Gerrish [?]
Ezekiel Goldthwait

Harrison Gray
John Gray
George Green
Joseph Green
John Greene
Thomas Greene

Hugh Hall
John Hancock
Thomas Hancock
Joseph Henshaw
Joshua Henshaw
Joshua Henshaw II
Joseph Hooper
Robert Hooper II
Daniel Hubbard
Ralph Inman
Jonathan Jackson
Woodbury Langdon
Jeremiah Lee
Thomas Lewis
Thomas Mifflin
Andrew Oliver
Peter Oliver

Charles Pelham
Benjamin Pickman
John Powell
Josiah Quincy
Isaac Royall
Epes Sargent
Epes Sargent II
Samuel P. Savage
Joseph Sherburne
Isaac Smith
Nathaniel Sparhawk
John Spooner
Ebenezer Storer
Ebenezer Storer II
Gulian Verplanck
Samuel Verplanck
George Watson

Isaac Winslow

Landowners (6)
Thaddeus Burr
Samuel Cary
James Murray
John Newton
Eleazer Tyng
James Warren

Shippers (4)
Nathaniel Allen
John Erving
Timothy Folger
Robert Hooper

Gentlemen (1)
James Allen

PROFESSIONS AND SERVICES (32; 28%)

Ministers (11)
Congregational
Nathaniel Appleton
Edward Barnard
Mather Byles
Thomas Cary
Samuel Cooper
William Welsteed

Anglican
Arthur Browne
Myles Cooper
Samuel Fayerweather
John Ogilvie

Presbyterian
Alexander MacWhorter

Public Officials (10)
Samuel Adams
Thomas Ainslie
Theodore Atkinson
Jonathan Belcher
Samuel Danforth
Benjamin Hallowell
Duncan Stewart
John Temple
John Wentworth
Samuel Winthrop

Lawyers (6)
Jabez Bowen

Peter Chardon
Richard Dana
Martin Howard
James Otis
Samuel Quincy

Physicians (3)
Sylvester Gardiner
Nathaniel Perkins
Joseph Warren

Teachers (2)
Edward Holyoke
John Winthrop

CRAFTS AND SMALL RETAIL BUSINESS (15; 12%)

Metalsmiths, Engravers,
Jewelers, Artists (5)
John S. Copley
Rufus Greene
Nathaniel Hurd
Andrew Oliver II
Paul Revere

Distillers (4)
Thomas Amory II

Joseph Green
Henry Hill
Joseph Mann

Braziers (3)
Moses Gill
Thomas Hubbard
Joseph Scott

Masons (1)
Joseph Blake

Shopkeepers (1)
John Scollay

Tailors (1)
Thomas Marshall

MILITARY (6; 5%)

William Brattle
Thomas Gage

James Gambier
Sir John St. Clair

George Scott
Joshua Winslow

EDUCATION — COLLEGE (50)

HARVARD (41)

	Class	Rank		Class	Rank
Samuel Adams	1740	6	Edward Holyoke	1705	2
James Allen	1754	13	Robert Hooper II	1763	1
Thomas Amory II	1741	17	Thomas Hubbard	1721	25
Nathaniel Appleton	1712	1	Jonathan Jackson	1761	13
Theodore Atkinson	1757	1	Andrew Oliver	1724	3
Edward Bernard	1736	11	Andrew Oliver II	1749	2
Jonathan Belcher	1728	3	Peter Oliver	1730	1
William Brattle	1722	1	Nathaniel Perkins	1734	1
Mather Byles	1725	13	Benjamin Pickman	1759	3
Thomas Cary	1761	14	Josiah Quincy	1728	7
Peter Chardon	1757	8	Samuel Quincy	1754	3
Samuel Cooper	1743	3	Epes Sargent	1712	15
Richard Dana	1718	18	Ebenezer Storer II	1747	17
Samuel Danforth	1715	1	Eleazer Tyng	1712	7
Samuel Fayerweather	1743	18	James Warren	1745	6
Joseph Green (A)	1726	13	Joseph Warren	1759	25
Hugh Hall	1713	3	William Welsteed	1716	1
John Hancock	1754	5	John Wentworth	1755	5
Joseph Henshaw	1748	22	Isaac Winslow	1727	9
Joshua Henshaw II	1763		John Winthrop	1732	1
Henry Hill	1756	10			

KING'S (COLUMBIA) (2)

Gulian Verplanck   1768   Samuel Verplanck

PRINCETON (2)

Thaddeus Burr   Alexander MacWhorter

YALE (2)

Jabez Bowen	1757	11	John Ogilvie	1748	13

COLLEGE OF PHILADELPHIA (UNIVERSITY OF PENNSYLVANIA) (1)

Thomas Mifflin

FOREIGN (2)

Arthur Browne (Trinity College, Dublin)   Myles Cooper (Oxford)

CHURCH (202)

CONGREGATIONAL (135; 67%)

Brattle Square (37)	William Brattle	The Gore Children
Mrs. Joseph Barrell (B)	Peter Chardon	Mrs. Edward Green
Nicholas Boylston	Samuel Cooper	John Hancock
Rebecca Boylston	Mrs. John S. Copley	Thomas Hancock
Mrs. Thomas Boylston	Richard Dana	Mrs. Thomas Hancock
Thomas Boylston II	Mrs. Benjamin Davis	Joseph Henshaw

Mrs. Joseph Henshaw
Joshua Henshaw
Joshua Henshaw II
Mrs. Joshua Henshaw II
Elizabeth Pitts
Samuel P. Savage
Mrs. Samuel P. Savage
John Scollay
Mrs. John Scollay
Joseph Scott
Mrs. Joseph Scott
Joseph Sherburne
Isaac Smith
Mrs. Isaac Smith
Ebenezer Storer
Mrs. Ebenezer Storer
Ebenezer Storer II
Mrs. Ebenezer Storer II
Joseph Warren

Old South (11)
Mrs. Alexander Cumming
Mrs. Joseph Green (A)
Benjamin Hallowell
Mrs. Benjamin Hallowell
Thomas Hubbard
Thankful Hubbard
Andrew Oliver
Mrs. Andrew Oliver
Andrew Oliver II
Elizabeth Oliver
Griselda Oliver

New Brick (5)
Ezekiel Goldthwait
Mrs. Ezekiel Goldthwait
Jonathan Mountfort
Paul Revere
William Welsteed

West Church (5)
James Allen
Harrison Gray
John Spooner
Mr. and Mrs. Isaac Winslow

King's (18)
John Amory
Mrs. John Amory
Joseph Barrell
Ann Gardiner
Sylvester Gardiner
Rufus Greene
Mrs. Rufus Greene

New North (3)
John Barrett
Mrs. John Barrett
Mrs. Henry Hill

Hollis Street (2)
Mrs. Gawen Brown
Mather Byles

First Church (1)
Joseph Green (A)

New South (1)
Samuel Adams

Old North (1)
Nathaniel Perkins

Other Congregational (69)
Nathaniel Allen
Mrs. Nathaniel Allen
Nathaniel Appleton
Mrs. Nathaniel Appleton
Mrs. Ebenezer Austin
Mrs. Adam Babcock
Edward Bernard
Mrs. Joseph Barrell (A)
Benjamin Blackstone
Mrs. Benjamin Blackstone
Mrs. Sylvanus Bourne
Jabez Bowen
Thaddeus Burr
Mrs. Thaddeus Burr
Samuel Cary
Mrs. Samuel Cary
Thomas Cary
Samuel Danforth
Mrs. Nathaniel Ellery
Thomas Flucker
Timothy Folger
Moses Gill
Mrs. Moses Gill
Mrs. Samuel Henley
John Bee Holmes
Edward Holyoke

Alice Hooper
Joseph Hooper
Mrs. Joseph Hooper
Robert Hooper
Mrs. Robert Hooper
Robert Hooper II
Nathaniel Hurd
Jonathan Jackson
Sarah Jackson
Woodbury Langdon
Mrs. Woodbury Langdon
Jeremiah Lee
Mrs. Jeremiah Lee
Mrs. John Murray
Peter Oliver
James Otis
Mrs. James Otis
Dorothy Quincy
Josiah Quincy
Samuel Quincy
Mrs. Samuel Quincy
Mrs. Daniel Rogers
Mrs. James Russell
Mrs. Daniel Sargent
Epes Sargent
Epes Sargent II
Mrs. Epes Sargent II
Mrs. Richard Skinner
Mrs. John Stevens
Mrs. William Stevens
Gregory Townsend
Mrs. Gregory Townsend
Mrs. Andrew Tyler
Eleazer Tyng
Mrs. Samuel Waldo
James Warren
Mrs. James Warren
George Watson
Mrs. George Watson
Mrs. Edward Watts
Mrs. Samuel Watts
John Winthrop
Mrs. John Winthrop
Samuel Winthrop

ANGLICAN (63; 31%)

Hugh Hall
Hannah Loring
Mrs. John Powell
John Powell II
Mrs. John Powell II
Isaac Royall
Mrs. Isaac Royall
Elizabeth and Mary Royall

William Turner
Mrs. William Turner
Elizabeth Wentworth

Trinity (14)
Thomas Amory II
Mrs. Thomas Amory II
Thomas Aston Coffin

CATEGORICAL LISTINGS

Mrs. William Coffin
John S. Copley
John Erving
John Greene
Mrs. John Greene
Joseph Greene
Mrs. Joseph Greene
Thomas Greene
Mrs. Daniel Hubbard
Lydia Lynde
Mrs. Duncan Stewart

Other Anglican (31)
Theodore Atkinson
Mrs. Theodore Atkinson

Jonathan Belcher
Mrs. Jonathan Belcher
John Bours
Mrs. Metcalf Bowler
Arthur Browne
Mrs. Arthur Browne
Jane Browne
Myles Cooper
Rhoda Cranston
Samuel Fayerweather
Thomas Gage
Mrs. Thomas Gage
James Gambier
Joseph Gerrish [?]
Martin Howard

Daniel Hubbard
Ralph Inman
Mary Martin
Dorothy Murray
James Murray
John Newton
John Ogilvie
Henry Pelham
Sir John St. Clair
George Scott
Duncan Stewart
Daniel Verplanck
Samuel Verplanck
John Wentworth

OTHER DENOMINATIONS (5; 2%)

Presbyterian (2)
Alexander MacWhorter
Mrs. Alexander MacWhorter

Quaker (2)
Mr. and Mrs. Thomas Mifflin

Baptist (1)
Adam Babcock

POLITICS (117)

TORY (64; 55%)

High Tory (38; 32%)
Thomas Ainslie
John Amory
Theodore Atkinson
Jonathan Belcher
Arthur Browne
Mather Byles
Myles Cooper
Thomas Flucker
Thomas Gage
James Gambier
Sylvester Gardiner
Harrison Gray
John Gray
Benjamin Hallowell
Joseph Hooper
Martin Howard
Daniel Hubbard
Thomas Hubbard
Ralph Inman
James Murray
John Murray
John Newton

Andrew Oliver
Peter Oliver
Nathaniel Perkins
Benjamin Pickman
John Powell II
Samuel Quincy
Isaac Royall
Joseph Scott
Joseph Sherburne
John Spooner
Duncan Stewart
Gregory Townsend
George Watson
John Wentworth
Isaac Winslow
Joshua Winslow

Moderate Tory (27; 23%)
Thomas Amory II
John Bours
Thomas Boylston
Samuel Cary

John S. Copley
Samuel Danforth
John Erving
Benjamin Gerrish
Joseph Gerrish [?]
George Green
John Greene
Joseph Greene
Rufus Greene
Hugh Hall
Thomas Hancock
Edward Holyoke
Robert Hooper
John Ogilvie
Andrew Oliver II
Charles Pelham
Epes Sargent
Epes Sargent II
Nathaniel Sparhawk
Sir John St. Clair
Eleazer Tyng
William Welsteed

WHIG (52; 45%)

Moderate Whig (33; 29%)
James Allen
Nathaniel Allen
Nathaniel Appleton

Adam Babcock
Edward Barnard
Joseph Barrell
John Barrett

Benjamin Blackstone
Joseph Blake
Jabez Bowen
Nicholas Boylston

CATEGORICAL LISTINGS

William Brattle
Thaddeus Burr
Thomas Cary
Peter Chardon
Samuel Fayerweather
Timothy Folger
Jacob Fowle
Ezekiel Goldthwait
Joseph Green (A)
Joseph Green (B)
Joseph Henshaw
Joshua Henshaw
Nathaniel Hurd
Thomas Lewis
John Scollay

Isaac Smith
Ebenezer Storer
John Temple
William Turner
Samuel Verplanck
John Winthrop
Samuel Winthrop

Radical Whig (19; 16%)
Samuel Adams
Samuel Cooper
Richard Dana
Moses Gill
John Hancock

Joshua Henshaw II
Henry Hill
Jonathan Jackson
Jeremiah Lee
Thomas Marshall
Alexander MacWhorter
Thomas Mifflin
James Otis
Josiah Quincy
Paul Revere
Samuel P. Savage
Ebenezer Storer II
James Warren
Joseph Warren

OFFICE (56)

APPOINTIVE OFFICES (42; 75%)

*Council of the
General Court* (13)
William Brattle
Samuel Danforth
John Erving
Benjamin Gerrish
Joseph Gerrish [?]
Harrison Gray
Thomas Hancock
Thomas Hubbard
James Murray
Andrew Oliver
Isaac Royall
Nathaniel Sparhawk
Isaac Winslow

Justice of the Peace (11)
Nathaniel Allen
Richard Dana
Joshua Henshaw
Robert Hooper
Ralph Inman

Jeremiah Lee
Epes Sargent II
John Scollay
Isaac Smith
Ebenezer Storer
Eleazer Tyng

Justice, Inferior Court (4)
Hugh Hall
Andrew Oliver II
Josiah Quincy
Epes Sargent

*Surveyor General
of Customs* (3)
Benjamin Hallowell
John Newton
John Temple

Chief Justice (2)
Jonathan Belcher
Martin Howard

Collector of Customs (2)
Thomas Ainslie
Duncan Stewart

Secretary of the Province (2)
Theodore Atkinson
Thomas Flucker

Clerk, Superior Court (1)
Samuel Winthrop

Governor (1)
John Wentworth

Justice, Superior Court (1)
Peter Oliver

Recorder of Deeds (1)
Ezekiel Goldthwait

Sheriff
Timothy Folger

ELECTIVE OFFICES — PROVINCE (6; 11%)

House of Representatives (5)
John Hancock
Thomas Mifflin

John Murray
James Otis
James Warren

*Clerk, House of
Representatives* (1)
Samuel Adams

ELECTIVE OFFICES — TOWN (8; 14%)

Miscellaneous Offices (7)
John Barrett
Moses Gill
John Gray

Nathaniel Hurd
Nathaniel Perkins
John Powell II
Joseph Sherburne

Selectman (1)
Ebenezer Storer II

126

CATEGORICAL LISTINGS

INCOME (121)

LOW (ESTIMATED AT UNDER £100 A YEAR) (9; 8%)

Nathaniel Appleton
Edward Barnard
Arthur Browne
Mather Byles
Myles Cooper
Samuel Fayerweather
Edward Holyoke
William Welsteed
John Winthrop

MEDIUM (ESTIMATED AT £100–500 A YEAR) (48; 39%)

Samuel Adams
Adam Babcock
John Barrett
Joseph Blake
John Bours
Jabez Bowen
William Brattle
Thaddeus Burr
Thomas Cary
Peter Chardon
Samuel Cooper
Richard Dana
Samuel Danforth
Timothy Folger
Thomas Gage
James Gambier
Moses Gill
Joseph Green (B)
John Greene
Joseph Greene
Hugh Hall
Joseph Henshaw
Joshua Henshaw II
Henry Hill
Joseph Hooper
Robert Hooper II
Daniel Hubbard
Nathaniel Hurd
Thomas Lewis
Joseph Mann
Thomas Marshall
Alexander MacWhorter
John Newton
James Ogilvie
James Otis
Charles Pelham
John Powell II
Samuel Quincy
Paul Revere
John Scollay
Joseph Scott
John Spooner
Duncan Stewart
Gregory Townsend
William Turner
James Warren
Mrs. Samuel Watts
Samuel Winthrop

HIGH (ESTIMATED AT £500–1000 A YEAR) (38; 31%)

James Allen
Nathaniel Allen
Joseph Barrell
Jonathan Belcher
Benjamin Blackstone
Samuel Cary
John S. Copley
Jacob Fowle
Benjamin Gerrish
Joseph Gerrish [?]
Ezekiel Goldthwait
John Gray
George Green
Joseph Green (A)
Rufus Greene
Thomas Greene
Joshua Henshaw
Daniel Hubbard
Woodbury Langdon
James Murray
John Murray
Andrew Oliver II
Peter Oliver
Nathaniel Perkins
Benjamin Pickman
Josiah Quincy
Epes Sargent
Epes Sargent II
Samuel P. Savage
Isaac Smith
Nathaniel Sparhawk
Sir John St. Clair
Ebenezer Storer
Ebenezer Storer II
Eleazer Tyng
Samuel Verplanck
Joseph Warren
Joshua Winslow

VERY HIGH (ESTIMATED AT OVER £1000 A YEAR) (26; 22%)

John Amory
Thomas Amory II
Theodore Atkinson
Nicholas Boylston
Thomas Boylston
John Erving
Thomas Flucker
Sylvester Gardiner
Harrison Gray
Benjamin Hallowell
John Hancock
Thomas Hancock
Robert Hooper
Thomas Hubbard
Ralph Inman
Jonathan Jackson
Jeremiah Lee
Thomas Mifflin
Andrew Oliver
Isaac Royall
Joseph Sherburne
John Temple
Gulian Verplanck
George Watson
John Wentworth
Isaac Winslow

Analysis of Data

The following analysis is based on statistical summaries and cross-references of the data. The primary category of information under discussion is given in capital letters; the name of the succeeding categories with which that information is cross-referenced is given in italics. In the cross-references salient information most often turns up in the form of radical departures from expected frequencies. To choose a simple example, let us suppose that data on "period of artistic production" and on "medium" are being cross-referenced. From our straight statistical tabulations we know that a certain number of pictures were painted in each of six elected periods. We also know the percentage of Copley's total American work in each medium — oil on canvas, pastel, watercolor on ivory, etc. In a cross-reference of "period of artistic production" and "medium," the percentages of work in each medium in each period might normally be expected to correspond with the percentages for the total American work. Thus, on the basis of the percentages for the total American work, we can predict a specific number of works in each medium in each period. This is called the expected frequency. If there should be a marked deviation from this expected frequency — for instance, if the number of pastels in a given period is double the number predicted — this suggests that there is some factor or combination of factors affecting the pattern of Copley's work which, if not immediately obvious, might be worth investigation. The following analysis presents the most important material that emerged from this cross-referencing procedure.

It must be borne in mind that these results pertain only to Copley's sitters and should not be given broader applications. Thus the percentage of Tories, or Anglicans, or Anglican Tories, among Copley's sitters may well differ considerably from the percentage for other groups, or for all of Boston, or for all of New England.[1]

PERIOD OF ARTISTIC PRODUCTION

To simplify calculations Copley's career was divided into six periods: 1753–57, 1758–61, 1762–64, 1765–67, 1768–70, and 1771–74. On the basis of known pictures Copley averaged about 6 paintings a year during 1753–57.[2] He appears to have more than doubled his output in

[1] As a rough indication of the limited extent of Copley's patronage, I estimate that he painted only about .1% of the population of Massachusetts (which was some 220,000 in 1770), less than 1% of the population of Boston (16,000), and at least one member from only about 5% of Boston's families. Copley's patrons were certainly more Anglican than average. Robert E. Brown, *Middle-Class Democracy and the Revolution in Massachusetts, 1691–* *1780* (Ithaca, 1955), p. 109, notes that the vast majority of people in Massachusetts were Congregationalists, even in Boston and Marblehead where the Anglicans were most active. Similarly Copley's sitters probably included a higher-than-average percentage of Tories, officeholders, merchants, and professional people; and a below-average percentage of craftsmen, Whigs, and low-income people.

[2] These estimates of output were arrived at by

1758–61, with most of the known pictures painted during the first part of the period. From 1762–70 he averaged about 24 currently known pictures a year, producing about 60% of his American paintings in that period. From 1771 until he left Boston in 1774, Copley's business fell off to an average of about 18 pictures per year. The sharpness of the decline becomes clearer with the realization that a large number of these pictures were produced during the successful New York trip at the beginning of the period.

SEX

All sitters (240):

Men	51%
Women	45%
Children	4%

Period. Copley painted an above-average percentage of women in 1762–67, especially in 1762–64 when two thirds of his sitters were females. He painted more men than average in 1758–61 and 1768–74.

RESIDENCE

All sitters (240):

Boston	50%	
Other Massachusetts	30%	
Total Massachusetts		80%
New York	5%	
New Hampshire (Portsmouth)	3%	
Maine	2½%	
Rhode Island	2½%	
Nova Scotia	2½%	
Other	4½%	

The largest concentration of Massachusetts sitters outside Boston was in Essex County, especially Marblehead and Gloucester.

Period. A high percentage of Copley's sitters came from outside Massachusetts during his early and late years, 1753–57 and 1771–74. In 1758–61 a particularly high percentage (40%) of his business came from Massachusetts outside Boston. He enjoyed less Boston business than average before 1762, with the proportion of Bostonians among his sitters rising to a high of two thirds in 1768–70 and then tapering off again in the final period, 1771–74, the beginning of which Copley spent in New York. During the first period, 1753–57, two thirds of the Boston sitters came from Central Boston, Copley's own section of town. In 1758–61 80% of the Boston sitters came from South Boston, and all but one of the rest came from Central Boston. In 1762–64 the Boston sitters came mostly from the Central and South sections; in 1765–67 there were few sitters from North and South Boston; in 1768–70 Copley became busy in North Boston; and in 1771–74 business in Central Boston fell off and was high once more in South Boston. The limited amount of business in West Boston did not deviate sharply from the pattern for the town as a whole.

OCCUPATION

Male sitters of known occupation (116):

Big business and landed gentry (shipper, merchant, landowner, gentleman)	55%
Professions (minister, lawyer, doctor, teacher, government official)	28%
Crafts or small retail trades (tailor, mason, distiller, shopkeeper, brazier, silver- or goldsmith, jeweler, engraver, artist, etc.)	12%
Military	5%

This analysis covers only male sitters, but it should be noted that over a third (35%) of all portrait subjects were housewives (not counting widows, daughters, and minors). Among the male sitters there were five times as many merchants (46%) as the next most popular

taking the results of the statistical analysis, based on 240 paintings, and applying them to Copley's total known American production of 350 paintings. If currently known pictures approximate three quarters of Copley's actual production, a rough estimate of the total during each period can be obtained by adding a factor of one third. Even if the given totals are incomplete, the important basic pattern of activity as reflected in the currently known pictures is probably accurate.

occupation groups, ministers and government officials (9% each).

Period. During 1762–64 Copley painted a particularly high percentage of big-business and landed-gentry sitters, including many wives and daughters, and had no sitters from the professions. To a lesser extent this was true of the following period, 1765–67, and in 1768–70 Copley painted a particularly high percentage of merchants. He painted few merchants at the very beginning of his career, 1753–57; few professional sitters in 1758–64; and few craftsmen after 1767.

Residence. The large landowners came from outlying areas, mostly rural Massachusetts; the officials were clustered around the provincial capitals, especially Boston, Portsmouth, and Halifax; almost all of the sitters in craft or small retail trades came from Boston, particularly Central Boston; and all of the teachers lived in Cambridge and taught at Harvard.[3] The sitters from outside Boston who were painted by Copley included an above-average number of professional people, soldiers, and landowners, or members of their families. The percentage of merchants was consistently high within and outside Boston. Sitters in the professions, including the military, tended not to have portraits painted of their wives and children, while the merchants, shippers, and landed gentry often ordered portraits of other members of their families, even when they themselves were not painted. Three of the Boston ministers depicted by Copley, William Welsteed, Mather Byles, and Alexander MacWhorter, came from North Boston, but few merchant sitters lived in that part of town.

EDUCATION

All male sitters (121):

Harvard	33%
Other colleges	8%

Period. The percentage of college-educated sitters was particularly high in 1758–61 and 1771–74, and low in 1762–64 when Copley painted a disproportionately large number of big-business and landed-gentry sitters and their wives.

Residence. A large percentage of Copley's customers from Marblehead and Gloucester, mostly merchants, did not have a college education. But college degrees were held by over three quarters of the male sitters in Salem and Newburyport (also Essex County), and in Cambridge, New York, and New Hampshire (Portsmouth).

Occupation. Except for lawyers, who were customarily trained in law offices, a very high percentage of the professional sitters (83% including lawyers) went to Harvard. Less than a third of the business and craft sitters were college-educated. Both of the sitters with foreign degrees, Arthur Browne and Myles Cooper, were ministers. Sylvester Gardiner, the physician, was also educated abroad.

CHURCH

Sitters of known church affiliation (202):

Congregational	67%
Anglican	31%
Other	2%

The handful of sitters who were neither Congregational nor Anglican included the Presbyterian MacWhorters, the Quaker Mifflins, and Adam Babcock, a Baptist.

Period. There is little proportional variation in religion from period to period, other than a slight increase in Anglicans during the early and final years, and a slight increase in Congregational sitters in 1762–70. But there is a noticeable introduction of portraits of sitters from Brattle Square Church in 1764, and a halt in 1772 when Copley's project for a new meetinghouse for that church was rejected.

Residence. The sitters from Massachusetts outside Boston were mostly Congregationalists, the exceptions being Ralph Inman of Cambridge, James Murray of Milton, and members of the Royall family in Medford, all of whom lived in the immediate environs of Boston. On the other hand, Copley's patronage from outside Massachusetts was decidedly Anglican (54%),

---

[3] Rev. Myles Cooper of New York, president of King's College, Columbia, should perhaps be considered a teacher as well as a minister. Rev. Edward Holyoke, a Congregational minister and president of Harvard when painted, is necessarily considered a teacher rather than a minister since he did not have an official congregation. Rev. Nathaniel Appleton, although considered a minister, lived in Cambridge and was connected with Harvard.

except for sitters from Maine, all of whom were Congregationalists. All sitters from New York, Nova Scotia, and Great Britain seem to have been Anglicans, as were at least three quarters of the sitters from New Hampshire and Rhode Island. In Boston, where the proportion of Congregationalists to Anglicans was close to that for all sitters, the Anglicans were clustered in South Boston, a part of town in which half of the sitters were Anglican and in which more than half of the Boston Anglicans lived. More than half of Copley's Boston Congregationalists and a third of all Boston sitters are known to have attended Brattle Square Church, four times as many as patronized the next most popular Congregational church, Old South, the church

of the Oliver family. Congregationalists in North Boston largely attended New Brick, and none is known to have attended Brattle. Boston Anglican sitters were quite evenly divided between King's and Trinity.

Occupation. Of the sitters from the professions, 61% were Anglicans, twice more than the average, whereas four fifths of the craft and small retail sitters were Congregationalists. All of the widows and widowers for whom religious affiliation is known were Congregationalists. Anglicans had a noticeable propensity for ordering portraits of their children.

Education. Harvard graduates included high percentage of Congregationalists (84%).

POLITICS [4]

Adult male sitters (117):

High Tory	32%	
Moderate Tory	23%	
Total Tory		55%
Moderate Whig	29%	
Radical Whig	16%	
Total Whig		45%

The percentages remain essentially unchanged when the politics of fathers or husbands, not painted by Copley, of dependent sitters are taken into consideration, except that the radical Whig percentage drops since Copley apparently did not paint any dependent wives or children of radical Whigs.

Period. During his early years, 1753–61, Copley painted a disproportionately high percentage of Tories (72%), while Whigs were above the average in 1762–64 and 1768–70 (56%), the latter period notably high in radical Whigs. Among husbands and fathers of dependent sitters, there is an almost straight progression from an above-average number of Tories before 1764 to an increasingly above-average number of Whigs after that (except for a Tory upswing in 1768–70), rising to a particularly strong Whig predominance (70%) at the end, 1771–74. As Copley moved up the economic and social ladder, one might expect his patronage to shift

from Whig to Tory. If anything, it goes the other way. This probably does not reflect any shift on Copley's part, but rather the fact that over these years the Whig position became more clearly defined, attracting more able adherents, and an increasing number of Whigs achieved prominence and wished to have portraits painted. Copley's Tory sitters, often identified with the ruling establishment, were more consistently on a level of political or social prominence that seems to have called for portraiture. Whigs seem to have been painted as and when they came into prominence, such as James Otis in 1758, John Hancock in 1765, and Samuel Adams in 1770–72.

Residence. Boston had a slightly above-average percentage of Whigs (53%), and more of them were radical than the average. But two thirds of the sitters from South Boston, an Anglican center among Copley's sitters, were Tories. Sitters from New Hampshire (Portsmouth), New York, and Nova Scotia, also Anglican centers, strongly tended toward Toryism.

Occupation. Government officials are, not unexpectedly, predominantly Tories, but otherwise the political division in various occupational groups is surprisingly close to the average, with only a slight tendency of professional and craft sitters to be Whigs, and businessmen and

[4] Political affiliations had to be gauged approximately. The political distinction between Tories and Whigs is obviously less clear during the early part of Copley's career than during the years immediately prior to the revolution. Before 1765 Tories are those who tended to favor hard money and to support the governor, while Whigs favored inflated paper money and tended to back the House of

Representatives against the governor, his council, and the customs officials. High Tories, as opposed to moderate Tories, were those who held high appointive office prior to the revolution, became refugees, or were connected with such people by marriage or business ties. Radical Whigs, as opposed to moderate Whigs, were active politically and tended to attain high office after 1776.

131

landed gentry to be Tories. Landowners were strongly Tory; lawyers were strongly Whig.

Education. There is little apparent relation between education and political position, but Harvard sitters tended slightly to be Whigs, and noncollege graduates tended to be slightly more Tory than average.

Church. Among sitters for whom both political and church affiliation are known:

	Tory	*Whig*
Anglican	87%	13%
Congregational	40%	60%

or considered another way:

	Anglican	*Congregational*
Tory	53%	47%
Whig	16%	84%

Anglicans tended to be Tories, and vice versa; Congregationalists tended to be Whigs, and vice versa. Although there were a considerable number of Congregational Tories among Copley's sitters, Anglican Whigs were rare (Joseph Barrell, Samuel Fayerweather, William Turner and Samuel Verplanck). Copley's sitters who attended Brattle Church (Congregational) were 78% Whig and 22% Tory. The statistics for husbands and fathers of dependent sitters show approximately the same results as above.

MARITAL STATUS

All sitters (240):
Married	75%
Single	18%
Widow(er)	7%

There is ample evidence that colonial Americans, at least on certain social and economic levels, had portraits painted at the time of marriage to celebrate the union. Among Copley's American sitters, approximately 10% seem to have been painted in the same year as their marriage, and 20% were painted in the same general period.

Among sitters for whom both the date of portrait and the date of marriage are specifically known, those painted in the year of marriage are:

Mr. and Mrs. Jonathan Belcher, 1756; Ann Tyng, 1756; Mrs. Thomas Marshall, 1757; Mrs. Daniel Sargent, 1763; Hannah Loring, 1763; Mrs. Edward Watts, 1765; Martin Howard, 1767; and John Wentworth, 1769.

Those painted in the year after marriage are:

Mrs. Benjamin Pickman, 1763; John Spooner, 1763; Mrs. Gregory Townsend, 1765; and Mr. and Mrs. Joseph Greene, 1767.

Those probably painted in or near the year of marriage are:

George Green, Mr. and Mrs. Thaddeus Burr, William Brattle, Mrs. Joseph Barrell [B], Mr. and Mrs. John S. Copley, Sylvester Gardiner, Mrs. Moses Gill [B], Mr. and Mrs. Joshua Henshaw II, Mr. and Mrs. Joseph Hooper,

Mr. and Mrs. Robert Hooper, Ralph Inman, Mr. and Mrs. Woodbury Langdon, Mr. and Mrs. Henry Marchant, Thomas Marshall, Mr. and Mrs. John Murray, John Ogilvie, Mrs. Samuel Alleyne Otis, Mrs. Samuel Quincy, Mrs. John Stevens, Deborah Scollay, Mrs. John Temple, and Joseph Warren.

The miniatures of Mr. and Mrs. Samuel Cary although clearly a pair, seem to have been painted before their marriage, presumably for the separated lovers. Mr. and Mrs. Jeremiah Lee were painted in 1769, which was their twenty-fifth wedding anniversary and perhaps the occasion for the portraits.

Period. During his early years Copley tended to paint more unmarried sitters, apparently reflecting the fact that he painted an above-average number of children and adolescents before 1762, especially the daughters of Tory fathers. In 1762–64 Copley painted an extremely high percentage of married women. He painted very few widows or widowers before 1765.

Occupation. All of Copley's widowed or widowered sitters came from the business–gentry level; there were no widows or widowers from the professional and craft or small retail groups.

Politics. A seemingly inexplicable, certainly exotic, and probably meaningless statistic is that an above-average proportion of the radical Whig sitters were married (89%).

OFFICE

Sitters holding office when painted (56):
Appointive office	75%
Provincial elective office	11%
Town elective office	14%

Among the officeholders who sat for Copley, the largest categories were members of the Governor's Council (appointive) and justices of the peace (appointive).

Period. The percentage of officials among all sitters was below the average during 1762–67, and the percentage of appointive officials was especially low in 1762–64. The majority of the justices of the peace were painted in 1768–70, and none of them sat to Copley before 1762.

Residence. Only a few officeholders came from outside the colony of Massachusetts, and these tended to be high appointed officials. All but one of the provincial elected officials were from Massachusetts, and virtually all elected town officials were Bostonians. Thus high officials came from afar to be painted by Copley, but not the lower provincial and town elected officials.

Occupation. A large proportion of the councillors, justices of the peace, justices of the Superior Court, and representatives of the House were merchants. Indeed being a successful merchant seems to have been a qualification for high appointive office.

Education. Officeholders were no better or worse educated than all of Copley's sitters, except that the justices of the Superior and Inferior Courts were all Harvard graduates, while a below-average proportion of the justices of the peace held college degrees.

Church. The high appointed officials tended to be Anglicans, but on a lower level of appointive office all of the justices of the peace for whom a religious affiliation is known were Congregationalists, except for Ralph Inman. Other than the Pennsylvania Quaker representative Thomas Mifflin, all town and provincial elective officeholders were Congregationalists.

Politics. The high appointed officials tended to be Tories, and high Tories at that. Among the sitters holding the offices of governor, chief justice, councillor, and justice of the Superior Court, 16 out of 17 were Tory, mostly high Tory (10). The one designated as a Whig, William Brattle, was painted very early, was quite moderate, and later became a Tory. If the list of high appointive officers is extended to include collectors and surveyors of customs and provincial secretaries, the Tory total is 22 out of 24, again mostly high Tory (16). But among the lower appointive positions, such as sheriff, clerk of the Superior Court, recorder of deeds, and justice of the peace, the pattern is reversed. Almost two thirds of the justices of the peace (64%) were Whigs. The lower appointive offices seem to have been political plums given to rising Whigs in an attempt, not entirely successful, to keep them content and malleable to the wishes of the ruling Tory oligarchy. If one compares the two largest groups of officials who sat to Copley, members of the Governor's Council and justices of the peace, the disparity between high and low appointive officeholders is illuminated. Council members were Tories (92%), included the average number of Anglicans and Congregationalists, had a very high income level, tended to be painted either on a very small scale, especially oil-on-copper miniatures, or on very large full-length canvases over 50″ x 40″, and tended not to be painted in pairs with their wives (15%), thus appearing more in an official rather than family role, even though an above-average percentage of the officials were married men. In contrast, justices of the peace were Whigs (64%), Congregationalists (91%), had only medium incomes, strongly preferred 50″ x 40″ canvases (64%), and were frequently painted in pairs with their wives (64%). In general the Tories held an above-average number of the appointive offices, especially the higher ones, and the Whigs held an above-average number of the elective positions. Of provincial elected officials, 5 out of 6 were radical Whigs, the exception being James Murray, a moderate Tory who was also one of the handful of Anglicans in Massachusetts outside Boston who sat to Copley. Copley painted remarkably few of the leaders of the British official and military establishment in America. Perhaps it was because these people thought of portraiture in terms of London, and could not conceive of being painted by a provincial portraitist, no matter what his skill. The crown officials that Copley did paint tended to be American loyalists rather than appointees sent over from England.

AGE

All sitters (240):

0–9	3%	50–59	15%
10–19	6%	60–69	9%
20–29	28%	70–79	3%
30–39	19%	over 80	1%
40–49	16%		

Period. Copley tended to have a younger clientele during the earlier part of his career and older sitters during his last years in the colonies. This reflects the fact that he painted a high proportion of women during the early years, and there was a marked preference on the part of female sitters to be painted young.

Sex. Half of the females were painted before they were thirty as opposed to one fifth of the men, and a decisively higher percentage of women (65%) than men (42%) were painted before the age of forty. Although less than half of all sitters were females, over two thirds of the sitters under thirty were females (68%).

Residence. Sitters from outside Massachusetts tended to be younger, with a decidedly low percentage over fifty, reflecting the large percentage of Copley's sitters from such provincial capitals as New York, Portsmouth, and Halifax and drawn from the ruling Tory-Anglican aristocracy, who tended to be painted young and to order children's portraits (see *Church* below).

Church. There was a slight but clear tendency for Anglican sitters to be painted younger and Congregational sitters to be painted older in life, with the percentage of Congregationalists increasing in each age group. The unusually high percentage of children and unmarried daughters from Anglican-Tory families indicates an inclination in that group to have family portraits of children, which is not found among Congregational-Whig families.

INCOME [5]

All sitters (240):

Low	8%
Medium	39%
High	31%
Very high	22%

With over half of the sitters ranked as high or very high in income, and only 8% ranked low, it may be judged that portraiture was indulged in by people of means, and that Copley's clientele was relatively well-to-do.

Period. Copley tended to paint wealthier clients as the years passed. About 90% of the very-high-income sitters were painted after 1765. This was accompanied, it should be recalled, by a steady rise in his scale of prices.

Residence. Just under two thirds of the very-high-income sitters came from Boston, but otherwise Boston was fairly close to the general distribution and surprisingly homogenous within the city, although there tended to be fewer low-income sitters in South and West Boston and more in North Boston, the latter because of the professional sitters, particularly ministers, in that area. Salem and Gloucester tended to be somewhat above average in income, and Charlestown and Cambridge (where several teachers lived) somewhat below average.

Occupation. Merchants, physicians, and some officials appear to have had fairly high incomes; other officials, lawyers, landowners, and craft and retail people were in the middle-income areas. The medium-income group contained about three times as many professional and craft sitters as the average, and a low percentage of the big-business sitters. The low-income group largely consisted of professionals, particularly ministers and teachers. Low-income craftsmen, retailers, laborers, farmers, etc., are not found among Copley's sitters. All of the ministers and teachers were college graduates, and presumably the low-income professional group enjoyed fairly high prestige.

Education. Since the low-income professionals were all college-educated, Harvard graduates as a group included more low-income sitters

[5] Because it is not possible to gauge the income of Copley's sitters with any precision, the division here is only a rough one. Estimates were based on the following guidelines: low, estimated gross annual income in local currency under £100; medium, £100–£500; high, £500–£1000; very high, over £1000. Obviously only a limited amount of evidence is available (official salaries, wills, tax records, landholdings, etc.), and the income statistics must be considered more as informed guess than fact. In the opinion of most historians, the overwhelming majority of colonial Americans rarely earned more than £100 a year, so that Copley's patrons by no means represent an average sample of the people of his day. It might be noted, too, that annual income then was not ordinarily used as an index of wealth.

To most colonists, property was wealth, and in urban maritime centers the volume and variety of a person's business indicated his financial status and, therefore, his credit. The colonists did most of their business on credit, involving complex manipulations of commodity prices, personal notes of hand, time payments, compound interest, public bills of credit, and very little cash. Thus the annual income of even the richest merchant was usually tied up in unpaid debts owed either to or by him. As a result, it is impossible for us today to gauge finances then with absolute accuracy. Of all the alternatives to indicate the financial status of Copley's clientele, the four groupings used appear to be the least arbitrary, the most accurate in the circumstances, and the closest to the system used by Copley's clients themselves.

than the average. Slightly more of the noncollege sitters had higher (but not very high) incomes than expected from a random distribution.

Church. Religion does not appear to have had any correlation with income level.

Politics. Among Copley's sitters a clear relation appears to have existed between income and political position; the higher the income, the more the inclination to be loyalist (and to favor the status quo), and vice versa. Over three quarters of the very-high-income group were Tories whereas almost two thirds of sitters with medium incomes were Whigs. The largest political group among very-high-income sitters was high Tory; the largest group among high-income sitters was moderate Tory; and most medium-income sitters were Whigs. But the low-income group was quite evenly divided, presumably because of its professional makeup.

Office. Four out of five appointive officials had high or very high incomes. Over half of the councillors, two out of three surveyors of customs, both provincial secretaries, and the one governor painted by Copley were in the very-high-income group. Among elective officials, half were in the upper two income groups and half in the medium-income group. The latter may be considered for all intents and purposes to be the low-income group among Copley's officeholders, since the handful of sitters classified as low-income were a special college-trained professional group of ministers and teachers who held no offices. The medium-income group was not strong politically.

Age. A disproportionately high percentage of the sitters in the medium-income group (60%) were in their twenties or thirties and at an early stage in their careers. The character of the lower-income half of Copley's sitters is colored by its disproportionately high percentage of professional sitters and of young people. So in terms of prestige and social position the lower-income sitters were a higher-ranking group than income alone would suggest.

PAIRS

Almost half (45%) of Copley's portrait business was in paired pictures. Of the married sitters, 58% were painted in pairs.

Period. Copley painted a high percentage of paired portraits in 1768–70 (62%), but he did a below-average number of pairs (17%) during and after his New York trip, 1771–74.

Occupation. A high percentage of housewives were of course painted in pairs. No Congregational ministers sat for pairs, and in general ministers tended to avoid them, being represented pictorially in terms of a professional rather than a family context. One of the exceptions, Alexander MacWhorter, was painted when he did not have a church and, with his wife, was visiting relatives in Boston. The other exception was Arthur Browne, an Anglican, whose wife and daughter were also painted. Craft and small-retail sitters favored pairs.

Education. Harvard graduates ordered considerably fewer pairs than average.

Church, Politics. There is no apparent relationship between church affiliation or politics and an inclination to be painted in pairs.

Office. The high appointive officials, such as members of the Council, tended not to be painted in pairs, perhaps because, like ministers, they were painted in official rather than familial roles. On the other hand, lower appointive officials, such as justices of the peace or surveyors and collectors of customs, did, like elective officials, order an above-average number of pairs. Perhaps since they largely represented the Whig faction, they were presented more as successful husbands and fathers rather than as part of the ruling officialdom.

Income. Pairs were slightly out of favor with the lowest and highest income groups, presumably because the former contained a number of professional subjects and the latter contained much of the political power elite.

Medium. Pastels were slightly in favor and oil-on-copper miniatures out of favor for paired portraits.

Size. The 50″ x 40″ canvases were used more often and 30″ x 25″ canvases less often for pairs than the average.

MEDIUM

All portraits (240):		Miniature (oil on copper)	4½%
Oil on canvas	80%	Miniature (watercolor on ivory)	1¼%
Pastel	14%	Mezzotint	¼%

Period. Copley painted over three quarters of the pastels in 1765–70. Most of the oil-on-copper miniatures were painted in 1758–61, with a second period of revived interest in 1765–70.

Sex. Very few women were painted in oil-on-copper miniatures, and no children are currently known to have been painted in pastels or miniatures.

Residence. Most pastel sitters (80%) came from Boston, and all of the rest came from Massachusetts except Governor John Wentworth of New Hampshire.

Church. Although there is virtually no relation between religion and choice of medium, a large number of pastels were ordered by members of Brattle Square Church (Congregational) and King's Chapel (Anglican). Almost a third of the Brattle sitters and a quarter of the King's sitters ordered pastels. The quarter of Copley's sitters of known religious affiliation who attended these two churches sat for over half of his pastels. Brattle was a fairly high church, though Congregational, and King's became Unitarian after the revolution, so the two churches were not too far apart in doctrine. They both seem to have been fashionable churches, and the taste for pastels and miniatures also seems to have been fashionable.

Education, Politics, Office. These factors do not seem to have been causally related to choice of medium, but it can be noted that the few sitters painted in oil-on-copper miniatures included a relatively high proportion of Tories, appointed officials, and Harvard graduates.

Age. Pastels were clearly favored by young sitters. Although only 28% of Copley's sitters were in their twenties, 45% of the sitters who sat for pastels were in their twenties. Less than half of Copley's sitters were between twenty and forty, but 69% percent of the pastels represent sitters in that age bracket.

Income. Little apparent relationship between income and medium is evident, except for a tendency for pastels and oil-on-copper miniatures to have been favored by wealthier sitters and not by low-income sitters, despite the fact that they were less costly than larger portraits.

SIZE

All portraits (240):

50″ x 40″	50%
Under 30″ x 25″	25%
30″ x 25″	15%
36″ x 28″	7%
Over 50″ x 40″	3%[6]

Period. The 50″ x 40″ canvases were particularly popular in 1762–64, and two thirds of the 30″ x 25″ canvases were painted after 1768.

Residence. Boston sitters ordered about 10% fewer 50″ x 40″ portraits and 10% more 30″ x 25″ portraits than the average. Conversely, sitters from elsewhere in Massachusetts overwhelmingly favored the 50″ x 40″ size, with only Rev. Edward Bernard currently known to have sat for a 30″ x 25″ portrait. In Boston there was a general tendency toward 50″ x 40″ canvases in Central Boston, toward pastels and miniatures under 30″ x 25″ in South Boston, and decidedly toward 30″ x 25″ canvases in North Boston, where only Mr. and Mrs. Ezekiel Goldthwait had large portraits.

Occupation. Merchants monopolized the full-length portraits, and along with shippers and landowners slightly favored 50″ x 40″ canvases over 30″ x 25″. On the other hand, ministers clearly preferred 30″ x 25″ portraits. Only two ministers were painted on 50″ x 40″ canvases, Thomas Cary (Congregational) and John Ogilvie (Anglican), both in the 1770's. In fact the entire professional group was somewhat inclined toward 30″ x 25″ portraits. Craft and small-retail sitters favored pictures measuring 36″ x 28″ and under 30″ x 25″.

Education. Although Harvard graduates slightly preferred pastels and miniatures, and noncollege graduates slightly favored large-size canvases, factors other than educational background appear to be responsible for this.

Church. There seems to be no general correlation between church affiliation and picture size. Three quarters of the portraits of members of Old South Church are under 30″ x 25″ because of the presence of the Olivers in the congregation (the family favored oil-on-copper miniatures and small oils). Dorothy Murray was the only Anglican painted on a 36″ x 28″ canvas, but the sample is too small to indicate any antipathy among Anglicans toward that size.

[6] Of the canvases over 50″ x 40″, half were full-length portraits (Thomas Hancock, Nathaniel Sparhawk, Mr. and Mrs. Jeremiah Lee), and the remainder were early childrens' group portraits (Gore, Royall) or late double portraits of adults (Mifflin, Winslow). Most of the pictures under 30″ x 25″ were pastels and miniatures. The rest were all oil on canvas.

Politics. No correlation between political position and picture size is discernible.

Office. The appointive officeholders ordered an above-average share of very large canvases and oil-on-copper miniatures. Three of the large canvas subjects were councillors (Nathaniel Sparhawk, Thomas Hancock, Isaac Winslow), and one was a justice of the peace (Jeremiah Lee). All of the provincial elective officials ordered portraits of the 50" x 40" or larger size.

Income. The very wealthy sitters ordered most of the very large canvases over 50" x 40", and they tended to order fewer 36" x 28" and 30" x 25" canvases than average.

SECOND PORTRAIT BY COPLEY

Slightly over 10% of Copley's sitters were painted by him more than once.

Residence, Church. Most of the repeat customers came from Boston (80%), were Congregationalists (87½%), and more than half attended Brattle Square Church.

Income. Most second portraits (70%) were ordered by sitters with high or very high incomes.

Genealogical Charts and Tables

In view of the limited society for which Copley painted, it is not surprising to find that many of his customers were related to one another. Over 80% of the sitters included in the statistical analysis appear on at least one of the 28 genealogical charts, developed and prepared by Gerard B. Warden, which are presented here. These charts display the pattern of family linkages, and the accompanying data tables suggest the character of different family groups. These are not full genealogical charts, but were simply constructed to clarify complicated relationships. Although the specific family groups are somewhat arbitrarily defined, footnotes guide the reader to connecting charts so that the continuum of related sitters can be followed. A guide to the charts is also provided.

In the charts the names of Copley's sitters are encased in boxes; for the married women, maiden names appear first in the box. Perforated boxes indicate that the person may also have been painted by Copley in America or England, but is not included in the statistical analysis. For general interest a chart has been inserted for the Copley family, without an accompanying table.

Guide to Sitters in Genealogical Charts

Adams, Samuel: *Adams*
Allen, James: *Allen (A); Waldo*
Allen, Nathaniel: *Allen (B); Hancock; Sargent*
Allen, Mrs. Nathaniel: *Allen (B); Hancock; Sargent*
Amory, John: *Amory; Greene*
Amory, Mrs. John: *Amory; Greene*
Amory II, Thomas: *Amory*
Amory II, Mrs. Thomas: *Amory*
Appleton, Nathaniel: *Rogers*
Appleton, Mrs. Nathaniel: *Rogers*
Apthorp, Mrs. John: *Greenleaf*
Atkinson, Theodore: *Greenleaf; Wentworth*
Atkinson, Mrs. Theodore: *Greenleaf; Wentworth*
Austin, Mrs. Ebenezer: *Adams*

Babcock, Adam: *Fayerweather*
Babcock, Mrs. Adam: *Fayerweather*
Barnard, Edward: *Russell*
Barrell, Joseph: *Green*
Barrell (A), Mrs. Joseph: *Green*
Barrell (B), Mrs. Joseph: *Green*
Barrett, John: *Clarke; Hancock*
Barrett, Mrs. John: *Clarke; Hancock*
Belcher, Jonathan: *Allen (A); Oliver; Waldo*
Belcher, Mrs. Jonathan: *Allen (A); Oliver; Waldo*

Blake, Joseph: *Gray*
Bourne, Mrs. Sylvanus: *Gray*
Bours, John: *Fayerweather*
Bowler, Mrs. Metcalf: *Fayerweather*
Boylston, Nicholas: *Adams*
Boylston, Rebecca: *Adams*
Boylston, Mrs. Thomas: *Adams*
Boylston II, Thomas: *Adams*
Brattle, William: *Allen (A); Green; Hancock*
Brown, Mrs. Gawen: *Oliver*
Byles, Mather: *Oliver*

Cary, Samuel: *Gray; Russell*
Cary, Mrs. Samuel: *Gray; Russell*
Cary, Thomas: *Russell*
Chardon, Peter: *Royall*
Coffin, Thomas Aston: *Amory*
Coffin, Mrs. William: *Amory*
Cooper, Samuel: *Royall*
Copley, John S.: *Clarke; Copley; Greene; Murray*
Copley, Mrs. John S.: *Clarke; Copley; Greene; Murray*
Cumming, Mrs. Alexander: *Hancock*

Danforth, Samuel: *Allen (A)*

139

Davis, Mrs. Benjamin: *Greenleaf*
Devereux, Mrs. Humphry: *Adams*

Ellery, Mrs. Nathaniel: *Sargent*
Eppes, Mrs. William: *Gardiner*
Erving, John: *Erving; Waldo*

Flucker, Thomas: *Waldo; Winslow*
Fowle, Jacob: *Hooper*

Gardiner, Ann: *Gardiner*
Gardiner, Sylvester: *Gardiner*
Gerrish, Benjamin: *Hancock*
Gerrish, Joseph: *Hancock*
Gill, Moses: *Adams*
Gill (B), Mrs. Moses: *Adams*
Goldthwait, Ezekiel: *Hancock*
Goldthwait, Mrs. Ezekiel: *Hancock*
Gray, Harrison: *Gray*
Gray, John: *Gray*
Gray, Mrs. John: *Gray*
Green, Mrs. Edward: *Green; Storer*
Green, George: *Green*
Green (B), Joseph: *Green*
Greene, John: *Greene*
Greene, Mrs. John: *Greene*
Greene, Joseph: *Greene*
Greene, Mrs. Joseph: *Greene*
Greene, Rufus: *Amory; Greene*
Greene, Mrs. Rufus: *Amory; Greene*
Greene, Thomas: *Allen (B); Greene*
Greene, Mrs. Thomas: *Allen (B); Greene*

Hall, Hugh: *Winslow*
Hallowell, Benjamin: *Adams*
Hallowell, Mrs. Benjamin: *Adams*
Hancock, John: *Hancock; Quincy*
Hancock, Thomas: *Hancock*
Hancock, Mrs. Thomas: *Hancock*
Henley, Mrs. Samuel: *Russell*
Henshaw, Joseph: *Henshaw*
Henshaw, Mrs. Joseph: *Henshaw*
Henshaw, Joshua: *Henshaw*
Henshaw II, Joshua: *Henshaw*
Henshaw II, Mrs. Joshua: *Henshaw*
Hill, Henry: *Clarke; Hancock*
Hill, Mrs. Henry: *Clarke*
Holmes, John Bee: *Amory*
Holyoke, Edward: *Rogers*
Hooper, Alice: *Hooper*
Hooper, Joseph: *Hooper*
Hooper, Mrs. Joseph: *Hooper*
Hooper, Robert: *Hooper*
Hooper, Mrs. Robert: *Hooper*
Hooper II, Robert: *Hooper*
Howard, Martin: *Greenleaf*
Hubbard, Daniel: *Greene*
Hubbard, Mrs. Daniel: *Greene*
Hubbard, Thankful: *Jackson*
Hubbard, Thomas: *Jackson; Wentworth*
Hurd, Nathaniel: *Hancock*

Inman, Ralph: *Murray*

Jackson, Jonathan: *Jackson; Quincy*
Jackson, Sarah: *Gray*

Langdon, Woodbury: *Amory; Storer; Wentworth*
Langdon, Mrs. Woodbury: *Amory; Storer; Wentworth*
Lee, Jeremiah: *Hooper*
Lee, Mrs. Jeremiah: *Hooper*
Lewis, Thomas: *Hooper*
Loring, Hannah: *Winslow*
Lynde, Lydia: *Oliver*

McEvers, Mrs. Charles: *Greenleaf*
MacWhorter, Alexander: *Hancock*
MacWhorter, Mrs. Alexander: *Hancock*
Marshall, Thomas: *Allen (B)*
Marshall, Mrs. Thomas: *Allen (B)*
Murray, Dorothy: *Murray*
Murray, James: *Murray*
Murray, John: *Allen (B)*
Murray, Mrs. John: *Allen (B)*

Newton, John: *Green*

Oliver, Andrew: *Allen (A); Clarke; Erving; Oliver; Waldo*
Oliver, Mrs. Andrew: *Erving; Oliver; Waldo*
Oliver II, Andrew: *Oliver*
Oliver, Elizabeth: *Oliver*
Oliver, Griselda: *Erving; Oliver; Waldo*
Oliver, Peter: *Clarke; Oliver*
Otis, James: *Gray*
Otis, Mrs. James: *Gray*
Otis, Mrs. Samuel A.: *Gray*

Pelham, Charles: *Clarke; Royall*
Pelham, Henry: *Clarke; Copley*
Perkins, Nathaniel: *Adams*
Pickman, Benjamin: *Gardiner*
Pickman, Mrs. Benjamin: *Gardiner*
Pitts, Elizabeth: *Winslow*
Powell, Mrs. John: *Murray; Rogers*
Powell II, John: *Murray; Rogers*
Powell II, Mrs. John: *Murray; Rogers*

Quincy, Dorothy: *Hancock; Quincy*
Quincy, Josiah: *Green; Hancock; Jackson; Quincy*
Quincy, Samuel: *Quincy*
Quincy, Mrs. Samuel: *Quincy*

Rogers, Mrs. Daniel: *Rogers*
Ross, Elizabeth: *Waldo*
Royall, Isaac: *Erving; Royall*
Royall, Mrs. Isaac: *Erving; Royall*
Royall, Elizabeth and Mary: *Erving; Royall*
Russell, Mrs. James: *Russell*

Sargent, Mrs. Daniel: *Osborne; Sargent*
Sargent, Epes: *Fayerweather; Osborne; Sargent*
Sargent II, Epes: *Osborne; Sargent*

140

Sargent II, Mrs. Epes: *Osborne; Sargent*
Savage, Samuel P.: *Royall*
Savage, Mrs. Samuel P.: *Royall*
Scollay, Deborah: *Greenleaf*
Scollay, John: *Greenleaf*
Scollay, Mrs. John: *Greenleaf*
Scott, George: *Erving*
Sherburne, Joseph: *Wentworth*
Skinner, Mrs. Richard: *Quincy*
Smith, Isaac: *Adams; Quincy; Storer*
Smith, Mrs. Isaac: *Adams; Quincy; Storer*
Smith, Mrs. James: *Murray*
Sparhawk, Nathaniel: *Royall*
Spooner, John: *Oliver*
Stevens, Mrs. John: *Allen (B); Sargent*
Stevens, Mrs. William: *Allen (B)*
Stewart, Duncan: *Erving*
Stewart, Mrs. Duncan: *Erving*
Storer, Ebenezer: *Storer*
Storer, Mrs. Ebenezer: *Storer*
Storer II, Ebenezer: *Green; Quincy; Storer*
Storer II, Mrs. Ebenezer: *Green; Storer*

Temple, John: *Erving*
Temple, Mrs. John: *Erving*
Townsend, Gregory: *Jackson*
Townsend, Mrs. Gregory: *Jackson*

Turner, William: *Osborne; Sargent*
Turner, Mrs. William: *Osborne; Sargent*
Tyler, Mrs. Andrew: *Clarke; Royall*
Tyng, Ann: *Waldo*
Tyng, Eleazer: *Waldo*

Verplanck, Daniel: *Greenleaf*
Verplanck, Gulian: *Greenleaf*
Verplanck, Samuel: *Greenleaf*

Waldo, Mrs. Samuel: *Erving; Oliver; Waldo*
Warren, James: *Gray*
Warren, Mrs. James: *Gray*
Watson, George: *Oliver*
Watson, Mrs. George: *Oliver*
Watts, Mrs. Edward: *Osborne*
Watts, Mrs. Samuel: *Osborne*
Welsteed, William: *Oliver*
Wentworth, Elizabeth: *Wentworth*
Wentworth, John: *Greenleaf; Wentworth*
Winslow, Isaac: *Clarke; Erving; Oliver; Waldo; Winslow*
Winslow, Joshua: *Green*
Winthrop, John: *Fayerweather; Waldo*
Winthrop, Mrs. John: *Fayerweather; Waldo*
Winthrop, Samuel: *Fayerweather*

ADAMS (14)

Period[1]:

1753–57: —

1758–61: —

1762–64: Moses Gill (1764)
Mrs. Moses Gill

1765–67: Mrs. Thomas Boylston (1766)
Nicholas Boylston (1767)
Rebecca Boylston (1767)
Mrs. Ebenezer Austin
Thomas Boylston II
Benjamin Hallowell
Mrs. Benjamin Hallowell

1768–70: Isaac Smith (1769)
Mrs. Isaac Smith (1769)

1771–74: Mrs. Humphrey Devereux (1771)
Samuel Adams
Nathaniel Perkins

Sex: men (7), women (7).

Residence[2]: Boston (12), Charlestown (1), Marblehead (1).

Occupation: merchant (3), official (2), doctor (1), brazier (1).

Education: Harvard (2).

Church: Congregational (12).

Politics: high Tory (2), moderate Tory (1), moderate Whig (2), radical Whig (2).

Marital status: single (4), married (8), widowed (2).

Office: surveyor of customs (1); justice of the peace (1); clerk, House of Representatives (1); town office (2).

Income: very high (3), high (2), medium (2).

Medium: oil on canvas (14).

Size: 50″ x 40″ (11), 36″ x 28″ (1), 30″ x 25″ (1), other (1).

Comment: A stable, older group of Boston Congregationalists, painted predominantly between 1765 and 1767.

---

[1] As in the other appendices, Copley's artistic career has been divided into six periods for convenience of reference.

[2] Towns are in Massachusetts unless otherwise specified.

ADAMS

Mary Charnock,
Mrs. H. Devereux
m.
Humphrey
Devereux

Joseph
Prince

Thomas
Prince

Sarah Prince,
Mrs. M. Gill

Mrs. J. Gill

Moses
Gill
m. 1759

Elizabeth Storer,
Mrs. I. Smith [3]

Rebecca
Boylston,
Mrs. M. Gill
m. 1773

Isaac
Smith
m. 1746

Thomas
Boylston

Sarah Morecock,
Mrs. T. Boylston
m.

Lucy
Boylston
m. 1745
Timothy [1]
Rogers

Mary Smith,
Mrs. E. Austin

William
Smith
m.

Elizabeth [2]
Quincy
m.

William
Smith

Sarah
Boylston

Peter
Boylston

Susannah
Boylston
m.

Abigail
Smith
m.

Abigail
Adams
m.
W. S. Smith

J. Q. Adams

Nicholas
Boylston

Thomas
Boylston

John
Adams

John
Adams

P. B. Adams

Mary Boylston,
Mrs. B. Hallowell
m. 1746

Benjamin
Hallowell

Samuel
Adams

Samuel
Adams

Samuel
Checkley

Elizabeth
Checkley *m.* 1749

Mary
Checkley

John
Perkins *m.*

Nathaniel
Perkins

1. See Rogers.   2. See Quincy.   3. See Storer.

ALLEN A (6)

Period:

1753–57: Jonathan Belcher (1756)
Mrs. Jonathan Belcher (1756)
William Brattle

1758–61: Samuel Danforth
Andrew Oliver

1762–64: —

1765–67: —

1768–70: James Allen

1771–74: —

Sex: men (5), women (1).

Residence: Boston (2), Nova Scotia (2), Cambridge (2).

Occupation: official (2), military (1), merchant (1), gentleman (1).

Education: Harvard (5).

Church: Anglican (2), Congregational (3).

Politics: high Tory (2), moderate Tory (1), moderate Whig (2).

Marital status: single (1), married (4), widowed (1).

Office: Council (3), chief justice (1).

Income: very high (1), high (2), medium (2).

Medium: oil on canvas (4), oil on copper (2).

Size: 50″ x 40″ (3), 30″ x 25″ (1), under 30″ x 25″ (2).

Comment: Unanimously Harvard-educated; high offices.

ALLEN (A)

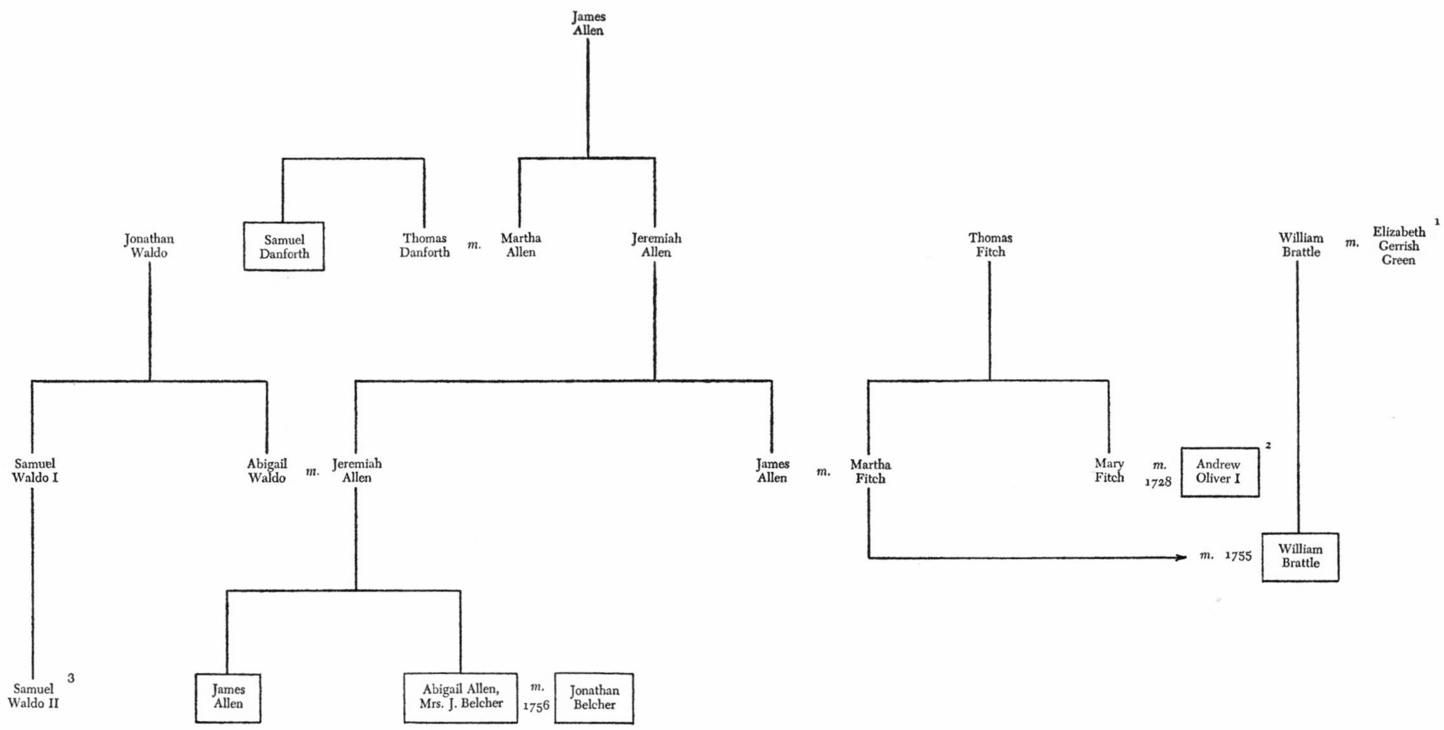

James Allen

Jeremiah Allen   Martha Allen

Thomas Danforth   m.

Samuel Danforth

Jonathan Waldo

Abigail Waldo   m.   Jeremiah Allen

Samuel Waldo I

Samuel Waldo II [3]

James Allen

Abigail Allen, Mrs. J. Belcher   m. 1756   Jonathan Belcher

James Allen   m.

Martha Fitch

Thomas Fitch

Mary Fitch   m. 1728   Andrew Oliver I [2]

William Brattle   m.   Elizabeth Gerrish Green [1]

m. 1755

William Brattle

1. See Green; Hancock.   2. See Oliver.   3. See Waldo.

ALLEN B (10)

Period:

1753–57: Thomas Marshall
Mrs. Thomas Marshall

1758–61: Thomas Greene (1758)
Mrs. Thomas Greene
Mrs. William Stevens

1762–64: Nathaniel Allen (1763)
Mrs. Nathaniel Allen
John Murray
Mrs. John Murray (1763)

1765–67: —

1768–70: —

1771–74: Mrs. John Stevens

Sex: men (4), women (6).

Residence: Boston (4), Gloucester (4), Rutland (2).

Occupation: merchant (1), shipper (1), tanner (1).

Education: —

Church: Anglican (1), Congregational (5).

Politics: high Tory (1), moderate Whig (1), radical Whig (1).

Marital status: married (10).

Office: justice of the peace (1), representative (1).

Income: high (3), medium (1).

Medium: oil on canvas (10).

Size: 50″ x 40″ (10).

Comment: Although there is considerable variety in residence, politics, and age, this family shows unusual homogeneity in medium, size, and the predilection for pairs. The group, early clients of Copley's, ranks low in education, and there is a high correlation of date of paintings with marriage (Marshall, Allen, Murray).

ALLEN (B)

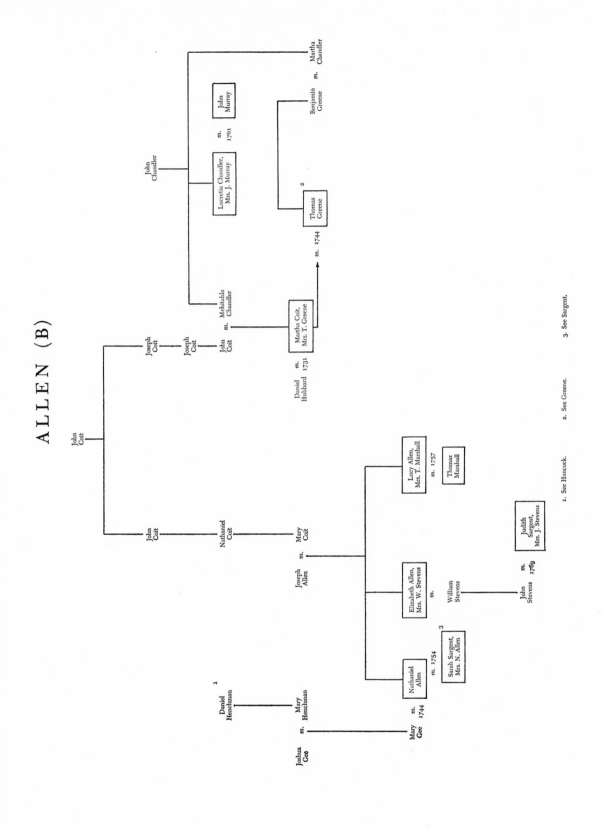

John Coit

Joseph Coit

Joseph Coit

John Coit

John Chandler

Mehitable Chandler

Lucretia Chandler, Mrs. J. Murray

m. 1701

John Murray

Martha Coit, Mrs. T. Greene

Daniel Hubbard   *m.* 1731

m. 1744

Thomas Greene   2

Benjamin Greene

Martha Chandler   *m.*

John Coit

Nathaniel Coit

Mary Coit   *m.*

Joseph Allen

Lucy Allen, Mrs. T. Marshall   *m.* 1757

Thomas Marshall

Elizabeth Allen, Mrs. W. Stevens   *m.*

William Stevens

John Stevens   *m.* 1769

Judith Sargent, Mrs. J. Stevens

Nathaniel Allen   *m.* 1754

Sarah Sargent, Mrs. N. Allen   3

Daniel Henchman   1

Mary Henchman

Joshua Gee   *m.*

Mary Gee   *m.* 1744

1. See Hancock.

2. See Greene.

3. See Sargent.

AMORY (11)

Period:

1753–57: —

1758–61: Thomas Aston Coffin
Rufus Greene
Mrs. Rufus Greene

1762–64: Mrs. John Amory

1765–67: John Bee Holmes (1765)
Woodbury Langdon
Mrs. Woodbury Langdon

1768–70: John Amory (1768)
Mrs. William Coffin

1771–74: Thomas Amory II
Mrs. Thomas Amory II

Sex: men (6), women (5).

Residence: Boston (8), Portsmouth, N.H. (2), Charleston, S.C. (1).

Occupation: merchant (2), distiller (1), metalsmith (1).

Education: Harvard (1).

Church: Anglican (7), Congregational (3).

Politics: high Tory (1), moderate Tory (2).

Marital status: single (2), married (9).

Office: —

Income: very high (2), high (2).

Medium: oil on canvas (11).

Size: 50″ x 40″ (5), 30″ x 25″ (3), under 30″ x 25″ (2),[1] other (1).

Comment: Like the Greenes, a rich, commercial, uneducated, Anglican group, with no officeholders.

[1] Although considered as under 30″ x 25″, the portraits of Mr. and Mrs. Rufus Greene were probably cut down from 50″ x 40″.

AMORY

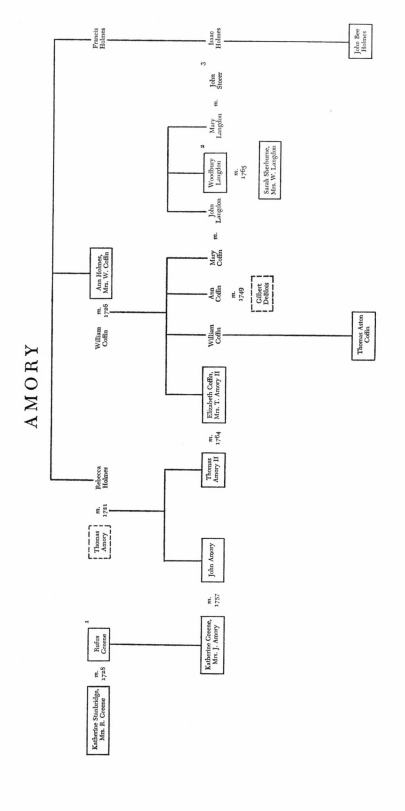

1. See Greene. 2. See Wentworth. 3. See Storer.

CLARKE (12)

Period:

1753–57: Charles Pelham

1758–61: John Barrett
Mrs. John Barrett
Andrew Oliver
Peter Oliver

1762–64: —

1765–67: Henry Pelham (1765)
Mrs. Andrew Tyler

1768–70: John S. Copley
Mrs. John S. Copley
Henry Hill
Mrs. Henry Hill

1771–74: Isaac Winslow (1774) [1]

Sex: men (8), women (4).

Residence: Boston (10), Middleboro (1), Westwood (1).

Occupation: merchant (5), painter (1), distiller (1)

Education: Harvard (4).

Church: Anglican (2), Congregational (8).

Politics: high Tory (3), moderate Tory (2), moderate Whig (1).

Marital status: single (2), married (10).

Office: Council (2); justice, Superior Court (1); town office (1).

Income: very high (2), high (2), medium (3).

Medium: oil on canvas (5), pastel (5), oil on copper (2).

Size: over 50″ x 40″ (1), 50″ x 40″ (2), 36″ x 28″ (1), 30″ x 25″ (1), under 30″ x 25″ (7).

Comment: Group is urban, Congregational, rich, influential; low in female subjects and large pictures.

[1] Counted as a single subject, although a double portrait.

CLARKE

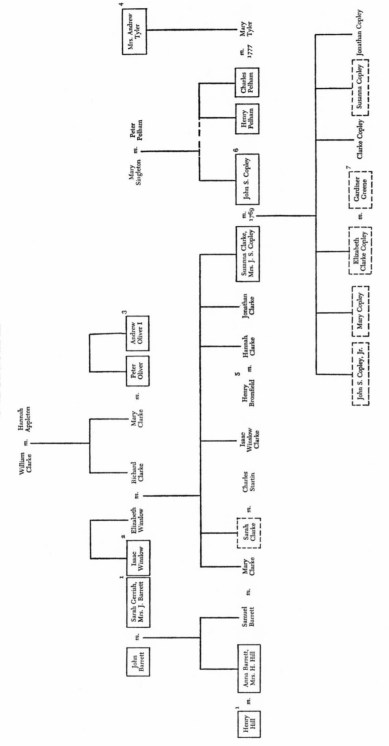

1. See Hancock.   5. See Rogers; Fayerweather.

2. See Winslow.   6. See Copley.

3. See Oliver.   7. See Greene.

4. See Royall.

[Statistical categories were not applied to the Copleys as a family.
The chart on the facing page is included for general interest.]

COPLEY

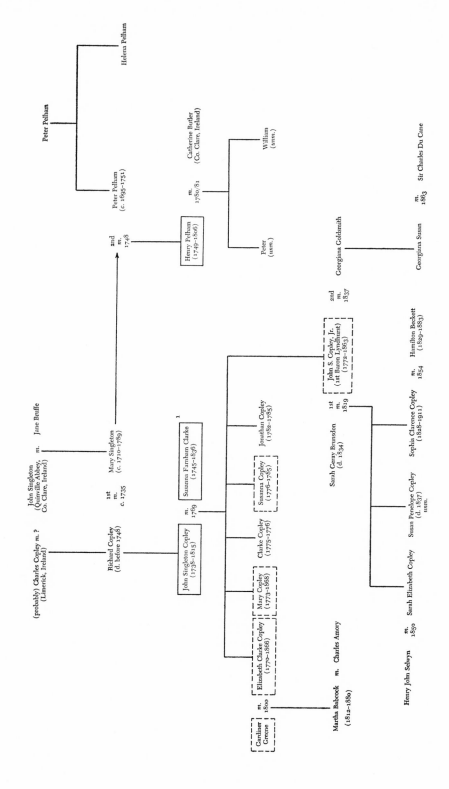

1. See Clarke.

ERVING (14)

Period:	*Sex:* men (7), women (7).
	Residence: Boston (10), Medford (3), Maine (1).
1753–57: George Scott	*Occupation:* merchant (3), military (1), shipper (1), official (2).
1758–61: Andrew Oliver	*Education:* Harvard (2).
Mrs. Andrew Oliver	*Church:* Anglican (7), Congregational (5).
Griselda Oliver	*Politics:* high Tory (4), moderate Tory (2), moderate Whig (1).
Mary and Elizabeth Royall [1]	*Marital status*[2]: single (3), married (9), widowed (1).
1762–64: —	*Office:* Council (4); surveyor of customs (1); collector of customs (1).
1765–67: John Temple (1765)	
Mrs. John Temple	*Income:* very high (5), medium (1).
Duncan Stewart (1767)	*Medium:* oil on canvas (10), pastel (2), oil on copper (2).
Mrs. Duncan Stewart	*Size:* over 50″ x 40″ (2), 50″ x 40″ (7), under 30″ x 25″ (5).
Mrs. Samuel Waldo	*Comment:* Very wealthy and influential Tory group.
1768–70: Isaac Royall (1769)	
Mrs. Isaac Royall (1769)	
1771–74: Isaac Winslow (1774) [1]	
John Erving	

[1] Counted as a single subject, although a double portrait.

[2] George Scott is not included in this category, since the date of his marriage to Abigail Erving is uncertain.

ERVING

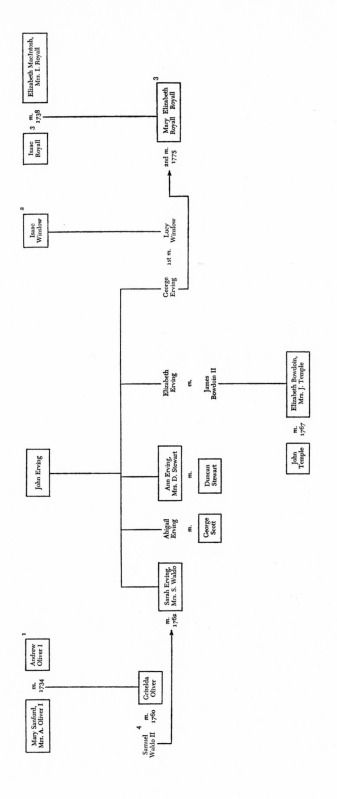

1. See Oliver; Allen (A).   2. See Clarke; Winslow.   3. See Royall.

4. See Waldo.

FAYERWEATHER (10)

Period:

1753-57:   —

1758-61:   John Bours
Rhoda Cranston
Samuel Fayerweather
Epes Sargent

1762-64:   Mrs. Metcalf Bowler

1765-67:   —

1768-70:   —

1771-74:   Mrs. John Winthrop (1773)
Adam Babcock
Mrs. Adam Babcock
John Winthrop
Samuel Winthrop

Sex: men (6), women (4).

Residence: Boston (1), Cambridge (2), Gloucester (1), Newport, R.I. (3), Westerly, R.I. (1), New Haven, Conn. (2).

Occupation: merchant (2), minister (1), teacher (1), official (1).

Education: Harvard (3).

Church: Anglican (4), Congregational (5), Baptist (1).

Politics: moderate Tory (2), moderate Whig (4).

Marital status: single (3), married (7).

Office: clerk, Superior Court (1); judge, Inferior Court (1).

Income: high (1), medium (3), low (2).

Medium: oil on canvas (9), oil on copper (1).

Size: 50″ x 40″ (8), 36″ x 28″ (1), under 30″ x 25″ (1).

Comment: A family largely outside of Boston, politically moderate, with a preponderance of large portraits.

FAYERWEATHER

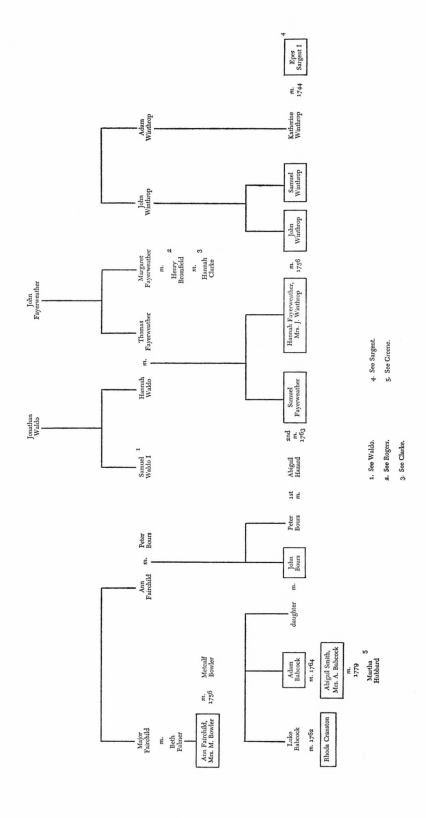

1. See Waldo.
2. See Rogers.
3. See Clarke.
4. See Sargent.
5. See Greene.

GARDINER (5)

Period:

1753–57: Ann Gardiner
1758–61: Benjamin Pickman
1762–64: Mrs. Benjamin Pickman (1763)
1765–67: —
1768–70: Mrs. William Eppes
1771–74: Sylvester Gardiner

Sex: men (2), women (3).

Residence: Boston (2), Salem (3).

Occupation: merchant (1), doctor (1).

Education: Harvard (1).

Church: Anglican (2).

Politics: high tory (2).

Marital Status: single (2), married (2), widowed (1).

Office: —

Income: very high (1), high (1).

Medium: oil on canvas (5).

Size: 50″ x 40″ (5).

Comment: Family is uniform in medium, size, politics, and religion.

GARDINER

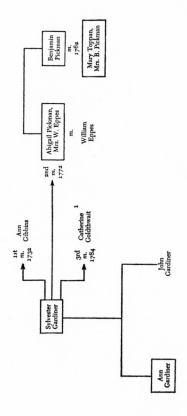

Sylvester Gardiner

1st m. 1732 — Ann Gibbins

2nd m. 1772 — Abigail Pickman, Mrs. W. Eppes — m. — William Eppes

Benjamin Pickman — m. 1762 — Mary Toppan, Mrs. B. Pickman

3rd m. 1784 — Catherine Goldthwait [1]

John Gardiner

Ann Gardiner

1. See Hancock; Sargent.

GRAY (13)

Period:

1753–57: —

1758–61: James Otis
Mrs. James Otis

1762–64: Mrs. John Gray
Mrs. Samuel Otis
James Warren
Mrs. James Warren

1765–67: Sarah Jackson (1765)
Mrs. Sylvanus Bourne (1766)
John Gray (1766)
Joseph Blake
Harrison Gray

1768–70: Samuel Cary [1]
Mrs. Samuel Cary [1]

1771–74: —

Sex: men (6), women (7).

Residence: Boston (6), Cape Cod (3), Plymouth (2), West Indies (2).

Occupation: merchant (2), landowner (2), mason (1), lawyer (1).

Education: Harvard (1).

Church: Congregational (9).

Politics: high Tory (2), moderate Tory (1), moderate Whig (1), radical Whig (2).

Marital status: single (1), married (10), widowed (2).

Office: Council (1), representative (2), town office (1).

Income: very high (1), high (2), medium (3).

Medium: oil on canvas (10), oil on copper (1), watercolor on ivory (2).

Size: 50'' x 40'' (8), 30'' x 25'' (1), under 30'' x 25'' (4).

Comment: A very diversified group, except for religion.

[1] Considered as a married couple, although stylistic evidence suggests that the miniatures were made as a pair before the date of marriage.

GRAY

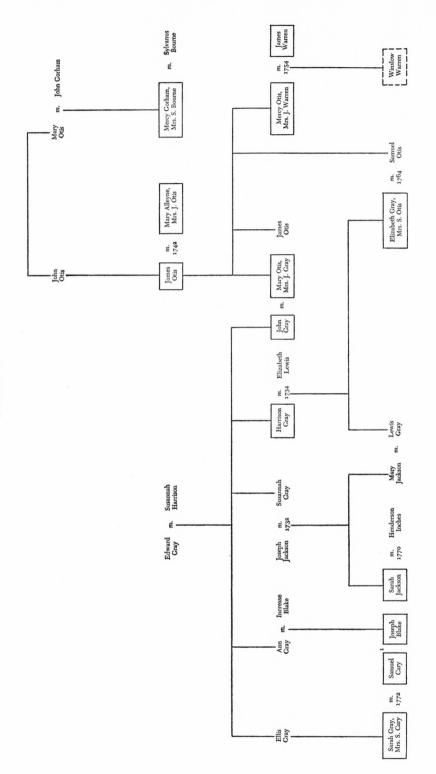

1. See Russell.

GREEN (12)

Period:

1753–57: Joshua Winslow (1755)
William Brattle

1758–61: —

1762–64: Joseph Green (B)

1765–67: Mrs. Edward Green (1765)
Josiah Quincy

1768–70: Joseph Barrell
Mrs. Joseph Barrell (A)
George Green
Ebenezer Storer II
Mrs. Ebenezer Storer II

1771–74: John Newton (1772)
Mrs. Joseph Barrell (B)

Sex: men (8), women (4).

Residence: Boston (8), Cambridge (1), Braintree (1), Marshfield (1), Nova Scotia (1).

Occupation: merchant (5), military (2), landowner (1).

Education: Harvard (3).

Church: Anglican (2), Congregational (7).

Politics: high Tory (2), moderate Tory (1), moderate Whig (3), radical Whig (2).

Marital status: single (1), married (9), widowed (1).

Office: Council (1); surveyor of customs (1); judge, Inferior Court (1); selectman (1).

Income: high (5), medium (3).

Medium: oil on canvas (4), pastel (7), oil on copper (1).

Size: 50″ x 40″ (2), 36″ x 28″ (1), 30″ x 25″ (1), under 30″ x 25″ (8).

Comment: The group has younger sitters ordering smaller pictures, many of them pastels. There are twice as many men as women, and the income level is moderate.

GREEN

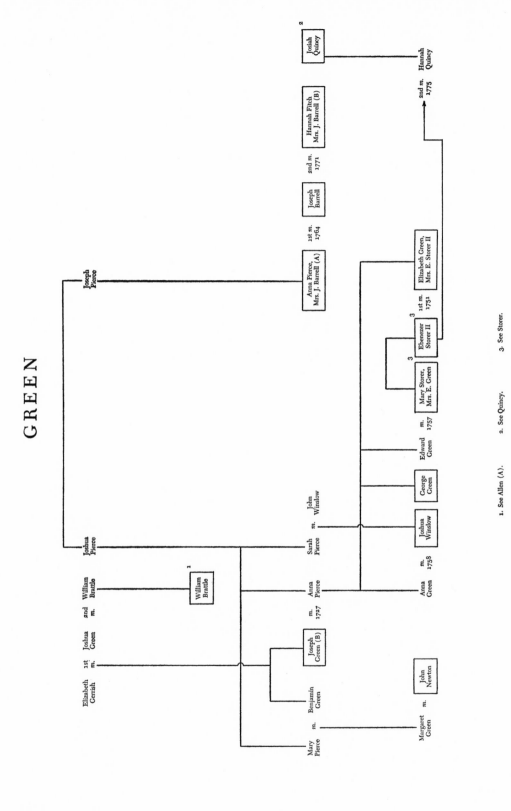

1. See Allen (A).   2. See Quincy.   3. See Storer.

GREENE (14)

Period:

1753–57: —

1758–61: Thomas Greene (1758)
Mrs. Thomas Greene
Rufus Greene
Mrs. Rufus Greene

1762–64: Daniel Hubbard (1764)
Mrs. Daniel Hubbard
Mrs. John Amory

1765–67: Joseph Greene (1767)
Mrs. Joseph Greene (1767)

1768–70: John Amory (1768)
Mrs. John Greene (1769)
John Greene
John S. Copley
Mrs. John S. Copley

1771–74: —

Sex: men (7), women (7).

Residence: Boston (14).

Occupation: merchant (4), painter (1), metalsmith (1).

Education: —

Church: Anglican (12), Congregational (1).

Politics: high Tory (2), moderate Tory (4).

Marital status: married (14).

Office: —

Income: very high (1), high (3), medium (3).

Medium: oil on canvas (10), pastel (4).

Size: 50″ x 40″ (8), under 30″ x 25″ (6).[1]

Comment: As a family group, this one is the most Anglican, the most Tory, the most married, the most paired, and the least educated.

[1] Although considered as under 30″ x 25″, the portraits of **Mr.** and **Mrs. Rufus** Greene were probably cut down from 50″ x 40″.

[164]

GREENE

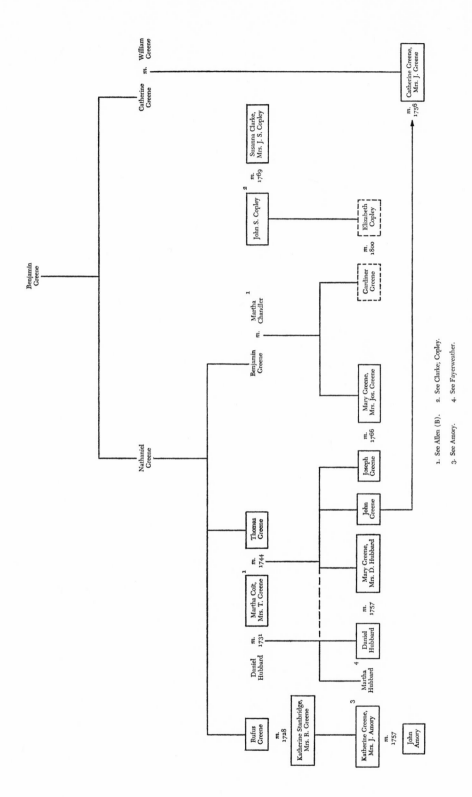

1. See Allen (B).   2. See Clarke; Copley.

3. See Amory.   4. See Fayerweather.

GREENLEAF (12)

Period:

1753–57: —

1758–61: Theodore Atkinson

1762–64: Mrs. John Scollay (1763)
John Scollay
Mrs. John Apthorp
Mrs. Benjamin Davis
Deborah Scollay

1765–67: Mrs. Theodore Atkinson (1765)
Martin Howard (1767)

1768–70: —

1771–74: Mrs. Charles McEvers (1771)
Daniel Verplanck (1771)
Gulian Verplanck (1771)
Samuel Verplanck (1771)

Sex: men (6), women (6).

Residence: Boston (5), New York (4), Portsmouth, N. H. (2), Charleston, S. C. (1).

Occupation: merchant (2), official (1), shopkeeper (1), lawyer (1).

Education: King's (Columbia) (2), Harvard (1).

Church: Anglican (5), Congregational (4).

Politics: high Tory (2), moderate Whig (2).

Marital status: single (4), married (8).

Office: chief justice (1); Council (1); justice of the peace (1).

Income: very high (2), high (2), medium (1).

Medium: oil on canvas (11), watercolor on ivory (1).

Size: 50″ x 40″ (4), 36″ x 28″ (3), 30″ x 25″ (4), under 30″ x 25″ (1).

GREENLEAF

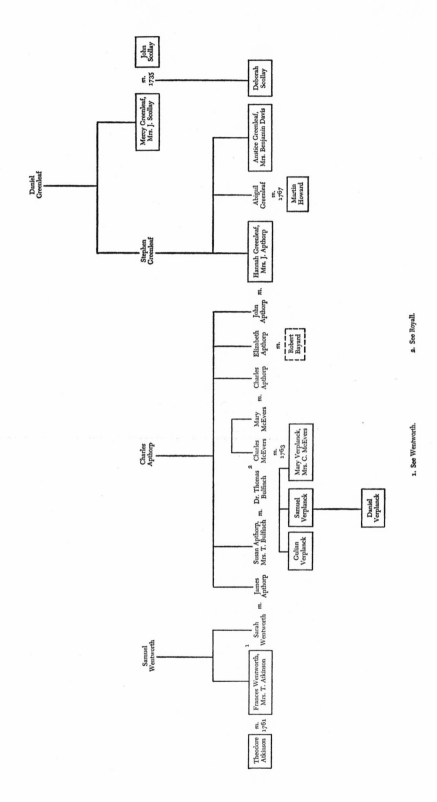

HANCOCK (20)

Period:

1753–57: William Brattle

1758–61: John Barrett
Mrs. John Barrett
Thomas Hancock

1762–64: Nathaniel Allen (1763)
Mrs. Nathaniel Allen

1765–67: John Hancock (1765)
Mrs. Thomas Hancock
Josiah Quincy

1768–70: Alexander MacWhorter (1769)
Mrs. Alexander MacWhorter (1769)
Mrs. Alexander Cumming (1770)
Ezekiel Goldthwait
Mrs. Ezekiel Goldthwait
Henry Hill
Mrs. Henry Hill
Nathaniel Hurd

1771–74: Benjamin Gerrish
Joseph Gerrish [?]
Dorothy Quincy

Sex: men (12), women (8).

Residence: Boston (13), Gloucester (2), Braintree (2), Cambridge (1), Nova Scotia (2).

Occupation: merchant (6), shipper (1), military (1), metalsmith (1), distiller (1), minister (1).

Education: Harvard (3), Princeton (1).

Church: Anglican (1), Congregational (15), Presbyterian (2).

Politics: moderate Tory (3), moderate Whig (5), radical Whig (4).

Marital status: single (3), married (14), widowed (2).

Office: Council (4); judge, Inferior Court (1); recorder of deeds (1); justice of the peace (1); representative (1); town office (2).

Income: very high (2), high (5), medium (5).

Medium: oil on canvas (16), pastel (2), oil on copper (2).

Size: 50″ x 40″ (9), 36″ x 28″ (1), 30″ x 25″ (6), under 30″ x 25″ (4).

Comment: This Boston group is wealthy, influential, Congregational, and Whiggish.

HANCOCK

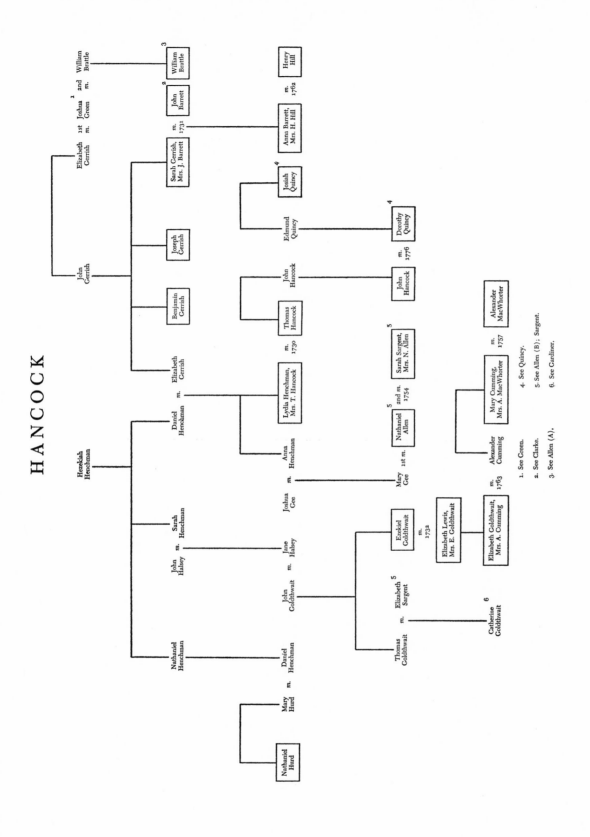

Elizabeth Gerrish m. 1st Joshua Green 2nd m. William Brattle [1] [3]

John Gerrish

Benjamin Gerrish

Joseph Gerrish

Sarah Gerrish, Mrs. J. Barrett m. 1731

John Barrett [2]

Anna Barrett, Mrs. H. Hill m. 1762 Henry Hill

Elizabeth Gerrish

Thomas Hancock m. 1730

John Hancock

Josiah Quincy [4]

Edmund Quincy

John Hancock m. 1776 Dorothy Quincy [4]

Hezekiah Henchman

Nathaniel Henchman

Daniel Henchman

Sarah Henchman

John Halsey m. Jane Halsey

Daniel Henchman m. Lydia Henchman, Mrs. T. Hancock

Anna Henchman

Mary Gee m. Joshua Gee

Nathaniel Allen 2nd m. 1754 Sarah Sargent, Mrs. N. Allen [5] [5]

Mary 1st m. Alexander Cumming Mary Cumming, Mrs. A. MacWhorter m. 1757 Alexander MacWhorter

John Goldthwait

Ezekiel Goldthwait m. 1732

Elizabeth [5] Sargent

Thomas Goldthwait m.

Elizabeth Lewis, Mrs. E. Goldthwait

Elizabeth Goldthwait, Mrs. A. Cumming m. 1763

Catherine Goldthwait [6]

Nathaniel Hurd

Mary Hurd m. Daniel Henchman

1. See Green.
2. See Clarke.
3. See Allen (A).
4. See Quincy.
5. See Allen (B); Sargent.
6. See Gardiner.

HENSHAW (5)

Period:

1753–57:	—
1758–61:	—
1762–64:	—
1765–67:	—
1768–70:	Joshua Henshaw
1771–74:	Joseph Henshaw
	Mrs. Joseph Henshaw
	Joshua Henshaw II
	Mrs. Joshua Henshaw II

Sex: Men (3), women (2).

Residence: Boston (5).

Occupation: merchant (3).

Education: Harvard (2).

Church: Congregational (5).

Politics: moderate Whig (2), radical Whig (1).

Marital status: married (5).

Office: justice of the peace (1).

Income: high (1), medium (2).

Medium: oil on canvas (4), pastel (1).

Size: 50″ x 40″ (1), 30″ x 25″ (3), under 30″ x 25″ (1).

Comment: The only family group of size not now demonstrably related to any other family group. This middle-class, mercantile, Whiggish family was painted late in Copley's American career, perhaps because of Copley's connection with Brattle Square Church, to which they all belonged.

HENSHAW

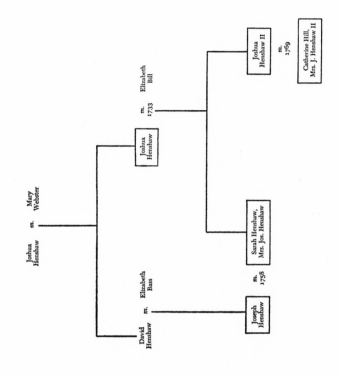

Joshua
Henshaw
m.
Mary
Webster

David
Henshaw
m.
Elizabeth
Bass

Joshua
Henshaw
m.
1733
Elizabeth
Bill

Joseph
Henshaw
m.
1758

Sarah Henshaw,
Mrs. Jos. Henshaw

Joshua
Henshaw II
m.
1769

Catherine Hill,
Mrs. J. Henshaw II

HOOPER (10)

Period:

1753-57: —

1758-61: Jacob Fowle

1762-64: Alice Hooper

1765-67: Robert Hooper (1767)
Mrs. Robert Hooper (1767)
Thomas Lewis

1768-70: Jeremiah Lee (1769)
Mrs. Jeremiah Lee (1769)
Joseph Hooper
Mrs. Joseph Hooper
Robert Hooper II

1771-74: —

Sex: men (6), women (4).

Residence: Marblehead (10).

Occupation: merchant (5), shipper (1).

Education: Harvard (1).

Church: Congregational (8).

Politics: high Tory (1), moderate Tory (1), moderate Whig (2), radical Whig (1).

Marital status: single (1), married (9).

Office: justice of the peace (2).

Income: very high (2), high (1), medium (3).

Medium: oil on canvas (10).

Size: over 50″ x 40″ (2), 50″ x 40″ (8).

Comment: This group is decidedly Marblehead-centered, Congregational, mercantile, low on education, partial to large paintings in oil on canvas. Most of the subjects were married; more than half of the pictures were painted close to the date of the sitter's marriage; and more than half of the paintings are paired.

HOOPER

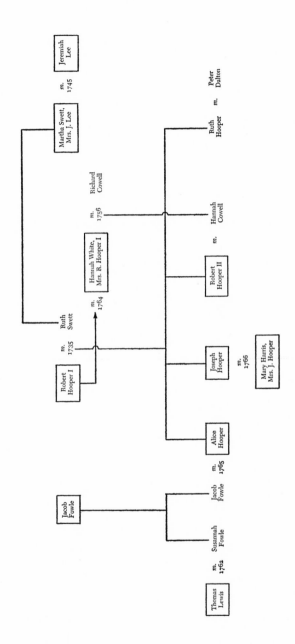

JACKSON (6)

Period:

1753–57: Thankful Hubbard
1758–61: Gregory Townsend
1762–64: —
1765–67: Mrs. Gregory Townsend (1765)
         Thomas Hubbard
         Josiah Quincy
1768–70: Jonathan Jackson
1771–74: —

Sex: men (4), women (2).

Residence: Boston (2), Needham (2), Braintree (1), Newburyport (1).

Occupation: merchant (2), brazier (1).

Education: Harvard (3).

Church: Congregational (6).

Politics: high Tory (2), radical Whig (2).

Marital status: single (3), married (2).

Office: Council (1); judge, Inferior Court (1).

Income: very high (2), high (1), medium (1).

Medium: oil on canvas (2), pastel (3).

Size: 50″ x 40″ (1), 36″ x 28″ (1), under 30″ x 25″ (4).

Comment: Family is well educated, Congregational, commercial, quite wealthy, given to political extremes, with a predilection for smaller pictures, especially pastels.

JACKSON

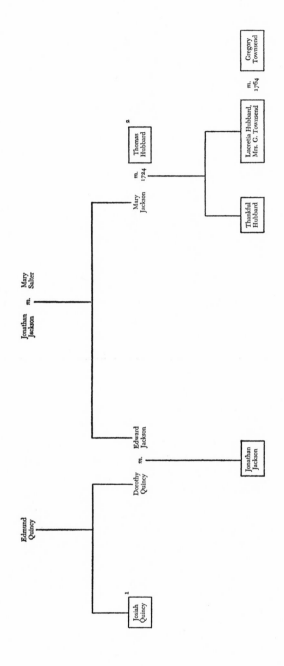

1. See Quincy.

2. See Wentworth.

MURRAY (9)

Period:

1753–57: —

1758–61: Dorothy Murray

1762–64: Mrs. John Powell (1764)
James Murray
John Powell II
Mrs. John Powell II

1765–67: —

1768–70: Mrs. James Smith (1769)
John S. Copley (1769)
Mrs. John S. Copley (1769)
Ralph Inman

1771–74: —

Sex: men (4), women (5).

Residence: Boston (7), Cambridge (1), Milton (1).

Occupation: merchant (2), artist (1), landowner (1).

Education: —

Church: Congregational (1), Anglican 7.

Politics: high Tory (3), moderate Tory (1).

Marital status: single (1), married (6), widowed (2).

Office: Council (1); justice of the peace (1); town office (1).

Income: very high (1), high (2), medium (1).

Medium: oil on canvas (4), pastel (5).

Size: 50″ x 40″ (2), 36″ x 28″ (2), under 30″ x 25″ (5).

Comment: A young, wealthy, Anglican group, of Tory inclination and with a penchant for pastels.

MURRAY

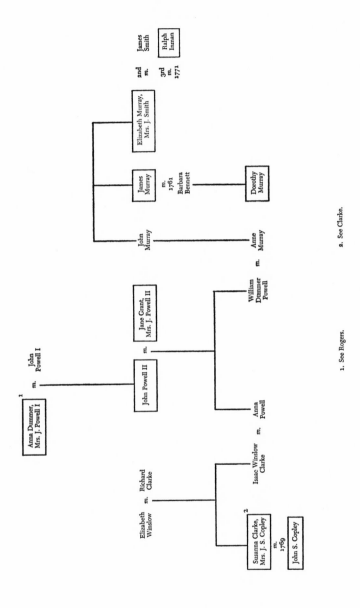

1. See Rogers.

2. See Clarke.

OLIVER (17)

Period:

1753–57: Jonathan Belcher (1756)
Mrs. Jonathan Belcher (1756)
William Welsteed [1]

1758–61: Andrew Oliver
Mrs. Andrew Oliver
Andrew Oliver II
Elizabeth Oliver
Griselda Oliver
Peter Oliver

1762–64: John Spooner (1763)
Mrs. Gawen Brown
Lydia Lynde

1765–67: Mrs. George Watson (1765)
Mather Byles
Mrs. Samuel Waldo

1768–70: George Watson (1768)

1771–74: Isaac Winslow (1774) [2]

Sex: men (9), women (8).

Residence: Boston (11), Plymouth (2), Middleboro (1), Nova Scotia (2), Maine (1).

Occupation: merchant (5), minister (2), official (1), jeweller (1).

Education: Harvard (7).

Church: Anglican (3), Congregational (14).

Politics: high Tory (7), moderate Tory (2).

Marital status: single (4), married (12), widowed (1).

Office: chief justice (1); Council (2); justice, Superior Court (1); justice, Inferior Court (1).

Income: very high (3), high (3), medium (1), low (2).

Medium: oil on canvas (12), oil on copper (4), engraving (1).

Size: over 50″ x 40″ (1), 50″ x 40″ (5), 30″ x 25″ (4), under 30″ x 25″ (8).

Comment: Largely painted in a ten-year period during the early half of Copley's American career, this group is very well educated, the most Tory of any group, very influential, and with a predilection for small pictures.

[1] Post-mortem portrait.
[2] Counted as a single subject, although a double portrait.

[178]

OLIVER

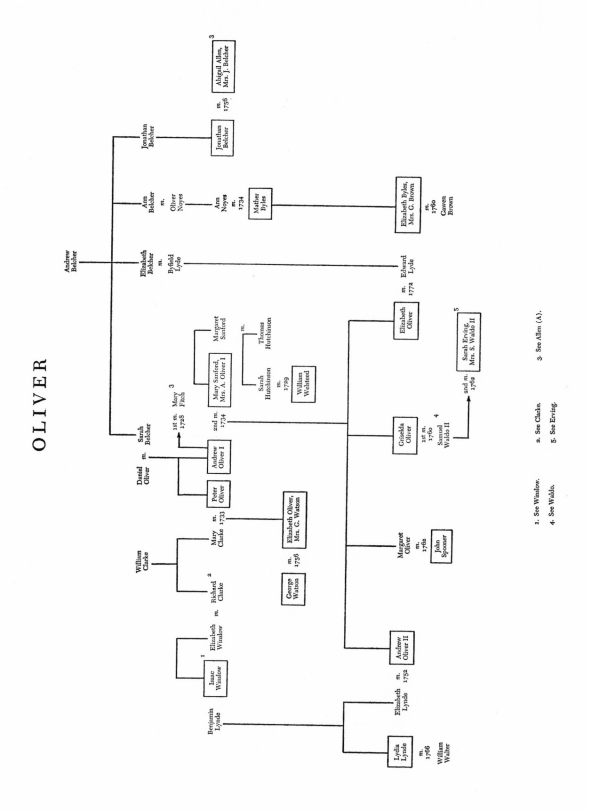

1. See Winslow.   2. See Clarke.   3. See Allen (A).

4. See Waldo.   5. See Erving.

OSBORNE (8)

Period:

1753–57: —

1758–61: Epes Sargent

1762–64: Mrs. Daniel Sargent (1763)
Mrs. Epes Sargent II (1764)
Epes Sargent II

1765–67: Mrs. Edward Watts (1765)
Mrs. William Turner (1767)
William Turner

1768–70: Mrs. Samuel Watts

1771–74: —

Sex: men (3), women (5).

Residence: Gloucester (4), Boston (3), Maine (1).

Occupation: merchant (2).

Education: Harvard (1).

Church: Anglican (2), Congregational (6).

Politics: moderate Tory (2), moderate Whig (1).

Marital status: married (7), widowed (1).

Office: justice, Inferior Court (1); justice of the peace (1).

Income: high (2), medium (1).

Medium: oil on canvas (6), pastel (2).

Size: 50″ x 40″ (4), 36″ x 28″ (1), 30″ x 25″ (1), under 30″ x 25″ (2).

OSBORNE

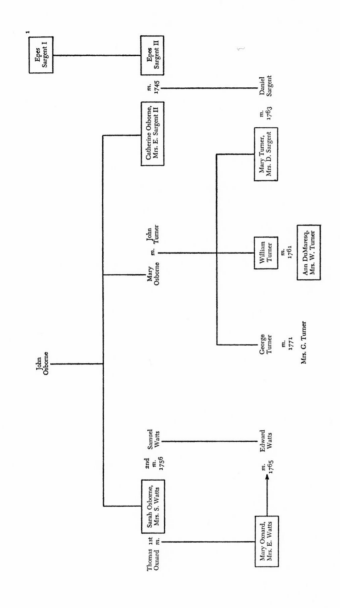

Epes Sargent I [1]

Epes Sargent II

Catherine Osborne, Mrs. E. Sargent II

John Osborne

Mary Osborne

Mary *m.* John Turner

Sarah Osborne, Mrs. S. Watts

Thomas Oxnard 1st *m.*

2nd Samuel Watts *m.* 1756

Mary Oxnard, Mrs. E. Watts *m.* 1765

Edward Watts

George Turner *m.* 1771 Mrs. G. Turner

William Turner *m.* 1761

Ann DuMaresq, Mrs. W. Turner

Mary Turner, Mrs. D. Sargent *m.* 1763

Daniel Sargent *m.* 1745

1. See Sargent.

QUINCY (10)

Period:

1753-57: —

1758-61: Mrs. Samuel Quincy

1762-64: —

1765-67: John Hancock (1765)
Josiah Quincy
Samuel Quincy

1768-70: Isaac Smith (1769)
Mrs. Isaac Smith (1769)
Jonathan Jackson
Ebenezer Storer II

1771-74: Mrs. Richard Skinner (1772)
Dorothy Quincy

Sex: men (6), women (4).

Residence: Braintree (4), Boston (4), Newburyport (1), Marble-head (1).

Occupation: merchant (5), lawyer (1).

Education: Harvard (5).

Church: Congregational (10).

Politics: high Tory (1), moderate Whig (1), radical Whig (4).

Marital status: single (3), married (6).

Office: justice, Inferior Court (1); justice of the peace (1); representative (1); selectman (1).

Income: very high (2), high (3), medium (1).

Medium: oil on canvas (8), pastel (2).

Size: 50″ x 40″ (4), 36″ x 28″ (3), under 30″ x 25″ (2), other (1).

Comment: Group is educated, influential, decidedly Whiggish, Congregational, wealthy, with varied tastes in picture sizes.

QUINCY

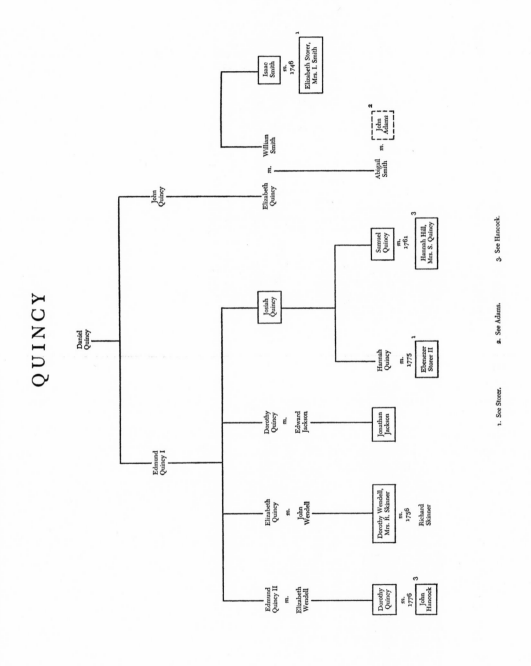

Daniel Quincy

Edmund Quincy I — John Quincy

John Quincy:
- Elizabeth Quincy
  - Abigail Smith m. [John Adams] [2]
- William Smith
- Isaac Smith m. 1746 — Elizabeth Storer, Mrs. I. Smith [1]

Edmund Quincy I:
- Edmund Quincy II m. Elizabeth Wendell
  - Dorothy Quincy m. 1776 — John Hancock [3]
- Elizabeth Quincy m. John Wendell
  - Dorothy Wendell, Mrs. R. Skinner m. 1756 — Richard Skinner
- Dorothy Quincy m. Edward Jackson
  - Jonathan Jackson
- Josiah Quincy
  - Hannah Quincy m. 1775 — Ebenezer Storer II [1]
  - Samuel Quincy m. 1761 — Hannah Hill, Mrs. S. Quincy [3]

1. See Storer.   2. See Adams.   3. See Hancock.

ROGERS (7)

Period:

1753–57: —

1758–61: Nathaniel Appleton
Edward Holyoke

1762–64: Mrs. Daniel Rogers (1762)
Mrs. Nathaniel Appleton (1763)
Mrs. John Powell II (1764)
John Powell II
Mrs. John Powell II

1765–67: —

1768–70: —

1771–74: —

Sex: men (3), women (4).

Residence: Boston (3), Cambridge (3), Gloucester (1).

Occupation: minister (1), teacher (1), merchant (1).

Education: Harvard (2).

Church: Anglican (3), Congregational (4).

Politics: high Tory (1), moderate Tory (1), moderate Whig (1).

Marital status: married (6), widowed (1).

Office: town office (1).

Income: medium (1), low (2).

Medium: oil on canvas (5), pastel (2).

Size: 50″ x 40″ (3), 36″ x 28″ (2), under 30″ x 25″ (2).

Comment: Largely painted during a ten-year span early in Copley's career, this small group tended to be well educated, older, professional, and relatively poor. The three Anglicans all came from Boston (King's Chapel).

ROGERS

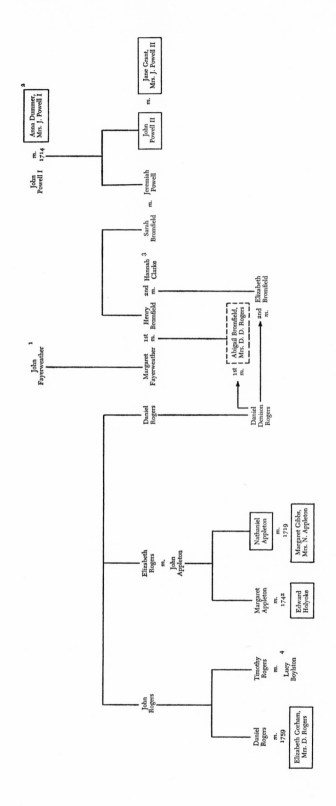

1. See Fayerweather. 2. See Murray. 3. See Clarke. 4. See Adams.

ROYALL (10)

Period:

1753–57: Charles Pelham

1758–61: Mary and Elizabeth Royall [1]

1762–64: Samuel Phillips Savage (1764)
Mrs. Samuel Phillips Savage (1764)
Nathaniel Sparhawk (1764)

1765–67: Peter Chardon
Mrs. Andrew Tyler

1768–70: Isaac Royall (1769)
Mrs. Isaac Royall (1769)
Samuel Cooper

1771–74: —

Sex: men (6), women (4).

Residence: Boston (5), Medford (3), Westwood (1), Maine (1).

Occupation: merchant (4), minister (1), lawyer (1).

Education: Harvard (2).

Church: Anglican (3), Congregational (5).

Politics: high Tory (1), moderate Tory (2), moderate Whig (1), radical Whig (2).

Marital status: single (3), married (6), widowed (1).

Office: Council (2).

Income: very high (1), high (2), medium (3).

Medium: oil on canvas (8), pastel (2).

Size: over 50″ x 40″ (2), 50″ x 40″ (4), 36″ x 28″ (1), 30″ x 25″ (1), under 30″ x 25″ (2).

Comment: A quite varied group.

---

[1] Counted as a single subject, although a double portrait.

[186]

ROYALL

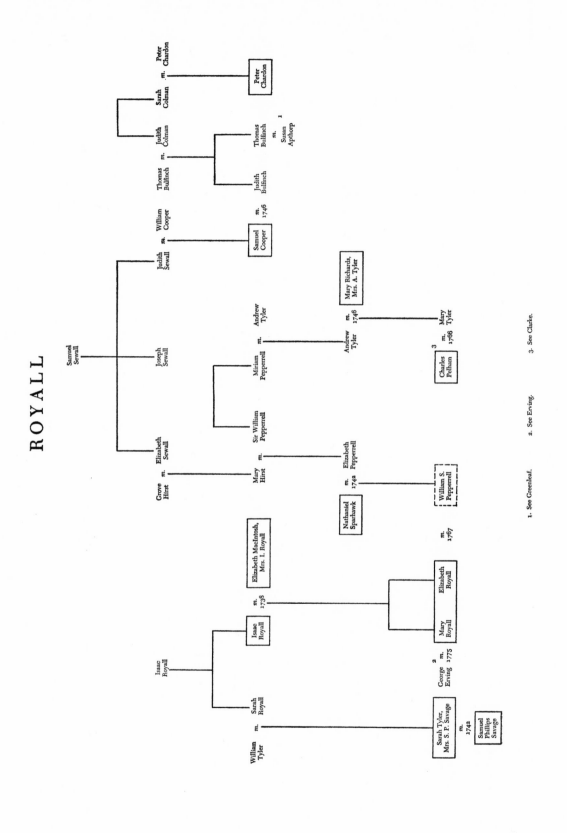

RUSSELL (6)

Period:

1753–57:	—
1758–61:	—
1762–64:	—
1765–67:	Mrs. Samuel Henley
1768–70:	Samuel Cary [1]
	Mrs. Samuel Cary [1]
	Mrs. James Russell
1771–74:	Thomas Cary (1773)
	Edward Barnard

Sex: men (3), women (3).

Residence: Charlestown (2), Haverhill (1), Newburyport (1), West Indies (2).

Occupation: minister (2), landowner (1).

Education: Harvard (2).

Church: Congregational (6).

Politics: moderate Tory (1), moderate Whig (2).

Marital status: married (5), single (1).

Office: —

Income: high (1), medium (1), low (1).

Medium: oil on canvas (3), pastel (1), watercolor on ivory (2).

Size: 50″ x 40″ (2), 30″ x 25″ (1), under 30″ x 25″ (3).

Comment: A diversified group in income, residence, medium, size, and age; educated, Congregational, largely professional, and wielding little political influence.

[1] Considered as a married couple, although stylistic evidence suggests that the miniatures were made as a pair before the date of marriage.

RUSSELL

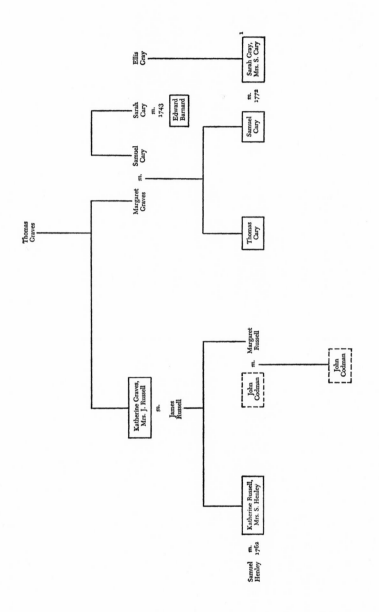

1. See Gray.

SARGENT (11)

Period:

1753–57:   —

1758–61:   Epes Sargent
           Mrs. William Stevens

1762–64:   Nathaniel Allen (1763)
           Mrs. Nathaniel Allen
           Mrs. Daniel Sargent (1763)
           Mrs. Epes Sargent II (1764)
           Epes Sargent II

1765–67:   Mrs. William Turner (1767)
           William Turner
           Mrs. Nathaniel Ellery

1768–70:   —

1771–74:   Mrs. John Stevens

Sex: men (4), women (7).

Residence: Gloucester (9), Boston (2).

Occupation: merchant (2), shipper (1).

Education: Harvard (1).

Church: Anglican (2), Congregational (9).

Politics: moderate Tory (2), moderate Whig (2).

Marital status: married (11).

Office: justice of the peace (2); justice, Inferior Court (1).

Income: high (3), medium (1).

Medium: oil on canvas (9), pastel (2).

Size: 50″ x 40″ (9), under 30″ x 25″ (2).

Comment: Both Anglicans are from Boston (King's Chapel); the out-of-towners are all Congregationalists. The canvases tend to be large.

SARGENT

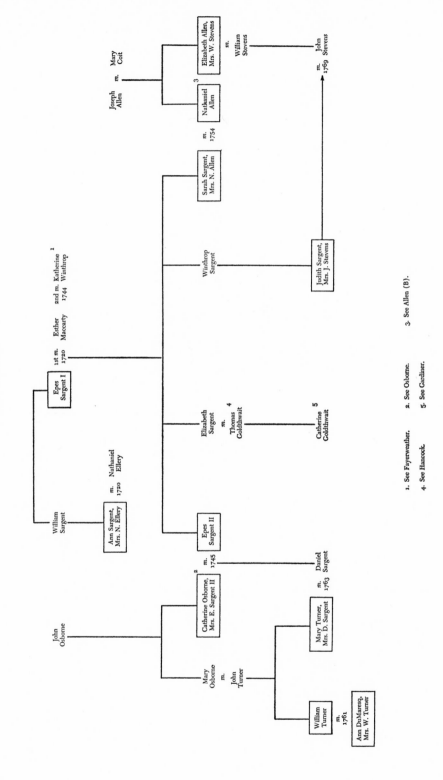

1. See Fayerweather. 2. See Osborne. 3. See Allen (B).

4. See Hancock. 5. See Gardiner.

STORER (9)

Period:

1753–57: —

1758–61: —

1762–64: —

1765–67: Mrs. Edward Green (1765)
Woodbury Langdon
Mrs. Woodbury Langdon

1768–70: Isaac Smith (1769)
Mrs. Isaac Smith (1769)
Ebenezer Storer[1]
Mrs. Ebenezer Storer
Ebenezer Storer II
Mrs. Ebenezer Storer II

1771–74: —

Sex: men (4), women (5).

Residence: Boston (7), Portsmouth (2).

Occupation: merchant (4).

Education: Harvard (1).

Church: Congregational (9).

Politics: moderate Whig (2), radical Whig (1).

Marital status: married (9).

Office: justice of the peace (2); selectman (1).

Income: high (4).

Medium: oil on canvas (4), pastel (5).

Size: 50″ x 40″ (4), under 50″ x 40″ (5).

Comment: Painted entirely in 1765–69, this is a uniform group, mostly from Boston, all merchant families, all Congregationalists, mostly Whig, quite wealthy, holding local offices, and with all of the sitters married. There is a high percentage of pairs and of pastels.

[1] Post-mortem portrait.

[192]

STORER

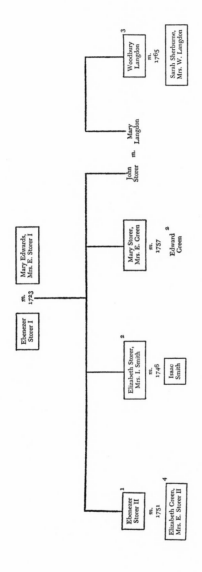

Ebenezer
Storer I

m.
1723

Mary Edwards,
Mrs. E. Storer I

Ebenezer
Storer II [1]

m.
1751

Elizabeth Green,
Mrs. E. Storer II [4]

Elizabeth Storer,
Mrs. I. Smith [2]

m.
1746

Isaac
Smith

Mary Storer,
Mrs. E. Green

m.
1757

Edward
Green [2]

John
Storer

m. Mary
Langdon

Woodbury
Langdon [3]

m.
1765

Sarah Sherburne,
Mrs. W. Langdon

---

1. See Quincy.   2. See Adams.   3. See Wentworth; Amory.   4. See Green.

WALDO (15)

Period:

1753–57: Mrs. Jonathan Belcher (1756)
Jonathan Belcher (1756)
Ann Tyng (1756)

1758–61: Andrew Oliver
Mrs. Andrew Oliver
Griselda Oliver

1762–64: —

1765–67: Elizabeth Ross
Mrs. Samuel Waldo II

1768–70: James Allen

1771–74: Eleazer Tyng (1772)
Mrs. John Winthrop (1773)
John Winthrop
Isaac Winslow (1774)[1]
John Erving
Thomas Flucker

Sex: men (8), women (7).

Residence: Boston (8), Cambridge (2), Tyngsboro (1), Maine (2), Nova Scotia (2).

Occupation: merchant (3), teacher (1), official (1), shipper (1), landowner (1), gentleman (1).

Education: Harvard (6).

Church: Anglican (2), Congregational (11).

Politics: high Tory (4), moderate Tory (2), moderate Whig (2).

Marital status: single (4), married (9), widowed (2).

Office: Council (3); chief justice (1); provincial secretary (1); justice of the peace (1).

Income: very high (4), high (3), low (1).

Medium: oil on canvas (13), oil on copper (2).

Size: over 50″ x 40″ (1), 50″ x 40″ (8), 36″ x 28″ (1), 30″ x 25″ (2), under 30″ x 25″ (3).

Comment: The paintings of Mrs. Belcher, Griselda Oliver, Elizabeth Ross, Ann Tyng, Mrs. Waldo, and Isaac Winslow come within two years of their marriage dates. This group seems richer, better educated, more Tory, more official, and more Congregational than average.

[1] Counted as a single subject, although a double portrait.

WALDO

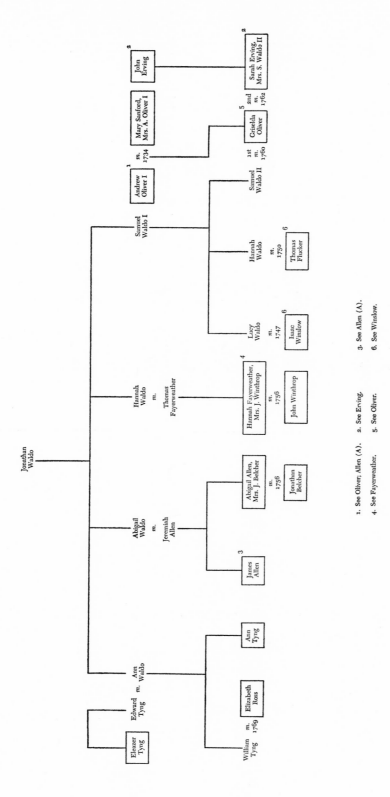

1. See Oliver; Allen (A).
2. See Erving.
3. See Allen (A).
4. See Fayerweather.
5. See Oliver.
6. See Winslow.

WENTWORTH (8)

Period:

1753-57: —

1758-61: Theodore Atkinson

1762-64: Mrs. Nathaniel Rogers

1765-67: Mrs. Theodore Atkinson (1765)
Thomas Hubbard
Woodbury Langdon
Mrs. Woodbury Langdon

1768-70: Joseph Sherburne
John Wentworth

1771-74: —

Sex: men (5), women (3).

Residence: Boston (3), New Hampshire (Portsmouth) (5).

Occupation: official (2), merchant (2), brazier (1).

Education: Harvard (3).

Church: Anglican (4), Congregational (4).

Politics: high Tory (4).

Marital status: single (1), married (7).

Office: governor (1); Council (1); provincial secretary (1); town office (1).

Income: very high (4), high (1).

Medium: oil on canvas (7), pastel (1).

Size: 50″ x 40″ (6), 30″ x 25″ (1), under 30″ x 25″ (1).

Comment: Group is very wealthy, Tory, educated, influential in Boston and Portsmouth.

WENTWORTH

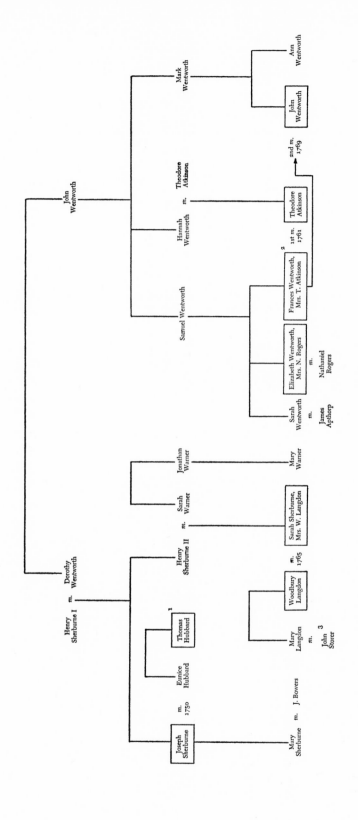

1. See Jackson. 2. See Greenleaf. 3. See Storer; Green.

WINSLOW (5)

Period:

1753–57: —

1758–61: Hugh Hall (1758)

1762–64: Hannah Loring (1763)
          Elizabeth Pitts

1765–67: —

1768–70: —

1771–74: Isaac Winslow (1774)[1]
          Thomas Flucker

Sex: men (3), women (2).

Residence: Boston (5).

Occupation: merchant (3).

Education: Harvard (2).

Church: Anglican (2), Congregational (3).

Politics: high Tory (2), moderate Tory (1).

Marital status: single (1), married (3), widowed (1).

Office: provincial secretary (1); Council (1); justice, Inferior Court (1).

Income: very high (2), high (1).

Medium: oil on canvas (3), pastel (2).

Size: over 50″ x 40″ (1), 50″ x 40″ (1), 30″ x 25″ (1), under 30″ x 25″ (2).

Comment: Quite uniform in occupation, residence, high offices, education, and politics.

[1] Counted as a single subject, although a double portrait.

WINSLOW

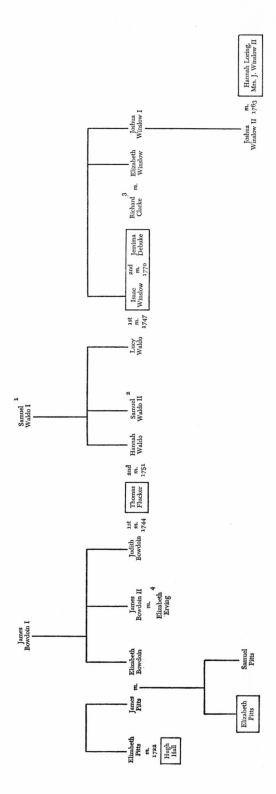

1. See Waldo.   2. See Oliver.   3. See Clarke.   4. See Erving.

Selected Bibliography

A special group of books was useful in gathering information about Copley's American sitters for the statistical study in this volume. (Works of more general interest are listed in the bibliography in Volume Two.) Particularly helpful, too, were such sources as *Appleton's Cyclopedia of American Biography*, *Dictionary of American Biography*, *Dictionary of National Biography*, and John Langdon Sibley and Clifford Kenyon Shipton, *Biographical Sketches of Graduates of Harvard University*, vols. I–III (Cambridge, Mass., 1873–1885), and vols. IV–XIII (Massachusetts Historical Society, 1933–1965); and the various publications of the Colonial Society of Massachusetts, the Essex Institute, the Maine Historical Society, the Massachusetts Historical Society, and the New England Historic Genealogical Society. The following books provided specific information:

Allan, Herbert S. *John Hancock: Patriot in Purple*. New York, 1948.

Austin, William. *William Austin, Creator of Peter Rugg*. Boston, 1925.

Blake, Francis Everett. *Increase Blake of Boston*. Boston, 1898.

Bowen, Clarence Winthrop. *History of Woodstock, Connecticut*. Norwood, Mass., 1926.

[Brattle Square Church.] *Records of the Church in Brattle Square*. Boston, 1902.

Brown, Robert E. *Middle-Class Democracy and the Revolution in Massachusetts, 1691–1780*. Ithaca, 1955.

Chapman, Frederick William. *The Coit Family*. Hartford, 1874.

Clarke, Hermann Frederick, and Henry Wilder Foote. *Jeremiah Dummer*. Boston, 1935.

Curry, Jabez Lamar Monroe. *Diplomatic Services of George W. Erving*. Cambridge, 1890.

Dana, John Jay. *Memoranda of Some of the Descendants of Richard Dana*. Boston, 1865.

Dexter, Franklin Bowditch. *Biographical Sketches of the Graduates of Yale College*. New Haven, 1885.

Doty, Ethan Allen. *The Doty-Doten Family*. Brooklyn, 1897.

Dows, Azro Milton. *The Dows or Dowse Family in America*. Lowell, 1890.

Eaton, Arthur Wentworth Hamilton. *The Famous Mather Byles*. Boston, 1914.

Fitch, Roscoe Conkling. *History of the Fitch Family*. Haverhill, 1930.

Foote, Henry Wilder. *Annals of King's Chapel*. Boston, 1896.

Forbes, Esther. *Paul Revere and the World He Lived In*. Boston, 1942.

Foster, Joseph, ed. *Alumni Oxonienses*. 8 vols. London, 1887–88.

French, Hollis. *Jacob Hurd*. Boston, 1939.

Goldthwaite, Charlotte. *Descendants of Thomas Goldthwaite*. Hartford, 1899.

Goss, Elbridge Henry. *Life of Colonel Paul Revere*. Boston, 1898.

The Greene Family in England and America [author anonymous]. Boston, 1901.

Greenleaf, James Edward. *Genealogy of the Greenleaf Family*. Boston, 1896.

Griffin, Edward Dorr. *Sermon on the Death of Reverend Alexander MacWhorter*. New York, 1807.

Harris, Edward Doubleday. *An Account of the Descendants of Captain Thomas Brattle*. Boston, 1867.

Hubbard, Harlan Page. *One Thousand Years of Hubbard History*. New York, 1895.

Jones, Edward Alfred. *Loyalists of Massachusetts*. London, 1930.

SELECTED BIBLIOGRAPHY

Jordan, Tristram Frost. *Family Record of Reverend Robert Jordan*. Boston, 1882.

Keith, Charles Penrose. *Provincial Councillors of Pennsylvania*. Philadelphia, 1883.

Lincoln, Waldo. *Genealogy of the Waldo Family*. Worcester, Mass., 1932.

Mather, Horace E. *Lineage of Reverend Richard Mather*. Hartford, 1890.

May, John Joseph. *Danforth Genealogy*. Boston, 1902.

Meredith, Gertrude Euphemia. *Descendents of Hugh Amory*. London, 1901.

Morse, Abner. *Genealogical Register*. Boston, 1861.

Oliver, Andrew. *Faces of a Family*. Privately printed, 1960.

Otis, Horatio Nelson. *The Family of Otis*. Boston, 1898.

Park, Lawrence. *Major Thomas Savage of Boston and His Descendants*. Boston, 1914.

Parker, Barbara Neville, and Anne Bolling Wheeler. *John Singleton Copley: American Portraits in Oil, Pastel and Miniature, with Biographical Sketches*. Boston, 1938.

Perkins, George Augustus. *Family of John Perkins of Ipswich*. Salem, 1889.

Prime, Temple. *Some Account of the Bowdoin Family*. New York, 1900.

Princeton University. *General Catalogue, 1746–1906*. Princeton, 1908.

Putnam, James Jackson. *Memoir of Dr. James Jackson*. Boston, 1905.

Raymond, Marcius Denison. *Gray Geneaology*. Tarrytown, New York, 1887.

Roebling, Mrs. Washington Augustus. *Richard Warren of the Mayflower*. Boston, 1901.

Roll of the Ancient and Honorable Artillery Company. Boston, 1895.

Rowe, John. *Letters and Diary*. Boston, 1903.

Salisbury, Edward Elbridge. *Family Memorials*. 4 vols. New Haven, 1885.

Sargent, Emma Worcester. *Epes Sargent of Gloucester and His Descendants*. Boston, 1923.

Seybolt, Robert Francis. *Town Officials of Colonial Boston*. Cambridge, Mass. 1939.

Todd, Charles Burr. *A General History of the Burr Family*. New York, 1902.

Torrey, Frederic Crosby. *The Torrey Families in America*. Lakehurst, N.J., 1924.

Venn, John A., ed. *Alumni Cantabrigienses*. 10 vols. Cambridge, Eng., 1922–24.

Ver Planck, William Edward. *History of Abner Isaacse Ver Planck*. Fishkill, N.Y., 1892.

Warren, John Collins. *Genealogy of Warren*. Boston, 1854.

Wentworth, John. *Wentworth Genealogy*. Boston, 1870.

Wheatley, Henry B. *London Past and Present*. London, 1891.

Wheildon, William Willder. *Beacon Hill*. Concord, Mass., 1877.

Whitmore, William Henry. *Genealogy of the Gore and Payne Families*. Boston, 1875.

————— *Massachusetts Civil List*. Albany, New York, 1870.

Winsor, Justin H. *Memorial History of Boston*. 4 vols. Boston, 1880.

Wyman, Thomas Bellows. *Genealogies and Estates of Charlestown*. 2 vols. Boston, 1890.

Checklist of American Pictures

Checklist of American Pictures

This checklist is intended for use in conjunction with Barbara N. Parker and Anne B. Wheeler, *John Singleton Copley: American Portraits* (Boston: Museum of Fine Arts, 1938). Page and plate references to Parker-Wheeler are given under the *Bibliography* for all objects included in that work, and it should be consulted for full catalogue entries and biographical information about the sitters. More comprehensive entries are presented here for objects not included in Parker-Wheeler, primarily paintings that have come to light since 1938. I have retained the still unlocated paintings listed in Parker-Wheeler and added a few others. An asterisk after the sitter's name indicates that he or she has been included in the statistical analysis presented in the appendices.

The first section of each entry includes title, medium, size, date of painting, present owner, and figure number used in this work [in brackets]. Provenance is given only when that information has not appeared in Parker-Wheeler. Bibliographies include only pertinent references and listings subsequent to or omitted from Parker-Wheeler. In addition to Parker-Wheeler, the following bibliographical abbreviations have been used:

Bayley: Frank W. Bayley, *The Life and Works of John Singleton Copley* (Boston, 1915).

Belknap: Waldron Phoenix Belknap, Jr., *American Colonial Painting: Materials for a History* (Cambridge, Mass., 1959).

BMFA '38: *John Singleton Copley, 1738–1815*, Loan Exhibition, Boston Museum of Fine Arts, Feb. 1–March 15, 1938.

Copley Exhib. '65: *John Singleton Copley, 1738–1815*, National Gallery of Art (Washington), Metropolitan Museum of Art (New York), and Museum of Fine Arts (Boston), Sept. 18, 1965–March 6, 1966. Text by Jules David Prown.

Copley-Pelham Letters: Letters and Papers of John Singleton Copley and Henry Pelham, 1739–1766, Guernsey Jones, ed. (Boston, 1914).

Gardner and Feld: Albert TenEyck Gardner and Stuart P. Feld, *American Paintings: A Catalogue of the Collection of the Metropolitan Museum of Art*, vol. I (New York, 1965).

Hipkiss: Edwin J. Hipkiss, *Eighteenth Century American Arts: The M. and M. Karolik Collection* (Boston, 1941).

New England Miniatures: New England Miniatures, 1750–1850, Museum of Fine Arts, Boston, April 24–May 28, 1957. Compiled and edited by Barbara Neville Parker.

Met '37: *An Exhibition of Paintings by John Singleton Copley*, Metropolitan Museum of Art, New York, Dec. 22, 1936–Feb. 14, 1937. Text by Harry B. Wehle.

Perkins: Augustus Thorndike Perkins, *A Sketch of the Life and a List of the Works of John Singleton Copley* (Boston, 1873).

Perkins, *Supplement*: Augustus Thorndike Perkins, *A Supplementary List of Paintings by John Singleton Copley* (Boston, [1875]).

Portraits

ADAMS, PETER BOYLSTON [?]. Oil on copper, 1765–70. J. William Middendorf, Greenwich, Conn. [245]

    Bibliography: Harriet Taylor Upton, "The Household of John Quincy Adams," *Wide Awake, an Illustrated Magazine*, XXVII (Nov. 8, 1888), 376.

    Once considered to be a portrait of Thomas Boylston Adams (b. 1772), and subsequently called Peter Boylston Adams (b. 1738), the subject of this miniature still eludes identification. The sitter may properly be a member of the Adams family, since Samuel Adams married Elizabeth Welles in 1764 and the miniature apparently descended in the Welles family.

ADAMS, SAMUEL.* Oil on canvas, 50″ x 40¼″, 1770–72. Museum of Fine Arts, Boston, on deposit from City of Boston. [302]

    Bibliography: Parker-Wheeler, pp. 17–19, plate 114; Copley Exhib. '65, pp. 69–70, 138 (48).

AINSLIE, THOMAS.* 1757. Unlocated.

    Bibliography: Copley-Pelham Letters, p. 23; Parker-Wheeler, p. 265.

ALLEN, JAMES.* Oil on canvas, 30″ x 25″, 1768–70. Massachusetts Historical Society, Boston. [268]

    Bibliography: Parker-Wheeler, p. 19, plate 65.

ALLEN, NATHANIEL.* Oil on canvas, 50″ x 40″, 1763. Charles S. Sargent, Jr., New York. [101]

    Inscribed: Signed lower left, "I. S. Copley. Pinx. 1763."

    Bibliography: Parker-Wheeler, p. 20, plate 32.

ALLEN, MRS. NATHANIEL (Sarah Sargent).* Oil on canvas, 49½″ x 40″, c. 1763. Minneapolis Institute of Arts, Minneapolis, Minn. [102]

    Bibliography: Parker-Wheeler, pp. 20–21, plate 30; "A Colonial Portrait by John Copley," *Bulletin of the Minneapolis Institute of Arts*, XXX (Oct. 4, 1941), 117–21; Copley Exhib. '65, pp. 29, 32, 136 (16).

AMORY, JOHN.* Oil on canvas, 50″ x 40″, 1768. Museum of Fine Arts, Boston (M. and M. Karolik Collection). [220]

    Bibliography: BMFA '38, p. 19 (2); Hipkiss, pp. 8–9 (4); Parker-Wheeler, pp. 21–22, plate 89.

AMORY, MRS. JOHN (Katherine Greene).* Oil on canvas, 49½″ x 40″, c. 1764. Museum of Fine Arts, Boston (M. and M. Karolik Collection). [140]

    Bibliography: BMFA '38, p. 19 (3); Hipkiss, pp. 10–11 (5); Parker-Wheeler, pp. 22–24, plate 41.

    Copies: Oil on canvas, 21¾″ x 18″. Mrs. Walter B. James, Dover, Mass. An interesting contemporary copy, overpainted in the lower area, possibly painted by an American artist and sent to the family in England after the death of Mrs. Amory there in 1777. *Bibliography*: Parker-Wheeler, pp. 23–24.

AMORY, THOMAS. Pastel, 23″ x 17¼″, c. 1770. Museum of Fine Arts, Boston (M. and M. Karolik Collection). [240]

    Bibliography: BMFA '38, p. 19 (4); Hipkiss, pp. 6–7 (3); Parker-Wheeler, p. 215.

    The Museum of Fine Arts, Boston, has a receipt for the pastel from the account book of John and Jonathan Amory, Aug. 16, 1770: John Amory paid Copley "in full for drawing his father's Picture — £9–16–." Thomas Amory died in 1728, and this Copley pastel was based on an earlier portrait.

    Copies: R. M. Staigg, oil on canvas, for William Amory, after a pastel copy of this pastel, 1880.

AMORY II, THOMAS.* Oil on canvas, 49½″ x 39¾″, 1770–72. Robert Amory, Jr., Washington, D.C. [303]

    Bibliography: Parker-Wheeler, p. 24, plate 102.

AMORY II, MRS. THOMAS (Elizabeth Coffin).* Oil on canvas, 29″ x 24″, 1770–72. Louisa Metcalf, Winthrop, Mass. [305]
    Bibliography: Parker-Wheeler, p. 25, plate 124.
ANDREWS, BENJAMIN. c. 1773. Unlocated.
    Bibliography: Copley-Pelham Letters, p. 197; Parker-Wheeler, p. 265.
    This portrait and the next one, possibly by Copley, are mentioned in a letter dated March 1773 from Andrews to Henry Pelham, who was to have made some alterations in the landscape background of Andrews' portrait.
ANDREWS, MRS. BENJAMIN. c. 1773. Unlocated.
    Bibliography: Copley-Pelham Letters, p. 197.
APPLETON, REV. NATHANIEL.* Oil on canvas, 35⁹⁄₁₆″ x 29⁷⁄₁₆″, 1759–61. Harvard University, Cambridge, Mass. [94]
    Bibliography: Parker-Wheeler, pp. 25–26, plate 22.
APPLETON, MRS. NATHANIEL (Margaret Gibbs).* Oil on canvas, 35⁵⁄₁₆″ x 29¹⁄₁₆″, 1763. Harvard University, Cambridge, Mass. [114]
    Inscribed: Signed center left, "J. S. Copley: Pinx / 1763."
    Bibliography: Met '37 (8); Parker-Wheeler, pp. 26–27, plate 38.
APPLETON-GREENLEAF FAMILY, BOY OF THE [?]. Oil on canvas, 21½″ x 17¾″, 1755–58. Mr. and Mrs. John Howard Joynt, Alexandria, Va. [86]
    Provenance: White family, before 1872 [?].
    Bibliography: Perkins, p. 113 [?]; *Antiques*, LIII (April 1948), 276–77; Belknap, pp. 311–12, plate XXXIX, 47A.
    This and the next painting are identified by family tradition only as portraits of twins in the Greenleaf family. They did not come to light until 1938 and were subsequently authenticated by William Sawitzky.
────── GIRL OF THE [?]. Oil on canvas, 21½″ x 17¾″, 1755–58. Mr. and Mrs. John Howard Joynt, Alexandria, Va. [87]
    Bibliography: Antiques, LIII (April 1948), 276–77.
    See previous item.
APTHORP, MRS. JOHN (Hannah Greenleaf).* Oil on canvas, 29¾″ x 24½″, c. 1764. Thomas Gilcrease Institute of American History and Art, Tulsa, Okla. [133]
    Provenance: R. E. Apthorp, 1873; Mrs. R. E. Apthorp; estate of an American owner deceased in Monaco.
    Bibliography: Perkins, p. 32; Bayley, p. 46; Parker-Wheeler, p. 251.
ATKINSON, THEODORE.* Oil on canvas, 49½″ x 39¾″, 1757–58. Museum of Art, Rhode Island School of Design, Providence. [53]
    Bibliography: Lawrence Park, *Joseph Blackburn* (Worcester, Mass., 1923), frontispiece and pp. 16–17 [as by Blackburn]; *American Collector*, XII (March 1943), p. 7; *Magazine of Art*, XXXVI (March 1943), pp. 114–15; *Art News*, XLII (March 15–31, 1943), pp. 9–11; Belknap, p. 292, plate XIX, 15C [as by Blackburn].
    This portrait, long attributed to Joseph Blackburn, was properly reattributed to Copley by William Sawitzky in 1943 at a seminar on American painting held at the Worcester Art Museum.
ATKINSON, MRS. THEODORE (Frances Deering Wentworth; later Mrs. John Wentworth).* Oil on canvas, 51″ x 40″, 1765. New York Public Library (Lenox Collection). [162]
    Inscribed: Signed lower right under the table, "John S. Copley Pinx / 1765."
    Bibliography: Met '37 (13); BMFA '38, p. 19 (7); Parker-Wheeler, pp. 27–28, plate 58; Copley Exhib. '65, pp. 40, 42, 136 (24).
AUSTIN, MRS. EBENEZER (Mary Smith).* Oil on canvas, 33½″ x 29″, 1766–70. Winthrop Kent, Buffalo, N.Y. [181]
    Bibliography: Parker-Wheeler, pp. 28–29, plate 71.

BABCOCK, ADAM.* Oil on canvas, c. 50" x 40", c. 1774. Dr. Henry A. Murray, Cambridge, Mass.
[333]
Bibliography: Parker-Wheeler, pp. 29–30, plate 120.
BABCOCK, MRS. ADAM (Abigail Smith).* Oil on canvas, c. 50" x 40", c. 1774. Mrs. Robert Low
Bacon, Washington, D.C. [334]
Bibliography: Parker-Wheeler, p. 31, plate 120.
BARBER, WILKES (Aged 4). Oil on canvas, 1770. Unlocated.
Bibliography: Bayley, pp. 50–51; *Copley-Pelham Letters*, pp. 95, 98.
BARNARD, REV. EDWARD.* Oil on canvas, 30" x 25", 1770–74. Essex Institute, Salem, Mass.
[309]
Bibliography: Parker-Wheeler, p. 32, plate 27.
BARRELL, JOSEPH.* Pastel, 23⅜" x 18¼", 1767–69. Worcester Art Museum, Worcester, Mass.
[230]
Bibliography: Parker-Wheeler, p. 216, plate 126.
——— Watercolor on ivory, 1¼" x 1⅛", 1762–70. Mrs. L. B. Dunham, New York.
Bibliography: Parker-Wheeler, p. 241, plate 129.
This miniature seems atypical stylistically in contrast to the few known Copley miniatures in
this medium. The strong stippling and the flatness of the depicted hand are not charac-
teristic. But the paucity of comparative materials and the long record of this picture as a
Copley argue against a premature change in the present attribution.
BARRELL [A], MRS. JOSEPH (Anna Pierce).* Pastel. 22¾" x 17", 1767–69. Mrs. Robert Lee Hale,
New Canaan, Conn. [231]
Bibliography: Parker-Wheeler, pp. 216–17.
This pastel is a pendant to the pastel portrait of *Joseph Barrell* [230].
——— Pastel, 23" x 17", 1769–71. William A. Putnam, Cornwall, N.Y. [232]
Bibliography: Met '37 (21); Parker-Wheeler, pp. 216–17.
BARRELL [B], MRS. JOSEPH (Hannah Fitch).* Pastel, 23" x 17¼", c. 1771. Museum of Fine Arts,
Boston. [233]
Bibliography: Parker-Wheeler, p. 218; Copley Exhib. '65, pp. 49, 52, 137 (33).
BARRETT, JOHN.* Oil on canvas, 50" x 39¾", c. 1758. Private collection. [59]
Bibliography: Parker-Wheeler, pp. 32–33, plate 24.
BARRETT, MRS. JOHN (Sarah Gerrish).* Oil on canvas, 50" x 40", c. 1758. Private collection. [58]
Bibliography: Parker-Wheeler, pp. 33–34, plate 24.
BARRETT, SAMUEL. Oil on copper, 5⅝" x 4⅞", 1765–70. George B. Foster, Montreal, Canada.
[246]
Provenance: Mrs. C. E. Temple, Rutland, Vt., 1873; Edward Temple, Windsor, Vt., 1915.
Bibliography: Perkins, p. 35; Bayley, p. 56; Arthur Wentworth Hamilton Eaton, "Old Boston
Families, No. 2, The Family of Capt. John Gerrish," *New England Historical and Gene-
alogical Register*, LXVII (April 1913), 110.
This miniature is not recorded in Parker-Wheeler.
BARRETT, MRS. SAMUEL (Mary Clarke). Oil on copper, 5½" x 4¾", 1765–70. Dr. and Mrs.
Monroe A. McIver, Cooperstown, N.Y. [247]
Bibliography: Parker-Wheeler, p. 243.
BARROW, MR. Oil on canvas, c. 50" x 40", 1771. Unlocated.
Bibliography: Copley-Pelham Letters, p. 114; Parker-Wheeler, p. 265.
Barrow subscribed for a "half-length" portrait by Copley in New York.
BAYARD, ROBERT. Watercolor on ivory, 1¼" x 1", 1765–71. Mrs. May W. Wace, Milton, Cam-
bridge, Eng. [248]
——— Pastel, before 1771. Unlocated.
Bibliography: Copley-Pelham Letters, pp. 126, 129, 134.
This picture was sent to Copley in New York by Pelham in the summer of 1771. The correspon-
dence suggests that it was a pastel.

BAYARD, MRS. ROBERT (Rebecca Apthorp; d. 1772). Pastel (probably), c. 1771. Mrs. May W. Wace, Milton, Cambridge, Eng.

This picture has been examined only in photograph. The figure is posed half-length, facing left. She wears a light-colored dress, a black ribbon around her throat tied in a bow in the front, pearl armbands, and her hair piled high. The photograph examined was very poor, and the portrait might be oil on canvas. But the possibility that the picture might be by Copley seems very high, with strong similarity to the portraits of *Mrs. Thomas Amory II* [305] and the second *Mrs. Joseph Barrell* [233]. The portrait has been known as a portrait of Robert Bayard's first wife, Elizabeth Apthorp, but the stylistic evidence dates the portrait after her death and hence makes it likely that it is of Rebecca Apthorp, his second wife.

BELCHER, JONATHAN.* Oil on canvas, 47″ x 39″, 1756. Beaverbrook Art Gallery, Fredericton, New Brunswick, Canada. [46]

Inscribed: Signed lower right, "J. S. Copley: Pinx 1756."

Bibliography: Parker-Wheeler, pp. 34–36, plate 9; Belknap, p. 286, plate XIV, 10A.

Copies: Oil on canvas, 49″ x 39″ (sight). Nova Scotia Barristers' Society, Halifax. *Bibliography*: Probably Parker-Wheeler, p. 36.

BELCHER, MRS. JONATHAN (Abigail Allen).* Oil on canvas, 47″ x 39″, 1756. Beaverbrook Art Gallery, Fredericton, New Brunswick, Canada. [45]

Inscribed: Signed lower left, "J. Singleton Copley. pinx 1756."

Bibliography: Parker-Wheeler, pp. 36–37, plate 9; Belknap, p. 326, plate XLV, 56A.

BERNARD, GOVERNOR FRANCIS. Oil on canvas, c. 50″ x 40″, before 1767. Unlocated.

Bibliography: Parker-Wheeler, p. 265.

In a 1767 manuscript at the Ridgeway Branch, Philadelphia Public Library, the artist Du Simitière notes seeing this three-quarter-length portrait in Cambridge, hanging in the dining room of Harvard Hall (at Harvard College) over the chimney, flanked by full-length portraits of Thomas Hollis and Thomas Hancock that are enclosed within folding doors and in elegant frames, all three painted by Copley. Copley subsequently painted a smaller portrait of Bernard in England [352].

BLACKSTONE, BENJAMIN.* Oil on canvas, 48″ x 37¼″, c. 1763. Amherst College, Amherst, Mass. [124]

Bibliography: Parker-Wheeler, p. 37, plate 66; Charles H. Morgan and Margaret C. Toole, "Benjamin West: His Times and His Influence," *Art in America*, XXXVIII (Dec. 1950), 237–39.

BLACKSTONE, MRS. BENJAMIN (Eleanor Phipps).* Oil on canvas, 48⅛″ x 37⅛″, c. 1763. Amherst College, Amherst, Mass. [125]

Bibliography: Parker-Wheeler, pp. 37–38, plate 67; Charles H. Morgan and Margaret C. Toole, "Benjamin West: His Times and His Influence," *Art in America*, XXXVIII (Dec. 1950), 237–39.

BLAKE, JOSEPH.* Oil on copper, 5″ x 4″, 1765–67. Winthrop Gardner Minot, Greenwich, Conn.

Bibliography: BMFA '38, p. 30 (89); Parker-Wheeler, p. 241, plate 128.

BOURNE, MRS. SYLVANUS (Mercy Gorham).* Oil on canvas, 50¼″ x 40″, 1766. Metropolitan Museum of Art, New York (Morris K. Jesup Fund, 1924). [179]

Inscribed: Signed center right, "Jnº. S. Copley / pinx 1766."

Bibliography: Met '37 (18); Parker-Wheeler, pp. 38–39, plate 70; Gardner and Feld, pp. 41–42.

BOURS, JOHN.* Oil on canvas, 50¼″ x 40⅛″, 1758–61. Worcester Art Museum, Worcester, Mass. [93]

Bibliography: Met '37 (36); BMFA '38, p. 20 (9); Parker-Wheeler, p. 39, plate 26; Copley Exhib. '65, pp. 29, 31, 136 (15).

BOWEN, JABEZ.* Oil on canvas, 29¹³⁄₁₆″ x 24⅞″, 1771–74. Mr. and Mrs. Donald Bowen, Providence, on loan at the Museum of Art, Rhode Island School of Design, Providence. [322]

Bibliography: Parker-Wheeler, p. 40, plate 124.

BOWEN, MRS. JABEZ (Sarah Brown).* Oil on canvas, 29¹³⁄₁₆″ x 24¾″, 1771–74. Mr. and Mrs.

Donald Bowen, Providence, on loan at the Museum of Art, Rhode Island School of Design, Providence. [323]

Bibliography: Parker-Wheeler, pp. 40–41, plate 124.

BOWERS, MRS. JERATHMAEL (Mary Sherburne). Oil on canvas, 49⅞″ x 39¾″, 1767–70. Metropolitan Museum of Art, New York (Rogers Fund, 1915). [219]

Bibliography: Parker-Wheeler, pp. 41–42, plate 39; Belknap, pp. 274, 313, 315, plate XLII, 52A; Gardner and Feld, pp. 39–41; Copley Exhib. '65, pp. 54–55, 137 (38).

The possibility exists that this is a portrait of Mrs. Joseph Sherburne (Mary Plaisted).

BOWLER, MRS. METCALF (Anne Fairchild).* Oil on canvas, 50¼″ x 40¼″, c. 1758. Mr. and Mrs. Ellerton M. Jette, Waterville, Maine, on indefinite loan at Colby College Art Museum. [84]

Bibliography: Met '37 (24); Parker-Wheeler, p. 43 [as a replica].

———— Oil on canvas, 50″ x 40″, c. 1763. Alida Livingston, Oyster Bay, Long Island, N.Y. [119]

Bibliography: Parker-Wheeler, pp. 42–43, plate 37; Copley Exhib. '65, pp. 29, 34, 136 (18).

BOY WITH A SQUIRREL. See *Pelham, Henry*.

BOYLSTON, NICHOLAS.* Oil on canvas, 49″ x 40″, 1767. Harvard University, Cambridge, Mass. [182]

Inscribed: Signed lower left, "JSC [monogram] 1767."

Bibliography: Parker-Wheeler, pp. 43–44, plate 78; Copley Exhib. '65, pp. 48–49, 137 (29).

———— Oil on canvas, 50¼″ x 40¼″, c. 1767. Museum of Fine Arts, Boston. [184]

Bibliography: Parker-Wheeler, p. 44.

Replica of previous item [182].

———— Oil on canvas, 94⅛″ x 58″, 1773. Harvard University, Cambridge, Mass. [330]

Bibliography: Parker-Wheeler, pp. 43–45, plate 79.

BOYLSTON, REBECCA.* Oil on canvas, 50″ x 40″, 1767. Mrs. Paul Webster Bean, Auburn, Maine, on loan at Museum of Fine Arts, Boston. [186]

Inscribed: Signed lower left, "JSC [monogram] p 1767."

Bibliography: BMFA '38, p. 20 (10); Parker-Wheeler, p. 45, plate 81.

———— See *Gill [B], Mrs. Moses*.

BOYLSTON, MRS. THOMAS (Sarah Morecock).* Oil on canvas, 50½″ x 40½″, 1766. Harvard University, Cambridge, Mass. [178]

Inscribed: Signed center right, "Jn⁰ S. Copley / pinx 1766."

Bibliography: Met '37 (19); BMFA '38, p. 20 (12); Parker-Wheeler, p. 47, plate 69; Copley Exhib. '65, pp. 44, 49, 137 (30).

BOYLSTON II, THOMAS.* Oil on canvas, 50″ x 40³⁄₁₆″, c. 1767. Harvard University, Cambridge, Mass. [183]

Bibliography: Met '37 (20); Parker-Wheeler, p. 46, plate 77.

BRATTLE, WILLIAM.* Oil on canvas, 49½″ x 39¾″, 1756. Thomas Brattle Gannett, Wayland, Mass. [36]

Inscribed: Signed lower left, "John: S: Copley. Pinx / 1756."

Bibliography: BMFA '38, p. 20 (13); Parker-Wheeler, pp. 47–48, plate 10.

BROWN, MRS. GAWEN (Elizabeth Byles).* Oil on canvas, 19″ x 17½″, c. 1763. Yale University Art Gallery, New Haven, Conn. [111]

Bibliography: Parker-Wheeler, pp. 49–50, plate 28.

———— Pastel, 17½″ x 14½″, 1763. Bayou Bend Collection of Americana, Museum of Fine Arts, Houston, Texas. [110]

Inscribed: Signed center right, "JS [monogram]. C. del. / 1763."

Bibliography: Met '37 (7); BMFA '38, p. 20 (14); Parker-Wheeler, p. 218, plate 126.

BROWNE, REV. ARTHUR.* Oil on canvas, 29½″ x 24½″, 1757. Heritage Foundation, Deerfield, Mass. [47]

Inscribed: Signed lower left, "I. S. Copley Pinx 1757."

Bibliography: Parker-Wheeler, p. 50, plate 12; Copley Exhib. '65, pp. 20, 25, 135 (8).

BROWNE, MRS. ARTHUR (Mary Cox).* Oil on canvas, 29″ x 25″, 1757. Heritage Foundation, Deerfield, Mass. [48]
    Bibliography: Parker-Wheeler, pp. 50–51, plate 12.

BROWNE, JANE (Mrs. Samuel Livermore).* Oil on canvas, 30⅛″ x 25⅛″, 1756. National Gallery of Art, Washington, D.C. (Andrew Mellon Collection, 1942). [40]
    Inscribed: Signed lower right, "I. S. Copley. Pinx. 1756."
    Bibliography: BMFA '38, p. 21 (15); Parker-Wheeler, pp. 51–52, plate 7; Copley Exhib. '65, pp. 20, 24, 135 (7).

BRUCE, CAPTAIN R. G. Pastel, 1766–67. Unlocated.
    Bibliography: Copley-Pelham Letters, pp. 43, 53.
    Captain Bruce asked Copley from London, Aug. 4, 1766, to send him a copy of his picture, which he had left with Mrs. Melville. That portrait may or may have not been by Copley. On June 11, 1767, he wrote again to thank Copley for the portrait, which had been sent directly to Benjamin West "that he may see your Performance in Crayons."

BULFINCH, SUSAN [?]. Pastel, 23⅞″ x 18⅛″. Milwaukee Art Center, Milwaukee, Wisc.
    Provenance: Vose Galleries, Boston, 1958.
    Attributed to Copley by Barbara N. Parker, 1958.
    This picture has been examined only in photograph.

BURR, THADDEUS.* Oil on canvas, 50⅝″ x 39⅞″, 1758–60. City Art Museum, St. Louis, Mo. [91]
    Bibliography: Met '37 (35); Parker-Wheeler, pp. 53, 54, plate 48; Perry T. Rathbone, "A Pair of Portraits by John Singleton Copley," *Bulletin of the City Art Museum of St. Louis*, XXXVIII, no. 1 (1953); Copley Exhib. '65, pp. 22, 29, 136 (13).

BURR, MRS. THADDEUS (Eunice Dennie).* Oil on canvas, 49⅞″ x 39⅜″, 1758–60. City Art Museum, St. Louis, Mo. [90]
    Bibliography: Parker-Wheeler, pp. 54–55, plate 49; Perry T. Rathbone, "A Pair of Portraits by John Singleton Copley," *Bulletin of the City Art Museum of St. Louis*, XXXVIII, no. 1 (1953).

BYLES, REV. MATHER.* Oil on canvas, 30¼″ x 25¼″, 1765–67. American Antiquarian Society, Worcester, Mass. [199]
    Bibliography: Parker-Wheeler, pp. 55–56, plate 62.

———— Oil on canvas, c. 30″ x 24″, 1771–74. University of King's College, Halifax, Nova Scotia. [200]

CALIF, MRS. JOSEPH (Hannah Jordan).* Oil on canvas, 36½″ x 30″, c. 1764. Lammot du Pont Copeland, Greenville, Del. [147]
    Bibliography: Parker-Wheeler, pp. 56–57.
    The picture is not signed and dated, as reported to Parker and Wheeler. But it seems probable that the portrait was cut down, since no other canvas of this size shows a three-quarter-length figure. This would account for the unusually high head placement, as well as possible loss of the signature.

CARSON, MRS. WILLIAM. c. 1772. Unlocated.
    Bibliography: Copley-Pelham Letters, p. 187; Parker-Wheeler, p. 265.
    William Carson praised his wife's portrait by Copley in a letter to the artist dated Aug. 16, 1772.

CARY, SAMUEL.* Watercolor on ivory, 1⁷⁄₁₆″ x 1³⁄₁₆″, c. 1769. Edward Cunningham, Dover, Mass. [252]
    Bibliography: BMFA '38, p. 30 (90); Parker-Wheeler, p. 242, plate 129; *New England Miniatures*, p. 10, fig. 11 (34); Copley Exhib. '65, pp. 55, 137 (36).
    Copies: Kate Cary, Lenox, Mass., 1930.

CARY, MRS. SAMUEL (Sarah Gray).* Watercolor on ivory, 1⅜″ x 1³⁄₁₆″, c. 1769. Edward Cunningham, Dover, Mass. [253]
    Inscribed: Signed lower right, "JSC [monogram]."

Bibliography: BMFA '38, p. 30 (91); Parker-Wheeler, p. 242, plate 129; *New England Miniatures*, p. 10, fig. 10 (35); Copley Exhib. '65, pp. 55, 137 (37).

Copies: Kate Cary, Lenox, Mass., 1930.

CARY, REV. THOMAS.* Oil on canvas, 50″ x 40¼″, 1773. Museum of Fine Arts, Boston. [324]

Bibliography: BMFA '38, p. 21 (16); Parker-Wheeler, pp. 57–58, plate 113; Copley Exhib. '65, pp. 73–74, 138 (52).

CHARDON, PETER.* Pastel, 22¼″ x 17¼″, c. 1766. Yale University Art Gallery, New Haven, Conn. [209]

Bibliography: Parker-Wheeler, p. 219.

CLARKE, DR. JOHN. Oil on canvas, three-quarter length. Destroyed.

Provenance: Peter Wainwright, Boston, 1872; destroyed in the Boston fire of 1872.

Bibliography: Augustus Thorndike Perkins, "Sketches," *New England Historical and Genealogical Register*, XXVII (Oct. 1873), 370; Perkins, p. 44; Bayley, p. 77.

Described as a three-quarter-length portrait of a noble-looking man in a white wig, white silk stockings, and a black velvet suit, "seated at a table on which stood a manikin." The sitter was a wealthy doctor.

CLARKE, MRS. JOHN (Elizabeth Breame). Oil on canvas, three-quarter length. Destroyed.

Provenance: Same as previous item.

Bibliography: Same as previous item.

The companion picture to the previous painting, this portrait was described as depicting a "handsome woman, dressed in a rich green silk, having pearl ornaments on her neck and in her hair. Her right hand rested on a table, while in her left she held a book."

CLARKE, WILLIAM. Oil on canvas, three-quarter length. Destroyed.

Provenance: Same as previous items.

Bibliography: Same as previous items.

The sitter wore a "rich pearl-colored suit. He was standing with his left hand upon his hip, and the background was a landscape with a house and some trees."

COFFIN, THOMAS ASTON.* Oil on canvas, 50⅛″ x 40³⁄₁₆″, 1757–59. Munson-Williams-Proctor Institute, Utica, N.Y. [85]

Bibliography: Parker-Wheeler, p. 58, plate 13.

COFFIN, MRS. WILLIAM (Ann Holmes).* Oil on canvas, 30¼″ x 20¾″, c. 1770. William Davies Sohier, Manchester, Mass. [271]

Bibliography: Parker-Wheeler, p. 59, plate 95.

COOPER, REV. MYLES.* Oil on canvas, 29½″ x 24½″, 1768. Columbia University, New York. [223]

Bibliography: Met '37 (26); Parker-Wheeler, pp. 59–61, plate 88.

COOPER, REV. SAMUEL.* Oil on canvas, 30″ x 25″, 1769–71. Williams College, Williamstown, Mass. [266]

Bibliography: Parker-Wheeler, pp. 61–62, plate 93A.

——— Oil on canvas, 26½″ x 20½″, 1767–69. Ralph Waldo Emerson House, Concord, Mass. [265]

Bibliography: Parker-Wheeler, pp. 61–63, plate 93B.

COPLEY, JOHN SINGLETON.* Pastel, 23¾″ x 17½″, 1769. Henry Francis du Pont Winterthur Museum, Winterthur, Del. [226 and frontispiece]

Bibliography: BMFA '38, p. 21 (20); Parker-Wheeler, p. 219.

——— Watercolor on ivory, 1½″ x 1⅛″, 1769. Katrine Rosalind Copley Greene, New York. [250]

Inscribed: Signed and dated lower right, "JSC [monogram] 176[9]" (the last number is hidden by the case).

Bibliography: BMFA '38, p. 30 (92); Parker-Wheeler, pp. 243–44, plate 129; *New England Miniatures*, pp. 9–10, figs. 1, 12 (44).

COPLEY, MRS. JOHN SINGLETON (Susanna Clarke).* Pastel, 23⅛″ x 17¼″, 1769. Henry Francis du Pont Winterthur Museum, Winterthur, Del. [227]

Bibliography: BMFA '38, p. 21 (21); Parker-Wheeler, pp. 219–20.

COTTON, MRS. ROLAND (Deborah Mason).* Oil on canvas, 50¼″ x 39½″, c. 1763. Mrs. Harold Buckminster Hayden, Plattsburg, N.Y., on loan at Museum of Fine Arts, Boston. [123]
    Bibliography: Parker-Wheeler, p. 63, plate 87.

COX, LEMUEL. Oil on canvas, 50″ x 40″, 1770. Baltimore Museum of Art, Baltimore, Md. (bequest of Elise Agnus Daingerfield). [282]
    Inscribed: Signed and dated lower left, "JSC [monogram] 1770."
    Bibliography: Parker-Wheeler, pp. 64–65, plate 102; Adelyn D. Breeskyn, "Cox by Copley," *Baltimore Museum of Art News*, V (March 1943), 4–5.

CRANSTON, RHODA (Mrs. Luke Babcock).* Oil on canvas, 50″ x 40″, 1756–58. Mrs. Alan Cunningham, Brookline, Mass. [44]
    Bibliography: BMFA '38, p. 22 (25); Parker-Wheeler, p. 65, plate 16.

CUMMING, MRS. ALEXANDER (Elizabeth Goldthwait; later Mrs. John Bacon).* Oil on canvas, 30″ x 25″, 1770. Brooklyn Museum, Brooklyn, N.Y. [269]
    Inscribed: Signed and dated lower right, "JSC [monogram] p. Bosᵗ 1770."
    Bibliography: Met '37 (29); Parker-Wheeler, pp. 66–67, plate 100.

DALTON, TRISTRAM. 1767. Unlocated.
    Bibliography: John Rowe, *Letters and Diary* (Boston, 1903), p. 129.
    The diary entry for April 23, 1767, reads, "Mrs. [Robert] Hooper went to Copley to have her Picture drawn as did Capt. Dalton & wife." Dalton lived in Marblehead.

DALTON, MRS. TRISTRAM (Ruth Hooper). 1767. Unlocated.
    Bibliography: See previous item.

DANA, RICHARD.* Oil on canvas, 50″ x 40″, c. 1770. Richard H. Dana, Jr., New York. [280]
    Bibliography: Met '37 (28); Parker-Wheeler, pp. 67–68, plate 68.
    Copies: Oil on canvas, c. 50″ x 40″, early nineteenth century. R. Dana Gibson, Washington, Conn. *Provenance*: Dana family, taken to England. *Bibliography*: Perkins, p. 50; Parker-Wheeler, p. 68 [as replica].

DANFORTH, SAMUEL.* Oil on copper, 6″ x 5″, c. 1758. Massachusetts Historical Society, Boston. [73]
    Bibliography: Parker-Wheeler, p. 244, plate 128.

DAVIS, MRS. BENJAMIN (Anstice Greenleaf).* Oil on canvas, 30″ x 25″, c. 1764. Brooklyn Museum, Brooklyn, N.Y. [134]
    Bibliography: Met '37 (30); BMFA '38, p. 22 (26); Parker-Wheeler, pp. 68–69, plate 56.

DEVEREUX, MRS. HUMPHREY (Mary Charnock; former Mrs. Samuel Greenwood; former Mrs. Joseph Prince).* Oil on canvas, 40⅛″ x 32″, 1770–71. On indefinite loan at National Art Gallery, Wellington, New Zealand, from the Greenwood family. [283]
    Bibliography: Bayley, pp. 95–96, 134; *Copley-Pelham Letters*, pp. 81–82, 105, 154; Parker-Wheeler, p. 265; Isaac John Greenwood, *The Greenwood Family of Norwich, England, in America* (privately printed, 1934); Copley Exhib. '65, pp. 66–67, 138 (46).

ELLERY, MRS. NATHANIEL (Ann Sargent).* Oil on canvas, 51″ x 40½″, c. 1766. Estate of Fanny Rogers, on loan at Museum of Fine Arts, Boston, through the executor of the estate, George E. Rogers, Cambridge, Mass. [180]
    Bibliography: Parker-Wheeler, p. 265; *New England Historical and Genealogical Register*, XXVIII (July 1874), 366.

EPPES, MRS. WILLIAM (Abigail Pickman; later Mrs. Sylvester Gardiner).* Oil on canvas, 50″ x 40″, c. 1769. Brooklyn Museum, Brooklyn, N.Y. [260]
    Provenance: Her daughter, Mrs. Richard Routh, Poole, Dorset; Routh family to Lieut. Col. A. E. Routh, Crewkerne, Somerset; Mrs. Elizabeth Norman and Other Properties Sale, Sotheby, May 15, 1963, to Weitzner; M. Knoedler & Co., New York.

ERVING, JOHN.* Oil on canvas, 50″ x 40″, c. 1772. Alice R. Erving, Santa Barbara, Calif. [319]
    Bibliography: Parker-Wheeler, pp. 69–70, plate 112.

ERVING, JOHN, JR. [?]. Oil on wood panel, 14″ x 10″, 1757–59. Stewart Society, Edinburgh. [80]

Inscribed: On envelope ". . . / Jo E. . .g / . . ."

Provenance: His daughter, Mrs. Duncan Stewart (Anne Erving); Stewart family to Sir James Haldane Stewart Lockhart, 1933; gift of Mrs. Stewart Lockhart, Andover, Hants.

The early date of this miniature, and the fact that the sitter appears to be too young for the elder John Erving, suggests that this may be a portrait of one of his sons. Perkins, *Supplement*, p. 3, records an oval miniature of James Erving, fourth son of John Erving, which according to family tradition "was the first miniature in oil that Copley made."

FAYERWEATHER, REV. SAMUEL.* Oil on copper, 3″ x 2½″, c. 1758. Yale University Art Gallery, New Haven, Conn. (Mabel Brady Garvan Collection) [74]

Bibliography: Perkins, pp. 53–54; Bayley, pp. 103–04; Parker-Wheeler, p. 260; *New England Miniatures*, p. 10, fig. 16 (59); Copley Exhib. '65, pp. 27, 135 (11).

FLUCKER, JAMES [?]. Oil on canvas, 30″ x 25″, 1769–74. Unlocated.

Bibliography: Parker-Wheeler, pp. 72, 265.

Medium and size are here presumed on the basis that this portrait cost the same amount as that of the subject's father, Thomas Flucker (*Copley-Pelham Letters*, p. 223).

FLUCKER, THOMAS.* Oil on canvas, 28″ x 23″, 1770–72. Bowdoin College Museum of Art, Brunswick, Maine. [311]

Bibliography: Met '37 (32); BMFA '38, p. 22 (29); Parker-Wheeler, pp. 71–72, plate 115; Copley Exhib. '65, pp. 70–71, 138 (49).

FOLGER, TIMOTHY.* Oil on canvas, 50″ x 40″, 1764. Metropolitan Museum of Art, New York. [132]

Inscribed: Lower left, "J. S. Copley pinx / 1764."

Bibliography: Parker-Wheeler, p. 71.

FOWLE, JACOB.* Oil on canvas, 50″ x 40½″, c. 1761. Corcoran Gallery of Art, Washington, D.C. [98]

Bibliography: Parker-Wheeler, pp. 73–74, plate 33.

GAGE, THOMAS.* Oil on canvas, 50″ x 39¾″, 1768–69. Mrs. Ronald V. C. Bodley, Newburyport, Mass. [285]

Provenance: A. L. Nicholson, London, 1935 (Witt).

Bibliography: Parker-Wheeler, pp. 74–75, plate 86; Copley Exhib. '65, pp. 67–68, 138 (47).

Copies: Exact duplicate, including inscription, oil on canvas, 36″ x 28″.

GAGE, MRS. THOMAS (Margaret Kemble).* Oil on canvas, 50″ x 40″, 1771. Viscount Gage, Firle Place, near Lewes, Sussex. [284]

Bibliography: Parker-Wheeler, p. 265; Charles Merrill Mount, "A Hidden Treasure in Britain, Part II: John Singleton Copley," *Art Quarterly*, XXIV (Spring 1961), 41, 43, and fig. 5.

This picture was misidentified as a portrait of Charlotte Ogle, born in 1773, the daughter of Mrs. Thomas Gage. The reidentification is by Barbara N. Parker. At Firle Place there is a full-length portrait of Mrs. Thomas Gage (Margaret Kemble) by David Martin, signed and dated 1775, which is strongly reminiscent in pose of the Copley portrait. The head rests on the arm and the sleeve is folded in exactly the same manner, an apparent instance of the influence of an American Copley on a subsequent English portrait.

GAMBIER, JAMES.* Oil on canvas, 50″ x 40″, 1773. Museum of Fine Arts, Boston (gift of Amelia Peabody). [325]

Inscribed: Signed and dated lower right, "J. S. Copley / 1773, Boston."

Provenance: Baron Aberdare, London; Vose Galleries, Boston, 1915.

Bibliography: Bayley, pp. 267–68 [as an English Copley].

Captain Gambier of the Royal Navy was Commander in Chief on the North American Station, 1770–73, headquartered in New York. He began his career as a lieutenant serving in the Mediterranean in 1743, and several years later was present at the battle of Louisburg. He became Rear Admiral of the Blue (1778), Rear Admiral of the Red (1779), and Vice Admiral of the Blue (1780).

GARDINER, ANN (Mrs. Arthur Brown).* Oil on canvas, 50″ x 40″, c. 1756. Gardiner family, Gardiner, Maine. [39]

    Bibliography: Perkins: p. 39; Parker-Wheeler, pp. 76–77, plate 11; Copley Exhib. '65, pp. 20, 23, 135 (6).

    Perkins, who incorrectly believed this portrait to have been painted in England, mentions another version owned by the Marquis of Sligo.

GARDINER, JOHN. Oil on canvas, 48″ x 38¾″, c. 1768. Tudor Gardiner, Boston. [193]

    Bibliography: Parker-Wheeler, p. 77, plate 104.

GARDINER, SYLVESTER.* Oil on canvas, 50″ x 40″, c. 1772. Gardiner family, Gardiner, Maine. [318]

    Bibliography: Parker-Wheeler, pp. 78–79, plate 103.

GERRISH, BENJAMIN.* Oil on canvas, 29½″ x 24½″, 1770–72. John Elwyn Stone, New York. [313]

    Bibliography: Parker-Wheeler, p. 80, plate 99.

GERRISH, JOSEPH [?].* Oil on canvas, 30″ x 25″, 1770–72. Chicago Art Institute, Chicago, Ill. [314]

    Bibliography: Parker-Wheeler, pp. 80–81, plate 99.

GILL, MRS. MICHAEL (Relief Dowse) [?]. Oil on canvas, 50″ x 40″, 1770–71. Mrs. Leonard Pinnell, Woking, Surrey. [276]

    Bibliography: Parker-Wheeler, p. 82, plate 17.

GILL, MOSES.* Oil on canvas, 49¾″ x 39½″, 1764. Museum of Art, Rhode Island School of Design, Providence. [128]

    Inscribed: Signed and dated lower left, "J S Copley Pinxt 1764."

    Bibliography: Parker-Wheeler, pp. 82–83, plate 43.

GILL [A], MRS. MOSES (Sarah Prince).* Oil on canvas, 49¾″ x 39½″, c. 1764. Museum of Art, Rhode Island School of Design, Providence. [129]

    Bibliography: Parker-Wheeler, pp. 83–84, plate 43.

——— Pastel, 23¼″ x 17¼″ (sight), c. 1764. Ward N. Boylston, Jr., Brattleboro, Vt., on loan at Museum of Fine Arts, Boston. [130]

    Bibliography: Parker-Wheeler, p. 220.

GILL [B], MRS. MOSES (Rebecca Boylston). Oil on canvas, 49¾″ x 39½″, c. 1773. Museum of Art, Rhode Island School of Design, Providence. [326]

    Bibliography: BMFA '38, p. 20 (11); Parker-Wheeler, pp. 45–46, plate 121; Copley Exhib. '65, pp. 70, 72, 138 (51).

——— See *Boylston, Rebecca*.

GOLDTHWAIT, EZEKIEL.* Oil on canvas, 50″ x 40″, 1770–71. Museum of Fine Arts, Boston. [274]

    Inscribed: Signed lower right, "JSC [monogram]."

    Bibliography: Parker-Wheeler, pp. 84–85, plate 106; Barbara N. Parker, "Portraits of the Goldthwait Family of Boston," *Bulletin of the Museum of Fine Arts*, XXXIX (June 1941), 40–44.

GOLDTHWAIT, MRS. EZEKIEL (Elizabeth Lewis).* Oil on canvas, 50″ x 39¾″, 1770–71. Museum of Fine Arts, Boston. [273]

    Bibliography: Parker-Wheeler, p. 85, plate 106; Barbara N. Parker, "Portraits of the Goldthwait Family of Boston," *Bulletin of the Museum of Fine Arts*, XXXIX (June 1941), 40–44; Copley Exhib. '65, pp. 61, 64, 138 (43).

GORE, A BROTHER AND SISTER OF CHRISTOPHER. Oil on canvas. Unlocated.

    Bibliography: Parker-Wheeler, p. 265.

GORE, THE BROTHERS AND SISTERS OF CHRISTOPHER.* Oil on canvas, 40½″ x 56¼″, c. 1755. Henry Francis du Pont Winterthur Museum, Winterthur, Del. [29]

    Bibliography: BMFA '38, p. 22 (31); Parker-Wheeler, pp. 85–86, plate 1.

GORE, TWO SISTERS OF CHRISTOPHER. Oil on canvas, 29½″ x 39½″, c. 1755. Mrs. Barrett P. Tyler and Mrs. L. Douglas Kingsland, on loan to Gore Place, Waltham, Mass. [30]

Bibliography: Parker-Wheeler, pp. 86–87, plate 1.

GRAY, HARRISON.* Oil on canvas, 30½″ x 21½″, c. 1767. Robert H. Thayer, Washington, D.C. [195]

Bibliography: Parker-Wheeler, pp. 87–88, plate 65.

GRAY, JOHN.* Oil on canvas, 49⁷⁄₁₆″ x 39⁵⁄₁₆″, 1766. Detroit Institute of Arts, Detroit, Mich. [171]

Inscribed: Signed and dated lower right, "J. S. Copley pinx 1766."

Bibliography: Met '37 (17); Parker-Wheeler, pp. 88–89, plate 76.

GRAY, MRS. JOHN (Mary Otis).* Oil on canvas, 50″ x 39¼″, c. 1763. Massachusetts Historical Society, Boston. [126]

Bibliography: BMFA '38, p. 23 (32); Parker-Wheeler, p. 89, plate 31.

GRAY, MRS. Pastel. Unlocated.

Bibliography: Copley-Pelham Letters, p. 187; Parker-Wheeler, p. 265.

Mentioned by William Carson in a letter to Copley dated Aug. 16, 1772. The context, in which this pastel is coupled with *Boy with a Squirrel*, suggests that it may have been one of the pastels sent to England by Copley for exhibition at the Society of Artists.

GREEN, MRS. EDWARD (Mary Storer).* Pastel, 23″ x 17½″, 1765. Metropolitan Museum of Art, New York (Curtis Fund, 1908). [204]

Inscribed: Signed and dated center left, "John S. Copley / fecᵗ 1765."

Bibliography: Parker-Wheeler, p. 220.

GREEN, GEORGE.* Oil on copper, 3¼″ x 2½″, 1765–70. Museum of Fine Arts, Boston. [244]

Bibliography: New England Miniatures, fig. 20 (76).

GREEN [A], JOSEPH.* Pastel, 24″ x 17″, 1767. Museum of Fine Arts, Boston. [215]

Inscriptions: Signed and dated center right, "JSC [monogram] 1767."

Bibliography: BMFA '38, p. 23 (34); Parker-Wheeler, p. 221, plate 126B.

GREEN [A], MRS. JOSEPH (Elizabeth Cross; former Mrs. Nathaniel Austin).* Pastel, 23¼″ x 17¼″, c. 1767. Museum of Fine Arts, Boston. [216]

Inscribed: Signed center left, "JSC [monogram, very faint]."

Bibliography: BMFA '38, p. 23 (35); Parker-Wheeler, pp. 221–22.

GREEN [B], JOSEPH.* Pastel, 22″ x 17″, c. 1764. Museum of Fine Arts, Boston. [151]

Bibliography: BMFA '38, p. 23 (33); Parker-Wheeler, pp. 220–21, plate 126A; *New England Historical and Genealogical Register*, XV (April 1861), 108.

GREENE, BENJAMIN. Oil on canvas, three-quarter length. Destroyed.

Provenance: Rev. John S. C. Greene, Longwood, Mass., 1872; destroyed in the Boston fire of 1872.

Bibliography: Augustus Thorndike Perkins, "Sketches," *New England Historical and Genealogical Register*, XXVII (Oct. 1873), 370; Perkins, p. 63; Bayley, p. 126.

GREENE, GARDINER. See *Murray, Mrs.*

GREENE, JOHN.* Oil on canvas, 50″ x 40″, c. 1769. Currier Gallery of Art, Manchester, N.H. [262]

Bibliography: BMFA '38, p. 23 (36); Parker-Wheeler, p. 90, plate 101.

GREENE, MRS. JOHN (Catherine Greene).* Oil on canvas, 48¾″ x 39¾″, 1769. Cleveland Museum of Art, Cleveland, Ohio (John Huntington Collection). [261]

Inscribed: Signed and dated lower right, "JSC [monogram] p. 1769."

Bibliography: Parker-Wheeler, p. 91, plate 98; Belknap, p. 307, plate XXXVI, 40A.

GREENE, JOSEPH.* Pastel, 23½″ x 17¼″, 1767. Mrs. Allan Forbes, Boston. [213]

Inscribed: Signed and dated center right, "J. S. Copley / fecᵗ 1767."

Bibliography: BMFA '38, p. 23 (37); Parker-Wheeler, p. 222, plate 127.

GREENE, MRS. JOSEPH (Mary Greene).* Pastel, 23¼″ x 17¼″, 1767. Mrs. Allan Forbes, Boston. [214]

Inscribed: Signed and dated lower left, "J. S. Copley / pinx 1767."

Bibliography: BMFA '38, p. 23 (38); Parker-Wheeler, pp. 222–23, plate 127; Copley Exhib. '65, pp. 49, 51, 137 (32).

GREENE, RUFUS.* Oil on canvas, 24″ x 20¾″, 1758–61. Senator Theodore F. Green, Providence, R. I. [61]
    Bibliography: Parker-Wheeler, pp. 91–92, plate 23.
GREENE, MRS. RUFUS (Katherine Stanbridge).* Oil on canvas, 24″ x 20¾″, 1758–61. Senator Theodore F. Green, Providence, R. I. [62]
    Bibliography: Parker-Wheeler, pp. 92–93, plate 23.
    The portraits of *Mr. and Mrs. Rufus Greene* have been dated 1760 on the basis of old inscriptions on the backs of the canvases. Both canvases were cut down, probably from 50″ x 40″. Perkins, p. 67, discusses these portraits as of *Mr. and Mrs. Benjamin Greene*, noting that the portraits were formerly full-length but "being injured by fire were reduced in size." In the *Supplement*, p. 13, he corrects the identification to *Mr. and Mrs. Rufus Greene*.
GREENE, THOMAS.* Oil on canvas, 50″ x 40″, 1758. Cincinnati Art Museum, Cincinnati, Ohio. [56]
    Inscribed: Letter in painting dated, "Sept 25, 1758."
    Bibliography: Parker-Wheeler, pp. 93–94, plate 12.
GREENE, MRS. THOMAS (Martha Coit).* Oil on canvas, 50½″ x 40″, c. 1758. Mr. and Mrs. Lawrence A. Fleischman, Detroit, Mich. [57]
    Bibliography: Parker-Wheeler, p. 94, plate 12; Copley Exhib. '65, pp. 20, 26, 135 (10).
HALL, HUGH.* Pastel, 15¾″ x 12⅞″ (sight), 1758. Michael C. Janeway, New York. [77]
    Inscribed: Signed and dated lower right, "J. S. Copley, / Pinx. 1758."
    Bibliography: Parker-Wheeler, p. 223; Copley Exhib. '65, pp. 27–28, 136 (12).
HALLOWELL, BENJAMIN.* Oil on canvas, 50″ x 40″, 1765–68. Vaughan family, Hallowell, Maine. [191]
    Bibliography: BMFA '38, p. 23 (39); Parker-Wheeler, p. 95, plate 64.
HALLOWELL, MRS. BENJAMIN (Mary Boylston).* Oil on canvas, 47″ x 37½″, 1766–67. Mrs. A. R. Wise, London. [190]
HANCOCK, BOY CALLED MASTER. See *Unknown Subject, Boy Called Master Hancock*.
HANCOCK, JOHN.* Oil on canvas, 49½″ x 40½″, 1765. Museum of Fine Arts, Boston, on deposit from City of Boston. [153]
    Inscribed: Signed and dated lower left, "J. S. Copley / pinx 1765."
    Bibliography: Met '37 (14); Parker-Wheeler, pp. 96–97, plate 60; Copley Exhib. '65, pp. 39, 42, 136 (23).
———— Oil on canvas, 29½″ x 24½″, 1770–72. Henry Lee Shattuck, Brookline, Mass. [300]
    Bibliography: Parker-Wheeler, pp. 96–98 [as replica or copy], plate 99.
    This picture is not a copy, and the question is unresolved whether this one or the following portrait [301] was painted first, with the other being a replica.
———— Oil on canvas, 30″ x 24½″, 1770–72. James S. Copley, La Jolla, Calif. [301]
    Bibliography: Parker-Wheeler, pp. 96–98.
    This picture has been examined only in photograph. See previous item.
———— Oil on canvas, full-length. Unlocated.
    Bibliography: Parker-Wheeler, pp. 98–99.
HANCOCK, THOMAS.* Oil on canvas, 95⅝″ x 59⁷⁄₁₆″, 1764–66. Harvard University, Cambridge, Mass. [154]
    Bibliography: Met '37 (6); Parker-Wheeler, pp. 99–100, plate 45.
———— Pastel, 18″ x 15″, c. 1758. Mrs. James A. Howe, Greenwich, Conn. [76]
———— Pastel, 24″ x 18½″, 1766. Unlocated. [157]
    Inscribed: Signed and dated lower left, "J. S. Copley 1766."
    Bibliography: BMFA '38, p. 23 (40); Parker-Wheeler, pp. 223–24, plate 127.
———— Oil on copper, 3⅞″ x 2⅞″ (sight); 3³⁄₁₆″ x 2½″ (original copper oval inset), c. 1758. Charles H. Wood, Wellesley, Mass. [75]
    Bibliography: Parker-Wheeler, pp. 244–45; *New England Miniatures* (85).

This miniature was originally smaller than the later matching portrait of *Mrs. Thomas Hancock* [155]. At some point, in order to make the pair visually harmonious, the earlier and smaller miniature was set into a larger cut-out copper oval and painted out to the new border.

HANCOCK, MRS. THOMAS (Lydia Henchman).* Pastel, 24″ x 18½″, c. 1766. Unlocated. [156]
Bibliography: BMFA '38, p. 24 (41); Parker-Wheeler, p. 224, plate 127.
———— Oil on copper, 3⅞″ x 2⅞″ (sight), c. 1766. Charles H. Wood, Wellesley, Mass. [155]
Bibliography: Parker-Wheeler, p. 245; *New England Miniatures* (86).

HENCHMAN, DANIEL [?]. Oil on canvas, 29¾″ x 24¼″, 1770–74. Concord Art Association, Concord, Mass. [320]
Bibliography: Met '37 (1); Parker-Wheeler, pp. 100–02.
Since Daniel Henchman died in 1761, the traditional identification of the portrait is unacceptable. Bayley, p. 137 (quoted in Parker-Wheeler), cites a 1766 bill to John Hancock for a quarter-length portrait of Daniel Henchman, but the present portrait, as noted in Parker-Wheeler, seems like a life portrait and its style indicates a later date.

HENLEY, MRS. SAMUEL (Katherine Russell).* Pastel, 22¾″ x 17¾″, c. 1765. Museum of Fine Arts, Boston. [205]
Bibliography: BMFA '38, p. 24 (42); Parker-Wheeler, pp. 224–25.

HENSHAW, JOSEPH.* Oil on canvas, 30¼″ x 24¾″, 1770–74. Mrs. Leon Little, Chestnut Hill, Mass. [308]
Bibliography: Parker-Wheeler, p. 102.

HENSHAW, MRS. JOSEPH (Sarah Henshaw).* Pastel, 24″ x 17¾″, 1769–72. Bayou Bend Collection of Americana, Museum of Fine Arts, Houston, Texas. [238]
Bibliography: BMFA '38, p. 24 (43); Parker-Wheeler, p. 225.

HENSHAW, JOSHUA.* Oil on canvas, 50¼″ x 40″, c. 1770. California Palace of the Legion of Honor, San Francisco. [279]
Bibliography: Parker-Wheeler, p. 103, plate 118; J[ermayne] M[acAgy], "Portrait of Joshua Henshaw," *Bulletin of the California Palace of the Legion of Honor Museum*, I (Oct. 1943), 57–61.

HENSHAW II, JOSHUA.* Oil on canvas, 30¼″ x 25¼″, 1770–74. Estate of Margarethe L. Dwight, on loan at Museum of Art, Rhode Island School of Design, Providence. [306]

HENSHAW II, MRS. JOSHUA (Catherine Hill).* Oil on canvas, 30″ x 25⅛″, 1770–74. Estate of Margarethe L. Dwight, on loan at Museum of Art, Rhode Island School of Design, Providence. [307]

HILL, HENRY.* Pastel, 23″ x 17″, c. 1770. Mrs. Joseph F. Knowles, Wellesley, Mass. [242]
Bibliography: BMFA '38, p. 24 (46); Parker-Wheeler, pp. 225–26 [as Thomas Hill]; Perkins, p. 72 [as Henry Hill].

HILL, MRS. HENRY (Anna Barrett).* Pastel, 21¾″ x 16¼″, c. 1770. Chicago Art Institute, Chicago, Ill. [243]
Bibliography: BMFA '38, p. 24 (44); Parker-Wheeler, p. 226; Arthur Wentworth Hamilton Eaton, "Old Boston Families, No. 2, The Family of Capt. John Gerrish," *New England Historical and Genealogical Register*, LXVII (April 1913), 110; *Art Institute of Chicago Quarterly*, LIII–LIV (Feb. 1960), 3.

HILL, MRS. SAMUEL (Miriam Kilby; former Mrs. Benjamin Clarke).* Oil on canvas, 50½″ x 40½″, c. 1764. Henry B. Cabot, Dover, Mass. [148]
Bibliography: BMFA '38, p. 24 (45); Parker-Wheeler, p. 104, plate 50.

HOLLIS, THOMAS. Oil on canvas, 94″ x 58″, 1766. Harvard University, Cambridge, Mass. [158]
Bibliography: Parker-Wheeler, pp. 104–05, plate 102.

HOLMES, JOHN BEE.* Oil on canvas, 29½″ x 24½″, 1765. H. Richard Dietrich, Jr., and Daniel Wellington Dietrich II, Philadelphia, Pa. [160]
Inscribed: Signed and dated lower right, "J. S. Copley / pinx 1765."
Bibliography: Parker-Wheeler, p. 106, plate 95.

HOLYOKE, REV. EDWARD.* Oil on canvas, 50½″ x 40½″, 1759–61. Harvard University, Cambridge, Mass. [92]
  Bibliography: Parker-Wheeler, pp. 107–08, plate 20.
  Copies: Copies (1) and (4), Parker-Wheeler, p. 108, are the same object, owned by Mrs. Robert F. King, Ashfield, Mass.
HOOPER, ALICE (Mrs. Jacob Fowle; Mrs. Joseph Cutler).* Oil on canvas, 49″ x 39″, c. 1763. Mrs. Ivan Hekimian, Buffalo, N. Y. [117]
  Bibliography: Parker-Wheeler, pp. 108–09, plate 35.
HOOPER, JOSEPH.* Oil on canvas, 50″ x 40″, 1770–71. Mr. and Mrs. Jacob Blaustein, Pikesville, Md. [277]
  Bibliography: Parker-Wheeler, pp. 109–10.
HOOPER, MRS. JOSEPH (Mary Harris).* Oil on canvas, 50″ x 40″, 1770–71. Mr. and Mrs. Jacob Blaustein, Pikesville, Md. [278]
  Bibliography: Parker-Wheeler, p. 110.
HOOPER, ROBERT.* Oil on canvas, 50″ x 39¾″, 1767. Robert C. Hooper, Cambridge, Mass. [201]
  Inscribed: Signed and dated right center, "JSC [monogram] p. 1767. Bosⁿ:".
  Bibliography: Parker-Wheeler, pp. 111–12, plate 80.
———— Watercolor on ivory, 1¼″ x 1″, c. 1767. Hirschl & Adler Galleries, New York.
  Provenance: Harriet Hooper; Sarah Bradbury Curtis; Bethia Curtis Reed, 1907; sale, Louis Joseph, Inc., Boston, 1951.
  Inscription on back of case, "Robert Hooper / Died at Marblehead / May 25, 1790. Age 80 / Copley Painter."
HOOPER, MRS. ROBERT (Hannah White).* Oil on canvas, 50″ x 39½″, c. 1767. New York Public Library (Lenox Collection). [202]
  Bibliography: Met '37 (10); Parker-Wheeler, pp. 112–13, plate 80.
HOOPER II, ROBERT.* Oil on canvas, 49¾″ x 40¼″, 1770–71. Robert Hooper Stevenson, Boston. [281]
  Bibliography: Parker-Wheeler, p. 113, plate 98.
HOOPER, MRS. STEPHEN (Sarah Woodbridge). Oil on canvas, c. 50″ x 40″, 1773. Unlocated.
  Bibliography: Copley-Pelham Letters, p. 200; Parker-Wheeler, p. 266.
  The original bill for this portrait, in the possession of Vose Galleries, Boston, made out to Stephen Hooper and dated Nov. 1773, reads: "To His Lady's Portrait, one-half length — £28 / To a case for ditto [—] .6" and on the reverse: "Received the within sum of 28 pounds six shillings / lawful money of Jonathan Snelling, Esq. / [signed] John Singleton Copley."
  Henry Pelham painted a miniature portrait of Stephen Hooper in the same year. *Copley-Pelham Letters*, pp. 199–200.
HOOPER, REV. WILLIAM (1702–1767). Oil on canvas, c. 30″ x 25″, 1767–69. Louis Graves, Chapel Hill, N. C. [267]
  Hooper was the rector of Trinity Church, 1747–67, and the portrait descended in his family. It is quite badly abraded, and the loss of impasto makes the figure look strangely soft. But the portrait seems all right typologically, and the basic brushwork is consistent with Copley's manner; hence the portrait is tentatively attributed to Copley. It has been examined only in photograph.
HOWARD, MARTIN.* Oil on canvas, 49½″ x 39¾″, 1767. Social Law Library, Boston, on loan at Museum of Fine Arts, Boston. [192]
  Inscribed: Signed and dated right center, "JSC [monogram] 1767."
  Bibliography: Met '37 (23); BMFA '38, p. 24 (47); Parker-Wheeler, pp. 114–15, plate 74; Copley Exhib. '65, pp. 49–50, 137 (31).
HUBBARD, DANIEL.* Oil on canvas, 49½″ x 39½″, 1764. Chicago Art Institute, Chicago, Ill. [138]
  Inscribed: Signed and dated center right, "John S. Copley pinx. 1764."

Bibliography: Parker-Wheeler, pp. 115–16; Frederick A. Sweet, "Mr. and Mrs. Daniel Hubbard by John Singleton Copley," *Bulletin of the Art Institute of Chicago*, XLII (Feb. 1948), 16–17.

HUBBARD, MRS. DANIEL (Mary Greene).* Oil on canvas, 49¼″ x 39½″, c. 1764. Chicago Art Institute, Chicago, Ill. [139]

Bibliography: Parker-Wheeler, p. 116; Frederick A. Sweet, "Mr. and Mrs. Daniel Hubbard by John Singleton Copley," *Bulletin of the Art Institute of Chicago*, XLII (Feb. 1948), 16–17.

HUBBARD, THANKFUL.* Miniature, 1758. Unlocated.

Bibliography: Parker-Wheeler, p. 266.

A dated bill for this miniature, made out to Mr. Thomas Fayerweather, is at the Massachusetts Historical Society.

HUBBARD, THOMAS.* Oil on canvas, 49″ x 39″, c. 1767. Harvard University, Cambridge, Mass. [185]

Bibliography: Parker-Wheeler, pp. 116–17, plate 75.

HURD, NATHANIEL.* Oil on canvas, 30″ x 25½″, c. 1765. Cleveland Museum of Art, Cleveland, Ohio (John Huntington Collection). [177]

Bibliography: Met '37 (16); Parker-Wheeler, pp. 117–119, plate 61 (portrait A); Copley Exhib. '65, pp. 45, 47, 137 (28).

Copies:

1. What appears in photograph to be an early copy, or possibly a replica, is owned by Miss H. L. Fenerty, Armdale, Halifax County, Nova Scotia, on loan to the Public Archives, Halifax.

2. By John Mason Furness, c. 1800. Emily Furness, Brookline, Mass. (Information courtesy of Barbara Parker.)

——— Oil on canvas, 28¾″ x 24½″, c. 1765. Memorial Art Gallery of the University of Rochester, Rochester, N. Y. (Marion Stratton Gould Fund). [176]

Bibliography: BMFA '38, p. 24 (48); Parker-Wheeler, pp. 117–19, plate 61 (portrait B).

——— Oil on copper, 2¾″ x 2″, 1755–58. Emily Furness, Brookline, Mass. [69]

Inscribed: Signed in red pigment center right, "I. S. C."

Bibliography: *New England Miniatures*, p. 10 (105).

HUST, M., AND LADY. 1771. Unlocated.

Bibliography: *Copley-Pelham Letters*, p. 114; Parker-Wheeler, p. 266.

"M Hust and Lady" subscribed for two bust portraits by Copley in New York.

HUTCHINSON, THOMAS. Unlocated.

Bibliography: *Copley-Pelham Letters*, p. 242; Parker-Wheeler, p. 266.

In a letter to Henry Pelham from London dated Aug. 25, 1774, Copley asked Pelham to send Hutchinson "the drawing I took of him with a pencil some years since."

INMAN, RALPH.* Pastel, 24″ x 18″, c. 1770. Boston Athenaeum. [241]

Provenance: Inman family to Mrs. Gouvernor K. Warren, 1875, great-great-granddaughter of the sitter; her daughter, Emily B. Warren, Newport, R. I.

Bibliography: Parker-Wheeler, p. 258.

The pastel was found to be backed with the *Boston Gazette* of March 26, 1770.

JACKSON, JONATHAN.* Pastel, 23″ x 17″ [sight], 1767–69. Francis W. Peabody, Chestnut Hill, Mass. [228]

Bibliography: Parker-Wheeler, p. 226 (portrait A); Copley Exhib. '65, pp. 49, 53, 137 (34).

An early photograph (Frick Art Reference Library) indicates that in its present framing the picture has been cropped or folded back several inches at the top.

——— Pastel, 22¼″ x 18″, 1767–69. Massachusetts Historical Society, Boston.

Bibliography: BMFA '38, p. 25 (50); Parker-Wheeler, pp. 226–27 (portrait B).

This pastel is in poor condition.

———— Watercolor on ivory, 1½″ x 1¼″, c. 1770. Mr. and Mrs. John M. Elliot, Boston. [251]

Inscribed: On back of case, "H. J. to H. J. Lee 1844 J. J. 1770."

Bibliography: *New England Miniatures*, fig. 13 (108).

JACKSON, SARAH (Mrs. Henderson Inches).* Oil on canvas, 49″ x 39¼″ (sight), c. 1765. Mrs. Oric Bates, Groton, Mass. [166]

Bibliography: Parker-Wheeler, p. 120, plate 57.

JOHNSTON, MISS. 1771. Unlocated.

Bibliography: *Copley-Pelham Letters*, p. 114; Parker-Wheeler, p. 266.

"Miss Johnston" subscribed for a half-length (50″ x 40″) portrait from Copley in New York, rather than a bust (as reported in Parker-Wheeler).

KEMP, MR. (John Taber Kemp?). 1771. Unlocated.

Bibliography: *Copley-Pelham Letters*, p. 114; Parker-Wheeler, p. 266.

"Mr. Kemp" subscribed for a portrait by Copley in New York.

LANE, JOHN. Unlocated.

John Lane died in 1829, aged eighty-six. A copy of his portrait by Copley is mentioned in his will (Somerset House). The portrait probably was painted during Lane's visit to America, Aug. 14, 1769 — July 22, 1771 (information on John Lane courtesy of Katherine Kellock, Washington, D.C.). The portrait of the unknown *Gentleman with a Cane* [304] was identified as *John Lane* prior to its acquisition by the Brooklyn Museum, and was purchased from the Lane family estate, King's Bromley, near Lichfield, England. That portrait accords stylistically with the dates of Lane's visit to America, and the only negative factor is that Lane at the time of the portrait would have been about twenty-seven, whereas the sitter in the portrait looks somewhat older. But the evidence seems strong that the portrait of the gentleman in Brooklyn is indeed *John Lane*.

LANGDON, WOODBURY.* Oil on canvas, 49⅝″ x 40″, 1765–66. Mrs. Thomas B. Foster, New York. [169]

Bibliography: Parker-Wheeler, pp. 121–22, plate 82.

LANGDON, MRS. WOODBURY (Sarah Sherburne).* Oil on canvas, 49¾″ x 39¾″, 1765–66. Mrs. Thomas B. Foster, New York. [170]

Bibliography: Parker-Wheeler, p. 122, plate 83; Copley Exhib. '65, pp. 45–46, 136–37 (27).

LEE, JEREMIAH.* Oil on canvas, 94⅞″ x 58⅞″, 1769. Wadsworth Atheneum, Hartford, Conn. [257]

Inscribed: Signed and dated center left, "JSC [monogram] P. 1769."

Bibliography: Parker-Wheeler, p. 123, plate 90; Copley Exhib. '65, pp. 58, 60–61, 137 (41).

———— Watercolor on ivory, 1½″ x 1¼″, c. 1769. Metropolitan Museum of Art, New York (Harrison Brisbane Dick Fund). [249]

Bibliography: Louise Burroughs, "Colonel Jeremiah Lee, a Miniature by Copley," *Bulletin of the Metropolitan Museum of Art*, XXXV (Dec. 1940), 236–37.

———— Watercolor on ivory, 1½″ x 1¼″, c. 1769. Marblehead Historical Society, Marblehead, Mass.

Bibliography: Louise Burroughs, "Colonel Jeremiah Lee, a Miniature by Copley," *Bulletin of the Metropolitan Museum of Art*, XXXV (Dec. 1940), 236–37. This appears to be a replica or copy of the previous item [249].

LEE, MRS. JEREMIAH (Martha Swett).* Oil on canvas, 94⅞″ x 58⅞″, 1769. Wadsworth Atheneum, Hartford, Conn. [258]

Inscribed: Signed and dated lower left at base of column, "JSC [monogram] P. 1769."

Bibliography: Parker-Wheeler, p. 124, plate 91; Copley Exhib. '65, pp. 59–61, 137–38 (42).

LEWIS, THOMAS.* Oil on canvas, 51″ x 40″, 1766–67. Glover Johnson, New Rochelle, N.Y. [194]

Bibliography: Parker-Wheeler, pp. 124–25.

LIVIUS. 1767. Unlocated.

Bibliography: *Copley-Pelham Letters*, pp. 60–61.

In Sept. 1767 George Livius in Portsmouth sent two "family pictures" to Copley in Boston, in order to have copies made that he could take with him to England. The originals were "painted by De Kelberg."

LORING, HANNAH (Mrs. Joshua Winslow).* Oil on canvas, 49¼″ x 38½″, 1763. William Caleb Loring, Prides Crossing, Mass. [122]

Inscribed: Signed and dated center left, "J. S. Copley Pinx 1763."

Bibliography: Parker-Wheeler, pp. 125–26, plate 37.

LYNDE, LYDIA (Mrs. William Walter).* Oil on canvas, 30¼″ x 25½″, 1762–64. Frederick S. Moseley, Jr., New York. [136]

Bibliography: Parker-Wheeler, pp. 126–27, plate 52.

McEVERS, MRS. CHARLES (Mary Verplanck).* Oil on canvas, 30″ x 24¼″, 1771. Mrs. Alfred Renshaw, Old Lyme, Conn. [297]

Bibliography: Parker-Wheeler, p. 266.

MACKINTOSH, MR. AND MRS. Unlocated.

In his bill of June 8, 1774, submitted immediately prior to his departure for England, to Isaac Royall for family portraits, Copley included an item for portraits of "Mr. Mackintosh & Lady — £14-0-0." Mrs. Isaac Royall was Elizabeth MacIntosh.

MacWHORTER, REV. ALEXANDER.* Oil on canvas, 30″ x 25″, 1769. Yale University Art Gallery, New Haven, Conn. [263]

Inscribed: Signed and dated lower right, "JSC [monogram] p. 1769."

Bibliography: BMFA '38, p. 25 (52); Parker-Wheeler, pp. 127–28, plate 94; John Marshall Phillips, "Two Copley Portraits," *Bulletin of the Associates in Fine Arts at Yale University,* VI (June 1937), 31–33.

MacWHORTER, MRS. ALEXANDER (Mary Cumming).* Oil on canvas, 30″ x 25″, 1769. Yale University Art Gallery, New Haven, Conn. [264]

Inscribed: Signed and dated lower right, "JSC [monogram] p. Bos: 1769."

Bibliography: Parker-Wheeler, pp. 128–29, plate 94; BMFA '38, p. 25 (53); John Marshall Phillips, "Two Copley Portraits," *Bulletin of the Associates in Fine Arts at Yale University,* VI (June 1937), 31–33.

MALLET, J. [Jonathan?]. c. 30″ x 25″, 1771. Unlocated.

Bibliography: Copley-Pelham Letters, p. 114; Parker-Wheeler, p. 266.

"J. Mallet" subscribed for a bust portrait by Copley in New York.

MALLETT, MRS. (Mary Livingston; 1748–1830). Oil on canvas, 36″ x 29¾″, 1771. Hirschl & Adler Galleries, New York. [299]

Provenance: Caleb S. Green, Trenton, N. J.

MANN, JOSEPH.* Oil on canvas, 36″ x 28¼″, 1754. Museum of Fine Arts, Boston. [21]

Inscribed: Signed and dated lower right, "I S Copley Pinx. 1754."

Bibliography: Parker-Wheeler, pp. 129–30, plate 3.

MANN, MRS. JOSEPH (Bethia Torrey).* Oil on canvas, 36″ x 27¼″, 1753. Museum of Fine Arts, Boston. [20]

Inscribed: Signed and dated lower right, "J S Copley Pinx 1753."

Bibliography: Parker-Wheeler, pp. 130–31, plate 3; Belknap, p. 293, plate XX, 16A; Copley Exhib. '65, pp. 17–18, 135 (4).

MARCHANT, HENRY (1741–1796). Oil on copper, 4¹³⁄₁₆″ x 3⅞″ (sight), c. 1765. William Marchant Prest, Brooklyn, N. Y., and Edward Clarke Prest, Rockville Centre, N. Y. [168]

Provenance: Frank E. Marchant, West Kingston, Rhode Island; Florence Clarke Prest (d. 1958) and Alice Clarke, Cohoes, N. Y.

Bibliography: Bayley, p. 171; Parker-Wheeler, p. 266.

MARCHANT, MRS. HENRY (Rebecca Cooke). Oil on copper, 4⅞″ x 4″ (sight), c. 1765. William Marchant Prest, Brooklyn, N. Y., and Edward Clarke Prest, Rockville Centre, N. Y. [167]

Provenance: Frank E. Marchant, West Kingston, Rhode Island; Florence Clarke Prest (d. 1958) and Alice Clarke, Cohoes, N. Y.

Bibliography: Bayley, p. 171; Parker-Wheeler, p. 266.

MARSHALL, THOMAS.* Oil on canvas, 49½″ x 38½″, c. 1755. Mrs. Franklin E. Campbell, West Medford, Mass. [52]

Bibliography: Parker-Wheeler, pp. 131–32, plate 6.

MARSHALL, MRS. THOMAS (Lucy Allen).* Oil on canvas, 49½″ x 39½″, c. 1757. George Barner, Melrose, Mass. [51]

Bibliography: Parker-Wheeler, pp. 132–33, plate 6.

MARTIN, MARY ELIZABETH.* Oil on canvas, 45½″ x 40″, 1771. Addison Gallery of American Art, Phillips Academy, Andover, Mass. [291]

Bibliography: Parker-Wheeler, pp. 123–24, plate 109.

MATURIN, GABRIEL. c. 30″ x 25″, 1771. Unlocated.

Bibliography: Copley-Pelham Letters, p. 114; Parker-Wheeler, p. 266.

"Captain Maturin" subscribed for a bust portrait in New York.

MAYHEW, REV. JONATHAN (1720–1756). Pastel, 1766–67. Destroyed.

Provenance: Peter Wainwright, Boston, 1872; destroyed in the Boston fire of 1872.

Bibliography: Perkins, pp. 84, 130; Bayley, p. 175; Perkins, "Sketches," *New England Historical and Genealogical Register*, XXVII (Oct. 1873), 370–71.

Perkins describes this picture as portraying the sitter half-length in black silk robes, wearing a large wig. Mayhew, it will be recalled, was the pastor of West Church whose sermon on civil liberty after the Stamp Act offended Copley's future father-in-law, Richard Clarke, and caused him to withdraw his family from the church.

———— Pastel, 1766–67. Unlocated.

Bibliography: Perkins, p. 130.

Copley received ten guineas for two pastel portraits of Mayhew on Feb. 25, 1767.

MAYHEW, MRS. JONATHAN (Elizabeth Clarke). Destroyed.

Provenance: Peter Wainwright, Boston, 1872; destroyed in the Boston fire of 1872.

Bibliography: Perkins, p. 84; Bayley, p. 175; Perkins, "Sketches," *New England Historical and Genealogical Register*, XXVII (Oct. 1873), 371.

This picture is described by Perkins as depicting the sitter in a "white muslin robe, blue mantle and a hat. In her right hand she held a rose-bud, while in her left she carried a basket of flowers."

MIFFLIN, MR. AND MRS. THOMAS (Sarah Morris).* Oil on canvas, 60½″ x 48″, 1773. Historical Society of Pennsylvania, Philadelphia. [331]

Inscribed: Signed and dated upper right, "J. Singleton Copley. Pinx. 1773. Boston."

Bibliography: Met '37 (33); Parker-Wheeler, pp. 134–36, plate 123; Copley Exhib. '65, pp. 74–77, 138 (55).

MONTRESOR, JOHN (1736–1799). Oil on canvas, 30″ x 25″, c. 1771. Detroit Institute of Arts, Detroit, Mich. [295]

Provenance: Mrs. Joan (Montresor) Read; Howard Young Galleries, London, c. 1934; Ferargil Galleries, New York, 1941.

MORRIS, MRS. ROGER (Mary Phillipse).* Oil on canvas, 30 1/16″ x 24 3/16″, 1771. Henry Francis du Pont Winterthur Museum, Winterthur, Del. [296]

Provenance: Morris family; Amherst Morris, England; Ehrich Galleries, New York, 1926; John Hay Whitney, New York; Wildenstein and Co., New York; Lawrence Fleischman, Detroit; Kennedy Galleries, New York.

Bibliography: Parker-Wheeler, p. 255 [as Mrs. Robert Morris].

MORTIER, MRS. (Mrs. Abraham Mortier?). 1771. Unlocated.

Bibliography: Copley-Pelham Letters, p. 114; Parker-Wheeler, p. 266.

"Mrs. Mortier" subscribed for a portrait in New York.

MOUNTFORT, JONATHAN.* Oil on canvas, 29¼″ x 24½″, c. 1753. Detroit Institute of Arts, Detroit, Mich. [26]

Inscribed: Signed lower right, "John S. Copley Pinx."
Bibliography: BMFA '38, p. 25 (54); Parker-Wheeler, p. 136, plate 4.
A close examination of the signature does not reveal the date recorded in Parker-Wheeler, but rather the word "Pinx."

MURRAY, DOROTHY (Mrs. John Forbes).* Oil on canvas, 36¼" x 28⅛", 1759–61. Fogg Art Museum, Harvard University, Cambridge, Mass. [96]
Bibliography: Parker-Wheeler, pp. 137–38, plate 36.

MURRAY, JAMES.* Oil on canvas, 49½" x 39½", c. 1763. Frank Lyman, Cambridge, Mass. [127]
Bibliography: Met '37 (27); Parker-Wheeler, pp. 138–140, plate 60.

MURRAY, JOHN.* Oil on canvas, 50" x 40", c. 1763. New Brunswick Museum, St. John, New Brunswick, Canada. [103]
Bibliography: Parker-Wheeler, pp. 140–141, plate 36.

MURRAY, MRS. JOHN (Lucretia Chandler).* Oil on canvas, 49¼" x 39½", 1763. H. Daland Chandler, Boston. [104]
Inscribed: Signed and dated lower right, "J. S. Copley Pinx 1763."
Bibliography: BMFA '38, p. 25 (55); Parker-Wheeler, p. 141, plate 40.

MURRAY, MRS., AND HER NEPHEW, GARDINER GREENE. Destroyed.
Provenance: Rev. John Singleton Copley Greene, Boston, 1872; destroyed in the Boston fire of 1872.
Bibliography: Perkins, "Sketches," *New England Historical and Genealogical Register*, XXVII (Oct. 1873), 370; Perkins, p. 63; Bayley, pp. 128–29.
Perkins describes the picture as being in Copley's early manner, with the subject seated and Gardiner Greene (the owner's grandfather and Copley's future son-in-law) standing by her side.

NEWTON, JOHN.* Oil on canvas, 30¼" x 25¼", 1772. Berkshire Athenaeum, Pittsfield, Mass. [312]
Inscribed: Signed and dated upper left, "John Singleton Copley / pinx 1772. Bo[s]ton."
Bibliography: Parker-Wheeler, p. 142, plate 115.

OGLE, CHARLOTTE. See *Gage, Mrs. Thomas*.

OGILVIE, REV. JOHN.* Oil on canvas, 50" x 40", 1771. Trinity Church, New York. [288]
Bibliography: Met '37 (31); Parker-Wheeler, pp. 102–04, plate 108.

OLIVER, ANDREW.* Oil on copper, 5" x 4", c. 1758. Seabury Oliver, Morristown, N.J. [67]
Bibliography: BMFA '38, p. 30 (93); Parker-Wheeler, pp. 245–46; Andrew Oliver, *Faces of a Family* (privately printed, 1960), p. 6, no. 5c.
———— Oil on copper, 2" x 1¾", c. 1758. Yale University Art Gallery, New Haven, Conn. [63]
Bibliography: Oliver, p. 5, no. 5a.
———— Oil on copper, 1¾" x 1½", c. 1758. Andrew Oliver, New York. [65]
Bibliography: Parker-Wheeler, pp. 245–46 [as replica of large miniature]; Oliver, p. 5, no. 5b.

OLIVER, MRS. ANDREW (Mary Sanford).* Oil on copper, 1¹¹⁄₁₆" x 1⅜", c. 1758. Yale University Art Gallery, New Haven, Conn. [64]
Bibliography: Oliver, p. 7, no. 7a.
———— Oil on copper, 1¾" x 1⅜", c. 1758. Andrew Oliver, New York. [66]
Bibliography: Parker-Wheeler, p. 246; Oliver, p. 6, no. 7.

OLIVER II, ANDREW.* Oil on copper, 2⅞" x 1⅜", c. 1758. Museum of Fine Arts, Boston. [71]
Bibliography: Parker-Wheeler, p. 246; Oliver, p. 11, no. 10a; *New England Miniatures* (135).

OLIVER, ELIZABETH (Mrs. Edward Lyde).* Oil on canvas, 17" x 14", c. 1758. Massachusetts Historical Society, Boston. [81]
Bibliography: BMFA '38, p. 25 (56); Parker-Wheeler, p. 144, plate 14; Oliver, p. 13, no. 13.

OLIVER, GRISELDA (Mrs. Samuel Waldo).* Oil on canvas, 17½" x 14½", c. 1758. Deerfield Academy, Deerfield, Mass. [82]
Bibliography: BMFA '38, p. 26 (57); Parker-Wheeler, p. 145, plate 14; Oliver, p. 12, no. 12.

———— Oil on copper, 3¼" x 2½", c. 1758. Yale University Art Gallery, New Haven, Conn. [72]

Bibliography: New England Miniatures, fig. 21 (188); Oliver, p. 12, no. 12a.

OLIVER, PETER.* Oil on copper, 5" x 4", c. 1758. Andrew Oliver, New York. [68]

Bibliography: BMFA '38, p. 30 (94); Parker-Wheeler, p. 247; Oliver, p. 7, no. 8a.

———— Oil on canvas, full-length. Unlocated.

Provenance: Oliver family to Miss Ware, Cambridge, Mass., a great-granddaughter, 1892.

Bibliography: Oliver, p. 10, no. 8h.

The portrait represented Chief Justice Peter Oliver in his scarlet judicial robes.

OTIS, JAMES.* Oil on canvas, 49½" x 39½", c. 1758. Wichita Art Museum, Wichita, Kansas (Roland P. Murdock Collection). [54]

Bibliography: Parker-Wheeler, pp. 145–46, plate 19.

OTIS, MRS. JAMES (Mary Alleyne).* Oil on canvas, 49½" x 39½", c. 1758. Wichita Art Museum, Wichita, Kansas (Roland P. Murdock Collection). [55]

Bibliography: Parker-Wheeler, pp. 146–47, plate 19.

OTIS, MRS. SAMUEL ALLEYNE (Elizabeth Gray).* Oil on canvas, 30¾" x 26¾", c. 1764. Robert H. Thayer, Washington, D.C. [137]

Bibliography: Parker-Wheeler, pp. 147–48, plate 52.

PELHAM, CHARLES.* Oil on canvas, 36" x 28", c. 1754. Charles P. Curtis, Southport, Conn. [27]

Bibliography: Perkins, p. 92; Bayley, p. 192; Parker-Wheeler, p. 255; Copley Exhib. '65, pp. 17, 19, 135 (5).

PELHAM, HENRY (BOY WITH A SQUIRREL).* Oil on canvas, 30¼" x 25", 1765. Private collection. [163]

Provenance: Lyndhurst Sale (85), to Bentley.

Bibliography: Met '37 (11); BMFA '38, p. 26 (58); Parker-Wheeler, pp. 148–50, plate 62 (portrait A); Copley Exhib. '65, pp. 41–42, 136 (26).

———— Oil on canvas, 16¾" x 13¾", 1758–61. Charles P. Curtis, Southport, Conn. [95]

Bibliography: BMFA '38, p. 26 (59); Parker-Wheeler, pp. 148–50, plate 51 (portrait B).

———— Drawing. Unlocated.

Inscribed: Signed and dated lower right, "JSC [monogram] 1767."

Provenance: Lawrence Park; Charles D. Childs, Boston; John Hill Morgan, Farmington, Conn.

Bibliography: Parker-Wheeler, p. 266.

Attributed to Copley by Parker-Wheeler on the basis of a heliotype.

PELHAM, PETER [William Pelham?]. Oil on canvas, 34½" x 27¾", 1753. Charles P. Curtis, Southport, Conn. [28]

Inscribed: Signed and dated center right, "John S. Copley. Fect: 1753."

Bibliography: Parker-Wheeler, pp. 151–52, plate 4.

PERKINS, NATHANIEL.* Oil on canvas, 30" x 25", 1770–74. Mrs. Charles B. Wiggin, New York. [321]

Bibliography: Parker-Wheeler, pp. 152–53, plate 40.

There is an inscription in Greek in the lower right. The first word, which presumably has something to do with healing, resists interpretation, but the remainder can be translated "or not to injure." The inscription relates to Perkins' profession as a physician. One of the books in his library behind him is marked "attus."

PICKMAN, BENJAMIN.* Oil on canvas, 50" x 40", 1758–61. Edith Wetmore, Newport, R. I. [99]

Bibliography: Met '37 (2); BMFA '38, p. 26 (60); Parker-Wheeler, pp. 153–54, plate 18.

PICKMAN, MRS. BENJAMIN (Mary Toppan).* Oil on canvas, 50" x 40", 1763. Edith Wetmore, Newport, R. I. [115]

Inscribed: Signed and dated center left, "J: S: Copley. Pinx. 1763 / A E. 19."

Bibliography: Met '37 (9); BMFA '38, p. 26 (61).

PITTS, ELIZABETH (Mrs. Jonathan Warner).* Pastel, 23¾" x 17⅞", c. 1764. Detroit Institute of Arts, Detroit, Mich. [131]

Bibliography: Parker-Wheeler, pp. 227–28.

POWELL, MRS. JOHN (Anna Susan Dummer).* Oil on canvas, 49½″ x 39½″, 1764. Ellery Sedgwick, Jr., Gates Mills, Ohio. [143]

Bibliography: Parker-Wheeler, p. 155, plate 49; Copley Exhib. '65, pp. 36–37, 136 (21).

———— Oil on canvas, 50″ x 40″, c. 1764. Yale University Art Gallery, New Haven, Conn. [146]

Bibliography: Parker-Wheeler, p. 155 [as replica].

This portrait is a replica of fig. 143.

POWELL II, JOHN.* Pastel, 22″ x 16½″, c. 1764. W. D. P. Jarvis, King City, Ontario, Canada. [149]

Bibliography: BMFA '38, p. 26 (62); Parker-Wheeler, p. 228.

POWELL II, MRS. JOHN (Jane Grant).* Pastel, 22″ x 16½″, c. 1764. W. D. P. Jarvis, King City, Ontario, Canada. [150]

Bibliography: BMFA '38, p. 26 (63); Parker-Wheeler, p. 228.

QUINCY, DOROTHY (later Mrs. John Hancock; Mrs. James Scott).* Oil on canvas, 50″ x 39½″, c. 1772. Mrs. Atherton Loring, Boston, on loan at Museum of Fine Arts, Boston. [316]

Bibliography: Parker-Wheeler, pp. 156–57, plate 118.

QUINCY, JOSIAH.* Oil on canvas, 36″ x 28½″, c. 1767. Private collection. [198]

Bibliography: Parker-Wheeler, pp. 157–58.

QUINCY, SAMUEL.* Oil on canvas, 35½″ x 28¼″, c. 1767. Grace W. Treadwell, Boston, on loan at Museum of Fine Arts, Boston. [197]

Bibliography: Parker-Wheeler, pp. 158–59, plate 64.

QUINCY, MRS. SAMUEL (Hannah Hill).* Oil on canvas, 35½″ x 28¼″, c. 1761. Grace W. Treadwell, Boston, on loan at Museum of Fine Arts, Boston. [97]

Bibliography: Parker-Wheeler, pp. 159–60, plate 27.

REA, MRS. DANIEL, AND HER DAUGHTER. Oil on canvas, 49″ x 39″, c. 1757. Butler Art Institute, Youngstown, Ohio. [50]

Provenance: Descended in family to William Charles Thompson, North Attleboro, Mass., great-great-great-grandson of sitter.

Bibliography: Parker-Wheeler, p. 255; Barbara N. Parker, "Problems of Attribution in Early Portraits by Copley," *Bulletin of the Museum of Fine Arts*, XL (June 1942), 54–57.

Mrs. Rea, whose third husband was Daniel Rea of Boston and Beverly, was a Miss Salter of Salem, Mass.

REVERE, PAUL.* Oil on canvas, 35″ x 28½″, 1768–70. Museum of Fine Arts, Boston. [272]

Bibliography: BMFA '38, p. 26 (64); Parker-Wheeler, pp. 160–61, plate 63; Copley Exhib. '65, pp. 61, 65, 138 (45).

RICHARD, MRS. PAUL (Elizabeth Garland).* Oil on canvas, 50″ x 39½″, 1771. Bayou Bend Collection of Americana, Museum of Fine Arts, Houston, Texas. [287]

Bibliography: BMFA '38, p. 27 (65); Parker-Wheeler, p. 162, plate 110.

RICHARDS, JOHN. Oil on canvas, 30″ x 24⅞″, 1770–71. Mrs. Frederic Milholland, Princeton, N. J. [294]

Bibliography: Parker-Wheeler, p. 255.

RICHARDS, CAPTAIN (Charles Lloyd?). 1771. Unlocated.

Bibliography: *Copley-Pelham Letters*, p. 128; Parker-Wheeler, p. 267.

This item and the preceding one [294] may be identical. Copley mentioned this portrait in a letter from New York dated July 14, 1771, to Henry Pelham.

ROGERS, DANIEL [?]. Oil on canvas, 50″ x 40½″, 1767. Museum of Fine Arts, Boston. [217]

Inscribed: Signed and dated lower right, "JSC [monogram] 1767."

Bibliography: Parker-Wheeler, pp. 162–63, plate 76.

ROGERS, MRS. DANIEL (Elizabeth Gorham).* Oil on canvas, 50″ x 40″, 1762. Mrs. Eugene Duffer, Arlington, Va. [100]

Inscribed: Signed and dated lower right, "John S. Copley Pinx / 1762."

Bibliography: Met '37 (4); Parker-Wheeler, p. 164, plate 25; *New England Historical and Genealogical Register*, L (Jan. 1896), 33–34.

ROGERS, JOHN (the Protomartyr). Oil on canvas, 24½″ x 20¼″ (sight), 1753–58, probably 1756–58. Massachusetts Historical Society, Boston [12]

Bibliography: Parker-Wheeler, p. 256; *New England Historical and Genealogical Register*, XII (Oct. 1858), 341.

Bayley, p. 210, says that this portrait was signed and dated 1759, but the signature is not in evidence. Barbara Parker, upon further examination of the painting, reversed her earlier opinion given in Parker-Wheeler and concluded that the portrait is by Copley and stylistically related to *Nathaniel Appleton* and *Rufus Greene* (Belknap folder, Museum of Fine Arts, Boston).

Copies: American Antiquarian Society, Worcester, Mass. This copy was supposedly taken from a painting owned by Governor Thomas Hutchinson. The original source remains unlocated.

ROGERS, MRS. TIMOTHY (Lucy Boylston) [?]. Oil on canvas, 50″ x 40″, 1766–67. Mrs. Paul Webster Bean, Auburn, Maine, on loan at Museum of Fine Arts, Boston. [187]

Bibliography: Parker-Wheeler, pp. 164–65, plate 17.

Since Mrs. Rogers died in 1759, it seems probable that this portrait, closely related stylistically to other Boylston portraits of 1766–67, is of another member of the Boylston family.

ROSS, ELIZABETH (Mrs. William Tyng).* Oil on canvas, 50″ x 40″, 1766–67. Museum of Fine Arts, Boston (M. and M. Karolik Collection). [175]

Bibliography: BMFA '38, p. 27 (67); Hipkiss, pp. 14–15 (7); Parker-Wheeler, pp. 165–66, plate 84.

ROYALL, ISAAC.* Oil on canvas, 50″ x 40″, 1769. Museum of Fine Arts, Boston (M. and M. Karolik Collection). [254]

Bibliography: BMFA '38, p. 27 (68); Hipkiss, pp. 4–5 (2); Parker-Wheeler, pp. 166–67, plate 112.

ROYALL, MRS. ISAAC (Elizabeth MacIntosh).* Oil on canvas, 50″ x 40″, 1769–80. Virginia Museum of Fine Arts, Richmond (Mrs. A. D. Williams, 1949). [364, vol. 2]

Bibliography: Parker-Wheeler, p. 168.

This portrait, begun in America and completed in England, is discussed and reproduced in Volume Two.

ROYALL, MARY MacINTOSH (Mrs. George Erving), AND ELIZABETH ROYALL (Mrs. William Sparhawk).* Oil on canvas, 57½″ x 48″, c. 1758. Museum of Fine Arts, Boston. [83]

Bibliography: Met '37 (3); Parker-Wheeler, pp. 169–70, plate 15; Copley Exhib. '65, pp. 20–21, 135 (9).

ROYALL, MISS POLLY. Pastel, 1769–74. Unlocated.

Bibliography: Parker-Wheeler, p. 267.

This pastel was listed in the bill for her parents' portraits.

RUSSELL, MRS. JAMES (Katherine Graves).* Oil on canvas, 50¼″ x 40¼″, 1770–71. Museum of Fine Arts, Boston. [275]

Bibliography: Parker-Wheeler, p. 170, plate 71.

ST. CLAIR, SIR JOHN.* Oil on copper, 1¾″ x 1⅜″, 1759. Historical Society of Pennsylvania, Philadelphia. [79]

Inscribed: Signed and dated lower right, "I S C 1759."

Bibliography: BMFA '38, p. 30 (95); Parker-Wheeler, p. 247.

SARGENT, MRS. DANIEL (Mary Turner).* Oil on canvas, 50″ x 40″, 1763. Mrs. Thomas R. Symington, New York, on loan at Corcoran Gallery of Art, Washington, D.C. [116]

Inscribed: Signed and dated lower left, "John Singleton Copley / pinx 1763."

Bibliography: Parker-Wheeler, pp. 170–71, plate 35; Copley Exhib. '65, pp. 29, 33, 35, 136 (17).

SARGENT, EPES.* Oil on canvas, 49⅞″ x 40″, 1759–61. National Gallery of Art, Washington, D.C. (gift of the Avalon Foundation, 1959). [89]

Bibliography: Met '37 (5); Parker-Wheeler, pp. 171–72, plate 21; Copley Exhib. '65, pp. 29–30, 136 (14).

SARGENT II, EPES.* Oil on canvas, 49″ x 39″, c. 1764. Oliver D. Knauth, Washington, D.C. [145]
Bibliography: BMFA '38, p. 27 (69); Parker-Wheeler, pp. 172–73, plate 47.

SARGENT II, MRS. EPES (Catherine Osborne).* Oil on canvas, 49″ x 39″, 1764. Oliver D. Knauth, Washington, D.C. [144]
Inscribed: Signed and dated lower right, "John S. Copley pin 1764."
Bibliography: BMFA '38, p. 27 (70); Parker-Wheeler, pp. 173–74, plate 47.

SAVAGE, SAMUEL PHILLIPS.* Oil on canvas, 49½″ x 39″, 1764. Mr. and Mrs. John Richard Savage, St. Paul, Minn. [141]
Inscribed: Signed and dated center right, "J. S. Copley, Pinx 1764."
Bibliography: Parker-Wheeler, pp. 176–77, plate 46.

SAVAGE, MRS. SAMUEL PHILLIPS (Sarah Tyler).* Oil on canvas, 50⅛″ x 40⅛″, c. 1764. Worcester Art Museum, Worcester, Mass. [142]
Bibliography: Parker-Wheeler, pp. 177–78, plate 46.

SCHILLING, G. W. (?). c. 1769. Unlocated.
Bibliography: *Copley-Pelham Letters*, pp. 76–77; Parker-Wheeler, p. 267.
Copley was sent a letter by this man, dated Oct. 18, 1769, Utrecht, noting that Copley's picture had been well received.

SCOLLAY, DEBORAH (Mrs. John Melville).* Watercolor on ivory, 1¼″ x 1½₂″ (sight), c. 1762. Worcester Art Museum, Worcester, Mass. [112]
Bibliography: BMFA '38, p. 30 (96); Parker-Wheeler, pp. 247–48, plate 129; *New England Miniatures*, p. 10, fig. 14 (167); Copley Exhib. '65, pp. 35, 136 (20).

SCOLLAY, JOHN.* Oil on canvas, 36″ x 28½″, 1763–64. Shelburne Museum, Shelburne, Vt. [105]
Bibliography: Parker-Wheeler, pp. 178–79, plate 22.
———— Pastel, 21⅞″ x 16⅞″ (sight), 1764. Mrs. Edward W. Kimball, Lexington, Mass. [107]
Inscribed: Signed and dated center right, "JSC [monogram] 1764."
Bibliography: Copley Exhib. '65, pp. 35–36, 136 (19).

SCOLLAY, MRS. JOHN (Mercy Greenleaf).* Oil on canvas, 35″ x 27″, 1763. Mrs. Calvin Josselyn Ellis, West Hanover, Mass. [106]
Inscriptions: Signed and dated lower left, "J. S. Copley. Pinx. 1763."
Bibliography: Parker-Wheeler, p. 179.
———— Pastel, 21¾″ x 17″, 1764. Fogg Art Museum, Harvard University, Cambridge, Mass. (Grenville L. Winthrop Collection). [108]
Inscribed: Signed and dated lower left, "JSC [monogram] 1764."

SCOTT, GEORGE.* Oil on canvas, 50″ x 40″, 1755–57. The Brook, New York. [35]
Provenance: General Joshua Winslow; Winslow family; purchased from Elizabeth C. Trott, 1909.
Bibliography: Parker-Wheeler, p. 256.

SCOTT, JAMES. c. 1766. Unlocated.
Bibliography: *Copley-Pelham Letters*, p. 46; Parker-Wheeler, p. 267.
Copley received a letter from this sitter in London, dated Sept. 5, 1766, noting, "I have got the portrait safe home. It gives great satisfn."

SCOTT, JOSEPH.* Oil on canvas, 49¾″ x 39″, c. 1765. Mrs. Theodore S. Watson, Greenwich, Conn. [172]
Bibliography: Parker-Wheeler, pp. 180–81, plate 54.

SCOTT, MRS. JOSEPH (Freelove Olney).* Oil on canvas, 50″ x 39¾″, c. 1765. Newark Museum, Newark, N. J. [173]
Bibliography: Parker-Wheeler, p. 181, plate 55.

SEWALL, REV. JOSEPH. Oil on canvas, 30″ x 25″, c. 1766. International Business Machines Corporation, New York. [196]

Provenance: Thomas Robie Sewall, Joseph F. Sewall, 1918; George C. Chapin; Robert Campbell, Boston, c. 1950.

Bibliography: Parker-Wheeler, p. 267.

SHERBROOK, MILES. Oil on canvas, c. 50″ x 40″, 1771. Unlocated.

Bibliography: Parker-Wheeler, p. 267.

SHERBURNE, JOSEPH.* Oil on canvas, 50″ x 40″, 1767–70. Metropolitan Museum of Art, New York. (Lazarus Fund, 1923). [218]

Bibliography: Parker-Wheeler, pp. 181–82, plate 105; Gardner and Feld, pp. 42–43.

SKINNER, MRS. RICHARD (Dorothy Wendell).* Oil on canvas, 39¾″ x 30¾″, 1772. Museum of Fine Arts, Boston. [315]

Inscribed: Signed and dated center right, "John Singleton Copley. pinx / 1772 / Boston."

Provenance: Lyndhurst Sale (60), to Timmins.

Bibliography: BMFA '38, p. 27 (72); Parker-Wheeler, pp. 182–83, plate 119; Copley Exhib. '65, pp. 70, 81, 138 (50).

SMALL, JOHN. Pastel, c. 1769. Unlocated.

Bibliography: *Copley-Pelham Letters*, pp. 77–78; Parker-Wheeler, p. 267.

Small mentions this pastel, and the miniature taken from it (next item), in a letter from New York dated Oct. 29, 1769. He also discusses a copy of the pastel that he wishes to order.

———— Miniature, c. 1769. Unlocated.

Bibliography: *Copley-Pelham Letters*, p. 77; Parker-Wheeler, p. 267.

SMITH, ISAAC.* Oil on canvas, 49¼″ x 39½″, 1769. Yale University Art Gallery, New Haven, Conn. [255]

Bibliography: Parker-Wheeler, pp. 183–84, plate 96; Copley Exhib. '65, pp. 55, 60, 63, 137 (39).

SMITH, MRS. ISAAC (Elizabeth Storer).* Oil on canvas, 50⅛″ x 40⅛″, 1769. Yale University Art Gallery, New Haven, Conn. [256]

Bibliography: Parker-Wheeler, p. 184, plate 97; Copley Exhib. '65, pp. 55, 57, 60, 137 (40).

SMITH, MRS. JAMES (Elizabeth Murray).* Oil on canvas, 49½″ x 40″, 1769. Museum of Fine Arts, Boston. [259]

Bibliography: BMFA '38, p. 28 (73); Parker-Wheeler, pp. 185–86, plate 92.

SPARHAWK, NATHANIEL.* Oil on canvas, 90″ x 57½″, 1764. Estate of Frederick H. Rindge, on deposit at Museum of Fine Arts, Boston. [152]

Inscribed: Signed and dated center right, "John S. Copley / pinx 1764."

Bibliography: Parker-Wheeler, pp. 186–87, plate 44; Copley Exhib. '65, pp. 36, 38–39, 136 (22).

SPOONER, JOHN.* Oil on canvas, 30″ x 25¾″, 1763. Hobart A. Spalding, Washington, D.C., on loan at Museum of Fine Arts, Boston. [113]

Inscribed: Signed and dated lower right, "J. S. Copley / Pinx 1763."

Bibliography: Parker-Wheeler, pp. 187–88, plate 28.

STEVENS, MRS. JOHN (Judith Sargent; later Mrs. John Murray).* Oil on canvas, c. 50″ x 40″, 1770–72. John P. Sargent, New York. [310]

Bibliography: Parker-Wheeler, pp. 174–75, plate 85 [as Judith Sargent].

STEVENS, MRS. WILLIAM (Elizabeth Allen).* Oil on canvas, 49½″ x 39½″, c. 1757. Montclair Art Museum, Montclair, N.J. [49]

Bibliography: Parker-Wheeler, p. 189, plate 20.

STEWART, DUNCAN.* Oil on canvas, 50″ x 40″, 1767. Stewart Society, Edinburgh. [189]

Inscribed: Signed and dated center left, "JSC [monogram] p. 1767."

Provenance: Family of Duncan Stewart, Sixth Earl of Ardsheal, Argyllshire, Scotland; Sir James Haldane Stewart Lockhart, London, 1933; Mrs. Stewart Lockhart, Andover, Hants.

STEWART, MRS. DUNCAN (Anne Erving).* Oil on canvas, 50″ x 40″, c. 1767. Stewart Society, Edinburgh. [188]

Provenance: Same as previous item.

STORER, EBENEZER.* Pastel, 24″ x 18″, 1767–69. Metropolitan Museum of Art, New York (purchased 1940, Thomas J. Watson Gift). [234]

Bibliography: Parker-Wheeler, p. 230 [as Ebenezer Storer, Jr., portrait A]; Herman W. Williams, Jr., "Two Early Pastels by Copley," *Bulletin of the Metropolitan Museum of Art*, (June 1941), 136–40, fig. 1.

Copies: Black and white chalk, 12½″ x 9⅝″. Amelia Peabody, Boston. *Bibliography*: Parker-Wheeler, p. 230 [as Ebenezer Storer, Jr., portrait B]; Williams, "Two Early Pastels by Copley," fig. 3.

STORER, MRS. EBENEZER (Mary Edwards).* Pastel, 24″ x 18″, 1767–69. Metropolitan Museum of Art, New York (purchased 1940, Thomas J. Watson Gift). [235]

Bibliography: Met '37 (22); Parker-Wheeler, p. 229; Herman W. Williams, Jr., "Two Early Pastels by Copley," *Bulletin of the Metropolitan Museum of Art*, XXXVI (June 1941), 136–40, fig. 5.

Copies: Black and white chalk, 12½″ x 9⅝″. Amelia Peabody, Boston. *Bibliography*: Parker-Wheeler, p. 231 [as Mrs. Ebenezer Storer, Jr.]; Williams, "Two Early Pastels by Copley," fig. 7.

———— Pastel, 23″ x 17¼″, 1767–69. Museum of Fine Arts, Boston.

Provenance: William Storer Eaton; Miss G. G. Eaton, 1915; gift of Mrs. Francis Storer Eaton, 1955.

Replica of previous item [235].

STORER II, EBENEZER.* Pastel, 23⅛″ x 17⅛″ (sight), 1767–69. John P. Sedgwick, Jr., Greensboro, N. C. [236]

Bibliography: Parker-Wheeler, p. 230 (portrait B); Herman W. Williams, Jr., "Two Early Pastels by Copley," *Bulletin of the Metropolitan Museum of Art*, XXXVI (June 1941), 136–40, fig. 2.

Copies:

1. Oil on panel, 10″ x 8″, c. 1800. Mrs. Helen F. Lambert, San Diego, Calif.

2. Watercolor on ivory, 1¼″ x 1″, by Joseph Dunkerley. Yale University Art Gallery, New Haven, Conn.

STORER II, MRS. EBENEZER (Elizabeth Green).* Pastel, 23⅞″ x 17⅝″, 1767–69. John P. Sedgwick, Jr., Greensboro, N. C. [237]

Bibliography: Parker-Wheeler, pp. 230–31; Herman W. Williams, Jr., "Two Early Pastels by Copley," *Bulletin of the Metropolitan Museum of Art*, XXXVI (June 1941), 136–40, fig. 6.

Copies:

1. Oil on panel, 10″ x 8″, c. 1800, Mrs. Helen F. Lambert, San Diego, Calif.

2. Watercolor on ivory, 1¼″ x 1″, by Joseph Dunkerley. Yale University Art Gallery, New Haven, Conn.

TEMPLE, JOHN.* Pastel, 23½″ x 18″, 1765. Dr. Irving Levitt, Southfield, Mich. [207]

Inscribed: Signed and dated lower right, "JS [monogram] Copley pinxit / 1765."

Provenance: Lady Temple, Boston; Elizabeth Bowdoin Temple Winthrop, Boston; Winthrop Tappan, Boston; Augusta Temple Tappan, Bound Brook, N.J.; Mr. and Mrs. Lawrence A. Fleischman, Detroit, Mich.

Bibliography: Perkins, pp. 110–11; Bayley, pp. 238–39; Theodore Bolton, *Early American Portrait Draughtsman in Crayons* (New York, 1923), p. 21; Parker-Wheeler, p. 267.

TEMPLE, MRS. JOHN.* Pastel, 23¼″ x 15¾″, c. 1767. Dr. Irving Levitt, Southfield, Mich. [208]

Provenance: Same as previous item.

Bibliography: Same as previous item.

THRALE, MRS. See *Unknown Subject, traditionally known as Mrs. Thrale*.

TOWNSEND, GREGORY.* Pastel, 21⁷⁄₁₆″ x 15⅞″ (sight), c. 1758. Col. George T. Derby, Princeton, N. J. [78]

Inscribed: Signed and dated center right, "J. S. Copley fec[t] 175 [last digit not visible]."

Bibliography: Parker-Wheeler, p. 231.

TOWNSEND, MRS. GREGORY (Lucretia Hubbard).* Pastel, 22⅜" x 17", 1765. Col. George T. Derby, Princeton, N. J. [203]

Bibliography: Met '37 (15); Parker-Wheeler, p. 231.

TRAILLE, PETER. Before 1763. Unlocated.

Bibliography: Copley-Pelham Letters, p. 28; Parker-Wheeler, p. 267.

Traille mentions his picture in a letter to Copley from Halifax, dated April 24, 1763.

TUFTS, RUTH (Mrs. Elijah Vose). Pastel, 23" x 16", 1769–72. Mrs. Samuel L. Fuller, West Chop, Martha's Vineyard, Mass. [239]

Bibliography: Parker-Wheeler, p. 232.

TURNER, MRS. GEORGE. Pastel, 22" x 13¾", c. 1767. Mr. and Mrs. Wright Morrow, Houston, Texas. [210]

Provenance: Turner family; Mrs. James M. Wolfe, Cambridge, Mass.; M. Knoedler & Co., New York.

This sitter has been identified as Elizabeth Cutty (1751–1790), but the style indicates that the pastel was painted before she married Captain Turner in 1771. Moreover, the subject of this portrait appears to have been born prior to 1751.

TURNER, WILLIAM.* Pastel, 22¾" x 17¼" (sight), c. 1767. Samuel E. Turner, St. Paul, Minn. [211]

Bibliography: Parker-Wheeler, p. 232.

TURNER, MRS. WILLIAM (Ann Dumaresq).* Pastel, 23¼" x 17½", 1767. Howard M. Turner, Marblehead, Mass. [212]

Inscribed: Signed and dated lower left, "JSC [monogram] 1767."

Bibliography: Parker-Wheeler, p. 233.

TYLER, MRS. ANDREW (Mary Richards).* Pastel, 22½" x 17¾", c. 1765. New England Historic Genealogical Society, Boston. [206]

Bibliography: Parker-Wheeler, p. 233.

TYNG, ANN (Mrs. Thomas Smelt).* Oil on canvas, 50" x 40¼", 1756. Museum of Fine Arts, Boston. [38]

Inscribed: Signed and dated center left, "J. S. Copley pinx. 1756."

Bibliography: Parker-Wheeler, pp. 189–90, plate 8.

TYNG, ELEAZER.* Oil on canvas, 49⅞" x 40⅛", 1772. National Gallery of Art, Washington, D.C. (gift of the Avalon Foundation). [317]

Inscribed: Signed and dated lower left, "John Singleton Copley / pinx 1772. / Boston."

Bibliography: BMFA '38, p. 28 (74); Parker-Wheeler, p. 190, plate 111; Copley Exhib. '65, pp. 74–75, 138 (53).

UNKNOWN SUBJECT, BOY CALLED MASTER HANCOCK. Oil on canvas, 50" x 40", 1758–59. Bayou Bend Collection of Americana, Museum of Fine Arts, Houston, Texas. [88]

Bibliography: Parker-Wheeler, p. 191.

——— GENTLEMAN WITH A CANE [John Lane?]. Oil on canvas, 49½" x 39½", 1770–72. Brooklyn Museum, Brooklyn, N.Y. [304]

Inscribed: Signed lower right, "J S Copley."

Bibliography: Parker-Wheeler, pp. 192–93, plate 92.

See also *Lane, John*.

——— A LADY. Oil on canvas, c. 50" x 40". Unlocated.

Inscribed: Signed and dated, Boston 1772.

Provenance: Perhaps Lyndhurst Sale (73), to Goldsmith.

Sir George Scharf, director of the National Portrait Gallery, on Nov. 26, 1863, saw at Lord Lyndhurst's London house a portrait of a lady in blue satin taking tea, life size, three-quarter length, with a watch hanging by a chatelaine, showing five minutes past ten, and a chimney piece behind the table ("Scharf Sketch Books," National Portrait Gallery, London, T.S.B. VII, 2).

—————— LADY IN A BLUE DRESS. Oil on canvas, 50″ x 40″, 1763. Museum of Fine Arts, Boston. [118]

Inscribed: Signed and dated center right, "J. S. Copley pinx 1763."

Bibliography: BMFA '38, p. 29 (87); Hipkiss, pp. 16–17 (8); Parker-Wheeler, pp. 193–94, plate 29.

—————— LADY IN A YELLOW DRESS. Oil on canvas, 36″ x 28″, c. 1771. Philbrook Art Center, Tulsa, Okla. [298]

Provenance: Baron Kuffner, Frankfurt, Germany; John Levy, New York; M. Knoedler & Co., New York; Paul Drey, New York.

—————— LITTLE GIRL WITH GRAPES. Oil on canvas, 27¼″ x 23″, 1765–70. Arthur Drinkwater, Cambridge, Mass. [292]

Bibliography: BMFA '38, p. 29 (88); Parker-Wheeler, p. 191, plate 57.

—————— MOTHER AND CHILD. Oil on canvas, 50¼″ x 40″, 1755–57. Museum of Fine Arts, Boston. [43]

Provenance: Martha Babcock Amory; Mrs. Franklin G. Dexter (Susan Greene Amory); Gordon Dexter; Mrs. Gordon Dexter; Thomas D. and Constance R. Williams, Litchfield, Conn., 1956; Vose Galleries, Boston; Amelia Peabody, Boston.

—————— PORTRAIT OF A WOMAN. Oil on canvas, 35″ x 28″, 1755. Mr. and Mrs. Leslie Muhlrad, Brooklyn, N. Y. [37]

Inscribed: Signed and dated lower right, "J. S. Copley / Pinx 1755."

—————— TRADITIONALLY KNOWN AS MRS. THRALE. Oil on canvas, 48½″ x 39½″, 1771. Hyde Collection, Four Oaks Farm, Somerville, N. J. [286]

Provenance: Lansdowne family; Windsor Sale, Christie, May 16, 1952, to Robinson [attributed to Nathaniel Dance].

Bibliography: Marquis of Lansdowne, ed., *Johnson and Queeney: Letters from Dr. Johnson to Queeney Thrale from the Bowood Papers* (London, 1932), opp. p. 24; James L. Clifford, *Hester Lynch Piozzi (Mrs. Thrale)* (Oxford, 1941), frontispiece; Charles Merrill Mount, "A Hidden Treasure in Britain, Part II; John Singleton Copley," *Art Quarterly*, XXIV (Spring 1961), 41, 43, and fig. 4.

This portrait has been known as Mrs. Henry Thrale for almost a century. Mrs. Thrale's daughter Hester Maria married into the Lansdowne family (her husband was George Elphinstone, Admiral Lord Keith), and the portrait first appeared in the possession of her daughter, Georgiana, when as Lady William Osborne she came into the ownership of the portrait, which she accepted as being of her grandmother (letter from James L. Clifford, Columbia University, May 12, 1965). The sitter indeed does have a resemblance to the known portraits of Mrs. Thrale, although her chin is less pointed. The provenance of the picture also supports the traditional identification, but the stylistic evidence seems to refute it. The portrait has strong stylistic and compositional affinities with Copley's New York portraits of 1771, especially *Mrs. Thomas Gage* (fig. 284). The sitter holds a letter dated 1771, and the date seems genuine. Since Mrs. Thrale was not then (or ever) in America, this would seem to eliminate the possibility that she was painted by Copley in 1771. Further stylistic considerations, as well as the date, eliminate the possibility that Copley later painted the portrait in England. Although the leading Thrale scholars do not feel that the stylistic evidence is sufficient to cause a change in the traditional identification of the subject, it is felt here that the internal evidence is convincing. It seems likely that the confusion of identity can be traced to the middle of the last century when, because of this sitter's strong resemblance to other likenesses of Mrs. Thrale, it was apparently identified or accepted as her portrait by her granddaughter.

—————— YOUNG LADY WITH A BIRD AND DOG [MARY WARNER?]. Oil on canvas, 48⅛″ x 40″, 1767. Toledo Museum, Toledo, Ohio (gift of Florence Scott Libbey, 1950). [164]

Inscribed: Signed and dated center left, "Jno: Singleton Copley pinx 1767".

Bibliography: BMFA '38, p. 28 (77); Parker-Wheeler, pp. 198–99, plate 73.

VERPLANCK, DANIEL CROMMELIN.* Oil on canvas, 49¾" x 40", 1771. Metropolitan Museum of Art, New York (gift of Bayard Verplanck, 1949). [293]

Bibliography: BMFA '38, p. 28 (75); Parker-Wheeler, pp. 194–95, plate 107; Gardner and Feld, pp. 44–45.

VERPLANCK, GULIAN.* Oil on canvas, 36" x 28", 1771. Metropolitan Museum of Art, New York (gift of Mrs. Bayard Verplanck, 1949). [290]

Bibliography: Metropolitan Museum of Art Bulletin, VII (June 1949), 262; Gardner and Feld, pp. 45–46.

VERPLANCK, SAMUEL.* Oil on canvas, 30" x 25", 1771. Metropolitan Museum of Art, New York (gift of James Delancey Verplanck, 1939). [289]

Bibliography: Parker-Wheeler, pp. 196–97, plate 116; Gardner and Feld, pp. 43–44.

WALDO, MRS. SAMUEL (Sarah Erving).* Oil on canvas, 50" x 40", 1764–65. Mrs. Charles E. Cotting, Boston, Mass. [161]

Bibliography: BMFA '38, p. 28 (76); Parker-Wheeler, pp. 197–98, plate 59; Copley Exhib. '65, pp. 42–43, 136 (25).

WARNER, MARY[?]. See *Unknown Subject, Young Lady with a Bird and Dog* [*Mary Warner?*].

WARREN, JAMES.* Oil on canvas, 51¼" x 41", 1761–63. Museum of Fine Arts, Boston. [120]

Bibliography: Parker-Wheeler, pp. 199–200, plate 42.

WARREN, MRS. JAMES (Mercy Otis).* Oil on canvas, 51¼" x 41", 1761–63. Museum of Fine Arts, Boston. [121]

Bibliography: Parker-Wheeler, pp. 200–01, plate 42.

WARREN, JOSEPH.* Oil on canvas, 50" x 40", c. 1765. Museum of Fine Arts, Boston (deposited by Buckminster Brown, 1895). [174]

Bibliography: Parker-Wheeler, pp. 202–03, plate 122.

Copies:

    1. Replica mentioned in Parker-Wheeler, p. 203.
    2. Adams National Historical Site, Quincy, Mass. (seen in photograph only).
    3. Massachusetts Historical Society, Boston.
    4. Williston Academy, East Hampton, Mass. (seen in photograph only).

Parker-Wheeler, p. 203, records a version of this painting cited by Perkins and by Bayley. Further evidence now indicates that that portrait, said to have been owned in 1872 by W. W. Corcoran, Washington, D.C., may in fact be identical with this picture, which in 1875 was owned by Henry E. Alvord and was on loan at the Corcoran Gallery (letter from Henry E. Alvord to Massachusetts Historical Society, 1875, Boston).

WATSON, GEORGE.* Oil on canvas, 50" x 40", 1768. Henderson Inches, Chestnut Hill, Mass. [222]

Inscribed: Signed and dated lower right, "JSC [monogram] P. 1768."

Bibliography: Met '37 (25); Parker-Wheeler, pp. 204–05, plate 86.

WATSON, MRS. GEORGE (Elizabeth Oliver).* Oil on canvas, 50" x 40", 1765. Henderson Inches, Chestnut Hill, Mass. [165]

Inscribed: Signed and dated lower right, "J: S: Copley. pinx / 1765."

Bibliography: Met '37 (12); BMFA '38, p. 28 (79); Parker-Wheeler, pp. 205–06, plate 53; Andrew Oliver, *Faces of a Family* (privately printed, 1960), p. 15, no. 18.

WATTS, MRS. EDWARD (Mary Oxnard).* Oil on canvas, c. 30" x 25", 1765. Frederick S. Moseley, Jr., New York. [159]

Inscribed: Signed and dated lower right, "J. S. Copley. Pix / 1765."

Bibliography: BMFA '38, p. 29 (81); Parker-Wheeler, pp. 206–07, plate 56.

WATTS, MRS. SAMUEL (Sarah Osborne; former Mrs. Thomas Oxnard).* Oil on canvas, 29" x 24", c. 1770. Frederick S. Moseley, Jr., New York. [270]

Bibliography: BMFA '38, p. 29 (82); Parker-Wheeler, p. 207, plate 100; Copley Exhib. '65, pp. 61–62, 138 (44).

WEBB, JOSEPH. Unlocated.

Bibliography: *Copley-Pelham Letters*, p. 219; Parker-Wheeler, p. 267.

Webb refers to the portrait in a letter to Henry Pelham sent from Wethersfield, Conn., June 3, 1774.

WELSTEED, REV. WILLIAM.* Mezzotint, 13⅝" x 9¹¹⁄₁₆", 1753. Yale University Art Gallery, New Haven, Conn. [5]

Bibliography: BMFA '38, p. 34 (134); Parker-Wheeler, pp. 237–38, plate 125; Copley Exhib. '65, pp. 13–14, 135 (1).

WENTWORTH, ANNE. Oil on copper, c. 1758. Unlocated. [70]

Provenance: W. A. Twiston Davies, loaned to National Museum of Wales, Cardiff; Sotheby, March 9, 1964 (9).

WENTWORTH, ELIZABETH DEERING (Mrs. Nathaniel Rogers).* Oil on canvas, 29⅞" x 24⅞", c. 1764. Atlanta Art Association, Atlanta, Ga. [135]

Provenance: Wentworth family; M. Knoedler & Co., New York.

WENTWORTH, John.* Pastel, 23" x 17½" (sight), 1769. Gordon Abbott, Manchester, Mass. [229]

Inscribed: Signed and dated center right, "JSC [monogram] p. 1769."

Bibliography: BMFA '38, p. 29 (83); Parker-Wheeler, p. 234 [as replica]; Copley Exhib. '65, pp. 55–56, 137 (35).

———— Pastel, 23¼" x 16½", 1769. Mrs. Everett Morss, Manchester, Mass.

Inscribed: Signed and dated center right, "JSC [monogram] p. 1769."

Bibliography: Parker-Wheeler, p. 234.

This may be the replica referred to by John Hurd of Portsmouth in a letter to Copley of May 4, 1770: "I am pleas'd with the Governor's Picture now sent, but I cant perswade Mrs. Hurd, nor my Children who were very fond of the first, that this Copy is equal to the Other. The Glass and frame is certainly not so good" (*Copley-Pelham Letters*, p. 88).

WENTWORTH, JOSHUA. c. 1774. Unlocated.

Bibliography: Parker-Wheeler, p. 267.

WENTWORTH, MRS. JOSHUA. c. 1774. Unlocated.

Bibliography: Parker-Wheeler, p. 267.

WINSLOW, MR. AND MRS. ISAAC (Jemima Debuke).* Oil on canvas, 40¼" x 48¾", 1774. Museum of Fine Arts, Boston (M. and M. Karolik Collection). [332]

Bibliography: BMFA '38, p. 29 (85); Hipkiss, pp. 2–3 (1); Parker-Wheeler, pp. 208–09, plate 116; Copley Exhib. '65, pp. 78–79, 139 (56).

WINSLOW, JOSHUA.* Oil on canvas, 50" x 40", 1755. Santa Barbara Museum of Art, Santa Barbara, Calif. (Preston Morton Collection). [31]

Inscribed: Signed and dated lower right, "J Copley 1755."

Provenance: Gen. Joshua Winslow; his nephew, John Winslow; his daughter, Mary Ann Winslow Trott; her son, James Fullerton Trott; J. W. Trott; M. Knoedler & Co., New York.

Bibliography: Perkins, p. 123; Bayley, p. 258; Parker-Wheeler, p. 257; Alan Burroughs, *John Greenwood in America, 1745–1752* (Andover, Mass., 1943), pp. 21, 42, 73, fig. 33; Alan Burroughs, "Young Copley," *Art in America* (Oct. 1943), pp. 163, 166, 170, fig. 5; Charles Coleman Sellers, "Mezzotint Prototypes of Colonial Portraiture: A Survey Based on the Research of Waldron Phoenix Belknap, Jr.," *Art Quarterly*, XX (Winter 1957), 426, 428; Belknap, pp. 291–92, plate XIX, 15B.

———— Oil on copper, c. 3" x 2", c. 1755. Andrew L. White, Rock Hill, S.C. [32]

Provenance: M. Knoedler & Co., New York, 1955.

Bibliography: Perkins, p. 123; Charles Coleman Sellers, "Mezzotint Prototypes of Colonial Portraiture: A Survey Based on the Research of Waldron Phoenix Belknap, Jr.," *Art Quarterly*, XX (Winter 1957), 426; Belknap, pp. 291–92.

WINTHROP, JOHN.* Oil on canvas, 50¼″ x 40¼″, c. 1773. Harvard University, Cambridge, Mass.
[328]
Bibliography: Parker-Wheeler, pp. 209–10, plate 114; Copley Exhib. '65, pp. 74, 76, 138 (54).
WINTHROP, MRS. JOHN (Hannah Fayerweather).* Oil on canvas, 35½″ x 28¾″, 1773. Metropolitan Museum of Art, New York (Morris K. Jesup Fund, 1931). [327]
Bibliography: Met '37 (34); BMFA '38, p. 29 (86); Parker-Wheeler, pp. 210–11, plate 117; Gardner and Feld, pp. 46–48.
WINTHROP, SAMUEL.* Oil on canvas, 49⅞″ x 40¼″, c. 1773. Harvard University, Cambridge, Mass. [329]
Bibliography: Parker-Wheeler, pp. 211–12, plate 68.
YOUNG LADY WITH A BIRD AND DOG. See *Unknown Subject, Young Lady with a Bird and Dog* [*Mary Warner?*].

Historical and Other Subjects

BOOK OF ANATOMICAL DRAWINGS. Ink, black and red crayon on white paper, 1756. British Museum, London. [Plate II, 19; Plate XI, 17]
Plate I. *Text for Arms.* Ink, 10¾″ x 16¾″.
Plate II. *Arms.* Ink, black and red crayon, 10¾″ x 17¹/₁₆″. [19]
Inscribed: Signed and dated lower right, "J: Singleton Copley Del: 1756."
Plate III. *Text for Legs.* Ink, 10¾″ x 17¹/₁₆″.
Plate IV. *Legs.* Ink, black and red chalk, 10¾″ x 17¹/₁₆″.
Inscribed: Signed and dated lower right, "J. Singleton Copley Dellin."
Plate V. *Text for Torso.* Ink, 10¾″ x 17¹/₁₆″.
Plate VI. *Torsos.* Ink and red crayon, 10¾″ x 17¹/₁₆″.
Inscribed: Signed and dated lower right, "J: Singleton Copley Delⁿ: / 1756."
Plate VII. *Front Figure.* Red ink and red crayon, 10¾″ x 17¹/₁₆″.
Inscribed: Signed and dated lower right, "J: Singleton Copley Dellin."
Plate VIII. *Side Figure.* Red ink and red crayon, 10¾″ x 17¹/₁₆″.
Inscribed: Signed and dated lower right, "J: Singleton Copley Dellin."
Plate IX. *Front Figure.* Red ink and red crayon, 10¾″ x 17¹/₁₆″.
Inscribed: Signed and dated lower right, "J. Singleton Copley Dellin."
Plate X. *Back Figure.* Red ink and red crayon, 10¾″ x 17¹/₁₆″.
Inscribed: Signed and dated lower right, "J. Singleton Copley Dellin."
Plate XI. *Medici Venus.* Ink, 10¾″ x 17¹/₁₆″. [17]
Provenance: Probably Lyndhurst Library Sale, Christie's, 1864 (676).
Bibliography: Laurence Binyon, *Catalogue of Drawings by British Artists . . . [in the British Museum]* (London, 1898–1907), pp. 247–48; Jules David Prown, "An 'Anatomy Book' by John Singleton Copley," *Art Quarterly*, XXVI (Spring 1963), 31–46; Copley Exhib. '65, pp. 16–17, 135 (3).
ESAU AND JACOB. Oil on canvas, large. Unlocated.
Bibliography: W. Carew Hazlitt, *Four Generations of a Literary Family*, I (London and New York, 1897), 35–36.
On a visit to Weymouth, Mass., in 1784 Margaret Hazlitt recorded in her diary "The first object we saw here was a very large and old picture in oil, of the meeting of Esau and Jacob. The embracing of the two brothers, the meeting of their followers on either side, with the groups of camels and other cattle, and the background winding up between the hills and seeming to vanish in the air, completed the enchantment. On this picture I used to gaze with delight, and wondered at the skill of the artist who had made so natural and lively a

representation of the scene . . . I have heard it was one of the first attempts of Copley; he was afterwards a painter of some note."

GALATEA. Oil on canvas, 37″ x 52″, c. 1754. Museum of Fine Arts, Boston. [7]
Bibliography: Parker-Wheeler, pp. 75–76, plate 5.
GRANICUS, BATTLE OF THE RIVER, from the Alexander Series, after Charles LeBrun (recto of next item [15]). Red, white, and black chalk on gray-green paper, 11⅞″ x 18¹³⁄₁₆″, 1753–58. Wickersham Gallery, New York. [14]
Inscribed: Lower left, "An early drawing of / J. S. Copley's given by his mother / to Miss Marcia [Mercy] Scollay. by her to Miss E. Lowell / who gave it to E. S. Quincy in 1832."
Bibliography: *Art Quarterly*, XXVI (Spring 1963), 124.
——— (verso of previous item [14]). Black chalk on gray-green paper, 11⅞″ x 18¹³⁄₁₆″, 1753–58. Wickersham Gallery, New York. [15]
Inscribed: In ink, "an early drawing of J. S. Copley's given by his mother to Miss Marcia Scollay who gave it to Miss E. Lowell by whom it was given to Eliza S. Quincy in 1835."
This drawing is related to the underdrawing in black chalk on the recto. Despite its faintness, it is a stronger drawing than the recto and more faithful to the LeBrun source.
MARS, VENUS AND VULCAN. Oil on canvas, c. 50″ x 30″, 1754. Mrs. James F. Chapman, Pueblo, Colo. [11]
Inscribed: Signed and dated lower left, "John S. Copley Pinx 1754."
Bibliography: Parker-Wheeler, p. 131, plate 5.
NEPTUNE, THE RETURN OF. Oil on canvas, 27½″ x 44½″, c. 1754. Metropolitan Museum of Art, New York (gift of Mrs. Orme Wilson, 1959, in memory of her parents, Mr. and Mrs. J. Nelson Borland). [9]
Bibliography: Albert TenEyck Gardner, "A Copley Primitive," *Metropolitan Museum of Art Bulletin*, XX (April 1962), 257–63; Gardner and Feld, pp. 38–39; Copley Exhib. '65, pp. 14–15, 135 (2).
——— Unlocated.
Provenance: Mrs. C. B. Raymond, Boston, 1872.
Bibliography: Perkins, p. 89. According to Perkins, this version is smaller and reversed in composition.
UNKNOWN SUBJECT, BATTLE SCENE. Pen and ink drawing, 3⅝″ x 7″, 1754. Addison Gallery of American Art, Phillips Academy, Andover, Mass. [13]
Inscribed: Signed and dated lower right, "J S Copely Del 1754."
Bibliography: Parker-Wheeler, p. 235; sale, property of Mrs. John F. Carroll, Anderson Galleries, New York, Feb. 5–6, 1920 (121).
——— STUDY OF A CHERUB (possibly John the Baptist as a child). Black chalk on blue paper, 13″ x 8½″, 1753–58 [possibly 1774–75]. Westmoreland County Museum of Art, Greensburg, Pa. [16]

Attributed Pictures

This list is a supplement to the extensive Parker-Wheeler checklists of attributed pictures, presenting subsequent information or emendations. Unless otherwise noted, objects listed are unlocated. Brackets are used to show whether an object has been examined or a photograph has been seen. When no source for the photograph is indicated, such as FARL (Frick Art Reference Library) or BMFA (Boston Museum of Fine Arts), it was in most cases supplied by the owner or appeared in a publication cited under the object's *Bibliography*.

Pictures that are unlocated or that I have not seen are in the attributed list unless there is positive documentary evidence that Copley painted the picture. Nevertheless, inclusion of a painting in the attributed list should not be regarded as necessarily implying that it is not a Copley, but merely as indicating that I have not examined it or that I have examined it and, in my opinion, its ascription to Copley has not been demonstrated beyond question.

ABERCROMBIE, JAMES, LORD. Miniature. [Photograph]
> *Bibliography*: Frederic Fairchild Sherman, "Recently Recovered Miniatures by John Singleton Copley," *Art in America*, XXIII (Dec. 1934), 34–38; hereafter cited, Sherman, "Miniatures."

APTHORP, CHARLES, JR. Pastel, 23″ x 18″, 1764. M. Knoedler & Co., New York. [Object]
> *Inscribed*: Signed and dated center right [by later hand], "Copley / 1764."
> *Bibliography*: BMFA '38, p. 19 (5); Parker-Wheeler, pp. 215–16.
> This is a good pastel of the period on which opinion about its attribution is divided. The modeling seems pinched in comparison with the broader and smoother modeling of known Copley pastels, and the figure is unusually recessed from the picture plane, leaving the space empty in contrast to most Copley pastels.

BAILEY, BARTLETT. Miniature, 1½″ tall. Haverhill Historical Society, Haverhill, Mass.
> Parker-Wheeler, p. 260, records a miniature of Christopher Bartlett in the same collection, formerly attributed to Copley, which the authors suggest is probably the work of Joseph Dunkerley.

BARRETT, SARAH. Oil on copper, 5½″ x 4½″.
> *Provenance*: Charles Follen, before 1872.
> *Bibliography*: Perkins, pp. 35–36.

BLACK, MRS.
> *Bibliography*: Perkins, pp. 36–37; Bayley, p. 59.

BLISS, REV. DANIEL (of Concord). Oil on canvas. Ralph Waldo Emerson House, Concord, Mass. [Object]
> A label on the back indicates that this portrait was thought by Lawrence Park in 1921 to be by Copley. Although it has some stylistic similarity to Copley's early portrait of *John Rogers (the Protomartyr)* at the Massachusetts Historical Society, it is more heavy-handed in execution and seems unlikely to be by Copley.

BORLAND, FRANCIS. [Photograph]
> *Bibliography*: *New England Miniatures*, fig. 15 (15).

BRATTLE, WILLIAM. Small copy. Alice Rogers Parsons, South Berwick, Maine.
> Examined by R. C. Vose, Jr., and Barbara N. Parker, 1955, and felt to be an early copy.
——— Miniature, c. 1760.
> *Bibliography*: *New England Miniatures* (22).

BROMFIELD, MRS. HENRY (Margaret Fayerweather). Oil on canvas, 36″ x 25¼″, before 1752. Mrs. Jean-Frederic Wagniere, on loan at Museum of Fine Arts, Boston. [Object]
> *Bibliography*: Parker-Wheeler, pp. 48–49, plate 2; Alan Burroughs, *John Greenwood in America, 1745–1752* (Andover, Mass., 1943), pp. 42–45, 63.
> This portrait has been convincingly attributed to John Greenwood by Alan Burroughs and is now exhibited as a Greenwood.

BROWER, JOHN.
> *Bibliography*: Perkins, pp. 41–42.

BURT, BENJAMIN. Miniature, oil on copper, 1769. [Photograph]
> *Bibliography*: Thomas Hamilton Ormsbee, "The Burts, Boston Silversmiths," *American Collector*, IX (Aug. 1940), 7.

COOPER, ABIGAIL. Pastel. [Photograph, BMFA]
>*Bibliography*: Parker-Wheeler, p. 258.
>Barbara N. Parker examined the object at the Museum of Fine Arts, Boston, in June 1938, and felt that the object was either a contemporary copy or was badly rubbed and restored; in its present condition it lacks the quality of known Copley pastels.

CRANSTON, THOMAS. Rhode Island Historical Society, Providence. [Object]
>*Bibliography*: Parker-Wheeler, p. 52.

CRANSTON, MRS. THOMAS (Mary Coggeshall). Oil on canvas, 50½″ x 40½″, c. 1758. [Photograph, BMFA]
>*Bibliography*: Parker-Wheeler, pp. 65–66, plate 16.
>In 1942 this painting was examined at the Museum of Fine Arts, Boston, and the Fogg Art Museum, and the consensus of opinion was that the attribution to Copley was erroneous.

CUNNINGHAM, MRS. WILLIAM (Elizabeth Barrett). Miniature.
>*Bibliography*: Arthur Wentworth Hamilton Eaton, "Old Boston Families, No. 2, The Family of Capt. John Gerrish," *New England Historical and Genealogical Register*, LXVII (April 1913), 110.

DANA, REV. EDMUND. Destroyed.
>*Bibliography*: Perkins, p. 50; Bayley, p. 89.

DUMARESQ, JAMES. Oil on canvas.
>*Provenance*: Francis Dumaresq, Jamaica, W.I.
>*Bibliography*: Perkins, p. 52; Bayley, p. 98.

DUMARESQ, REBECCA. Pastel, 12″ x 8″.
>*Provenance*: Mrs. John Rice Blake, Boston; Mrs. W. Austin Wadsworth, Boston, 1915.
>*Bibliography*: Perkins, p. 52, Bayley, pp. 98–99.

ELIOT, JOSIAH. Oil on panel, 16⅜″ x 12⅜″. [Photograph]
>*Provenance*: Miss Hull, Fairfield, Conn., 1872.
>*Bibliography*: Parker-Wheeler, p. 258 [possibly, listed there as a pastel, information taken from Perkins, p. 53].

FOSTER, ELEANOR (Mrs. Nathaniel Coffin). 1755.
>*Bibliography*: Bayley, p. 108.

FRANCIS, ANNE.
>*Provenance*: Col. F. C. Goldsborough, Maryland, 1915.
>*Bibliography*: Bayley, p. 267.

FRANKLIN, MICHAEL. Oil on canvas, 29½″ x 24″, oval.
>*Provenance*: Christie, Dec. 18, 1953 (100), to John Mitchell, London.
>*Bibliography*: Parker-Wheeler, p. 253.
>This picture is said to be a replica of a destroyed portrait in Town Hall, Brunswick, Halifax, Nova Scotia. A copy of the portrait was reported to be at the University of Kings College, Halifax, but it has not been located. Michael Franklin was lieutenant-governor of Nova Scotia.

FRANKLIN, MRS. MICHAEL. Oil on canvas, 29½″ x 24″, oval.
>*Provenance*: Christie, Dec. 18, 1953 (100), to John Mitchell, London.
>*Bibliography*: Parker-Wheeler, p. 253.
>This picture is said to be a replica of a destroyed portrait in Town Hall, Brunswick, Halifax, Nova Scotia.

GARDINER, MRS. SYLVESTER (Ann Gibbins). Oil on canvas, 49″ x 39″, c. 1760. Gardiner family, Gardiner, Maine. [Object]
>*Bibliography*: Parker-Wheeler, p. 79, plate 11.
>A studied comparison of this portrait with other American colonial paintings strongly argues that it is an excellent example of the work of Joseph Blackburn, c. 1760. It shows close similarities to the Blackburn portraits of *Mrs. Theodore Atkinson* (Cleveland Art Museum),

Mrs. Jonathan Simpson (Museum of Fine Arts, Boston), *Lettice Mitchell* (Brooklyn Museum), *Mrs. Joshua Babcock* (private collection), and in reverse pose the Blackburn portraits of *An Unidentified Woman* (Isabella Stewart Gardner Museum, Boston) and *Susan Apthorp* (Museum of Fine Arts, Boston). In comparison with these paintings, *Mrs. Sylvester Gardiner* is similar in pose, with the drapery flowing in the same manner over her right shoulder and down to her left hand. In special comparison with the portrait of *Mrs. Theodore Atkinson*, there are identical folds in the drapery of the sleeve on the right and a similar puff of drapery in the lower right, which is a virtual Blackburn trademark. The handling of the drapery, the softer value contrasts and gentler brushwork, and the palette, as well as the diagonal alternation of lights and darks, are all characteristic of Blackburn.

GERRISH, MRS. BENJAMIN (Rebecca Dudley).
> *Provenance*: Mrs. H. H. Braddlee, 1892.
> *Bibliography*: Arthur Wentworth Hamilton Eaton, "Old Boston Families, No. 2, The Family of Capt. John Gerrish," *New England Historical and Genealogical Register*, LXVII (April 1913), 114.

GIST, GENERAL MORDECAI.
> *Provenance*: Miss Mary S. Gist, Carroll County, Md., 1875.
> *Bibliography*: Perkins, *Supplement*, p. 18.

GLOVER, JONATHAN. Pastel.
> *Bibliography*: Parker-Wheeler, p. 258.
> Examined by Barbara N. Parker, Jan. 1943, who felt it probably not to be by Copley.

GLOVER, MRS. JONATHAN. Pastel.
> *Bibliography*: Parker-Wheeler, p. 258.
> Examined by Barbara N. Parker, Jan. 1943, who felt it probably not to be by Copley.

HABERSHAM, JAMES.
> *Bibliography*: Perkins, *Supplement*, pp. 25–26.

HANCOCK, EBENEZER. Miniature. [Photograph]
> *Bibliography*: Sherman, "Miniatures," pp. 34–38.

HANCOCK, JOHN. Miniature. [Photograph]
> *Bibliography*: Sherman, "Miniatures," pp. 34–38.

HANCOCK, THOMAS. Watercolor on ivory, c. 1″ x ⅝″, oval. John Hancock Life Insurance Co., Boston. [Object]
> *Provenance*: Mrs. Walling.
> *Bibliography*: Sherman, "Miniatures," pp. 34–38.

HART, DR. THOMAS. Miniature. [Photograph]
> *Bibliography*: Sherman, "Miniatures," pp. 34–38.

HICKS, WHITEHEAD. Museum of the City of New York. [Object]
> *Bibliography*: Belknap, p. 321, plate XLIX, 62A.
> This portrait seems to be by an unidentified New York contemporary of Copley's, perhaps the artist who painted *Gabriel Ludlow*, also at the Museum of the City of New York.

HOOPER, JOSEPH[?]. Watercolor on ivory, 1½″ x 1¼″, c. 1770. Museum of Fine Arts, Boston. [Object]
> *Bibliography*: Parker-Wheeler, p. 245.
> Although there is some stylistic similarity to Copley's few miniatures on ivory, especially his self-portrait, the style seems closer to the signed Henry Pelham miniature of *Adam Babcock*, a copy of the Copley portrait of that subject.

HILL, MR. AND MRS.
> *Provenance*: Sidney Everett, Boston, 1915.
> *Bibliography*: Bayley, p. 143.

HURD, NATHANIEL. Watercolor on ivory, 1½″ x 1″. Emily P. Furness, Brookline, Mass. [Object]
> A delightful small miniature, which appears to be by another hand.

HUTCHINSON, MRS. THOMAS.
> *Provenance*: Mrs. F. Gordon Dexter, Boston, 1915.
> *Bibliography*: Bayley, p. 154.

JACKSON, DR. HALL. Oil on canvas, 36″ x 28½″. Amherst College, Amherst, Mass. [Object]
> *Bibliography*: Charles H. Morgan and Margaret C. Toole, "Benjamin West: His Times and His Influence," *Art in America*, XXXVIII (Dec. 1950), 234–37.

JACOCKS, REBECCA SCOLLAY. Pastel. Mrs. A. T. Wickersham, New York. [Object]
> An eighteenth-century pastel by another hand.

LEIGH, JUDGE PETER.
> *Bibliography*: Bayley, p. 163.

LEONARD, THE REV. ABIEL. Oil on canvas. Mr. and Mrs. Mason C. Shoup, Carmel, N.Y. [Object]
> *Bibliography*: Parker-Wheeler, p. 254.
> A well-painted eighteenth-century portrait, apparently done under the influence of Copley, but by another hand.

MACPHEADRIS, MRS. Oil on canvas, 50″ x 39″.
> *Bibliography*: Perkins, p. 85; Bayley, pp. 173–74.

LUDLOW, GABRIEL. Oil on canvas. Museum of the City of New York. [Object]
> Not by Copley; possibly by the same artist who painted *Whitehead Hicks* in the same collection. A portrait of Gabriel Ludlow, said to have been painted by Copley in 1753, was exhibited at the American Academy of Fine Arts in 1833 and discussed in a review in *American Monthly Magazine* (Aug. 1833), p. 402.

LUDLOW, WILLIAM. Oil on canvas, 30″ x 25″. Metropolitan Museum of Art, New York. [Object]
> *Bibliography*: Parker-Wheeler, p. 254; Gardner and Feld, pp. 51–52.
> This nineteenth-century portrait may well be a copy of an unlocated Copley original.

LUDLOW, MRS. WILLIAM (Mary Duncan). Oil on canvas, 29½″ x 24½″. Metropolitan Museum of Art, New York. [Object]
> *Bibliography*: Parker-Wheeler, p. 254; Gardner and Feld, p. 52.
> This nineteenth-century portrait may well be a copy of an unlocated Copley original.

MacWHORTER, ALEXANDER. Oil on panel, 11½″ x 9½″. [Photograph, FARL]
> *Provenance*: Dr. and Mrs. Forbes Hawkes, New York.

MacWHORTER, MRS. ALEXANDER. Oil on panel, 11½″ x 9½″. [Photograph, FARL]
> *Provenance*: Dr. and Mrs. Forbes Hawkes, New York.

MIFFLIN, MR. AND MRS. SAMUEL. Metropolitan Museum of Art, New York.
> *Bibliography*: Parker-Wheeler, p. 255.
> This painting is signed and dated by Charles Willson Peale, 1777.

OLIVER, DR. PETER, JR. Watercolor on ivory, 1⅜″ x 1³⁄₁₆″. Yale University Art Gallery, New Haven, Conn. [Object]
> *Bibliography*: *New England Miniatures*, pp. 10–11, fig. 5 (136); Andrew Oliver, *Faces of a Family* (privately printed, 1960), p. 14, no. 16.
> Probably an English miniature.

PARSONS, MRS. JONATHAN. Pastel, 22⅞″ x 17⅛″. James Andrew Clarkson, West Medford, Mass. [Object]
> Very badly rubbed and impossible to attribute; perhaps originally by Copley.

PELHAM, HENRY. 22″ x 17¼″. [Photograph]
> *Provenance*: Harry Stone.
> *Bibliography*: Sherman, "Miniatures," pp. 82–83.

PELHAM, HENRY[?]. Watercolor on ivory, miniature. Museum of Fine Arts, Boston. [Object]
> *Bibliography*: *New England Miniatures*, p. 11, fig. 17 (144).
> Appears to be a good English miniature.

—— Museum of Fine Arts, Boston. [Object]
> Copy of the previous item.

PEPPERRELL, SIR WILLIAM. Oil on canvas, 36″ x 28″. Destroyed.
  Provenance: Mrs. Mary Wheeler Smith.
  Bibliography: Bayley, p. 194.
PEPPERRELL, LADY. Oil on canvas, 36″ x 28″.
  Provenance: Mary Pepperrell Sparhawk Cutts; David E. Wheeler; Everett Pepperrell Wheeler, 1915.
  Bibliography: Bayley, p. 194.
PIERPONT FAMILY, A CHILD OF THE. Oil on canvas, 34½″ x 28″. Museum of Fine Arts, Boston. [Object]
  Bibliography: Parker-Wheeler, p. 255; Barbara N. Parker, *Museum of Fine Arts Bulletin* (June 1942), pp. 54–57.
  This portrait seems to predate Copley's earliest works, and the attribution to Copley is not convincing.
PITTS, SAMUEL. Oil on wood panel, 23½″ x 19½″, Detroit Institute of Arts, Detroit, Mich. [Object]
  Bibliography: Parker-Wheeler, p. 227 [as a pastel].
  This painting appears to be a contemporaneous oil copy of an unlocated pastel original by Copley. Even though painted in oil, the palette is pastel-like.
PRINGLE, MRS.
  Bibliography: Perkins, p. 96.
REVERE, MRS. PAUL. Miniature.
  Provenance: Dr. John P. Reynolds, Boston, 1875.
  Bibliography: Perkins, *Supplement*, p. 22.
ROGERS, DANIEL DENISON. [Object]
Bibliography: New England Miniatures, p. 11; fig. 19 (162).
RUSSELL, CHARLES. Oil on canvas. Massachusetts Historical Society, Boston. [Object]
SHEPHEARD, SAMUEL. Oil on canvas. City Art Gallery, Temple Newsam House, Leeds, Eng. [Photograph, FARL]
  Bibliography: *Apollo*, XXXII (Dec. 1940), 165; *City Art Gallery (Leeds) Catalogue* (1954), p. 25.
  The previous attribution to Thomas Hudson was changed to Copley in the 1954 Leeds museum catalogue. The portrait represents a full-length figure standing before an elaborate marble-top table, very much like the 1764 portraits of *Nathaniel Sparhawk* and *Thomas Hancock*. The attribution seems possible, but the painting has not been examined and a good photograph was not available.
SPARHAWK, NATHANIEL[?]. Miniature. Amherst College, Amherst, Mass. [Object]
TILLEY, JAMES. Oil on copper, 13¾″ x 10¼″.
  Bibliography: Parker-Wheeler, p. 248, plate 128; Theodore Sizer, *The Works of Colonel John Trumbull* (New Haven, 1950), p. 41.
  This miniature has been reidentified by Theodore Sizer as a portrait of *Alexander Moore* [?] by John Trumbull.
TURNER, CAPTAIN GEORGE. Pastel, 22″ x 13½″. [Object]
  Provenance: M. Knoedler & Co., New York.
TYNG, COLONEL WILLIAM. Miniature.
  Bibliography: Bayley, p. 245.
UNKNOWN SUBJECT, PORTRAIT OF A MAN. Oil on canvas, 50″ x 40″. North Carolina Museum of Art, Raleigh. [Photograph]
  Bibliography: George Wiswell, "A Copley Rescued," *Art in America*, L (1962), 86–87.
  In photograph the attribution to Copley seems possible, but is not completely convincing.
——— GENTLEMAN IN A BLUE SUIT. Oil on canvas, 29½″ x 25½″. Mrs. Oric Bates, Groton, Mass. [Object]
  Bibliography: Parker-Wheeler, p. 192, plate 99.

Although this portrait bears a number of stylistic similarities to Copley's American paintings, close examination suggests that it is an English portrait by a contemporary of Copley's.

—— GENTLEMAN IN A BROWN SUIT. Oil on canvas, 29½″ x 24¼″. Arthur Drinkwater, Cambridge, Mass. [Object]

Bibliography: Parker-Wheeler, p. 192, plate 32.

This is a difficult picture to attribute. It is somewhat rubbed and quite dirty. It is very close to Copley's style of 1763–67, although it has a dry scumbly quality that is atypical. A firm decision on the attribution will have to await cleaning and closer examination.

—— A MAN. Watercolor on ivory, 1⅜″ x ⅞″. National Collection of Fine Arts, Washington, D.C. [Photograph]

Inscribed: Signed and dated 1773 over the sitter's left shoulder.

—— PORTRAIT OF A GENTLEMAN.

Bibliography: Sherman, "Miniatures," pp. 34–38.

—— PORTRAIT OF A WOMAN. Oil on canvas. Mr. and Mrs. Henry Flynt, Deerfield, Mass. [Object]

Although this picture seems to predate Copley's earliest work and consideration of it is hampered by a considerable amount of repainting, the strong color and bold brushwork, particularly in the drapery, is reminiscent of Copley's early work and suggests the possibility that Copley's hand is present in some way.

—— A LADY. William Rockhill Nelson Gallery of Art, Kansas City, Mo. [Object]

Bibliography: Parker-Wheeler, p. 256.

This portrait may date from the early nineteenth century and is quite possibly a copy of an earlier picture.

—— LADY IN A WHITE DRESS. Oil on canvas, 50″ x 40″.

Bibliography: Bayley, p. 265 [as *Mrs. Oliver Whipple*]; Parker-Wheeler, p. 194, plate 10.

This picture, when restored, was found to have been inscribed by Allan Ramsay, to whom the portrait is now attributed.

—— LADY WITH A PEARL NECKLACE. Watercolor on ivory, 1½″ x 1¼″. Metropolitan Museum of Art, New York. [Object]

Inscribed: Signed and dated center right, "JSC [monogram] / 1762."

—— MOTHER AND CHILD. Red and white crayon on brown paper, 12⅜″ x 9½″. Fogg Art Museum, Harvard University, Cambridge, Mass. [Object]

Inscribed: Signed in black ink, lower left.

—— MOTHER AND CHILD (sometimes called Mary Pelham and son Henry). Fogg Art Museum, Harvard University, Cambridge, Mass. [Object]

This appears to be an English or Irish portrait, similar to Copley's English style but clearly by another hand.

—— STUDY OF A HAND RESTING ON BOOK. Black and red chalk on white paper, 7¼″ x 6½″, 1758. Mrs. Harold Willcox, Boston.

Inscribed: Lower left, "Copley Del 1758" [perhaps by a later hand].

Bibliography: Parker-Wheeler, pp. 235–36.

The attribution of this drawing to Copley is not completely convincing though it is possible. There is little to compare it with.

—— TAPESTRY DESIGN.

Bibliography: Perkins, *Supplement*, p. 10; Bayley, p. 237.

VANS, WILLIAM, AND HIS WIFE

Bibliography: Perkins, *Supplement*, p. 8; Bayley, p. 245.

VERPLANCK, MARY C., AND HER DAUGHTER ANNE (Mrs. Gabriel Ludlow).

Provenance: Robert Ludlow, Westchester, N.Y.; Mrs. T. W. Fearing, 1892.

Bibliography: W. E. Verplanck, *History of Abraham Verplanck and His Descendants* (1892), p. 108.

VASSALL, COLONEL HENRY. Massachusetts Historical Society, Boston. [Photograph, FARL]

VOSE, ROBERT. Miniature. Museum of Fine Arts, Boston. [Object]

WALDO, COLONEL SAMUEL. Miniature, 1⅝″ x 1¼″. Walters Art Gallery, Baltimore, Md. [Photograph]

WARD, GOVERNOR RICHARD. Museum of Art, Rhode Island School of Design, Providence. [Object]

> Bibliography: Parker-Wheeler, p. 259.

> This is a good early pastel, but the attribution to Copley seems unlikely. The signature and date, 1754, are scratched in and seem to be by another hand.

WARREN, MRS. JOSEPH (Elizabeth Hooten). Oil on canvas, 50″ x 40″, 1771–75. Museum of Fine Arts, Boston (deposited by Buckminster Brown, 1895). [Object]

> Bibliography: Parker-Wheeler, pp. 203–04, plate 121.

> Although this portrait is typical of Copley's latest American work in its organization, the actual handling indicates that it was executed by another hand. This suggests that the painting is either a copy of an unlocated Copley original of the same subject or a painting that was planned and begun by Copley and finished by someone else. In composition the picture would come at the very end of Copley's American career, echoing New York portraits like *Mrs. Thomas Gage* but also looking forward to *Mr. and Mrs. Ralph Izard*. Work that Copley left behind him, such as the portraits of *Mr. and Mrs. Joshua Wentworth*, might have been finished by Henry Pelham. The stylistic similarity between this portrait and Pelham's *Miss Catherine Byles*, 1770–71, reproduced in Alan Burroughs, "A Pelham Portrait," *Antiques*, LXXI (April 1957), 359, reinforces this hypothesis. But verification is not possible until more is known about the work of Henry Pelham.

WASHINGTON, GEORGE. Watercolor on ivory, 1½″ x 1¼″. Metropolitan Museum of Art, New York.

> Bibliography: Perkins, p. 117; Bayley, p. 13.

WATSON, GEORGE. Watercolor on ivory, 2¹⁵⁄₁₆″ x 2⅜″. Yale University Art Gallery, New Haven, Conn. [Object]

> A copy of the 1768 Copley portrait, by another hand.

WATSON, MRS. GEORGE (Elizabeth Oliver). Watercolor on ivory, 2¹³⁄₁₆″ x 2⅜″. Yale University Art Gallery, New Haven, Conn. [Object]

> Bibliography: *New England Miniatures*, fig. 22 (193); Andrew Oliver, *Faces of a Family*, p. 15, no. 18A.

> An early copy of the 1765 Copley portrait, by another hand.

WEBB, JOSEPH. Pastel. Kent–De Lord, House Museum, Plattsburg, N.Y. [Photograph]

> Bibliography: Parker-Wheeler, p. 267 [possibly].

WENTWORTH, JOHN. Pastel, 32″ x 26″. [Photograph, FARL]

> Provenance: Mrs. Walter Jennings, Cold Spring Harbor, Long Island, N.Y.

WENTWORTH, MRS. JOHN.

> Provenance: Asa Freeman, Dover, N.H., 1850.

> Bibliography: *New England Historical and Genealogical Register*, IV (1850), 323.

WHIPPLE, MRS. WILLIAM (Katherine Moffatt). Oil on canvas, 35″ x 27½″. [Photograph]

> Bibliography: Parker-Wheeler, pp. 207–08, plate 2; Alan Burroughs, *John Greenwood in America, 1745–1752* (Andover, Mass., 1943), pp. 42–45, 68; Charles Coleman Sellers, "Mezzotint Prototypes of Colonial Portraiture: A Survey Based on the Research of Waldron Phoenix Belknap, Jr.," *Art Quarterly*, XX (Winter 1957), 429, 431; Belknap, pp. 293, 326, plate XX, 17B.

> Like the portrait of *Mrs. Henry Bromfield*, this picture has been convincingly reattributed to John Greenwood by Alan Burroughs.

WHITE, REV. MR.

> Bibliography: Perkins, p. 123.

WILMOT, CAPTAIN. 12″ x 9″.
    Provenance: J. B. Wilmot, M.D., Tunbridge Wells, Eng., 1875.
    Bibliography: Perkins, *Supplement*, pp. 23–24.
WILMOT, JOHN. 20″ x 16″, c. 1758.
    Provenance: Belgravia House, New York.
    Bibliography: *Antiques*, LXX (Nov. 1956), 428.
WINSLOW, ANNA GREEN. Miniature.
    Provenance: Miss E. C. Trott, Niagara Falls, N.Y., before 1915.
    Bibliography: Bayley, p. 266.

Illustrations

(Figures 1-334)

1. John Smibert: Dean Berkeley and His Entourage (The Bermuda Group)   *1729*

2. Robert Feke: Isaac Royall and Family   *1741*

3. John Greenwood: The Greenwood-Lee Family   *c. 1747*

4. Peter Pelham: Rev. William Cooper   *1743*

5. Rev. William Welsteed   *1753*

7. Galatea   *c. 1754*

8. Greg. Lazarini: Galatea

6. Joseph Badger: Rev. William Welsteed
    before 1753

9. The Return of Neptune   *c. 1754*

10. Simon François Ravenet, after Andrea
Casali: The Return of Neptune   *1749*

11. Mars, Venus and Vulcan   *1754*

12. John Rogers (the Protomartyr)
1753–58, probably 1756–58

13. Unknown Subject, Battle Scene   *1754*

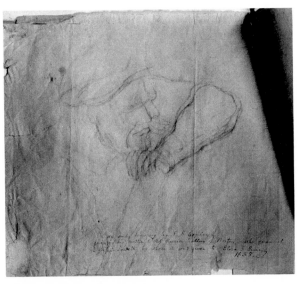

14. Figure from The Battle of the River Granicus, after Charles LeBrun (recto of 15)   *1753–58*

15. Figure from The Battle of the River Granicus, after Charles LeBrun (verso of 14)   *1753–58*

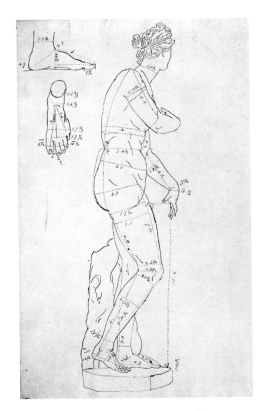

16. Unknown Subject, Study of a Cherub
1753–58 (or 1774–75)

17. Plate XI, Book of Anatomical Drawings
1756

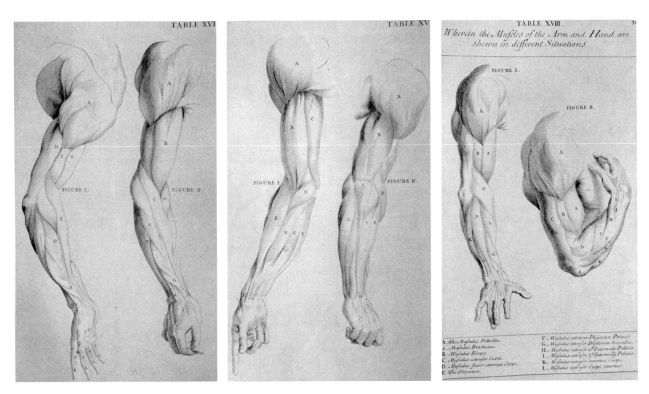

18. Bernardino Genga and Giovanni Maria Lancisi,
Anatomy Improv'd and Illustrated (1691), tables XVI, XV, XVIII

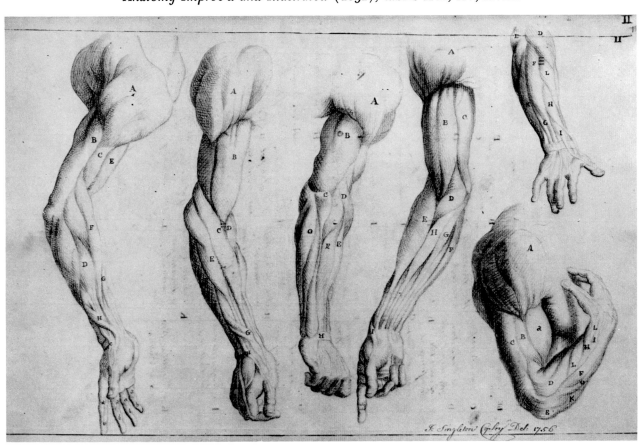

19. Plate II, Book of Anatomical Drawings   *1756*

20. Mrs. Joseph Mann   *1753*

21. Joseph Mann   *1754*

22. Robert Feke: Mrs. James Bowdoin II   *1748*

23. Robert Feke: James Bowdoin II   *1748*

25. John Greenwood: Robert Jenkins   *c. 1750*

24. John Smibert: Mrs. Nathaniel Cunningham
c. 1733

26. Jonathan Mountfort   *c. 1753*

27. Charles Pelham   *c. 1754*

28. Peter Pelham [?]   *1753*

29. The Brothers and Sisters of Christopher Gore   *c. 1755*

30. Two Sisters of Christopher Gore   *c. 1755*

31. Joshua Winslow   *1755*

32. Joshua Winslow   *c. 1755*

33. Robert Feke: Isaac Winslow   *c. 1748*

34. Robert Feke: Tench Francis   *1746*

35. George Scott   *1755–57*

36. William Brattle   *1756*

37. Unknown Subject, Portrait of a Woman   *1755*

38. Ann Tyng   *1756*

39. Ann Gardiner   *c. 1756*

40. Jane Browne   *1756*

41. Joseph Blackburn: Mrs. Benjamin Pollard
1756

42. Joseph Blackburn: Joseph Dwight   *1756*

43. Unknown Subject, Mother and Child
1755–57

44. Rhoda Cranston   *1756–58*

45. Mrs. Jonathan Belcher   *1756*

46. Jonathan Belcher   *1756*

48. Mrs. Arthur Browne   1757

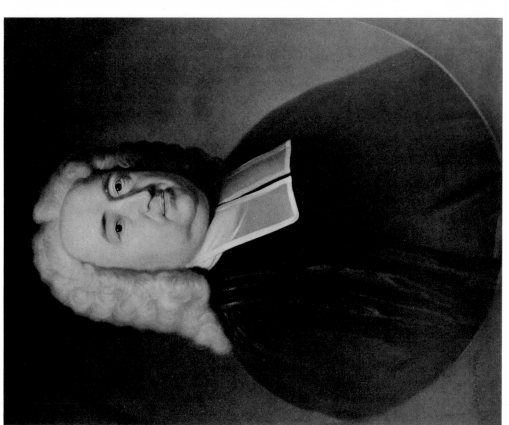

47. Rev. Arthur Browne   1757

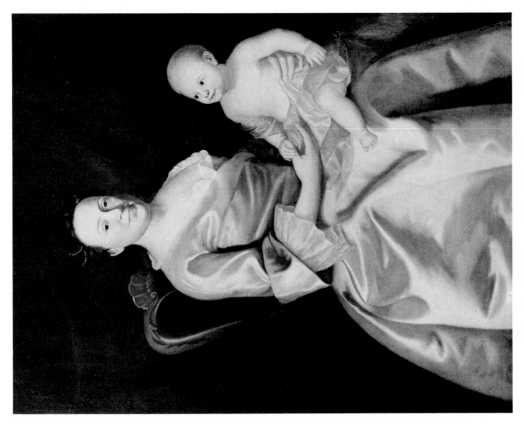

50. Mrs. Daniel Rea and Her Daughter   c. 1757

49. Mrs. William Stevens   c. 1757

52. Thomas Marshall   c. 1755

51. Mrs. Thomas Marshall   c. 1757

53. Theodore Atkinson   *1757–58*

55. Mrs. James Otis   c. 1758

54. James Otis   c. 1758

57. Mrs. Thomas Greene   c. 1758

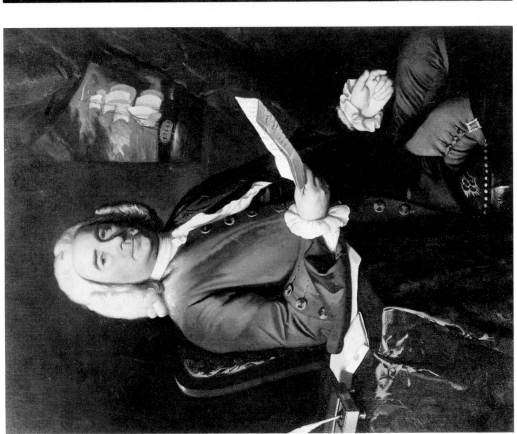

56. Thomas Greene   1758

59. John Barrett   *c. 1758*

58. Mrs. John Barrett   *c. 1758*

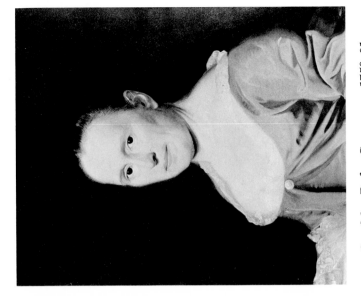

62. Mrs. Rufus Greene   *1758–61*

61. Rufus Greene   *1758–61*

60. John Smibert: Mrs. Daniel
    Oliver   *before 1732*

63. Andrew Oliver   *c. 1758*

64. Mrs. Andrew Oliver   *c. 1758*

65. Andrew Oliver   *c. 1758*

66. Mrs. Andrew Oliver   *c. 1758*

67. Andrew Oliver   *c. 1758*

68. Peter Oliver   *c. 1758*

69. Nathaniel Hurd   *1755–58*

70. Anne Wentworth   *c. 1758*

71. Andrew Oliver II   *c. 1758*

72. Griselda Oliver   *c. 1758*

73. Samuel Danforth   *c. 1758*

74. Rev. Samuel Fayerweather   *c. 1758*

75. Thomas Hancock   *c. 1758*

76. Thomas Hancock   *c. 1758*

77. Hugh Hall   *1758*

78. Gregory Townsend   *c. 1758*

79. Sir John St. Clair   *1759*

80. John Erving, Jr. [?]   *1757–59*

81. Elizabeth Oliver   *c. 1758*

82. Griselda Oliver   *c. 1758*

83. Mary MacIntosh Royall and Elizabeth Royall   *c. 1758*

85. Thomas Aston Coffin   1757–59

84. Mrs. Metcalf Bowler   c. 1758

86. Boy of the Appleton-Greenleaf
Family   *1755–58*

87. Girl of the Appleton-Greenleaf
Family   *1755–58*

88. Unknown Subject, Boy Called Master Hancock
1758–59

89. Epes Sargent   *1759–61*

90. Mrs. Thaddeus Burr   *1758–60*

91. Thaddeus Burr   *1758–60*

92. Rev. Edward Holyoke   *1759–61*

93. John Bours   *1758–61*

95. Henry Pelham   1758–61

94. Rev. Nathaniel Appleton   1759–61

97. Mrs. Samuel Quincy   c. 1761

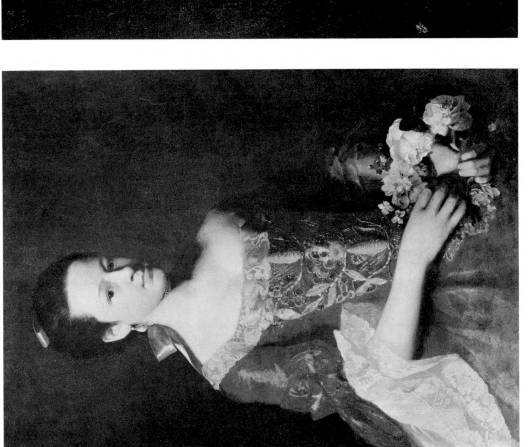

96. Dorothy Murray   1759–61

98. Jacob Fowle   *c. 1761*

99. Benjamin Pickman   *1758–61*

100. Mrs. Daniel Rogers   *1762*

102. Mrs. Nathaniel Allen   c. 1763

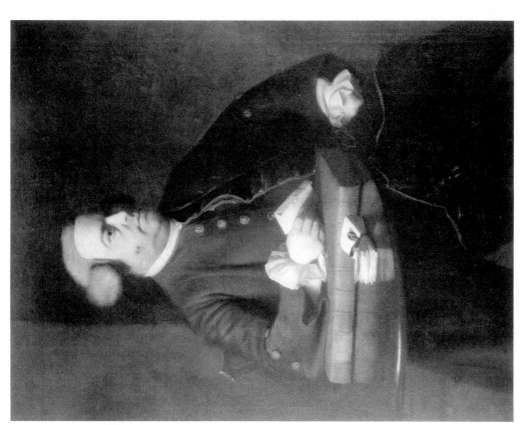

101. Nathaniel Allen   1763

104. Mrs. John Murray   1763

103. John Murray   c. 1763

105. John Scollay   *1763–64*

106. Mrs. John Scollay   *1763*

107. John Scollay   *1764*

108. Mrs. John Scollay   *1764*

109. Thomas Fry: Maria, Countess of
Coventry, engraving   *1761*

110. Mrs. Gawen Brown   *1763*

111. Mrs. Gawen Brown   *c. 1763*

112. Deborah Scollay   *c. 1762*

114. Mrs. Nathaniel Appleton   1763

113. John Spooner   1763

115. Mrs. Benjamin Pickman   *1763*

116. Mrs. Daniel Sargent   *1763*

118. Unknown Subject, Lady in a Blue Dress   1763

117. Alice Hooper   c. 1763

119. Mrs. Metcalf Bowler   *c. 1763*

120. James Warren   *1761–63*

121. Mrs. James Warren   *1761–63*

123. Mrs. Roland Cotton   *c. 1763*

122. Hannah Loring   *1763*

125. Mrs. Benjamin Blackstone   c. 1763

124. Benjamin Blackstone   c. 1763

126. Mrs. John Gray   *c. 1763*

127.   James Murray   *c. 1763*

128. Moses Gill   *1764*

129. Mrs. Moses Gill [A]   *c. 1764*

130. Mrs. Moses Gill [A]   *c. 1764*

131. Elizabeth Pitts   *c. 1764*

132. Timothy Folger   *1764*

133. Mrs. John Apthorp   *c. 1764*

134. Mrs. Benjamin Davis   *c. 1764*   135. Elizabeth Deering Wentworth   *c. 1764*

136. Lydia Lynde   *1762–64*   137. Mrs. Samuel Alleyne Otis   *c. 1764*

139. Mrs. Daniel Hubbard   c. 1764

138. Daniel Hubbard   1764

140. Mrs. John Amory   *c. 1764*

142. Mrs. Samuel Phillips Savage   c. 1764

141. Samuel Phillips Savage   1764

143. Mrs. John Powell   *1764*

144. Mrs. Epes Sargent II   *1764*

145. Epes Sargent II   *c. 1764*

147. Mrs. Joseph Calif   c. 1764

146. Mrs. John Powell   c. 1764

148. Mrs. Samuel Hill   *c. 1764*

149. John Powell II   *c. 1764*

150. Mrs. John Powell II   *c. 1764*

151. Joseph Green [B]   *c. 1764*

152. Nathaniel Sparhawk   *1764*

153. John Hancock   *1765*

154. Thomas Hancock   *1764–66*

155. Mrs. Thomas Hancock   *c. 1766*

156. Mrs. Thomas Hancock   *c. 1766*

157. Thomas Hancock   *1766*

158. Thomas Hollis   *1766*

160. John Bee Holmes   1765

159. Mrs. Edward Watts   1765

161. Mrs. Samuel Waldo   *1764–65*

162. Mrs. Theodore Atkinson   *1765*

163.   Henry Pelham (Boy with a Squirrel)   *1765*

164. Young Lady with a Bird and Dog [Mary Warner?]   *1767*

165. Mrs. George Watson   *1765*

166. Sarah Jackson   *c. 1765*

168. Henry Marchant   c. 1765

167. Mrs. Henry Marchant   c. 1765

169. Woodbury Langdon   *1765–66*

170. Mrs. Woodbury Langdon   *1765–66*

171. John Gray   *1766*

173. Mrs. Joseph Scott   *c. 1765*

172. Joseph Scott   *c. 1765*

175. Elizabeth Ross   1766–67

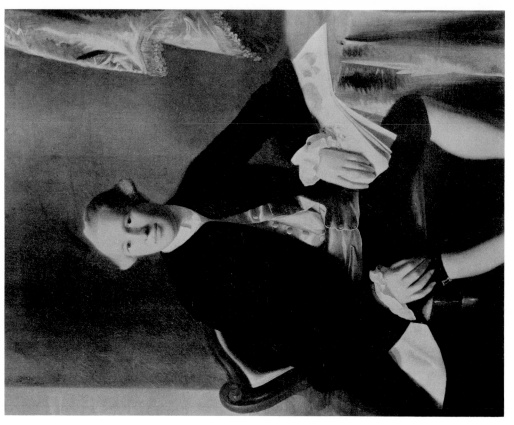

174. Joseph Warren   c. 1765

177. Nathaniel Hurd   c. 1765

176. Nathaniel Hurd   c. 1765

178. Mrs. Thomas Boylston   *1766*

185. Thomas Hubbard   c. 1767

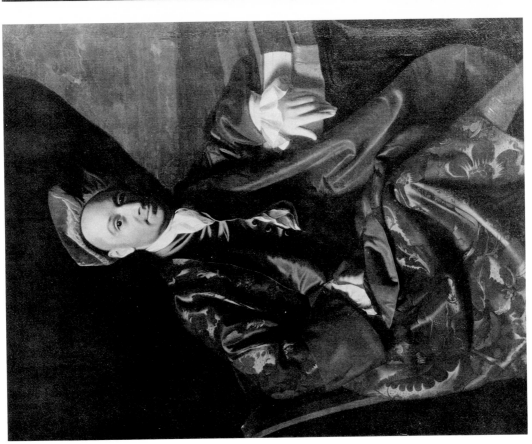

184. Nicholas Boylston   c. 1767

183. Thomas Boylston II   *c. 1767*

182. Nicholas Boylston   1767

179. Mrs. Sylvanus Bourne   *1766*

180. Mrs. Nathaniel Ellery   *c. 1766*

181. Mrs. Ebenezer Austin   *1766–70*

187. Mrs. Timothy Rogers [?]   1766–67

186. Rebecca Boylston   1767

189. Duncan Stewart   *1767*

188. Mrs. Duncan Stewart   *c. 1767*

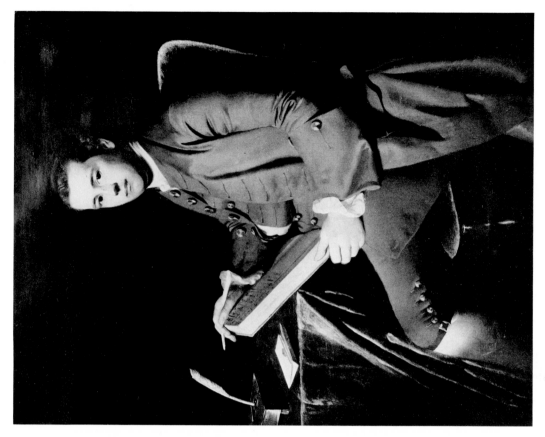

191. Benjamin Hallowell   1765–68

190. Mrs. Benjamin Hallowell   1766–67

192. Martin Howard   *1767*

193. John Gardiner   *c. 1768*

194. Thomas Lewis   *1766–67*

195. Harrison Gray   *c. 1767*

196. Rev. Joseph Sewall   *c. 1766*

197. Samuel Quincy   *c. 1767*

198. Josiah Quincy   *c. 1767*

199. Rev. Mather Byles   *1765–67*

200. Rev. Mather Byles   *1771–74*

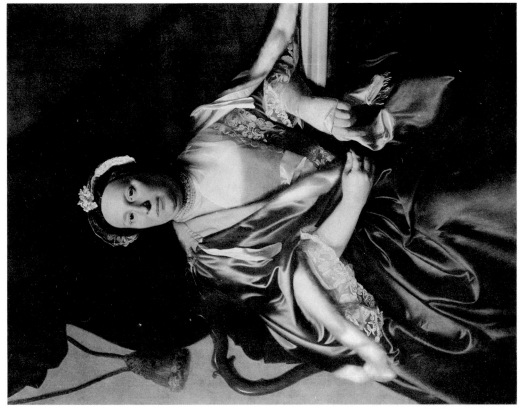

201. Robert Hooper   1767

202. Mrs. Robert Hooper   c. 1767

203. Mrs. Gregory Townsend   *1765*

204. Mrs. Edward Green   *1765*

205. Mrs. Samuel Henley   *c. 1765*

206. Mrs. Andrew Tyler   *c. 1765*

207. John Temple   *1765*   208. Mrs. John Temple   *c. 1767*

209. Peter Chardon   *c. 1766*   210. Mrs. George Turner   *c. 1767*

211. William Turner   *c. 1767*

212. Mrs. William Turner   *1767*

213. Joseph Greene   *1767*

214. Mrs. Joseph Greene   *1767*

215. Joseph Green [A]   *1767*   216. Mrs. Joseph Green [A]   *c. 1767*

217. Daniel Rogers [?]   *1767*

218. Joseph Sherburne   *1767–70*

219. Mrs. Jerathmael Bowers *1767–70*

221. Thomas Hudson: Samuel Scott   1732–34

220. John Amory   1768

223. Rev. Myles Cooper   *1768*

222. George Watson   *1768*

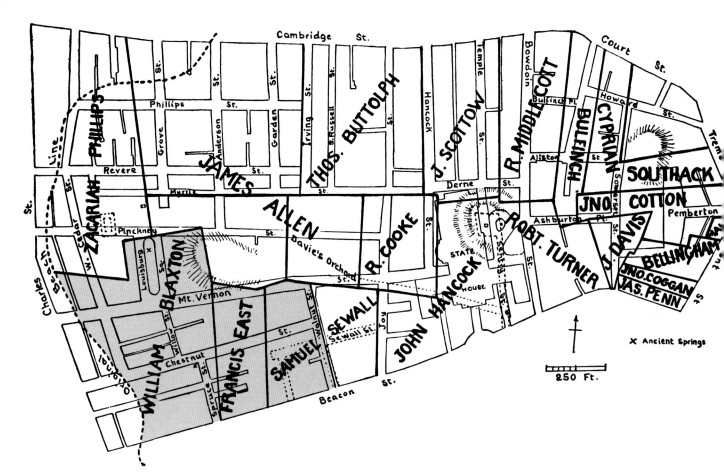

224. Beacon Hill, marked with ancient pasture fence lines (from Allen Chamberlain, *Beacon Hill: Its Ancient Pastures and Early Mansions* [Boston and New York, 1925], opp. p. 2) — shaded area shows Copley's property

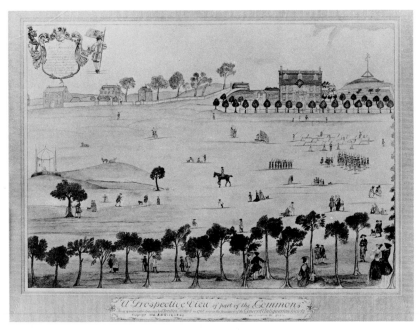

225. A Prospective View of Part of the Commons, 1768, engraved after the watercolor by Christian Remick (Concord Antiquarian Society)

226. John Singleton Copley   *1769*

227. Mrs. John Singleton Copley   *1769*

228. Jonathan Jackson   *1767–69*

229. John Wentworth   *1769*

230. Joseph Barrell   *1767–69*

231. Mrs. Joseph Barrell [A]   *1767–69*

232. Mrs. Joseph Barrell [A]   *1769–71*

233. Mrs. Joseph Barrell [B]   *c. 1771*

234. Ebenezer Storer   *1767–69*

235. Mrs. Ebenezer Storer   *1767–69*

236. Ebenezer Storer II   *1767–69*

237. Mrs. Ebenezer Storer II   *1767–69*

238. Mrs. Joseph Henshaw   *1769–72*

239. Ruth Tufts   *1769–72*

240. Thomas Amory   *c. 1770*

241. Ralph Inman   *c. 1770*

242. Henry Hill   *c. 1770*

243. Mrs. Henry Hill   *c. 1770*

245. Peter Boylston Adams [?]
1765–70

244. George Green   *1765–70*

246. Samuel Barrett   *1765–70*   247. Mrs. Samuel Barrett   *1765–70*

248.   Robert Bayard   *1765–71*   249. Jeremiah Lee   *c. 1769*

250.   John Singleton Copley
1769

251.   Jonathan Jackson   *c. 1770*

252. Samuel Cary   *c. 1769*   253. Mrs. Samuel Cary   *c. 1769*

254. Isaac Royall   *1769*

255. Isaac Smith   *1769*

256. Mrs. Isaac Smith   *1769*

257. Jeremiah Lee   *1769*

258. Mrs. Jeremiah Lee   *1769*

260. Mrs. William Eppes   c. 1769

259. Mrs. James Smith   1769

262. John Greene   c. 1769

261. Mrs. John Greene   1769

264. Mrs. Alexander MacWhorter   1769

263. Rev. Alexander MacWhorter   1769

265. Rev. Samuel Cooper   *1767–69*

266. Rev. Samuel Cooper   *1769–71*

267. Rev. William Hooper   *1767–69*

268. James Allen   *1768–70*

269. Mrs. Alexander Cumming   *1770*

270. Mrs. Samuel Watts   *c. 1770*

271. Mrs. William Coffin   *c. 1770*

272. Paul Revere   *1768–70*

273. Mrs. Ezekiel Goldthwait   *1770–71*

274. Ezekiel Goldthwait   *1770–71*

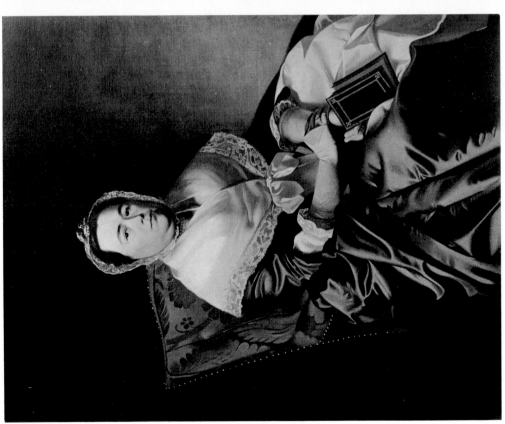

276. Mrs. Michael Gill [?] 1770–71

275. Mrs. James Russell 1770–71

278. Mrs. Joseph Hooper   *1770–71*

277. Joseph Hooper   *1770–71*

279. Joshua Henshaw   *c. 1770*

280. Richard Dana   *c. 1770*

282. Lemuel Cox   1770

281. Robert Hooper II   1770–71

283. Mrs. Humphrey Devereux   *1770–71*

284. Mrs. Thomas Gage   *1771*

286. Unknown Subject, traditionally known as Mrs. Thrale
1771

285. Thomas Gage 1768-69

288. Rev. John Ogilvie   1771

287. Mrs. Paul Richard   1771

289. Samuel Verplanck   *1771*

290. Gulian Verplanck   *1771*

291. Mary Elizabeth Martin   *1771*

292. Unknown Subject, Little Girl with Grapes   *1765–70*

293. Daniel Verplanck   *1771*

294. John Richards   *1770–71*

295. John Montresor   *c. 1771*

296. Mrs. Roger Morris   *1771*

297. Mrs. Charles McEvers   *1771*

298. Unknown Subject, Lady in a Yellow Dress
c. 1771

299. Mrs. Mallett (Mary Livingston)
1771

300. John Hancock *1770–72*

301. John Hancock *1770–72*

302. Samuel Adams   *1770–72*

303. Thomas Amory II   *1770–72*

304. Unknown Subject, Gentleman with a Cane
[John Lane?]   *1770–72*

305. Mrs. Thomas Amory II   *1770–72*

306. Joshua Henshaw II   *1770–74*

307. Mrs. Joshua Henshaw II   *1770–74*

308. Joseph Henshaw   *1770–74*

309. Rev. Edward Barnard   *1770–74*

310. Mrs. John Stevens   *1770–72*

311. Thomas Flucker   *1770–72*

312. John Newton   *1772*

313. Benjamin Gerrish   *1770–72*

314. Joseph Gerrish [?]   *1770–72*

316. Dorothy Quincy   c. 1772

315. Mrs. Richard Skinner   1772

318. Sylvester Gardiner   c. 1772

317. Eleazer Tyng   1772

319. John Erving   *c. 1772*

320. Daniel Henchman [?]   *1770–74*

321. Nathaniel Perkins   *1770–74*

322. Jabez Bowen   *1771–74*

323. Mrs. Jabez Bowen   *1771–74*

324. Rev. Thomas Cary   *1773*

325. James Gambier   *1773*

326. Mrs. Moses Gill [B]   *c. 1773*

327. Mrs. John Winthrop   *1773*

329. Samuel Winthrop   c. 1773

328. John Winthrop   c. 1773

330. Nicholas Boylston   *1773*

331. Mr. and Mrs. Thomas Mifflin   *1773*

332. Mr. and Mrs. Isaac Winslow   1774

334. Mrs. Adam Babcock   c. 1774

333. Adam Babcock   c. 1774